urdu

David Matthews

and

Mohamed Kasim Dalvi

TEACH YOURSELF BOOKS

For UK orders: please contact Bookpoint Ltd., 78 Milton Park, Abingdon, Oxon OX14 4TD. Telephone: (44) 01235 400414, Fax: (44) 01235 400454. Lines are open from 9.00 - 6.00, Monday to Saturday, with a 24 hour message answering service.
Email address: orders@bookpoint.co.uk.

For U.S.A. & Canada orders: please contact NTC/Contemporary Publishing, 4255 West Touhy Avenue, Lincolnwood, Illinois 60646-1975, U.S.A. Telephone: (847) 679 5500, Fax: (847) 679 2494.

Long renowned as the authoritative source for self-guided learning – with more than 30 million copies sold worldwide – the *Teach Yourself* series includes over 200 titles in the fields of languages, crafts, hobbies, business and education.

British Library Cataloguing in Publication Data
A catalogue record for this title is available from The British Library

Library of Congress Catalog Card Number: On file

First published in UK 1999 by Hodder Headline Plc, 338 Euston Road, London, NW1 3BH.

First published in US 1999 by NTC/Contemporary Publishing, 4255 West Touhy Avenue, Lincolnwood (Chicago), Illinois 60646-1975, U.S.A.

Typeset by Thomson Press (India) Ltd, New Delhi.
Printed in Great Britain for Hodder & Stoughton Educational, a division of Hodder Headline Plc, 338 Euston Road, London NW1 3BH by Cox & Wyman Ltd, Reading, Berkshire.

Impression number	10	9	8	7	6	5	4	3	2	1
Year	2005	2004	2003	2002	2001	2000	1999			

CONTENTS

INTRODUCTION

Urdu, the official language of Pakistan and one of the 15 officially recognised languages of India, is spoken as a mother tongue by an estimated 50 million people. To this we may add the millions of people both inside and outside the subcontinent who use Urdu in addition to their own language as a primary means of spoken and written communication. Like its 'sister', Hindi, Urdu came into being in Delhi and its surrounding areas as the result of the Muslim conquests of India in the 11th and 12th centuries AD. The Persian- and Turkish-speaking invaders adopted the language of the capital to communicate with the local inhabitants, and quickly added a vast stock of Persian (and through Persian, Arabic) words to its vocabulary. At first the Muslim rulers referred to this growing language simply as 'Hindi', i.e. 'Indian'. Much later it acquired the name 'Urdu', a Turkish word meaning 'barracks' from the area of Old Delhi with which it was closely associated – the *Urdu-e Mu'allā* 'the Exalted Royal Army Camp'. In English we find the word Urdu as 'horde', the armies of Genghis Khan and the Mongols.

By the end of the 16th century, Urdu written in a modified form of the Arabic alphabet, with an ever increasing number of Arabic and Persian loanwords, became a flourishing literary language, and over the last three centuries has been the major vehicle for the literature of the Muslims of the subcontinent. From the beginning Urdu functioned as a convenient lingua franca, and was not linked to any one geographical area, so its appeal became universal, and it was much favoured by the British, who often referred to it as 'Hindustani' ('Indian'). Although it is fair to say that the language is now mainly connected with the Muslims of the subcontinent, its literature also boasts a number of prominent Hindu and Sikh writers. After Partition in 1947, Urdu was the natural choice for the national or official language of Pakistan.

Wherever they have migrated, Urdu speakers have taken their language and culture with them. In parts of East Africa, the Persian Gulf and, of course, Britain and the USA, Urdu still maintains its role as a major means of general communication.

At the basic, conversational level, Urdu and Hindi are virtually identical, differing from each other in script, technical and literary vocabulary, and, of course, cultural background. The debate about whether one is speaking Hindi or Urdu is endless, and fraught with subtle problems. Suffice it to say that if you chat in Urdu to a Hindi speaker, he will naturally assume you are speaking Hindi, and vice versa.

Urdu belongs to the Indo-European family of languages and is ultimately related to English and many other European languages, with which you will find it has much in common. Like English, French and German it has the familiar patterns of nouns, verbs, gender, case, etc. It is a very regular, but at the same time an extremely precise language, making clear distinctions in its pronouns between people of lower and higher orders, and in its verbs between what happens now and what happens generally. Because it is written in a script which does not employ vowels, and which, like English, has a number of letters used to represent the same sound, spelling is something which requires constant attention.

How to use this book

First, you must thoroughly master the script, which is introduced gradually in the first section. At the same time, you should make sure that you fully understand the system of phonetic transcription, which is used throughout to indicate correct pronunciation. The dialogues of the first five units are fully transcribed, as are all new words and phrases in the following units. Examples of the Urdu script, often beautifully written, can often be found outside Indian and Pakistani restaurants and shops in almost any town in Britain and the USA. Practise your reading skills by trying to decipher them as you pass.

Each unit contains two or three dialogues composed in practical, everyday Urdu. From the outset care has been taken to give you practice in the 'polite' style of speaking, which is characteristic of Urdu. Literal translations of many polite phrases may sometimes seem a little quaint, but in Urdu such expressions are part of ordinary speech.

First, try to understand each dialogue by reading and listening to the recording in conjunction with the vocabulary that follows.

Only then should you have recourse to the transliterated and translated versions provided. When you have finished a unit, it is a good idea to read the dialogues out loud to yourself. The more you can commit to memory, the easier it will be to speak without hesitation.

The spelling and grammar notes in each unit relate directly to the new material contained in the dialogues. They also contain a certain number of additional words and expressions which will be of use. The precision of Urdu means that grammar should be mastered as thoroughly as the vocabulary. You will find that committing very logical rules to memory will pay great dividends in the future.

The exercises within and at the end of the units are of a practical nature and will help you check your progress. For those who wish to learn how to compose Urdu some English–Urdu translation exercises are also included.

It goes without saying that you should make sure you have completely mastered one unit before going on to the next. When testing yourself on vocabulary it is a good idea to proceed from the English side of the list to the Urdu. If you know the Urdu word for ‘book’, you will naturally know the meaning of the Urdu word in English!

Because of the somewhat illogical nature of the Urdu counting system, the numbers have been given in an appendix. Whatever your purpose in learning Urdu, numbers will always be essential, and once learnt should be constantly practised.

The English translations of the dialogues in the first five units deliberately follow the Urdu as closely as possible, at the expense of making the English seem a little stilted. Once you have been through the dialogue, it would be good practice to recast the translation into a more idiomatic style.

Reading and writing Urdu:

Pronunciation, transcription and script

The Urdu alphabet

Urdu is written in an adapted form of the script which was first used to write Arabic in the 6th and 7th centuries AD. During the 8th century the Persians began to use the Arabic script for their own language, adding a few extra letters for sounds which did not occur in Arabic. After the 12th century the Central Asian invaders of India, who had already adopted the Arabic script for writing Turkish, used it to write the language of Delhi, which eventually became modern Urdu.

The Arabic script, like that of Hebrew, is written from right to left, the opposite direction from English:

میں اُردو سیکھ رہا ہوں ←

The script is **cursive**, that is most of the letters join each other, and cannot be 'printed' separately. There are no capital letters, and for the most part only *consonants* are written. Although there are special signs for indicating vowels, these are rarely used. Since there is no way of telling which vowels are to be employed, each word has to be learnt with its pronunciation. This is indicated in simple phonetic transcription in the book. In the vocabulary sections each word will be noted thus:

Urdu script	Phonetic transcription	Meaning
سبب	*sabab*	cause
کلکتہ	*kalkatta*	Calcutta

Many letters of the alphabet have the same shape, and are differentiated from one another by the arrangement of dots which may be written either above or below the letter. Reading from right to left, compare the following basic shapes:

ث	ت	پ	ب
s	*t*	*p*	*b*

The dots play a crucial role and must never be left out.

There are two major styles of printed script, both of which follow handwriting very closely. The first is known as *naskh* (the Arabic word for 'writing'). This is used for typing Arabic and Persian, but has never been popular with Urdu speakers. The second is known as *nasta'līq* (literally 'hanging *naskh*'), an ornate, sloping version of the script, developed in Persia and India during the Middle Ages. This is the style preferred for Urdu. At its best, *nasta'līq* possesses great natural beauty, and for this reason Urdu speakers have always resisted the more commonplace *naskh*. There is not a vast difference between the two styles, although this may not seem the case at first sight.

Brief examples of verse are written in *naskh* and *nasta'līq* respectively as follows:

مَن کی دولت ہاتھ آتی ہے تو پھر جاتی نہیں
تَن کی دولت چھاؤں ہے، آتا ہے دھن جاتا ہے دھن
مَن کی دنیا میں نہ پایا میں نے افرنگی کا راج
مَن کی دنیا میں نہ دیکھے میں نے شیخ و برہمن
پانی پانی کر گئی مجکو قلندر کی یہ بات
تُو جھکا جب غیر کے آگے نہ مَن تیرا نہ تن

مَن کی دولت ہاتھ آتی ہے تو پھر جاتی نہیں
تن کی دولت چھاؤں ہے، آتا ہے دھن جاتا ہے دھن
مَن کی دنیا میں نہ پایا میں نے افرنگی کا راج
مَن کی دنیا میں نہ دیکھے میں نے شیخ و برہمن
پانی پانی کر گئی مجکو قلندر کی یہ بات
تو جھکا جب غیر کے آگے نہ مَن تیرا نہ تن

Since the Urdu alphabet is cursive, most letters have four forms: **independent** (the letter written in its full form, standing alone); **initial** (the letter coming at the beginning of a word; **medial** (the letter in the middle of a word); **final** (the letter at the end of a word). This can be demonstrated with the Urdu letter ظ *z*, which starting from right to left is joined thus:

← ظ ظظظ

ظ is ***independent***; ظـ is ***initial***; ـظـ is ***medial***; ـظ is ***final.***

Some sounds are represented by more than one letter of the alphabet. For example, the sound *z* is represented by four letters:

ظ ض ز ذ

The Urdu alphabet has 35 letters, plus a number of signs which are written above the letters to indicate the doubling of a consonant, the absence of a vowel, a break in the middle of a word, etc.

Most letters fall into sets of the same basic pattern of shapes, members of the set being distinguished from one another only by the dots written above or below the basic shapes. For example, the basic shapes ب and ج have in their sets:

ب	*b*	ج	*j*
پ	*p*	چ	*c*
ت	*t*	ح	*h*
ٹ	*ṭ*	خ	*x*
ث	*s*		

Vowels may be indicated by a sign written either over or under the letter:

ـَ *a*   ـِ *i*   ـُ *u*

or by one of the consonants which in certain circumstances also function as vowel markers. The use of three vowel signs is very restricted and is usually only found in dictionaries, where exact pronunciation needs to be indicated. Otherwise vowel signs are hardly ever used.

Transcription

As we can never ascertain the correct pronunciation of an Urdu word from the way in which it is written, it is necessary to transcribe the words into

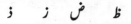

'Roman' letters. The simple phonetic transcription used in this book indicates as accurately as possible how the Urdu word is pronounced and how the letters reflect the sounds. The dialogues in the first five units are transcribed in full. Thereafter transcription is only used where absolutely necessary.

The following features of the transcription should be carefully noted:

- A line written over a vowel indicates that it is 'long':

tab 'then'	short *a* which sounds like the *u* in English 'tub'
bāb 'gate'	long *ā* which sounds like the *a* in English 'barb'
kis 'whom'	short *i* which sounds like the *i* in English 'kiss'
sīm 'silver'	long *ī* which sounds like the *ee* in English 'seem'
pul 'bridge'	short *u* which sounds like the *u* in English 'pull'
kū 'lane'	long *ū* which sounds like the *oo* in English 'coo'.

- A dot under the letter *ṭ* and *ḍ* indicates the distinctive 'Indian' *t* and *d* sounds, which are produced by turning back (retroflexing) the tongue onto the roof of the mouth. These are known as retroflex sounds and must be distinguished from *t* and *d* (without a dot), which are produced by putting the tip of the tongue behind the top front teeth. These are known as *dental* sounds.
- Urdu has a set of strongly **aspirated** consonants, which are produced by exerting breath pressure when pronouncing them. In Urdu, the presence or absence of aspiration is crucial. For example, Urdu *khā* (strongly aspirated) means 'eat'; *kā* (no breathiness) means 'of'. In our transcription *h* written after a consonant means that it is aspirated.
- Pay special attention to the letter *c* which is pronounced like the *ch* in 'church' but with no breathiness. Its aspirated counterpart *ch* is like English *ch* but this time with strong aspiration. The Urdu word *cāe* 'tea' sounds like 'chy' (rhyming with 'by') with no breath; the word *che* 'six' sounds like *chhay* with lots of breath. Always remember that in our transcription *c* is always pronounced *ch* and never like *k*.
- The letter *x* is pronounced like the *ch* in Scottish *loch*.
- The letter *q* is similar to English *k* but pronounced further towards the back of the throat.
- The letter *š* is pronounced like *sh* in English *ship*.

- The letter *ğ* is pronounced something like the French *r* in Paris. The Modern Greek *g* in *Georgiou* is closer.
- The letter *ž* is pronounced like the *si* in English televi**sion**. In fact, the only common Urdu word in which it makes an appearance is *ṭelīvižan*.
- The letter *ṅ* coming after a vowel indicates that the vowel is 'nasalised' (pronounced through the nose). The final syllable of Urdu *kitāboṅ* 'books' sounds like French *bon*.

Other consonants are pronounced in much the same way as their English counterparts.

The table of Urdu sounds below follows the traditional order of the alphabet. Reading from **right** to **left** you will see the **independent** form of the Urdu letter followed by its name, e.g. *alif, be, ce, dāl* like *a, b, c, d* in English; the symbol used in transcription; a rough equivalent of the sound in English (or in one of the better known European languages); an Urdu word containing the sound.

We begin with the vowels, which do not form part of the alphabet as such. These are followed by the consonants, several of which (*t, s, z, h*) have the same sound. The letter *'ain'* will be discussed later. The letter *ṛ* is a quickly produced *ḍ* sounding something like the *tt* in the American pronunciation of *butter*.

There are two letters for *h* : ح known as *baṛī he* 'big *he*' and ہ known as *choṭī he* 'little *he*'.

Urdu Word	**Sound in English (etc.)**	**Phonetic symbol**	**Urdu letter**
Vowels			
ab 'now'	among, but	*a*	اَ
āp 'you'	after, father	*ā*	آ
in 'those'	in, bin	*i*	اِ
tīn 'three'	teen	*ī*	اِی
un 'those'	pull	*u*	اُ
ūpar 'upon'	pool	*ū*	اُو
ek 'one'	(French) été	*e*	اے
fon 'phone'	(French) *beau*	*o*	او
aisā 'such'	hen	*ai*	اَے
aur 'and'	or, because	*au*	اَو

Consonants

amīr 'rich'	(discussed later)	*none*	*alif*	ا
bāp 'father'	bar	*b*	*be*	ب
bhāī 'brother'	aspirated *b*	*bh*	*bhe*	بھ
par 'on'	unaspirated *p*	*p*	*pe*	پ
phal 'fruit'	aspirated *p*	*ph*	*phe*	پھ
tum 'you'	dental *t*	*t*	*te*	ت
thā 'was'	aspirated *t*	*th*	*the*	تھ
ṭaiksī 'taxi'	retroflex *ṭ*	*ṭ*	*ṭe*	ٹ
ṭhīk 'all right'	aspirated *ṭ*	*ṭh*	*ṭhe*	ٹھ
sābit 'proved'	sing	*s*	*se*	ث
jānā 'to go'	jar	*j*	*jīm*	ج
jhīl 'lake'	aspirated *j*	*jh*	*jhe*	جھ
calnā 'to walk'	church	*c*	*ce*	چ
chat 'roof'	aspirated *c*	*ch*	*che*	چھ
hāl 'condition'	hall	*h*	*baṛī he*	ح
xān 'Khan'	Scottish loch	*x*	*xe*	خ
dāl 'lentils'	dental *d*	*d*	*dāl*	د
dhūl 'dust'	aspirated *d*	*dh*	*dhe*	دھ
ḍāk 'post'	retroflex *ḍ*	*ḍ*	*ḍāl*	ڈ
ḍhāī '2½'	aspirated retroflex *ḍ*	*ḍh*	*ḍhe*	ڈھ
rājā 'king'	(Italian) Roma	*r*	*re*	ر
baṛā 'big'	(American) butter	*ṛ*	*ṛe*	ڑ
baṛhā 'increased'	aspirated *ṛ*	*ṛh*	*ṛhe*	ڑھ
zabān	zoo	*z*	*z*	ز
ṭelīvižan 'TV'	television	*ž*	*že*	ژ
sāl 'year'	seven	*s*	*sīn*	س
šer 'tiger'	share	*š*	*šīn*	ش
sadī 'century'	seven	*s*	*svād*	ص
zarūr 'certainly'	zoo	*z*	*zvād*	ض
tālib 'student'	dental *t*	*t*	*toe*	ط
zālim 'cruel'	zoo	*z*	*zoe*	ظ
'arab 'Arab'	(discussed later)	*'*	*'ain*	ع
ğarīb 'poor'	(Greek) Georgiou	*ğ*	*ğain*	غ
fārsī 'Persian'	farm	*f*	*fe*	ف
qurān 'Quran'	back '*k*'	*q*	*qāf*	ق

karnā 'to do'	keep	*k*	*kāf*	ک
khānā 'to eat'	aspirated *k*	*kh*	*khe*	کھ
gānā 'to sing'	go	*g*	*gāf*	گ
ghar 'house'	aspirated *g*	*gh*	*ghe*	گھ
lāhaur 'Lahore'	lamp	*l*	*lām*	ل
madrās 'Madras'	Madras	*m*	*mīm*	م
nām 'name'	name	*n*	*nūn*	ن
vālid 'father'	between '*v*' and '*w*'	*v*	*vāū*	و
ham 'we'	home	*h*	*choṭī he*	ہ
yār 'friend'	yard	*y*	*ye*	ی

Reading and writing Urdu

Connectors and non-connectors

We have seen that the Urdu script is **cursive** and in both type and handwriting most letters are joined to one another from both the front and the back. Letters fall into two categories, connectors and non-connectors.

Connectors These are letters which join from both directions.

The letter ب *be*, *b*, being connector has four shapes:

Final	**Medial**	**Initial**	**Independent**
ـب	ـبـ	بـ	ب

The initial and medial shapes lose their long 'flourish', and the shapes connect as follows:

ببب ب b b + b + b

Non connectors These are letters which cannot be joined to a following letter. The first letter of the alphabet ا *alif*, whose function is discussed later in this section, is one of these, and has only an independent final shape:

Final	**Independent**
ـا	ا

با *be* + *alif* BUT اب *alif* + *be*

Funtions of ا *alif*; vowel signs

We have seen that there are three optional vowel signs, two of which are written above another letter, and one which is written below. These are:

َ known as *zabar*, representing the short vowel '*a*'

ِ known as *zer*, representing the short vowel '*i*'

ُ known as *peš*, representing the short vowel '*u*'.

These names are Persian, *zabar* meaning 'above', *zer* 'below' and *peš* 'forward'.

With the letter ب they are written:

بَ	*ba*	بِ	*bi*	بُ	*bu*
بَب	*bab*	بِب	*bib*	بُب	*bub*

When one of the short vowels is required at the beginning of the word, that is if we want to write *ab*, *ib* or *ub*, the vowel sign is written over or under ا *alif*, one of whose main functions is to 'carry' initial vowels. Thus:

اَب	*ab*	اِب	*ib*	اُب	*ub*

When ا *alif* follows a letter it represents the long vowel *ā*

با	*bā*	باب	*bāb*	بابا	*bābā*

When the sign ~ (known as *madd*, 'increasing') is written over *alif* آ at the beginning of a word it represents the long vowel *ā*

آب *āb*

Usually the signs for the short vowels '*a*, *i*, *u*' are not used. Therefore, unless we know beforehand, there is no way in which we can tell whether اب is to be pronounced *ab*, *ib* or *ub*. The Urdu word اب *ab* means 'now', but there are no words *ib* and *ub*, i.e. there is only one way in which اب can be pronounced.

The short vowels are optional, but the sign ~ *madd* must never be omitted.

Letters 1–10

The first letter, ا *alif*, is a non-connector and has only independent and initial shapes. Letters 2–6 are connectors and have the basic shape ب while letters 7–10 are also connectors with ح as the basic shape.

In the table below, reading from **right** to **left**, you will find the independent, initial, medial and final shapes of the letters; their 'phonetic' values; the Urdu name and number of the letter.

Name	Phonetic value	Final	Medial	Initial	Independent
1 *alif*	—	ـا	—	—	ا
2 *be*	b	ـب	ـبـ	بـ	ب
3 *pe*	*p*	ـپ	ـپـ	پـ	پ
4 *te*	*t*	ـت	ـتـ	تـ	ت
5 *ṭe*	*ṭ*	ـٹ	ـٹـ	ٹـ	ٹ
6 *se*	s	ـث	ـثـ	ثـ	ث
7 *jīm*	*j*	ـج	ـجـ	جـ	ج
8 ce	c	ـچ	ـچـ	چـ	چ
9 *baṛī he*	*h*	ـح	ـحـ	حـ	ح
10 *xe*	x	ـخ	ـخـ	خـ	خ

Script exercise 1

Read the following words, and write them out, omitting the vowel signs, *zabar*, *zer* and *peš*, but be sure to write ~ *madd* and all the dots.

اَب	*ab*	'now'	بُت	*but*	'idol'
تَب	*tab*	'then'	باپ	*bāp*	'father'
ثابِت	*sābit*	'proved'	جَب	*jab*	'when'
چَچا	*cacā*	'uncle'	جَج	*jaj*	'judge'
آپ	*āp*	'you'	آٹا	*āṭā*	'flour'
بَچَت	*bacat*	'savings'	پِتا	*pitā*	'father'

Letters 11–19

Letters 11–13 have the basic shape د and are non-connectors. Letters 14–17 have the basic shape ر and are also non-connectors.

It is important to keep the د set distinct from the slightly similar ر set.

Letters 18–19 are connectors with the basic shape س or alternatively, ﺳـ both shapes equally common and often alternate with one another in the same word.

Name	Phonetic value	Final	Medial	Initial	Independent
11 *dāl*	d	ـد	—	—	د
12 *ḍāl*	ḍ	ـڈ	—	—	ڈ
13 *zāl*	z	ـذ	—	—	ذ
14 *re*	r	ـر	—	—	ر
15 *ṛe*	ṛ	ـڑ	—	—	ڑ
16 *ze*	z	ـز	—	—	ز
17 *že*	ž	ـژ	—	—	ژ
18 *sīn*	s	ـس	ـسـ	سـ	س
		ـس	ـسـ	سـ	س
19 *šīn*	š	ـش	ـشـ	شـ	ش
		ـش	ـشـ	شـ	ش

We now have two letters for the sound *z* : ذ *zāl* and ز *ze* and two for the sound *s* ث *se* and س *sīn*. The letters ذ and ث only occur in words of Arabic and Persian origin and are much less commonly used than ز and س. You should, of course, make sure that you recognise them.

The sign ْ sukun

The sign ْ written above a letter, known as *sukūn* (an Arabic word meaning 'rest', 'pause'), indicates the absence of a vowel.

In the word سَخْت *saxt* 'hard', the sign ْ shows that no vowel is to be pronounced after the letter خ *xe*. Similarly, بَحْث is pronounced *bahs* 'discussion', ْ indicating that no vowel is to be pronounced after ح *barī he*. Like the vowel signs, ْ *sukūn* is optional and is rarely used.

Script exercise 2

Read the following words and write them out, omitting the vowel signs and *sukūn*.

آخِر	*āxir*	'finally'	زَبَر	*zabar*	'zabar'
اُس	*us*	'that'	سُسْت	*sust*	'lazy'
بَڑا	*baṛā*	'big'	دَس	*das*	'ten'
بُخار	*buxār*	'fever'	سَخْت	*saxt*	'hard'
اَژدَر	*aždar*	'python'	شَراب	*šarāb*	'wine'
ذات	*zāt*	'caste'	بارِش	*bāriš*	'rain'

Letters 20 – 29

All these letters are connectors.

Letters 20 and 21 have the basic shape ص.

Letters 22 and 23 have the basic shape ط. The upright stroke is written separately after the oval: ط ط. Letters 24 and 25 have the basic shape ع. Note that the medial shape has a flat top.

Letters 26 and 27 are similar in shape, but note that the final and independent shape of ف *fe* has a flat flourish, while that of ق *qāf* is circular.

Letters 28 and 29 resemble each other, but ک *kāf* has one sloping stroke at the top, while گ *gāf* has two.

Name	Phonetic value	Final	Medial	Initial	Independent
20 *svād*	s	ـص	ـصـ	صـ	ص
21 *zvād*	*z*	ـض	ـضـ	ضـ	ض
22 *toe*	*t*	ـط	ـطـ	طـ	ط
23 *zoe*	*z*	ـظ	ـظـ	ظـ	ظ
24 *'ain*	'	ـع	ـعـ	عـ	ع
25 *ğain*	*ğ*	ـغ	ـغـ	غـ	غ
26 *fe*	*f*	ـف	ـفـ	فـ	ف
27 *qāf*	*q*	ـق	ـقـ	قـ	ق
28 *kāf*	*k*	ـک	ـکـ	کـ	ک
29 *gāf*	*g*	ـگ	ـگـ	گـ	گ

We now have more letters representing the sounds *t*, *s* and *z*. ط *toe*, ص *svād*, ض *zvād* and ظ *zoe* are only used in words of Arabic origin.

The letter ع *'ain*

In Arabic the letter ع *'ain*, which we are transcribing as ', represents a rasping sound produced at the back of the throat. In Urdu and Persian the sound is ignored, even though the letter is preserved in the spelling of Arabic words in which it occurs. In practice, at the beginning of a word it functions in the same way as ا *alif*, carrying an initial vowel: in Urdu, the word عرب *'arab* 'Arab' sounds exactly the same as the word اَرب *arab* 'necessity'.

Double consonants – the sign ّ *tašdīd*

In Urdu doubled consonants must be given their full force, as in Italian *bello*, *ragazzo* or in English *bookcase* (with a double *k* sound).

A doubled consonant may be indicated by writing the sign ّ *tašdīd* 'strengthening' over the letter.

اَبّا	*abbā*	'daddy'	سَتّر	*sattar*	'seventy'

More often than not, as with vowel signs and *sukūn*, the sign ّ is not written, and you just have to know that the word has a double consonant.

Script exercise 3

Read the following words and write them out, omitting the optional signs.

صاحِب	*sāhib*	'Sahib'	باغ	*bāğ*	'garden'
ضِد	*zid*	'stubbornness'	قَحْط	*qaht*	'famine'
خَط	*xat*	'letter'	دَفْتَر	*daftar*	'office'
عَرَب	*'arab*	'Arab'	اَکْثَر	*aksar*	'most'
عادَت	*'ādat*	'habit'	گِرْتا	*girtā*	'falls'

Double consonants:

اَبّا	*abbā*	'daddy'	عِزَّت	*izzat*	'honour'
کُتّا	*kuttā*	'dog'	اَڈّا	*aḍḍā*	'office'

Letters 30–32

All these letters are connectors. Care should be taken to distinguish initial lām لـ and medial lām ـلـ which join the following letter, from ا alif which does not. The initial and medial forms of ن nūn are the same shape as the ب set.

Name	Phonetic value	Final	Medial	Initial	Independent
30 *lām*	*l*	ـل	ـلـ	لـ	ل
31 *mīm*	*m*	ـم	ـمـ	مـ	م
32 *nūn*	*n*	ـن	ـنـ	نـ	ن

ن *nūn* and ں *nūn ğunna*

The letter ن *nūn* represents the sound n:

آسْمان	*āsmān*	'sky'	بَنْد	*band*	'closed'

In final position when ں is written without a dot it indicates that the preceding vowel is nasalised. This undotted *nūn* is known as *nūn ğunna* 'nasalising' *nūn*. In transcription it is written *ṅ*, with a dot above the *n*.

Nasalised vowels are produced by diverting the airstream through the nose. French has a number of such vowels which are usually indicated by the letter *n*: *bon, élan, rapidement*, etc. In Urdu, all vowels can be nasalised.

The undotted *nūn* can only be used at the end of a word:

ماں	*māṅ*	'mother'
جاں	*jāṅ*	'darling'

If a nasalised vowel occurs in the middle of the word then the normal dotted *nūn* must be used, since omitting the dot would make the letter illegible:

مانگ	*māṅg*	'demand'
ٹانگ	*ṭāṅg*	'leg'

ک **kāf** and گ **gāf** followed by ا *alif* and ل **lām**

When the letters *kāf* and *gāf* are followed by *alif* and *lām*, they have a special 'rounded' shape: ک *kāf* گ *gāf*. Thus:

کا	*kā*	'of'	شکار	*šikār*	'hunting'
گام	*gām*	'step'	پکار	*pukār*	'calling'
کل	*kal*	'yesterday'	شکل	*šakl*	'form'
گل	*gul*	'rose'	جنگل	*jangal*	'jungle'

ل **lām followed by** ا *alif*

Before ا *alif*, ل *lām* is usually written, لا *lā*:

عِلاج	*'ilāj*	'cure'	لادْنا	*lādnā*	'to load'
گِلاس	*gilās*	'glass'	بَلا	*balā*	'disaster'

Sometimes, especially in words of Arabic origin, *lām-alif* is written ﻻ ﻻ , ﻻ *lā* is the Arabic word for '*no, not*' and is used in many Urdu words as an equivalent to the prefix 'un' or 'in' in English:

لا علاج ﻻعلاج *lā-'ilāj* 'incurable'

Script exercise 4

Read the following words and write them out, omitting the optional signs:

قَلَم	*qalam*	'pen'	کانٹا	*kāṅṭā*	'fork'
اَلگ	*alag*	'separate'	مُشکِل	*muškil*	'difficult'
ماں	*māṅ*	'mother'	مُمکِن	*mumkin*	'possible'
لَڑکا	*laṛkā*	'boy'	کالا	*kālā*	'black'
مَکان	*makān*	'house'	مُحَمَّد	*muhammad*	'Muhammad'

Letter 33 و vāū

The letter و *vāū*, which is pronounced something like a cross between English 'w' and 'v', has two functions:

(i) representing the consonant *v*

(ii) representing the three long vowels *ū*, *o* and *au*

Note that, although it is transcribed with two letters, *au* is a single long vowel, something like the *oa* in English '*oar*'.

It is a non-connector and has only two shapes.

Name	Phonetic value	Final	Medial	Initial	Independent
33 *vāū*	*v, ū, o, au*	ـو	—	—	و

و vāū as the consonant *v*

والِد	*vālid*	'father'
سَوال	*savāl*	'question'
رَو	*rav*	'going'

و vāū as a vowel marker

When the three vowels *ū*, *o*, *au*, stand at the beginning of a word, they are written with ا *alif* followed by و *vāū*:

اوپر	*ūpar*	'above'
اوس	*os*	'dew'
اور	*aur*	'and'

In the middle or at the end of a word, they are indicated with و used alone:

پورا	*pūrā*	'full'
لوگ	*log*	'people'
شوق	*šauq*	'keenness'
لوگو	*logo*	'oh people!'

These vowels can be nasalised, and at the end of a word this is indicated by و followed by ں *nūn gunna*:

کروں	*karūṅ*	'I may do'
لڑکوں کا	*laṛkoṅ kā*	'of the boys'

When necessary, the vowels may be indicated more precisely by writing ُ *peš* over the preceding letter for *ū* and writing َ *zabar* over the preceding letter for *au*.

There is no mark for representing *o*.

اُوپر	*ūpar*	اَور	*aur*
پُورا	*pūrā*	شَوق	*šauq*

If no sign is used, you may assume that the vowel is *o*:

اوس	*os*	لوگ	*log*

Again, *zabar* and *peš* are rarely used, and only when confusion is likely to arise. For example, to distinguish between different words:

اور	*or*	'direction'	اَور	*aur*	'and'			
سُو	*sū*	'direction'	سو	*so*	'thus'	سَو	*sau*	'100'

Even in this case, where real confusion can arise, the vowel signs are more often than not omitted.

خو xe-vāū

Urdu has a number of very common words of Persian origin which begin with *xe* followed by *vāū*. If ا *alif* (making the vowel *ā*) follows *vāū*, the *vāū* is not pronounced. This so-called 'silent *vāū*' is written in transcription as *w*.

خواب	*xwāb*	'dream' (pronounced *xāb*)

After خ, و may indicate the long vowels *ū, o, au,* in the normal way:

خوب	*xūb*	'good'
خون	*xūn*	'blood'

خود	*xod*	'helmet'
خوف	*xauf*	'fear'

But in two very common words, *vāū* represents the **short** vowel *u*:

خود	*xud*	'self'
خوش	*xuš*	'happy'

Script exercise 5

Read the following words and write them out, omitting the optional signs.

والِد	*vālid*	'father'	دَور	*daur*	'period'
اِتْوار	*itvār*	'Sunday'	اُونْچا	*ūncā*	'high'
نَوَمْبَر	*navambar*	'November'	گورا	*gorā*	'white'
خُون	*xūn*	'blood'	اَولاد	*aulād*	'children'
خواب	*xwāb*	'dream'	خُود	*xud*	'self'

Letter 34 choṭī he

The next letter of the Urdu alphabet is called *choṭī he* 'little *he*' (as opposed to *baṛī he* ح which we have already seen). Both *choṭī* and *baṛī he* represent the 'h' sound. *baṛī he* is used only in words of Arabic origin.

The initial shape of *choṭī he* is written with a hook underneath it, The medial form is written either with or without a hook.

Name	Phonetic value	Final	Medial	Initial	Independent
34 *Choṭī he*	*h*	ـہ	(ـہـ) ـہـ	ہـ	ہ

choṭī he as a consonant

The normal function of *choṭī he* is to represent the consonant *h*. In the following examples note its slightly different shapes according to what precedes and follows it:

ہِنْدُو	*hindū*	'Hindu'	مُنْہ	*munh*	'mouth'
ہونا	*honā*	'to be'	واہ	*vāh*	'bravo!'
کہاں	*kahāṅ*	'where'	کوہ	*koh*	'mountain'

In the final position, *he* must be pronounced and given its full force.

Initial *choṭī he* has a special form written before ا *alif* and ل *lām*:

ہاں	*hāṅ*	'yes'
وہاں	*vahāṅ*	'there'
ہل	*hal*	'plough'
اہل	*ahl*	'people'

Silent *he*

Urdu derives a large number of its most commonly used nouns and adjectives from Arabic and Persian. Many of these words end in *choṭī he* which is not pronounced. This so-called 'silent *he*' is written in the transcription with the vowel *a*, which is pronounced exactly as the long vowel *ā*:

بچّہ	*bacca*	'child'	مکّہ	*makka*	'Mecca'
ارادہ	*irāda*	'intention'	آہستہ	*āhista*	'slow'

The symbol *a* at the end of such words indicates that the word is written with *choṭī he*, and not with *alif*. There is, however, no difference in the pronunciation of pairs of words such as the following:

دانا	*dānā*	'wise'
دانہ	*dāna*	'seed'

The word راجا *rājā* 'king' is of Indian origin and properly spelt with a final *alif*. It was taken into Persian, and according to Persian convention was spelt راجہ *rāja* with a final 'silent *he*'. It was then borrowed back into Urdu in that form. Consequently, in Urdu, both spellings راجا and راجہ are acceptable. Whichever spelling is used, the pronunciation is, of course, the same.

Aspirated consonants *do cašmī he*

We have seen that Urdu has a set of aspirated consonants which are produced with a strong emission of breath. In the transcription, these are indicated by the consonant immediately followed by *h*: *bh, ph, dh, th, kh, gh*, etc. In the script the *h* marking aspiration is indicated by a variant of *choṭī he*, which is known as *do cašmī he* ('two-eyed *he*'). *do cašmī he* has independent, initial, medial and final forms as shown in Table below.

Name	Phonetic value	Final	Medial	Initial	Independent
34(a) *do cašmī he*	*-h*	ـھ	ـھـ	ھـ	ھ

The aspirated consonants are written as follows:

بھ	bh	دھ	dh
پھ	ph	ڈھ	ḍh
تھ	th	ڑھ	ṛh
ٹھ	ṭh	کھ	kh
جھ	jh	گھ	gh
چھ	ch		

Until recently, *choṭī he* ہ and *do cašmī he* ھ were regarded as alternative foms of the letter *h*, and could be used interchangeably. In other words, what is now properly written in Urdu as ہاں *hāṅ* 'yes' or ہونا *honā* 'to be' was also written as ھاں or ھونا. The modern convention is to use *choṭī he* as a consonant, while *do cašmī he* is used exclusively for aspirates. Many people, however, still confuse the two letters. You should follow the modern convention.

Script exercise 6

Read the following words and write them out, omitting the optional signs.

***Choṭī he* as a consonant :**

وَہاں	*vahāṅ*	'there'	کوہ	*koh*	'mountain'
ہونا	*honā*	'to be'	لاہَور	*lāhaur*	'Lahore'
ہَم	*ham*	'we'	گَہْنا	*gahnā*	'jewel'

Silent *he* :

آہِسْتَہ	*āhista*	'slow'	بارَہ	*bāra*	'twelve'
بَچّہ	*bacca*	'child'	سَتْرَہ	*satra*	'seventeen'

Aspirated consonants with *do casmi he*:

بھات	*bhāt*	'cooked rice'	کھانا	*khānā*	'to eat'
پَھل	*phal*	'fruit'	مُجھ	*mujh*	'me'
اَچّھا	*acchā*	'good'	دُودھ	*dūdh*	'milk'

Letter 35 *ye*

The last letter of the Urdu alphabet is *ye*, written in the transcription as *y*. Like *vāū* it is used both as a consonant and to represent long vowels. The initial and medial shapes are the same as the ب set. There are two forms of the independent and final shapes, which are explained below:

Name	Phonetic value	Final	Medial	Initial	Independent
35 *ye*	*y*	ی	ید	یـ	ی
		ے	—	—	ے

ye as a consonant

At the beginning and in the middle of a word *ye* usually represents the consonant *y*:

یار *yār* 'friend' بایاں *bāyāṅ* 'left'
سایہ *sāya* 'shadow' سَیِّد *sayyid* 'Sayyid', 'Syed' (a Muslim title)

ye as a vowel marker

The letter *ye* is also used to represent the three long vowels *ī*, *e*, and *ai*. Note that, although transcribed with two letters, *ai* is one long vowel pronounced similarly to the *e* in English *hen*.

When these three vowels occur at the beginning of a word they are written with *alif* followed by *ye*:

ایمان *īmān* 'faith' ایک *ek* 'one' ایسا *aisā* 'such'

In the middle of a word, these vowels are indicated by *ye* used alone:

سینہ *sīna* 'breast' دینا *denā* 'to give' جیسا *jaisā* 'as'

At the end of a word, the first final shape ی indictes the long vowel *ī*:

لڑکی *laṛkī* 'girl' بھی *bhī* 'also'

At the end of word, the second final shape ے represents both the long vowels *e* and *ai*:

لڑکے *laṛke* 'boys' ہے *hai* 'is'

All three vowels may be nasalised with *nūn gunna*:

تھیں *thīṅ* 'were' ہمیں *hameṅ* 'us' میں *maiṅ* I

When it is necessary to indicate pronunciation more precisely, the vowel sign ِ *zer* may be written under the letter preceding ی to indicate *ī*:

اِیمان *īmān* سِینہ *sīna* تھِیں *thīṅ*

َ *zabar* may be used to indicate the vowel *ai* :

اَیسا	*aisā*	جَیسا	*jaisā*	ہَے	*hai*

No sign is used for indicating *e*:

لڑکے	*laṛke*	دینا	*denā*

You will notice that this is a similar convention to that used for precisely indicating *ū*, *o* and *au* written with *vaū*. Again, the vowel signs are rarely used.

Script exercise 7

Read the following words and write them out, omitting the optional signs:

یہاں	*yahāṅ*	'here'	کھیلنا	*khelnā*	'to play'
دایاں	*dāyāṅ*	'right'	میں	*meṅ*	'in'
پیر	*pīr*	'Monday'	کَیسے	*kaise*	'how?'
اینٹ	*īṅṭ*	'brick'	نَوّے	*navve*	'ninety'
بیٹی	*beṭī*	'daughter'	ہَے	*hai*	'is'

More on vowels

Pronunciation of short vowels before *h*

When coming immediately before *h* either ح or ہ – the short vowels have special pronunciations.

a before *h* is pronounced *ai* like the *e* in English *hen* :

اَحمد	*ahmad*	'Ahmad'
رَہنا	*rahnā*	'to remain'
شَہر	*šahr*	'city'

i before *h* also sounds like the *e* in English *hen* :

مِہربانی	*mihrbānī*	'kindness'
واضِح	*vāzih*	'clear'

u before *h* sounds like the *o* in English *cot*:

شُہرت	*šuhrat*	'fame'
تَوَجُّہ	*tavajjuh*	'attention'

Note the pronunciation of three very important words which end in 'unpronounced' *choṭī he* :

Transcription		Pronunciation	
کہ	*ki*	*ke*	'that'
یہ	*yih*	*ye*	'this, he, she, it'
وہ	*vuh*	*vo*	'that, he, she, it'

Pronunciation of short vowels before ع *'ain*

When the short vowels come before ع *'ain,* which is itself ignored in pronunciation, ع *'ain* has the effect of changing the quality of the vowel:

َ *a* before *'ain* is pronounced *ā*
ِ *i* before *'ain* is pronounced *e*
ُ *u* before *'ain* is pronounced *o*

Transcription		Pronunciation	
بَعد	*ba'd*	*bād*	'after'
جَمع	*jama'*	*jamā*	'collected'
شِعر	*ši'r*	*šer*	'verse'
واقِع	*vāqi'*	*vāqe*	'situated'
شُعلہ	*šu'la*	*šola*	'flame'
تَوَقُّع	*tavaqqu'*	*tavaqqo*	'hope'

Vowel junctions with ء *hamza*

In many Urdu words, one vowel may follow another, and both must be given their full value. For example: *āo* 'come' is clearly pronounced *ā-o* (not rhyming with English 'cow'); similarly *kaī* 'several' is pronounced *ka-ī* (not like English 'kay').

The junction between vowels is marked by the sign ء which is known as *hamza*. In Arabic *hamza* is a catch in the throat, sounding like *tt* in the Cockney pronunciation of 'bottle'.

When *ye* indicates the vowels *ī* or *e* coming immediately after another vowel, it must be preceded by the sign ء *hamza*. The *hamza* is written over a base which has the shape ـیـ traditionally, this is called the 'chair' on which *hamza* 'sits'.

کئی	*kaī*	'several'
تیئیس	*teīs*	'twenty-three'

کوئی	*koī*	'someone'
گئے	*gae*	'they went'
گائے	*gāe*	'they sang'

The short vowel *i* coming after another vowel is indicated by *hamza* 'sitting on its chair':

کوئلہ *koila* 'coal' آئس کریم *āis krīm* 'ice cream' لائن *lāin* 'queue'

When و *vāū* represents the long vowels *ū* and *o* coming after another vowel, *hamza* is usually placed directly over و – without a 'chair':

آؤ	*āo*	'come'	جاؤں	*jāūṅ*	'I may go'

Often the *hamza* over و is omitted:

آو	*āo*	جاوں	*jāūṅ*

If you mentally split the two vowels, *ka-ī, ko-ila, ā-o,* you may think of *hamza* as the line /-/ you put between them.

There are many words which have the vowel combinations [*īā, īe, īo*] in which *hamza* is not generally employed. For example:

لڑکیاں	*laṛkīāṅ*	'girls'	چلیے	*calīe*	'come on'
احتیاط	*ihtīāt*	'caution'	لڑکیوں کا	*laṛkīoṅ kā*	'of the girls'
چاہیے	*cāhīe*	'is needed'	کھڑکیوں میں	*khiṛkīoṅ meṅ*	'in the windows'

Script exercise 8

Read the following words and write them out, omitting the optional signs, but writing the *hamza* in all cases:

اَحْمَد	*ahmad*	'Ahmad'	شُعْلَہ	*šu'la*	'flame'
اِحْتِیاط	*ihtīāt*	'caution'	بَمْبَئی	*bam̊baī*	'Bombay'
عُہْدَہ	*'uhda*	'position'	مَئی	*maī*	'May'
بَعض	*ba'z*	'some'	چائے	*cāe*	'tea'
اِعْتِراض	*i'tirāz*	'objection'	لاؤں	*lāūṅ*	'let me bring'

The Arabic definite article

The Arabic word for 'the' (the 'definite article') is ال *al*, and is joined to the word it precedes:

الاکسیر	*al-iksīr*	'elixir' ('the potion')
الکحل	*al-kuhl*	'alcohol' ('the powdered lead')
القرآن	*al-qurān*	the Quran (Koran)

Note that, exceptionally, آ *alif madd* is used for the *ā* in the word for Quran. The word ال *al-* is employed in many Urdu expressions borrowed from Arabic. When the word following ال *al-* begins with a letter representing one of the sounds *d, n, r, s,* š, *t, n, l* or *z*, the *lām* of the article is pronounced like the following letter. The most common example of this is the Muslim greeting:

السلام علیکم *as-salāmu 'alaikum* 'the peace upon you'

i.e. 'peace be upon you' *(l + s > s - s).*

The letters which 'attract' *lām* in this way are:

ت	*te*	ش	*šīn*
ث	*se*	ص	*svād*
د	*dāl*	ض	*zvād*
ذ	*zāl*	ط	*toe*
ر	*re*	ظ	*zoe*
ز	*ze*	ل	*lām*
س	*sīn*	ن	*nūn*

The most common examples of this 'attraction' are proper names taken from Arabic. In this case the vowel of the article is changed to *u*:

شمس الدین	*šams ud dīn*	Shams ud Din
عبدالرحمان	*'abd ur rahmān*	'Abd ur Rahman
نورالزمان	*nūr uz zamān*	Nur uz Zaman

Before other letters, the *lām* of the article retains its value *l*:

عبدالعزیز	*'abd ul 'azīz*	'Abd ul 'Aziz
خورشیدالاسلام	*xuršīd ul Islām*	Khurshid ul Islam

These names literally mean Sun (of) the Faith, Servant (of) the Compassionate, Light (of) the Age, Servant (of) the Noble and Sun (of) the Islam.

Punctuation

Punctuation is a fairly recent innovation in Urdu. The only regularly employed punctuation marks are:

۔	full stop	،	comma	؟	question mark

Even in the most carefully printed Urdu books, the use of punctuation is still erratic.

Compound words

Like English, Urdu has many 'compound' words, i.e. one word made up of two, e.g. 'tea-house', 'fruit-seller'. The modern convention in Urdu is to write the two words separately without a hyphen:

چائے خانہ	*cāe xāna*	'tea shop'
پھل والا	*phal vālā*	'fruit seller'
دو پہر	*do pahr*	'two watch' = 'afternoon'

or as one word:

چائیخانہ *cāexāna*   پھلوالا *phalvālā*   دوپہر *dopahar*

In this book compounds are written as separate words.

Numerals

Unlike the rest of the alphabet, the numerals are written from left to right, as in English:

→									
۱	۲	۳	۴	۵	۶	۷	۸	۹	۰
1	2	3	4	5	6	7	8	9	0

۱۰	۲۵	۱۴۷	۱۰۸۹۲
10	25	147	10892

1 السلام علیکم، وکٹوریہ روڈ کہاں ہے؟

assalām 'alaikum, vikṭoria roḍ kahāṅ hai?

Hello! Where is Victoria Road?

In this unit you will learn how to:

- say hello and goodbye
- ask directions
- address strangers
- obtain information

مکالمہ ایک *mukālima ek* Dialogue 1

John stops Aslam in a Karachi street and asks him the way to Victoria Road.

جان : السلام علیکم

اسلم : وعلیکم السلام

جان : یہ بتائیے وکٹوریہ روڈ کہاں ہے؟

اسلم : وکٹوریہ روڈ وہاں ہے۔ دیکھیے بہت دور نہیں۔ کیا آپ امریکن ہیں۔

جان : جی نہیں، میں انگریز ہوں۔

اسلم : آپ کا نام کیا ہے؟

جان : میرا نام جان ہے۔ اور آپ کا؟

اسلم : میرا نام اسلم ہے۔

جان : اچھا، اسلم صاحب۔ میرا ہوٹل یہاں ہے۔ اجازت۔

اسلم : اچھا جان صاحب۔ خدا حافظ۔

جان : خدا حافظ۔

jān : *assalāmu 'alaikum.*

aslam : *va 'alaikum assalām*

jān : *yih batāīe, vikṭorīa roḍ kahāṅ hai?*

aslam : *vikṭorīa roḍ vahāṅ hai. dekhīe. bahut dūr nahīṅ hai. kyā āp amrīkan haiṅ?*

jān : *jī nahīṅ. maiṅ angrez hūṅ.*

aslam : *āp kā nām kyā hai?*

jān : *merā nām jān hai. aur āp kā?*

aslam : *merā nām aslam hai.*

jān : *acchā, aslam sāhib. merā hotel yahāṅ hai. ijāzat.*

aslam : *acchā, jān sāhib. xudā hāfiz.*

jān : *xudā hāfiz.*

John : Hello.

Aslam : Hello.

John : Tell (me) this. Where is Victoria Road?

Aslam : Victoria Road is there. Look. (It) is not very far. (What), are you American?

John : No. I am English.

Aslam : What is your name?

John : My name is John. And your name?

Aslam : My name is Aslam.

John : Very well, Aslam Sahib. My hotel is here. Excuse me (may I take leave?)

Aslam : Very well, John Sahib. Goodbye.

John : Goodbye.

جان	*jān*	John	وکٹوریہ روڈ	*vikṭorīa roḍ*	Victoria Road
اسلام علیکم	*assalāmu 'alaikum*	hello	کہاں	*'kahāṅ*	where?
اسلم	*aslam*	Aslam	ہے	*hai*	is
وعلیکم السلام	*va'alaikum assalām*	hello (in answer)	وہاں	*vahāṅ*	there
			دیکھیے	*dekhīe*	look!, see!
یہ	*yih*	this	بہت	*bahut*	very
بتائیے	*batāīe*	(please) tell (me)	دور	*dūr*	far
			نہیں	*nahīṅ*	not

کیا	*kyā*	what?; introduces questions	آپ کا	*āp kā*	your
			نام	*nām*	name
			میرا	*merā*	my
آپ	*āp*	you [polite]	اور	*aur*	and
			اچھا	*acchā*	good, very well
امریکن	*amrīkan*	American, American person	صاحب	*sāhib*	Mr
			ہوٹل	*hoṭal*	hotel
ہیں	*haiṅ*	are	یہاں	*yahāṅ*	here
جی نہیں	*jī nahīṅ*	no	اجازت	*ijāzat*	Excuse me [lit.:may I take leave?]
میں	*maiṅ*	I			
انگریز	*angrez*	English, English person			
			خدا حافظ	*xudā hāfiz*	goodbye
ہوں	*hūṅ*	am			

قواعد *qavā'id* Grammar

ہجے *hijje* Spelling

Note the special way in which the Arabic word السلام *assalāmu* 'the peace' is spelt in the phrase السلام علیکم *assalāmu 'alaikum* '(the) peace (be) upon you'. In such phrases the ل *lām* of ال *al* becomes *s* before a following س *s*.

Greetings: hello and goodbye; صاحب *sāhib*

The normal greeting used by Muslims is السلام علیکم *assalāmu 'alaikum*. It literally means 'the peace upon you', and can be used at any time of day for 'hello', 'good morning', 'good evening', etc. It is answered by saying وعلیکم السلام *va 'alaikum assalām* 'and upon you peace'. When taking leave of someone you can say اجازت *ijāzat* 'excuse me', literally '(give me) leave'. The phrase for 'goodbye' is خدا حافظ *xudā hāfiz*, a Persian expression meaning 'God (be your) Protector'. The word صاحب *sāhib* 'Mr' follows the person's name. It may be added to any of the person's names. Thus John Smith جان اسمتھ *jān ismith* could be addressed either as جان صاحب *jān sāhib* or as اسمتھ صاحب *ismith sāhib*.

The verb to be, 'am, is, are'

A verb is a word which denotes action, feeling, existing and so on. English examples are 'to do', 'to seem', 'to be', 'I do, you seem, he is', etc. In Urdu the verb 'to be' is *honā*.

In Dialogue 1 you met the forms :

میں ہوں	*main hūṅ*	I am
یہ ہے	*yih hai*	
وہ ہے	*vuh hai*	} he, she, it is
آپ ہیں	*āp haiṅ*	you are

Note that the words یہ *yih* 'this' and وہ *vuh* 'that' can also mean 'he, she, it', and that verb always comes at the end of the sentence:

وکٹوریہ روڈ دور ہے	*viktoriā roḍ dūr **hai***	Victoria Road is far away
میں امریکن نہیں ہوں	*main amrīkan nahīṅ **hūṅ***	I am not American
وہ وہاں ہے	*vuh vahāṅ **hai***	He is there

Personal pronouns 'I' and 'you'; polite commands 'tell me' and 'look!'

Personal pronouns are words such as 'I', 'you', 'he', 'they', etc. The Urdu pronoun *main* 'I' is used like its English counterpart:

میں پاکستانی ہوں   ***main*** *pākistānī hūṅ*   I am Pakistani

We shall see that Urdu has three words for 'you', which indicate various degrees of familiarity and respect. The word most commonly used when addressing adults and elders (including one's father, elder brother, etc.) is آپ *āp*. This requires a special form of the verb which conveys respect. The polite form of command, which always ends in ـے *-īe*, e.g. بتائے *batāīe'* (please) tell me, دیکھے *dekhīe* '(please) look, see', is only used with آپ and is in itself respectful. Urdu therefore, requires no word for 'please'.

یہ بتائے	*yih batāīe*	'please tell me'
دیکھے	*dekhīe*	'please look'

یہ *yih* وہ *vuh* 'this, that; he, she, it'

یہ *yih* means 'this' and وہ *vuh* means 'that', and may be used like their English equivalents:

یہ انگریز	*yih aṅgrez*	this English (man)
وہ امریکن	*vuh amrīkan*	that American
یہ بتائیے	*yih batāīe*	tell (me) this
وہ ہوٹل ہے	*vuh hoṭel hai*	that is a/the hotel

Urdu has no special word for 'a' or 'the', thus ہوٹل *hoṭal* can mean either 'a hotel' or 'the hotel'.

یہ *yih* and وہ *vuh* are also used as pronouns meaning 'he, she, it'. The actual meaning can be determined only from the context. یہ *yih* refers to a person or thing nearby: 'this person/thing here', وہ *vuh* refers to a person or thing further away: 'that person/thing there':

یہ انگریز ہے اور وہ پاکستانی ہے

yih aṅgrez hai aur vuh pākistānī hai

He/she (here) is English and he/she (there) is Pakistani

یہ کیا ہے؟

yih kyā hai?

What is it (this thing here)?

وہ کیا ہے؟

vuh kyā hai?

What is it (that thing there)?

In neutral circumstances when no contrast of distance is implied وہ *vuh* is more commonly used:

وہ پاکستانی ہے	*vuh pākistānī hai*	He/she is Pakistani
وہ کیا ہے؟	*vuh kyā hai?*	What is it?

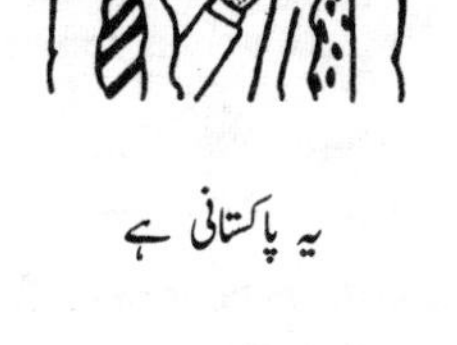

یہ پاکستانی ہے

وہ انگریز ہے

یہ ہوٹل ہے

Leaving out the pronoun

The personal pronoun is often omitted when the sense is clear:

آپ امریکن ہیں؟ جی نہیں، انگریز ہوں

āp amrīkan haiṅ? jī nahīṅ, angrez hūṅ

Are you American? No, (I) am English

Questions

Questions to which the answer may be either جی ہاں *jī hāṅ* 'yes' or جی نہیں *jī nahīṅ* 'no', as in English, are asked with rise in intonation, but in Urdu the word order remains that of the statement:

آپ امریکن ہیں؟ *āp amrīkan haiṅ?* Are you American?

Such questions are often prefaced by the word کیا *kyā* 'what?.

کیا آپ انگریز ہیں؟ *kyā āp angrez haiṅ?* (What), are you English?

کیا آپ کا ہوٹل یہاں ہے؟ *kyā āp kā hotal yahāṅ hai?* Is your hotel here?

Putting کیا *kyā* at the start of the question makes little difference to the sense and its inclusion is optional.

In questions which ask 'what is?', 'where is?', the question word کیا *kyā* 'what? or کہاں *kahāṅ* 'where?' always comes immediately before the verb:

یہ کیا ہے؟	*yih kyā hai?*	What is this?
پاکستان کہاں ہے؟	*pākistān kahāṅ hai?*	Where is Pakistan?
آپ کا نام کیا ہے؟	*āp kā nām kyā hai?*	What is your name?

میرا **merā my** آپ کا **āp kā your**

These words come before the word to which they refer. Note that آپ کا *āp kā* 'your' consists of two elements which are written separately:

میرا نام	*merā nām*	my name
آپ کا ہوٹل	*āp kā hotal*	your hotel

مکالمہ دو **mukālima do Dialogue 2**

John meets Aslam again and after asking him about Karachi invites him to have tea in a nearby cafe.

جان : السلام علیکم، اسلم صاحب۔ کیا حال ہے؟
اسلم : آپ کی دعا ہے، سب ٹھیک ہے۔ اور آپ ٹھیک ہیں؟
جان : جی ہاں، میں بالکل ٹھیک ہوں۔ اسلم صاحب، یہ بتائیے، یہ بڑی عمارت کیا ہے؟
اسلم : یہ عمارت حبیب بینک ہے۔ کافی نئی عمارت ہے۔
جان : اور وہ کیا ہے وہاں؟
اسلم : وہ بوہری بازار ہے۔ بہت پرانا بازار ہے اور بہت دلچسپ ہے۔
جان : اور وہ آدمی کون ہے؟ وہ سندھی ہے؟
اسلم : جی نہیں۔ وہ پنجابی ہے۔ لیکن یہ عورت یہاں، یہ سندھی ہے۔
جان : اچھا اسلم صاحب، کراچی بہت دلچسپ شہر ہے۔ دیکھیے، یہاں چائے خانہ ہے۔ چلیے چائے پیئیں۔

jān : *assalāmu 'alaikum, aslam sāhib. kyā hāl hai?*

aslam : *āp kī du'ā hai. sab ṭhīk hai. aur āp ṭhīk haiṅ?*

jān : *jī hāṅ, maiṅ bilkul ṭhīk hūṅ. aslam sāhib, yih batāīe. yih baṛī 'imārat kyā hai?*

aslam : *yih 'imārat habīb baiṅk hai. kāfī naī 'imārat hai.*

jān : *aur vuh kyā hai vahāṅ?*

aslam : *vuh bohrī bāzār hai. bahut purānā bāzār hai aur bahut dilcasp hai.*

jān : *aur vuh ādmī kaun hai? vuh sindhī hai?*

aslam : *jī nahīṅ. vuh panjābī hai. lekin yih 'aurat yahāṅ, yih sindhī hai.*

jān : *acchā, aslam sāhib. karācī bahut dilcasp šahr hai. dekhīe, yahāṅ cāe xāna hai. calīe, cāe pīeṅ.*

John : Hello, Aslam Sahib. How are you?

Aslam : (It is your prayer), all is well. And are you all right?

John : Yes, I am extremely well. Aslam Sahib, tell (me) this. What is this big building?

Aslam : This building is the Habib Bank. (It) is quite a new building.

John : And what is that there?

Aslam : That is Bohri Bazaar. It's a very old bazaar and very interesting.

John : And who is that man? Is he a Sindhi?

Aslam : No. He's a Panjabi. But this woman here. She is a Sindhi.

John : I see, Aslam Sahib. Karachi is a very interesting city. Look. There's a tea shop here. Come on, let's have ('drink') tea.

حال	*hāl*	condition (m.)	بازار	*bāzār*	bazaar, market (m.)
کیا حال ہے؟	*kyā hāl hai*	how are you?	پرانا	*purānā*	old
دعا	*du'ā*	prayer (f.)	دلچسپ	*dilcasp*	interesting
آپ کی دعا ہے	*āp kī du'ā hai*	'it is (your) prayer'	آدمی	*ādmī*	man (m.)
سب	*sab*	all, everything	کون	*kaun?*	who?
ٹھیک	*ṭhīk*	all right	سندھی	*sindhī*	Sindhi
بالکل	*bilkul*	absolutely	پنجابی	*panjābī*	Panjabi
جی ہاں	*jī hāṅ*	yes	لیکن	*lekin*	but
شکریہ	*šukrīa*	thank you	عورت	*'aurat*	woman (f.)
بڑا	*baṛā*	big	کراچی	*karācī*	Karachi
عمارت	*'imārat*	building (f.)	شہر	*šahr*	city, town (m.)
حبیب بینک	*habīb baiṅk*	Habib Bank (m.)	چائے خانہ	*cāe xāna*	tea shop, restaurant (m.)
کافی	*kāfī*	quite	چلیے	*calīe*	come on
نیا	*nayā*	new	چائے	*cāe*	tea (f.)
بوہری بازار	*bohrī bāzār*	Bohri Bazaar (m.)	پئیں	*pīeṅ*	let's drink

قواعد *qavā'id* Grammar

ہجے *hijje* Spelling

Note the way in which the word بالکل *bilkul* 'absolutely' is spelt. It is, in fact, a borrowing from Arabic composed of three elements ب *bi* 'in' ال *al* 'the' کل *kul* 'all'. In Urdu it functions as an adverb meaning 'absolutely', 'extremely': بالکل ٹھیک *bilkul ṭhīk* 'extremely well', بالکل شاندار *bilkul šāndār* 'absolutely fabulous!'.

Many Urdu nouns (words for things and people such as boy, city, John) and adjectives (descriptive words such as big, good, blue), mostly borrowed from Persian, end in *choṭī he*, which is not pronounced. The ending in transcription is written as *-a*: وکٹوریہ *vikṭorīa* 'Victoria', چائے خانہ *cāe xāna* 'tea shop', تازہ *tāza* 'fresh'. In pronunciation the ending ہ *-a* is the same as ا *-ā*: دعا *du'ā* 'prayer', بڑا *baṛā* 'big', پرانا *purānā* 'old'.

More greetings

A common way of saying 'how are you?' is کیا حال ہے؟ *kyā hāl hai*?, literally 'what is (your) condition?'. It may be answered by the phrase آپ کی دعا ہے *āp kī du'ā hai* 'it is your prayer (which makes me well)'.

These phrases may be used by both Muslims and non-Muslims.

شکریہ *šukrīa* is a common word for 'thank you' used by people of any religion.

Masculine and feminine

Urdu nouns fall into two groups or genders: masculine and feminine. Nouns denoting males such as آدمی *ādmī* 'man' and صاحب *sāhib* 'gentleman' are always masculine; those denoting females such as عورت *'aurat* 'woman' and صاحبہ *sāhiba* 'lady' are always feminine. Other nouns may be of either gender. Thus بازار *bāzār* 'bazaar' and شہر *šahr* 'town/city' are masculine, while دعا *du'ā* 'prayer' and عمارت *'imārat* 'building' are feminine. There are, unfortunately, no hard and fast rules for determining gender, which simply has to be learnt. In the first dialogue all the nouns were masculine. From now on each noun listed in the vocabulary will have its gender indicated with m. for masculine and f. for feminine; m.p. is used for masculine plural, and f.p. for feminine plural.

Adjectives in certain cases must agree with the following noun in gender, i.e.

change their gender to correspond with that of the noun.

Adjectives which have their masculine form ending in ا *-ā* '*alif*' such as اچھا *acchā* 'good', بڑا *baṛā* 'big', نیا *nayā* 'new' change the ending ا- *-ā* to ی- *-ī* before feminine nouns:

Masculine			**Feminine**		
اچھا شہر	*acchā šahr*	good city	اچھی چائے	*acchī cāe*	good tea
نیا بازار	*nayā bāzār*	new bazaar	نئی عمارت	*naī 'imārat*	new building
پرانا ہوٹل	*purānā hoṭal*	old hotel	پرانی کتاب	*purānī kitāb*	old book

Note the spelling of نیا *nayā* (masculine) and نئی *naī* (feminine).

Agreement must be made wherever the adjective appears in the sentence:

یہ آدمی اچھا ہے	*yih ādmī acchā hai*	this man is good
وہ عورت اچھی ہے	*vuh 'aurat acchī hai*	this woman is good
وہ ہوٹل پرانا ہے	*vuh hoṭal purānā hai*	this hotel is old
یہ عمارت پرانی ہے	*yih 'imārat purānī hai*	this building is old

Adjectives ending in any other letter e.g. دلچسپ *dilcasp* 'interesting', انگریز *angrez* 'English' make no change for gender:

دلچسپ آدمی	*dilcasp ādmī*	an interesting man
انگریز عورت	*angrez 'aurat*	an English woman

The words میرا *merā* 'my' and آپ کا *āp kā* 'your' are also adjectives and agree accordingly in gender with the noun:

میرا شہر	*merā šahr*	my city
میری کتاب	*merī kitāb*	my book
آپ کا پورا نام	*āp kā pūrā nām*	your full name
آپ کی چائے	*āp kī cāe*	your tea

Note that the words انگریز *angrez*, امریکن *amrīkan*, پاکستانی *pākistānī*, ہندوستانی *hindustānī* 'Indian' may function as both adjectives and nouns:

پاکستانی عورت	*pākistānī 'aurat*	a Pakistani woman
یہ پاکستانی ہے	*yih pākistānī hai*	he/she is a Pakistani
وہ ہندوستانی ہے	*vuh hindustānī hai*	he/she is an Indian

Although ہندوستانی *hindustānī* is written with و *vau*, the *u* is pronounced short.

Who is that? Who is he/ she?

The word for 'who?' is کون *kaun*, and like all other 'question' words, such as کیا *kyā* 'what?' and کہاں *kahāṅ* 'where?' must come immediately before the verb:

وہ کون ہے؟ وہ پنجابی ہے Who is he/she (there)? He/she is a Panjabi
vuh kaun hai? vuh panjābī hai

یہ کون ہے؟ یہ سندھی ہے؟ Who is this? This is a Sindhi
yih kaun hai? yih sindhī hai

چلیے‘ چائے پییں **calīe, cāe pīeṅ** 'Come on, let's have tea'

The polite command form چلیے *calīe* means 'come on' or please get a move on'. The useful expression چائے پییں *cāe pīeṅ* means 'let's drink/have tea'.

مشق *mašq* Exercise

1.1 Fill in the blanks

Fill in the blanks with the correct masculine or feminine form of the adjective given in brackets (watch out for those that require no change). Before writing, check the gender of the noun.

(good)	یہ چائے ______ ہے۔	1
(interesting)	بوہری بازار ______ ہے۔	2
(new)	وہ عمارت بالکل ______ ہے۔	3
(big)	میرا شہر ______ ہے۔	4
(Indian)	کیا آپ ______ ہیں۔	5

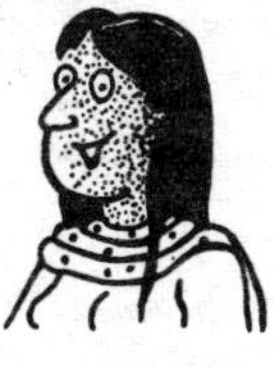

مکالمہ ۳ mukālima tīn Dialogue 3

John and Aslam go to have tea in a tea shop. In the course of the conversation they exchange personal details and telephone numbers. John is invited to Aslam's home.

جان : یہ چائے خانہ واقعی بہت اچھا ہے۔ چائے اچھی ہے اور کھانا بہت مزے دار ہے۔

اسلم : جی ہاں، یہاں سب کچھ ہے۔ جان صاحب بتائیے، آپ کا پورا نام کیا ہے؟

جان : میرا پورا نام جان اسمتھ ہے۔ اور آپ کا پورا نام کیا ہے؟

اسلم : میرا پورا نام محمد اسلم خان ہے۔ میں یہاں کراچی میں انجنیر ہوں اور آپ؟

جان : میں کراچی میں سیاح ہوں۔ لندن میں میں ڈاکٹر ہوں۔ کراچی میں آپ کا گھر کہاں ہے؟

اسلم : میرا گھر بندر روڈ پر ہے۔ بہت دور نہیں۔ گھر پرانا ہے لیکن اچھا ہے۔ آپ کبھی آئیے۔ ایک پاکستانی گھر دیکھیے۔

جان : شکریہ، اسلم صاحب۔ آپ کا ٹیلیفون نمبر کیا ہے؟

اسلم : میرا نمبر دو، چار، سات، تین، پانچ ہے۔

جان : شکریہ۔ اور میرا نمبر ایک، چھے، آٹھ، صفر، نو ہے۔

jān : *yih cāe xāna vāqa'ī bahut acchā hai. cāe acchī hai aur khānā bahut mazedār hai.*

aslam : *jī hāṅ, yahāṅ sab kuch hai. jān sāhib, batāīe. āp kā pūrā nām kyā hai?*

jān : *merā pūrā nām jān ismith hai. aur āp kā pūrā nām kyā hai?*

aslam : *merā pūrā nām muhammad aslam xān hai. maiṅ yahāṅ karācī meṅ injinīr hūṅ. aur āp?*

jān : *maiṅ karācī meṅ sayyāh hūṅ, landan meṅ maiṅ ḍākṭar hūṅ. karācī meṅ āp kā ghar kahāṅ hai?*

aslam : *merā ghar bandar roḍ par hai. yahāṅ se bahut dūr nahīṅ hai. purānā ghar hai, lekin bahut acchā hai. āp kabhī āīe. ek pākistānī ghar dekhīe.*

jān : *šukrīa, aslam sāhib. āp kā ṭelifon nambar kyā hai?*

aslam : *merā nambar do cār sāt tīn pāṅc hai.*

jān : *šukrīa. aur merā nambar ek che āṭh sifr nau hai.*

John : This tea shop is really very good. The tea is good and the food is very tasty.

Aslam : Yes. (There's) everything here. John Sahib, tell me. What is your full name?

John : My full name is John Smith. And what is your full name?

Aslam : My full name is Muhammad Aslam Khan. I am an engineer here in Karachi. And you?

John : I am a tourist in Karachi. In London I am a doctor. Where is your house in Karachi?

Aslam : My house is on Bandar Road. It's not very far from here. It's an old house, but it is very good. (You) come sometime. See a Pakistani house.

John : Thank you, Aslam Sahib. What is your telephone number?

Aslam : My number is 24735.

John : Thank you. And my number is 16809.

واقعی	*vāqa'ī*	really	بندر روڈ	*bandar roḍ*	Bandar Road (m.)
کھانا	*khānā*	food (m.)			
مزےدار	*mazedār*	tasty	پر	*par*	on, upon
سب کچھ	*sab kuch*	everything	سے	*se*	from
پورا	*pūrā*	full	کبھی	*kabhī*	sometime
اسمتھ	*ismith*	Smith	آیئے	*āīe*	please come
محمد	*muham-mad*	Muham-mad	ایک	*ek*	one, a
خان	*xān*	Khan	ٹیلیفون	*ṭelīfon*	telephone (m.)
میں	*meṅ*	in			
انجینیر	*injinīr*	engineer (m.)	نمبر	*nambar*	number (m.)
سیاح	*sayyāh*	tourist (m.)	دو	*do*	two
لندن	*landan*	London (m.)	چار	*cār*	four
			سات	*sāt*	seven
ڈاکٹر	*ḍākṭar*	doctor (m.)	تین	*tīn*	three
گھر	*ghar*	house, home (m.)	پانچ	*pāṅc*	five

قواعد *qavā'id* Grammar

Names نام

In India and Pakistan the western concept of Christian/given name and surname rarely applies. Many Muslims have three elements in their name, e.g. محمد اسلم خان *muhammad aslam xān* 'Muhammad Aslam Khan', any of which might be used when addressing or referring to the person. This man might be called محمد صاحب *muhammad sāhib*, اسلم صاحب *aslam sāhib*, or خان صاحب *xān sāhib*. From the dialogues he obviously likes to be known as اسلم *aslam*. To find out a person's full name, you may ask: آپ کا پورا نام کیا ہے؟ *āp kā pūrā nām kyā hai*? 'What is your full name?'.

'in', 'on', 'from' – postpositions

In English, words such as 'in', 'on, 'from' are known as prepositions and come before the word they modify: '*in* London', '*from* here', etc. In Urdu their equivalents میں *meṅ* 'in', پر *par* 'on', سے *se* 'from' follow the word they modify and are termed postpositions.

بریڈ فورڈ میں	*braiḍforḍ meṅ*	in Bradford	گھر سے	*ghar se*	from the house
بندر روڈ پر	*bandar roḍ par*	on Bandar Road	یہاں سے دور	*yahāṅ se dūr*	far from here

Place names

So far we have met various names for countries, towns and streets, the spelling of which should be carefully noted:

ہندوستان	*hindustān*	India
پاکستان	*pākistān*	Pakistan
سندھ	*sindh*	Sindh
پنجاب	*panjāb*	Panjab
کراچی	*karācī*	Karachi
لندن	*landan*	London
بریڈ فورڈ	*braiḍforḍ*	Bradford
وکٹوریہ روڈ	*vikṭorīa roḍ*	Victoria Road (Karachi)
بندر روڈ	*bandar roḍ*	Bandar Road (Karachi)
بوہری بازار	*bohrī bāzār*	Bohri Bazaar (Karachi)

Numbers

The Urdu numbers from 0–10 are given in Appendix 1. These should now be learnt.

ثقافت *siqāfat* Culture

Urdu is one of the major languages of India as well as of Pakistan and is spoken by people of various religious and cultural backgrounds. In Pakistan, the majority of people you will meet will be Muslims, and so the customary Muslim greetings السلام علیکم for 'hello' and خداحافظ for 'goodbye' will usually be sufficient. When greeting or taking leave of one another, Hindus use the word نمستے *namaste*, which can be used at any time for both 'hello' and 'goodbye'. A greeting used by people of all faiths is آداب عرض ہے *ādāb 'arz hai* literally meaning 'respect is presented'.

Karachi is a huge cosmopolitan port بندر *bandar* 'port' (hence Bandar Road) in which both western and Asian influences are visible. In its colourful bazaars, of which the central Bohri Bazaar is the biggest, you will see not only native Sindhis (people from the province of Sindh), but Panjabis, Balochis, Afghans and many people who have migrated there from India.

مشقیں *mašqeṅ* Exercises

1.2 Write these sentences in Urdu.

1 Say hello to Mr Khan and ask him how he is.

2 Ask him where Bandar Road is.

3 Tell him your name.

4 Tell him your hotel is not far away.

5 Take your leave and say goodbye.

1.3 Give your part in the dialogue.

Aslam	السلام علیکم۔ کیا حال ہے؟
You	Answer the greeting and say you are fine
Aslam	کیا آپ انگریز ہیں؟
You	Tell him that you are
Aslam	آپ ہوٹل میں ہیں؟
You	Say yes, you are
Aslam	آپ کا ہوٹل یہاں سے دور ہے؟
You	Say that it is not
Aslam	اچھا' اجازت۔ خدا حافظ
You	Say goodbye

1.4 Sums

Work out the answers to these sums and write them out in words and figures.

1 دو اور پانچ = (۲ + ۵)

2 چھے اور تین = (۶ + ۳)

3 چھے اور چھے = (۶ + ۶)

4 ایک اور سات = (۱ + ۷)

5 تین اور تین = (۳ + ۳)

1.5 Comprehension

Listen to the dialogue and tick the appropriate answers.

1 Where is Mr Khan's house?	In London ( )	In Karachi ( )
2 Where is Mr Khan originally from?	India ( )	Pakistan ( )
3 Is Mr Khan's house far away?	Yes ( )	No ( )
4 What is Mr Khan's house like?	New ( )	Old ( )

1.6 Answer the questions

Look at the visitor's entry form and answer the questions.

Name	محمد خان
Country of Origin	پاکستان
Place of Residence	کراچی
Address	۳۵ بندر روڈ
Occupation	انجینیر
Place of Residence in UK	بریڈ فورڈ
Duration of stay (days)	۱۰ (دس)

1 Which country does Mr Khan come from?

2 He lives in Victoria Road. True or false?

3 He is a doctor. True or false?

4 How many days is he staying in the UK?

5 He is visiting London. True or false?

2 آیئے۔ تشریف لائیے۔ تشریف رکھیے

āīe, tašrīf lāīe, tašrīf rakhīe

Please come in and take a seat

In this unit you will learn how to:

- introduce yourself
- make polite conversation
- describe your family
- address children

مکالمہ ایک *mukālima ek* Dialogue 1

John and his wife, Helen, are invited to dinner by Aslam and his wife, Bilqis, who introduce them to their children.

اسلم : آیئے' جان صاحب' تشریف لائیے۔ کیا حال ہے؟

جان : آپ کی دعا ہے' اسلم صاحب۔ میں ٹھیک ہوں شکریہ۔ میری بیگم سے ملیے۔ ان کا نام ہیلن ہے۔ لندن میں وہ بھی ڈاکٹر ہیں۔

اسلم : السلام علیکم' ہیلن صاحبہ۔ آیئے' تشریف رکھیے۔ آپ لوگ میری بیگم سے ملیے۔ ان کا نام بلقیس ہے۔

ہیلن : آداب عرض ہے' بلقیس صاحبہ۔ کیا یہ آپ کے بچے ہیں؟

بلقیس : جی ہاں۔ ہمارے چار بچے ہیں۔ دو لڑکے اور دو لڑکیاں۔ یہ ہمارا بڑا بیٹا ہے۔ اس کا نام حامد ہے۔ اور یہ ہمارا چھوٹا بیٹا ہے۔ اس کا نام اقبال ہے اور یہ ہماری دو بیٹیاں ہیں۔ نرگس اور جمیلہ۔ جمیلہ بہت چھوٹی ہے۔ صرف دو سال۔ دیکھیے ان کی چیزیں ہر جگہ بکھری پڑی ہیں۔

ہیلن : کوئی بات نہیں۔ بچے ہیں' اور کیا!

بلقیس : کیا آپ کے بھی بچے ہیں؟

ہیلن : جی نہیں۔ ہمارے بچے نہیں ہیں۔

aslam : *āīe, jān sāhib, tašrīf lāīe. kyā hāl hai?*

jān : *āp kī du'ā hai, aslam sāhib. maiṅ ṭhīk hūṅ šukrīa. merī begam se milīe. in kā nām helan hai. landan meṅ vuh bhī ḍākṭar haiṅ.*

aslam : *assalāmu 'alaikum, helan sāhiba. āīe, tašrīf rakhīe. āp log merī begam se milīe. in kā nām bilqīs hai.*

helan : *ādāb arz hai, bilqīs sāhiba. kyā yih āp ke bacce haiṅ?*

bilqīs : *jī hāṅ. hamāre cār bacce haiṅ, do laṛke aur do laṛkīāṅ. yih hamārā baṛā beṭā hai. is kā nām hāmid hai. aur yih hamārā choṭā beṭā hai. is kā nām iqbāl hai. aur yih hamārī do beṭīāṅ haiṅ, nargis aur jamīla. jamīla bahut choṭī hai. sirf do sāl. dekhīe. in kī cīzeṅ har jagah bikhrī-paṛī haiṅ.*

helan : *koī bāt nahīṅ. bacce haiṅ. aur kyā?*

bilqīs : *kyā āp ke bhī bacce haiṅ?*

helan : *jī nahīṅ. hamāre bacce nahīṅ.*

Aslam : Come (in), John. Please come in. How are you?

John : Well ('it is your prayer'), Aslam Sahib. I am all right, thank you. Meet my wife. Her name is Helen. In London she is also a doctor.

Aslam : Hello, Helen Sahiba. Come, please take a seat (You people) meet my wife. Her name is Bilqis.

Helen : Hello, Bilqis Sahiba. Are these your children?

Bilqis : Yes, we have four children. Two boys and two girls. This is our elder ('big') son. His name is Hamid. And this is our younger son. His name is Iqbal. And these are our two daughters, Nargis and Jamila. Jamila is very small. Only two years (old). Look. Their things are scattered around everywhere.

Helen : It doesn't matter. (They) are children. So what?

Bilqis : Do you also have children?

Helen : No. We don't have children.

آیئے	āīe	come
آنا	ānā	to come
تشریف	tašrīf	honour (f.)
لایئے	lāīe	bring
لانا	lānā	to bring
تشریف لایئے	tašrīf lāīe	please come (in)
رکھیے	rakhīe	place, put
رکھنا	rakhnā	to put, place
تشریف رکھیے	tašrīf rakhīe	please sit down
بیگم	begam	wife (f.)
سے ملیے	se milīe	please meet (with)
ان کا (کی، کے)	in kā, -ī, -e	his, her, their
ہیلن	helan	Helen
بھی	bhī	also, too
ہیں	haiṅ	are
صاحبہ	sāhiba	Mrs, Miss
لوگ	log	people (m.p.)
آپ لوگ	āp log	you (plural)
بلقیس	bilqīs	Bilqis
بچہ، بچے	bacca, bacce	child (m.), children (m.p.)
یہ آپ کے بچے ہیں؟	yih āp ke bacce haiṅ	are these your children?
ہمارا -ی -ے	hamārā, -ī, -e	our
ہمارے چار بچے ہیں	hamāre cār bacce haiṅ	we have four children
اور کیا	aur kyā	so what?
لڑکا، لڑکے	laṛkā, laṛke	boy (m.), boys (m.p.)
لڑکی، لڑکیاں	laṛkī, laṛkīāṅ	girl (f.), girls (m.f.)
بڑا -ی -ے	baṛā, -ī, -e	elder
بیٹا، بیٹے	beṭā, beṭe	son (m.), sons (m.p.)
اس کا	is kā	his, her, its
حامد	hāmid	Hamid
چھوٹا	choṭā -ī, -e	small, younger
اقبال	iqbāl	Iqbal
بیٹی، بیٹیاں	beṭī, beṭīāṅ	daughter (f.), daughters (f.p.)
نرگس	nargis	Nargis
جمیلہ	jamīla	Jamila
صرف	sirf	only
سال	sāl	year (m.)
دو سال	do sāl	two years (old)
ان کا، کی، کے	un kā, -ī, -e	their
چیز، چیزیں	cīz, cīzeṅ	thing (f.), things (f.p.)
ہر جگہ	har jagah	everywhere
بکھری پڑی	bikhrī-paṛī	scattered
کوئی	koī	some, any
بات	bāt	matter, thing (f.)
کوئی بات نہیں	koī bāt nahīṅ	it doesn't matter
آپ کے بچے ہیں	āp ke bacce haiṅ	do you have children?

قواعد *qavā'id* Grammar

Polite commands: 'please do this!'; the Urdu verb

The Urdu verb is referred to (e.g. in dictionaries) by its *infinitive* which is the equivalent of the English 'to tell', 'to see', 'to come'. The infinitive always ends with نا *-nā*: بتانا *batānā* 'to tell', دیکھنا *dekhnā* 'to see', چلنا *calnā* 'to come (on)'.

By removing the ending نا *-nā*, we find the stem, the part of the verb from which all other parts are formed. A parallel in English might be: 'to love' infinitive; 'love' stem; 'loved', 'loving' other parts of the verb.

We met the verbs بتانا *batānā* 'to tell', دیکھنا *dekhnā* 'to see', چلنا *calnā* 'to come (on)', in Unit 1. In Dialogue 1 of this unit we have four more verbs: آنا *ānā* 'to come', لانا *lānā* 'to bring', رکھنا *rakhnā* 'to place/put' and ملنا *milnā* 'to meet'. The stems of these verbs are: آ *ā-*, لا *lā-*, رکھ *rakh-*, مل *mil-*.

The polite command form (*imperative*) is formed by adding the ending یے *-īe* to the stem. When the stem ends in a vowel, e.g. ا *-ā*, the junction is effected by ء *hamza*: دیکھیے *dekhīe* 'see!' but بتائیے *batāīe* 'tell!'.

The polite imperative of verbs met so far are:

Infinitive		**Stem**		**Polite imperative**		
بتانا	*batānā*	بتا	*batā-*	بتائیے	*batāīe*	tell!
دیکھنا	*dekhnā*	دیکھ	*dekh-*	دیکھیے	*dekhīe*	see!, look!
چلنا	*calnā*	چل	*cal-*	چلیے	*calīe*	come on!
آنا	*ānā*	آ	*ā-*	آئیے	*āīe*	come!
لانا	*lānā*	لا	*lā-*	لائیے	*lāīe*	bring!
رکھنا	*rakhnā*	رکھ	*rakh-*	رکھیے	*rakhīe*	put/place
ملنا	*milnā*	مل	*mil-*	ملیے	*milīe*	meet!

Polite language

In the past, Urdu was heavily influenced by the Persian of the Indian courts, and still has many rather flowery polite expressions, which in normal conversation are used in place of everyday words. When asking someone into your house, as well as saying آئیے *āīe* 'come (in)', you can also say تشریف لائیے *tašrīf lāīe*, which literally means 'bring (your) honour'. When asking someone to sit down, as well as the ordinary بیٹھیے *baiṭhīe* from بیٹھنا *baiṭhnā* 'to sit', you may also say تشریف رکھیے *tašrīf rakhīe* 'place (your) honour'.

سے ملنا se milnā 'to meet'

The verb ملنا *milnā* 'to meet' is always used with the postposition سے *se*. In Urdu you 'meet *from* someone'.

میری بیگم سے ملیے	*merī begam se milīe*	(Please) meet my wife (may I introduce you?)
خان صاحب سے ملیے	*xān sāhib se milīe*	(Please) meet Mr Khan

Plurals

Urdu nouns fall into four major groups.

Masculine nouns which end in ا -ā or 'silent' ہ -a

لڑکا	*laṛkā*	'boy'	بیٹا	*beṭā*	'son'
بچہ	*bacca*	'child'	چائے خانہ	*cāe xāna*	'tea shop'

Masculine nouns which end in *any* other letter

گھر	*ghar*	'*house/home*'	آدمی	*ādmī*	'*man*'

Feminine nouns which end in ی -ī

لڑکی	*laṛkī*	'girl'	بیٹی	*beṭī*	'daughter'

Feminine nouns which end in *any* other letter

عورت	*'aurat*	'woman'	کتاب	*kitāb*	'book'

Nouns in the first group form their plural by changing ا -ā and ہ -a to ے e:

لڑکا	*laṛkā*	'boy'	لڑکے	*laṛke*	'boys'
بیٹا	*beṭā*	'son'	بیٹے	*beṭe*	'sons'
بچہ	*bacca*	'child'	بچے	*bacce*	'children'
چائے خانہ	*cāe xāna*	'tea shop'	چائے خانے	*cāe xāne*	'tea shops'

Sometimes the plural of nouns ending in ہ such as بچہ *bacca* is written simply with ہ – بچہ – but the plural is still pronounced *bacce*. In other words, the written form does not change but the pronunciation does. In this book the plural is alway written with ے – i.e. بچے *bacce*.

Nouns in the second group make no change for the plural:

گھر	*ghar*	'house'	گھر	*ghar*	'houses'
آدمی	*ādmī*	'man'	آدمی	*ādmī*	'man'

Nouns in the third group form their plural by adding اں *-āṅ*:

لڑکی	*laṛkī*	'girl'	لڑکیاں	*laṛkīāṅ*	'girls'
بیٹی	*beṭī*	'daughter'	بیٹیاں	*beṭīāṅ*	'daughters'

Nouns in the fourth group form their plural by adding یں *-eṅ* :

عورت	*'aurat*	'woman'	عورتیں	*'auratеṅ*	'women'
کتاب	*kitāb*	'book'	کتابیں	*kitābeṅ*	'books'

مشق *mašq* Exercise

2.1 Complete the list using transcription and the Urdu script.

ایک لڑکا	*ek laṛkā*	one boy
تین لڑکے	*tīn laṛke*	three boys
چار بچے	*cār bacce*	four children
دو لڑکیاں	*do laṛkīāṅ*	two girls
سات عورتیں	*sāt 'auratеṅ*	seven women
	__________	five daughters
	__________	seven sons
	__________	eight books
	__________	six houses
	__________	ten men

Plural adjectives

Adjectives must agree with the noun they precede. Adjectives ending in ا *-ā* such as اچھا *acchā* 'good', بڑا *baṛā* 'big' 'elder' form their masculine plural by changing ا *-ā* to ے *-e*:

اچھا لڑکا	*acchā laṛkā*	'good boy'	اچھے لڑکے	*acche laṛke*	'good boys'
بڑا گھر	*baṛā ghar*	'big house'	بڑے گھر	*baṛe ghar*	'big houses'

The feminine form of the adjective in ی *-ī* makes no change for the plural:

بڑی بیٹی	*baṛī beṭī*	'big/elder daughter'	بڑی بیٹیاں	*baṛī beṭīāṅ*	'big/elder daughters'
اچھی عورت	*acchī 'aurat*	'good woman'	اچھی عورتیں	*acchī 'auratеṅ*	'good women'

Adjectives ending in any other letter make no change for the plural:

دلچسپ شہر	*dilcasp šahr*	'interesting town'	دلچسپ شہر	*dilcasp šahr*	'interesting towns'
انگریز عورت	*angrez 'aurat*	'English woman'	انگریز عورتیں	*angrez 'auratein*	'English women'

یہ *yih* 'these', وہ *vuh* 'those'

Before plural nouns یہ *yih* means 'these', وہ *vuh* means 'those':

یہ کتابیں	*yih kitāben*	'these books'	وہ لڑکے	*vuh laṛke*	'those boys'

Personal pronouns

In Unit 1 we met the pronouns میں *main* 'I', آپ *āp* the polite word for '*you*', یہ ، وہ *yih, vuh* 'he, she, it'. We now look at some of the other pronouns.

تو *tū* 'thou', 'you' is a singular pronoun which is used to address only one person. It is now used rarely in conversation, but is frequently used in poetry and film songs. It is also used when talking to animals and addressing God. The form of the verb ہونا *honā* it takes is ہے *hai*:

تو کہاں ہے، میری جان؟	*tū kahān hai, merī jān?*	Where are you my darling?

تم *tum* 'you' is a second person plural pronoun, which like English 'you' may be used to address one person or more. تم *tum* is used for people 'lower' in the social order than oneself. It may, for example, be used for children, younger relations, waiters, taxi drivers, servants, and often for your mother, wife and very close friends. It is never used by a woman for her husband, who like her father, boss and most equals, would only be addressed as آپ *āp*. When males are addressed the pronoun requires plural agreement in both the noun and the adjective. The form of ہونا *honā* it takes is ہو ho:

تم اچھے بچے ہو	*tum acche bacce ho*	you are a good child

Obviously, this sentence could also mean 'you are good children'. The context usually determines the meaning, but if any confusion is likely to arise, this is avoided by placing the masculine plural word لوگ *log* 'people' after the pronoun:

تم لوگ اچھے بچے ہو	*tum log acche bacce ho*	you (people) are good children

When one female is addressed, however, the noun remains singular:

تم اچھی لڑکی ہو	*tum acchī laṛkī ho*	you are a good girl
تم لوگ اچھی لڑکیاں ہو	*tum log acchī laṛkīāṅ ho*	you are good girls

The same considerations apply to آپ *āp*, which is used for people to whom respect is due. آپ *āp* is obligatory for elder male relations and for anyone who is addressed as صاحب *sāhib* 'Mr' or صاحبہ *sāhiba* 'Mrs/Miss'. In practice it is better to use آپ to any adult, even to waiters, servants, etc., although you will often hear Urdu speakers using تم for such people. It must be remembered that آپ is a plural pronoun and like تم requires plural agreement:

اسلم صاحب، آپ واقعی بڑے آدمی ہیں

aslam sāhib, āp vāqa'ī baṛe ādmī haiṅ

Aslam Sahib, you are really a great man

بیگم صاحبہ، آپ پاکستانی ہیں؟

begam sāhiba, āp pākistānī haiṅ?

Madame, are you a Pakistani?

بیگم *begam* can mean both 'wife' and 'lady'. A woman whose name is not known may be addressed as بیگم صاحبہ *begam sāhiba* 'Madame'.

آپ *āp* may also be 'pluralised' by adding لوگ *log*:

آپ لوگ پاکستانی ہیں؟ *āp log pakistānī haiṅ?* Are you (people) Pakistanis?

ہم *ham* is a plural pronoun like English 'we'; the form of ہونا *honā* it takes is ہیں *haiṅ*:

ہم امریکن ہیں، ہم انگریز نہیں ہیں

ham amrīkan haiṅ; ham angrez nahīṅ haiṅ

We are Americans; we are not English

Again, لوگ *log* may be added to ہم to show the plural:

ہم لوگ لندن میں ڈاکٹر ہیں

ham log landan meṅ ḍākṭar haiṅ

We are doctors in London.

یہ *yih* and وہ *vuh*, the words we have met for 'he, she, it', when used with the plural verb ہیں *haiṅ* 'are', mean 'they'. Again the word لوگ may be placed after the pronoun to emphasise plurality:

وہ عورتیں کون ہیں؟ وہ سندھی ہیں

vuh 'auraten kaun hain? vuh sindhī hain

Who are those women? They are Sindhis

یہ بچے کون ہیں؟ یہ میرے بچے ہیں

yih bacce kaun hain? yih mere bacce hain

Who are those children? They are my children

The verb ہونا *honā* 'to be' is used with the personal pronouns as follows:

	Singular			**Plural**	
میں ہوں	*main hūn*	I am	ہم ہیں	*ham hain*	we are
تو ہے	*tū hai*	you are	تم ہو	*tum ho*	you are
یہ' وہ ہے	*yih/vuh hai*	he, she, it is	آپ ہیں	*āp hain*	you are (polite)
			یہ' وہ ہیں	*yih/vuh hain*	they are

Leaving out ہونا *honā*

In negative sentences such as میں پاکستانی نہیں ہوں *main pākistānī nahīn hūn* 'I am not a Pakistani' or وہ لوگ ڈاکٹر نہیں ہیں *vuh log ḍākṭar nahīn hain* 'they are not doctors', the verb 'to be' is often dropped. These sentences could equally well expressed: میں پاکستانی نہیں *main pākistānī nahīn* وہ لوگ ڈاکٹر نہیں *vuh log ḍākṭar nahīn*.

Note the expression کوئی بات نہیں *koī bāt nahīn* 'some matter (is) not', which can be translated as 'it doesn't matter'.

Possessive adjectives: 'my, your, his, her, its, our, their'

The possessive adjectives corresponding to the personal pronouns are:

میں	*main*	میرا	*merā*	my
تو	*tū*	تیرا	*terā*	your
یہ	*yih*	اِس کا	*is kā*	his, her, its
وہ	*vuh*	اُس کا	*us kā*	his, her, its
ہم	*ham*	ہمارا	*hamārā*	our
تم	*tum*	تمہارا	*tumhārā*	your
آپ	*āp*	آپ کا	*āp kā*	your
یہ	*yih*	اِن کا	*in kā*	their
وہ	*vuh*	اُن کا	*un kā*	their

The possessive adjectives form their feminine and plural like other adjectives ending in ا *-ā*:

ہمارا	*hamārā*	ہماری	*hamārī*	ہمارے	*hamāre*	our
اُس کا	*us kā*	اُس کی	*us kī*	اُس کے	*us ke*	his, etc.
اُن کا	*un kā*	اُن کی	*un kī*	اُن کے	*un ke*	their

Plural of respect

As we have seen Urdu is much more polite than English and many other European languages. Along with the three words for 'you', the use of which has social implications, and the honorific phrases which we have met for 'come in' and 'sit down', there are many other ways of indicating respect. One of these is the use of the plural when referring to one person to whom respect is due, e.g. the sentence 'this is Mr Aslam; he is my good friend; his house is in Karachi' must be translated into Urdu as 'these are Mr Aslam; they are my good friends; their house is in Karachi':

یہ اسلم صاحب ہیں' یہ میرے اچھے دوست ہیں' ان کا گھر کراچی میں ہے۔

yih aslam sāhib haiṅ; yih mere acche dost haiṅ; in kā ghar karācī meṅ hai

The 'plural of respect' must be used when talking about people who are present in your company and people who are known to and respected by the person to whom you are talking. Thus you would always say:

یہ میری بیگم ہیں' ان کا نام بلقیس ہے

yih merī begam haiṅ; in kā nām bilqīs hai
This is my wife; her name is Bilqis

کیا آپ کے والد کراچی میں ہیں؟

kyā āp ke vālid karācī maiṅ haiṅ?
Is your father in Karachi?

بیگم رحیم بہت اچھی خاتون ہیں

begam rahīm bahut acchī xātūn haiṅ
Mrs Rahim is a very good woman

The word خاتون *xātūn* 'woman' is respectful and is used in preference to عورت *'aurat* in circumstances where respect is due. Remember that feminine nouns, when referring to one person remain singular even though the verb is plural; masculine nouns, however, have the plural form:

یہ آپ کے بیٹے ہیں؟ ان کا نام کیا ہے؟

yih āp ke beṭe haiṅ? in kā nām kyā hai?

Is this your son? What is his name?

یہ آپ کی بیٹی ہیں؟ ان کا نام کیا ہے؟

yih āp kī beṭī haiṅ? in kā nām kyā hai?

Is this your daughter? What is her name?

When referring to your own son or daughter, it is more usual to use the singular, although some people use the 'plural of respect' even for their own children:

یہ میرا بیٹا ہے، اس کا نام اقبال ہے؟

yih merā beṭā hai; is kā nām iqbāl hai

This is my son; his name is Iqbal

Relations

Urdu has no verb meaning 'to have'. 'We have two sons' is expressed as 'our two sons are':

ہمارے دو بیٹے اور دو بیٹیاں ہیں

hamāre do beṭe aur do beṭīāṅ haiṅ

We have two sons and two daughters ('our sons and daughters are')

کیا اپ کے بچے ہیں؟

kyā āp ke bacce haiṅ?

Do you have children? ('your children are?')

جی نہیں، ہمارے بچے نہیں

jī nahīṅ, hamāre bacce nahīṅ

No, we do not have children ('our children are not')

مشق *mašq* Exercise

2.2 Plural of respect

The following sentences all demand 'plural of respect'. Give the correct plural form of the adjectives and the verb 'to be' written in brackets.
For example:

رحیم صاحب کراچی میں بہت (اچھا) ڈاکٹر (ہونا)۔

رحیم صاحب کراچی میں بہت اچھے ڈاکٹر ہیں۔

1 جان صاحب (اچھا) آدمی (ہونا)۔

2 بیگم صاحبہ، آپ (انگریز) (ہونا)؟

3 وہ خاتون کون (ہونا)؟ کیا وہ (پاکستانی) (ہونا)۔

4 (آپ کا) والد بھی یہاں (ہونا)۔

5 (ان کا) (بڑا) بیٹے (اچھا) انجینر (ہونا)۔

یہ میری بیگم ہیں۔ ان کا نام جمیلہ ہے

وہ میری چھوٹی بیٹی ہے

یہ میرے والد ہیں

یہ حامد اور اقبال ہیں۔ یہ ہمارے بیٹے ہیں

وہ کون ہیں۔ وہ ہمارے ڈاکٹر ہیں

مکالمہ دو *mukālima do* Dialogue 2

While dinner is being prepared, John asks Hamid about his school.

جان : اسلم صاحب، یہ بتائیے کراچی میں اسکول اچھے ہیں؟

اسلم : جی ہاں۔ لیکن میرا بیٹا، حامد، یہاں ہے۔ حامد سے پوچھیے۔ اے حامد، تم ادھر آؤ۔ یہ ہمارے انگریز دوست، اسمتھ صاحب، ہیں۔

حامد : السلام علیکم، اسمتھ صاحب۔

جان :	وعلیکم السلام۔ حامد، یہ بتاؤ۔ تمہارا اسکول کہاں ہے؟
حامد :	میرا اسکول کلفٹن میں ہے۔ بڑا امریکن اسکول ہے۔
جان :	اچھا۔ تم امریکن اسکول میں ہو۔ وہاں کتنے بچے ہیں؟
حامد :	بہت بچے ہیں۔ دو تین سو بچے ہیں۔
جان :	وہاں لڑکیاں بھی ہیں یا صرف لڑکے؟
حامد :	صرف لڑکے ہیں۔ لڑکیاں نہیں۔
جان :	اور اسکول میں تم خوش ہو؟
حامد :	جی ہاں، ہم لوگ وہاں بہت خوش ہیں۔
جان :	اور کلفٹن کہاں ہے؟ یہاں سے دور ہے؟
حامد :	جی ہاں، یہاں سے کافی دور ہے۔ لیکن اچھی جگہ ہے۔

jān : *aslam sāhib, yih batāīe. karācī meṅ iskūl acche haiṅ?*

aslam : *jī hāṅ. lekin merā beṭā, hāmid, yahāṅ hai. hāmid se pūchīe. e hāmid tum idhar āo. yih hamāre angrez dost, ismith sāhib, haiṅ.*

hāmid : *assalāmu 'alaikum, ismith sāhib.*

jān : *va 'alaikum assalām. hāmid, yih batāo. tumhārā iskūl kahāṅ hai?*

hāmid : *merā iskūl kliftan meṅ hai. baṛā amrīkan iskūl hai.*

jān : *acchā. tum amrīkan iskūl meṅ ho. vahāṅ kitne bacce haiṅ?*

hāmid : *bahut bacce haiṅ. do tīn sau bacce haiṅ.*

jān : *vahāṅ laṛkīāṅ bhī haiṅ yā sirf laṛke?*

hāmid : *sirf laṛke haiṅ. laṛkīāṅ nahīṅ.*

jān : *aur iskūl meṅ tum xuš ho?*

hāmid : *jī hāṅ, ham log vahāṅ bahut xuš haiṅ.*

jān : *aur kliftan kahāṅ hai? yahāṅ se dūr hai?*

hāmid : *jī hāṅ, yahāṅ se kāfī dūr hai, lekin acchī jagah hai.*

John : Aslam Sahib. Tell (me) this. Are the schools in Karachi good?

Aslam : Yes. But my son, Hamid, is here. Ask (from) Hamid. Eh, Hamid! Come here. This is our English friend, Mr Smith.

Hamid : Hello, Mr Smith

John : Hello Hamid. Tell (me) this. Where is your school?

Hamid : My school is in Clifton. It's a big American school.

John : I see. You're in an American school. How many children are there?

Hamid : There are a lot of children. There are two (or) three hundred children.

John : Are there girls there too, or only boys?

Hamid : There are only boys. There aren't (any) girls.

John : And are you happy at school?

Hamid : Yes. We are very happy there.

John : And where is Clifton? Is it far from here?

Hamid : Yes, it's quite far from here. But it's a good place.

اسکول	*iskūl*	school (m.)	ہو	*ho*	are (familar)
سے پوچھیے	*se pūchīe*	ask (from)	کتنا	*kitnā?*	how much?
پوچھنا	*pūchnā*	to ask			
اے	*e*	hey!	کتنے	*kitne?*	how many?
تم	*tum*	you (familiar)	بہت	*bahut*	many
ادھر	*idhar*	to here, here	سو	*sau*	hundred
			دو تین سو	*do tīn sau*	two (or) three hundred
ادھر آؤ	*idhar āo*	come here (familiar)			
دوست	*dost*	friend (m.)	یا	*yā*	or
بتاؤ	*batāo*	tell (familiar)	خوش	*xuš*	happy
			ہم	*ham*	we
تمہارا	*tumhārā*	your (familiar)	ہم لوگ	*ham log*	we (plural)
			جگہ	*jagah*	place (f.)
کلفٹن	*kliftan*	Clifton (a Karachi suburb)			

قواعد *qavā'id* Grammar

ہجے *hijje* Spelling

Although the word خوش *xuš* 'happy' is written with و *vāu*, the vowel *u* is pronounced short.

In words taken from English beginning with an 's' followed by another consonant like 'Smith', 'school', etc., Urdu adds the vowel *i* before the *s*. Here are a few common examples:

اسکول	*iskūl*	school (m.)
اسٹیشن	*isṭešan*	station (m.)
بس اسٹاپ	*bas isṭāp*	bus stop (m.)
اسمتھ	*ismith*	Smith

سے پوچھنا *se pūchnā* to ask

The verb پوچھنا *pūchnā* 'to ask' is construed with the postposition سے *se* 'from'. In Urdu you ask *from* someone:

حامد سے پوچھیے	*hāmid se pūchīe*	ask (from) Hamid

Commands with تم *tum* and تو *tū*

We have already seen that the stem of the verb is obtained by removing the ending *-nā* from the infinitive. The imperative for تم *tum* is formed simply by adding the ending و *-o* to the verb stem. When the stem ends in a vowel, the junction is effected with ء *hamza*:

آؤ	*āo*	come
بتاؤ	*batāo*	tell
بیٹھو	*baiṭho*	sit
کھاؤ	*khāo*	eat

The imperative for تو *tū* is simply the stem:

آ	*ā*	come
بتا	*batā*	tell
بیٹھ	*baiṭh*	sit
کھا	*khā*	eat

It is not uncommon to use the pronoun with the imperative, although this is not obligatory:

آپ بتائیے	*āp batāīe*	please tell
تو کھا	*tū khā*	eat
حامد، تم ادھر آؤ	*hāmid, tum idhar āo*	Hamid come here

The word ادھر *idhar* 'here' is an alternative for یہاں *yahāṅ*, but is mainly used in the sense of 'to here/hither'.

کتنا، کتنی؟ kitnā, kitnī? 'how much?'; کتنے؟ kitne? 'how many?'

The adjective کتنا *kitnā* with singular nouns is translated as 'how much?'

کتنا کھانا؟	*kitnā khānā?*	how much food?
کتنی چائے؟	*kitnī cāe?*	how much tea?

With a plural noun it must be translated as 'how many?'.

کتنے لڑکے؟	*kitne laṛke?*	how many boys?
کتنی چیزیں؟	*kitnī cīzeṅ?*	how many things?

When used before an adjective, کتنا means 'how!', 'what!':

کتنا اچھا کھانا	*kitnā acchā khānā!*	what good food!

بہت bahut 'very', 'much', 'many'

We have already met the word بہت *bahut* used in the sense of 'very':

کھانا واقعی بہت مزے دار ہے The food is really tasty

khānā vāqa'ī bahut mazedār hai

Used before a singular noun it also means 'much', 'a lot of'; with plural nouns it means 'many':

یہاں بہت کھانا ہے There is much/ a lot of food here

yahāṅ bahut khānā hai

اسکول میں بہت بچے ہیں There are many children in the school

iskūl meṅ bahut bacce haiṅ

'One or two', 'two or three'

To express approximate numbers, such as 'two or three girls', 'three or four hundred children', two consecutive numerals are used without a word for 'or':

دو تین لڑکیاں	*do tīn laṛkīāṅ*	two or three girls
تین چار سو بچے	*tīn cār sau bacce*	three or four hundred children

The word سو *sau* 'hundred' is used after other numerals as in English:

١٠٠	ایک سو	*ek sau*	100
٢٠٠	دو سو	*do sau*	200

کتنا؟ کتنے؟ کتنی؟

یہاں کتنے بچے ہیں؟

یہاں کتنی عورتیں ہیں؟

یہاں کتنے گھر ہیں؟

یہاں کتنی لڑکیاں ہیں؟

یہاں کتنے لڑکے ہیں؟

مکالمہ تین **mukālima tīn** Dialogue 3

Over dinner, Aslam and Bilqis describe their family.

بلقیس : آیئے۔ کھانا تیار ہے۔ آپ لوگ یہاں بیٹھیے۔

جان : اوہو! میز پر کتنی مزے دار چیزیں ہیں۔ کیا تکلف ہے!

اسلم : جی نہیں۔ کوئی تکلف نہیں۔ مرغی ہے، روٹی ہے، چاول ہے، دال ہے۔ بس۔

ہیلن : آپ کا گھر بہت اچھا ہے۔ یہاں کتنے کمرے ہیں؟

اسلم : ہمارا گھر بہت بڑا نہیں۔ سات کمرے ہیں۔ لیکن یہاں بہت لوگ ہیں۔ ہم ہیں، ہمارے بچے ہیں، میرے والدین، یعنی والد صاحب اور والدہ . . .

بلقیس : . . . اور میرے چچا ہیں، میری نانی بھی ہیں اور دو تین نوکر۔

جان : کیا، سب لوگ ایک گھر میں؟

اسلم : جی ہاں۔ یہ پاکستان ہے۔ انگلستان نہیں۔ یہ مشکل نہیں ہے۔

بلقیس : لیکن ہر جگہ آپ کی کتابیں بکھری پڑی ہیں۔ یہ بہت مشکل ہے۔

اسلم : کیا مشکل ہے؟ یہ سب میری کتابیں ہیں۔ اور کیا؟

جان : کوئی بات نہیں۔ کتابیں بہت اچھی چیزیں ہیں۔

bilqīs : *āīe. khānā tayyār hai. āp log yahāṅ baiṭhīe.*

jān : *oho! mez par kitnī mazedār cīzeṅ haiṅ. kyā takalluf hai!*

aslam : *jī nahīṅ. koī takalluf nahīṅ. murğī hai, roṭī hai, cāval hai, dāl hai. bas.*

helan : *āp kā ghar bahut acchā hai. yahāṅ kitne kamre haiṅ?*

aslam : *hamārā ghar bahut baṛā nahīṅ. sāt kamre haiṅ. lekin yahāṅ bahut log haiṅ. ham haiṅ, hamāre bacce, mere vālidain, ya'nī vālid sāhib aur vālida ...*

bilqīs : *... aur mere cacā haiṅ, merī nānī bhī haiṅ aur do tīn naukar.*

jān : *kyā, sab log ek ghar meṅ?*

aslam : *jī hāṅ. yih pākistān hai. inglistān nahīṅ. yih muškil nahīṅ hai.*

bilqīs : *lekin har jagah āp kī kitābeṅ bikhrī-paṛī haiṅ. yih bahut muškil hai.*

aslam : *kyā muškil hai? yih sab merī kitābeṅ haiṅ. aur kyā?*

jān : *koī bāt nahīṅ. kitābeṅ bahut acchī cīzeṅ haiṅ.*

Bilqis : Come on. The food is ready. (You people) sit here.

John : Oho! How many tasty things there are on the table. What trouble (you have gone to)!

Aslam : No. It's no trouble. There's chicken, bread, rice, lentils. That's all.

Helen : Your house is very nice. How many rooms are (there) here?

Aslam : Our house is not very big. There are seven rooms. But there a lot of people here. There's us ('we are'), our children, my parents, that is father and mother ...

Bilqis : ... and my uncle, there's also my grandmother and two (or) three servants.

John : What, all (people) in one house?

Aslam : Yes. This is Pakistan. Not England. This is no problem ('not difficult').

Bilqis : But your books are scattered around everywhere. This is very difficult.

Aslam : What's difficult? They are all my books. So what?

John : Never mind. Books are very good things.

تیار	*tayyār*	ready	والدین	*vālidain*	parents (m.p.)
بیٹھیے	*baiṭhīe*	sit down	یعنی	*ya'nī*	that is, I mean
بیٹھنا	*baiṭhnā*	to sit	والد	*vālid*	father (m.)
اوہو	*oho*	oh	والدہ	*vālida*	mother (f.)
تکلف	*takalluf*	formality, trouble (m.)	چچا	*cacā*	uncle (m.)
کیا تکلف ہے	*kyā takalluf hai*	how much trouble (you have taken)	نانی	*nānī*	grand-mother (f.)
کوئی ... نہیں	*koī ... nahīṅ*	no ... (trouble)	دو تین	*do tīn*	two (or) three
مرغی	*murğī*	chicken (f.)	نوکر	*naukar*	servant (m.)
روٹی	*roṭī*	bread	انگلستان	*inglistān*	England
چاول	*cāval*	rice (m.)	کتاب	*kitāb*	book (f.)
دال	*dāl*	lentils (f.)	مشکل	*muškil*	difficult
بس	*bas*	that's all	کیا مشکل ہے	*kyā muškil hai?*	what (do you mean) difficult?
کمرہ	*kamra*	room (m.)			
یہ سب	*yih sab*	all these			

قواعد *qavā'id* Grammar

تکلف *takalluf*

The nearest English equivalent of تکلف *takalluf* is 'formality'. We might translate the expression کیا تکلف ہے *kyā takalluf hai*, literally 'what formality (there) is!', as 'what trouble you have gone to!'. The answer is کوئی تکلف نہیں *koī takalluf nahīn* 'some fomality (is) not', i.e 'it's no trouble'.

Relations

Urdu is very precise with relationship terms, and has many more of them than English. There are different terms for 'uncle', according to whether he is the father's brother or the mother's brother; for 'grandfather' according to whether he is the father's father or mother's father and so on (a fuller list is given in Appendix 2). It must be remembered that elder relations are always given the plural of respect, including elder brothers and sisters, and must be addressed as آپ *āp*.

Your parents, والدین *vālidain*, are والد *vālid* 'father' and والدہ *vālida* mother'. The word صاحب *sāhib* is frequently used with والد *vālid* to denote respect:

میرے والد صاحب آج کراچی میں ہیں

mere vālid sāhib āj karācī men hain

My father is in Karachi today

The more familiar and affectionate word ماں *mān* is often used for 'mother':

میری ماں آج گھر پر ہیں

merī mān āj ghar par hain

My mother is at home ('on home') today

چچا *cacā* or چچا صاحب *cacā sāhib* is 'strictly speaking' your younger paternal uncle; نانی *nānī* is your mother's mother.

In the context of relations, بڑا *baṛā* 'big' is used for 'elder' and چھوٹا *choṭā* 'small' for 'younger':

آپ کے بڑے بیٹے	*āp ke baṛe beṭe*	your older son (plural of respect)
آپ کی چھوٹی بیٹی	*āp kī choṭī beṭī*	your younger daughter

It should be noted that the word چچا *cacā* 'uncle' does not change in the plural:

میرے چچا صاحب گھر پر نہیں ہیں

mere cacā sāhib ghar par nahīṅ haiṅ

My uncle is not at home (plural of respect)

یہ سب *yih sab* 'all this', 'all these'

The word order in the phrase یہ سب *yih sab* 'all this' is the opposite of the English:

یہ سب میری کتابیں ہیں *yih sab merī kitābeṅ haiṅ* All these are my books

کیا *kyā* in exclamations

کیا *kyā* 'what' is, as in English, often used in exclamations:

کیا مشکل ہے؟	*kyā muškil hai?*	What (do you mean), it's difficult?
بچے ہیں۔ اور کیا؟	*bacce haiṅ, aur kyā?*	They're (only) children. So what?

یعنی *ya'nī* 'I mean', 'that is', 'in other words'

The word یعنی *ya'nī* is used much as the English expressions 'I mean', 'in other words' to clarify or expand an explanation:

یہ حامد اور اقبال ہیں، یعنی میرے بڑے اور چھوٹے بیٹے

yih hāmid aur iqbāl haiṅ, ya'nī mere baṛe aur choṭe beṭe

They are Hamid and Iqbal, in other words my elder and younger sons

ثقافت *siqāfat* Culture

In India and Pakistan, people often have big families, and even in large cities family life is considered to be extremely important. It is not uncommon to find several generations living under one roof, and elders are treated with great respect. This is shown in the language when an elder is addressed or talked about using the 'plural of respect' and appropriate 'honorific' expressions such as تشریف لائیے 'come' and تشریف رکھیے 'sit down'. Hospitality مہمان نوازی *mihmān navāzī* is also important aspect of life, and people go to a great deal of trouble تکلف *takalluf* when entertaining guests. Foreigners are always welcome and are often greeted with a certain element of good-natured curiosity, especially if they can speak the language.

مشقیں *mašqeṅ* Exercises

2.3 Correct form of the verb

In the following sentences give the correct form of the verb ہونا :

1 اے اقبال، آج تم اسکول میں نہیں ______ ؟
2 ہم لوگ امریکن ______ ۔ کیا آپ بھی امریکن ______ ؟
3 آپ کی کتابیں ہر جگہ بکھری پڑی ______ ۔
4 یہ میری بیگم ______ ۔ وہ بھی ڈاکٹر ______ ۔
5 وہ آدمی کون ______ ؟ کیا وہ پنجابی ______ ؟

2.4 Correct form of the imperative

In the following sentences give the correct form of the imperative (آ، آو، آیئے etc.) :

1 اے حامد ادھر (آنا)۔ تمہارا اسکول کہاں ہے؟
2 بیگم صاحبہ، تشریف (لانا) اور تشریف (رکھنا)
3 اسلم صاحب (دیکھنا)۔ وہاں اچھا چائے خانہ ہے۔
4 (چلنا)، چائے پیئیں۔
5 (بتانا)، تمہارے والد صاحب کہاں ہیں۔

2.5 Comprehension

Listen to the dialogue and tick the appropriate answers.

1 How many children does Rahim have?	Two ( )	Three ( )
2 Are all Rahim's children at school?	Yes ( )	No ( )
3, Which kind of school do the boys attend?	American ( )	Pakistani ( )
4 How many rooms are there in Rahim's house?	Seven ( )	Five ( )
5 Do Rahim's parents live with him?	Yes ( )	No ( )

3 آپ کو پاکستانی کھانا پسند ہے؟

āp ko pākistanī khānā pasand hai?

Do you like Pakistani food?

In this unit you will learn how to:

- say what you like
- express your needs
- take a taxi
- order a meal in a restaurant

مکالمہ ایک *mukālima ek* Dialogue 1

John meets Aslam's friend, Dr Rahim, who invites him to lunch.

اسلم : جان صاحب، یہ ڈاکٹر رحیم ہیں۔ ان سے ملیے، رحیم صاحب میرے بہت اچھے دوست ہیں۔ کراچی میں یہ بہت مشہور ڈاکٹر ہیں۔

جان : السلام علیکم، رحیم صاحب، آپ کو معلوم ہے، میں بھی ڈاکٹر ہوں لیکن آج کل میں کراچی میں چھٹی پر ہوں۔ میں سیاح ہوں۔

رحیم : اچھا، یہ بہت دلچسپ بات ہے۔ مجھے معلوم ہے کہ آپ ڈاکٹر ہیں۔ یہ بتایئے۔ آج آپ کو فرصت ہے؟

جان : جی ہاں۔ آج مجھے فرصت ہے۔

رحیم : اچھا۔ تو آج ہم ساتھ کھانا کھائیں! میرا اسپتال گلشن اقبال میں ہے۔ یہاں سے زیادہ دور نہیں ہے۔ اور وہاں ایک بہت اچھا ریستراں ہے۔ اس کا نام کوہِ نور ہے۔ کیا آپ کو پاکستانی کھانا پسند ہے؟

جان : جی ہاں، مجھے بہت پسند ہے۔ لیکن میری بیوی اس وقت ہوٹل میں ہیں۔ ان کو معلوم نہیں ہے کہ میں کہاں ہوں۔

رحیم : ٹھیک ہے۔ آپ انہیں یہاں سے ٹیلیفون کیجیے اور ان کو بتایئے کہ ہم کہاں ہیں۔

جان : اچھا۔ یہاں کوئی ٹیلیفون ہے؟

رحیم : جی ہاں، وہاں ہے۔ آپ بیگم صاحبہ کو جلدی ٹیلیفون کیجیے۔

aslam : *jān sāhib, yih ḍākṭar rahīm hain. in se milīe. rahīm sāhib mere bahut acche dost haiṅ. karācī meṅ yih bahut mašhūr ḍākṭar haiṅ.*

jān : *assalāmu 'alaikum, rahīm sāhib. āp ko ma'lūm hai, maiṅ bhī ḍākṭar hūṅ. lekin āj kal maiṅ karācī meṅ chuṭṭī par hūṅ. maiṅ sayyāh hūṅ.*

rahīm : *acchā, yih bahut dilcasp bāt hai. mujhe ma'lūm hai ki āp ḍākṭar haiṅ. yih batāīe, āj āp ko fursat hai?*

jān : *jī hāṅ, āj mujhe fursat hai.*

rahīm : *acchā, to āj ham sāth khānā khāeṅ? merā aspatāl gulšan-e iqbāl meṅ hai. yahāṅ se ziyāda dūr nahīṅ hai. aur vahāṅ ek bahut acchā restarāṅ hai. us kā nām koh-e nūr hai. kyā āp ko pākistānī khānā pasand hai?*

jān : *jī hāṅ, mujhe bahut pasand hai. lekin merī bīvī is vaqt hoṭal meṅ haiṅ. un ko ma'lūm nahīṅ hai ki maiṅ kahāṅ hūṅ.*

rahīm : *ṭhīk hai. āp unheṅ yahāṅ se ṭelīfon kījīe aur un ko batāīe ki ham kahāṅ haiṅ.*

jān : *acchā. yahāṅ koī ṭelifon hai?*

rahīm : *jī hāṅ, vahāṅ hai. āp begam sāhiba ko jaldī ṭelīfon kījīe.*

Aslam : John! This is Doctor Rahim. (Please) meet him. Rahim Sahib is my very good friend. In Karachi he is a very famous doctor.

John : Hello, Rahim Sahib. Do you know I am also a doctor? But these days I am on holiday in Karachi. I am a tourist.

Rahim : Really? (Then) this is (a) very interesting (matter). I know that you are a doctor. Tell me (this). Do you have (some) free time today?

John : Yes. I have time.

Rahim : Good. Then let's have ('eat') lunch together today. My hospital is in Gulshan-e Iqbal. It's not very far. And there's a very good restaurant there. Its name is Koh-e Nur. Do you like Pakistani food?

John : Yes, I like it very (much). But my wife is at this moment in the hotel. She does not know (that) where I am.

Rahim : It's all right. Telephone (to) her and tell (to) her (that) where we are.

John : Very well. Is there any telephone here?

Rahim : Yes. It's there. Telephone (your) wife quickly.

آپ کو...پسند ہے	*āp ko... pasand hai*	do you like...?	اسپتال	*aspatāl*	hospital (m.)
رحیم	*rahīm*	Rahim	گلشنِ اقبال	*gulšan-e iqbāl*	Gulshan-e Iqbal (a Karachi suburb) (m.)
ان سے ملیے	*in se milīe*	meet him			
مشہور	*mašhūr*	famous			
کو	*ko*	to, for			
معلوم	*ma'lūm*	known			
آپ کو معلوم ہے؟	*āp ko ma'lūm hai?*	do you know?	زیادہ	*ziyāda*	very, more, most
			ریستراں	*restarāṅ*	restaurant (m.)
آج کل	*āj kal*	nowadays			
چھٹی	*chuṭṭī*	holiday (f.)	کوہِ نور	*koh-e nūr*	Koh-e Nur (m.)
چھٹی پر	*chuṭṭī par*	on holiday			
مجھے معلوم ہے	*mujhe ma'lūm hai*	I know	مجھے پسند ہے	*mujhe pasand hai*	I like
کہ	*ki*	that	بیوی	*bīvī*	wife (f.)
فرصت	*fursat*	leisure, (free) time (f.)	اس وقت	*is vaqt*	at this time
			اُن کو معلوم نہیں ہے	*un ko ma'lum nahīṅ hai*	she doesn't know
آپ کو فرصت ہے	*āp ko fursat hai?*	do you have time?	ٹھیک ہے	*ṭhīk hai*	it's all right
آج	*āj*	today			
مجھے فرصت ہے	*mujhe fursat hai*	I have time	انہیں	*unheṅ*	(to) her
			انہیں ٹیلیفون کیجیے	*unheṅ ṭelīfon kījīe*	telephone her
اچھا تو	*acchā to*	good, then...			
ساتھ	*sāth*	together	جلدی	*jaldī*	quickly, soon
کھانا کھائیں	*khānā khāeṅ*	let's have lunch			

قواعد **qavā'id Grammar**

ہجے **hijje** Spelling

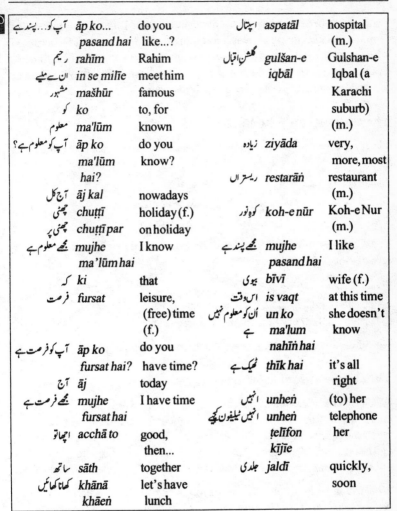

In Urdu there are many expressions of Persian origin which consist of two words joined to each other with the sign ِ pronounced e, which can often be translated as 'of'. This sign is known as اضافت *izāfat* (f.) 'addition'. A familiar example is کوہِ نور *koh-e nūr* 'Mountain of Light', the name of the famous diamond in the Crown Jewels. The ـِ *izāfat* must not be confused with the vowel sign ـِ *zer* which we use in اِس کا *is kā*, اِن کا *in kā*. Another example of the *izāfat* is in the name of a Karachi suburb گلشنِ اقبال *gulšan-e iqbāl* which literally means 'Garden of Prosperity'.

The postposition کو ko 'to, for'

The postposition کو *ko* has a number of uses, but may often be translated as 'to':

آپ کو	*āp ko*	to you
رحیم صاحب کو	*rahīm sāhib ko*	to Mr Rahim
میری بیوی کو	*merī bīvī ko*	to my wife

The word بیوی *bīvī* is another word for 'wife' and like بیگم *begam* normally requires the plural of respect:

میری بیوی اِس وقت ہوٹل میں ہیں

merī bīvī is vaqt hoṭal meṅ haiṅ

My wife at this time/moment is in the hotel

Note the expression اِس وقت *is vaqt* 'at this moment/time'.

The oblique case of pronouns

When we talk of case, we mean the way in which a word changes its form or ending according to its position in the sentence. In English, for example, when the pronouns 'I', 'he', 'she', etc. are the object (i.e. on the receiving end) of a verb or are preceded by a preposition like 'in', 'to', 'on', they change their form to '*me, him, her*', etc.: 'I see *him*'; 'to *me*'; 'on *him*'.

Similarly in Urdu, when میں *maiṅ* is followed by a postposition such as سے *se*, پر *par*, کو *ko* it changes its form to مجھ *mujh* 'me':

مجھ سے	*mujh se*	from me
مجھ کو	*mujh ko*	to me
مجھ پر	*mujh par*	on me

میں *maiṅ* is the direct case and مجھ *mujh* is the oblique case. The direct and oblique cases of the personal pronouns are as follows:

		Direct			Oblique	
Singular	میں	*main̈*	I	مجھ	*mujh*	me
	تو	*tū*	you	تجھ	*tujh*	you
	یہ	*yih*	he, she, it	اِس	*is*	him, her, it
	وہ	*vuh*	he, she, it	اُس	*us*	him, her, it
Plural	ہم	*ham*	we	ہم	*ham*	us
	تم	*tum*	you	تم	*tum*	you
	آپ	*āp*	you	آپ	*āp*	you
	یہ	*yih*	they	اِن	*in*	them
	وہ	*vuh*	they	اُن	*un*	them

Notice that with the pronouns آپ تم ہم the direct and oblique cases are the same.

The oblique case must be used when the pronoun is followed by a postposition: مجھ میں *mujh men̈* 'in me'; تجھ کو *tujh ko* 'to you'; اُس سے *us se* 'from him, her, it'; اُن پر *un par* 'on them'; آپ کو *āp ko* 'to you', etc.

یہ میری بیوی ہیں۔ ان سے ملیے

yih merī bīvī hain̈; in se milīe

This is my wife; (please) meet (from) her

میرا بیٹا حامد یہاں ہے۔ اس سے پوچھیے

merā beṭā, hāmid, yahān̈ hai. is se pūchīe

My son, Hamid, is here. Ask (from) him

Special forms + کو ko: the extended oblique case

The oblique form of the pronoun may be followed by the postposition کو *ko*: مجھ کو *mujh ko* 'to me', اُس کو *us ko* 'to him/her/it' تم کو *tum ko* 'to you', etc.

With the exception of آپ *āp* there are special forms which are the equivalent of the pronoun+ کو *ko*. This is known as the extended oblique:

مجھ کو	*mujh ko*	⟶	مجھے	*mujhe*	to me
اُس کو	*us ko*	⟶	اُسے	*use*	to him / her / it
ہم کو	*ham ko*	⟶	ہمیں	*hamen̈*	to us

The extended oblique forms of the pronouns are as follows:

کو + ko		Extended oblique		
مجھ کو	mujh ko	مجھے	mujhe	to me
تجھ کو	tujh ko	تجھے	tujhe	to you
اِس کو	is ko	اِسے	ise	to him, her, it
اُس کو	us ko	اُسے	use	to him, her, it
ہم کو	ham ko	ہمیں	hameṅ	to us
تم کو	tum ko	تمہیں	tumheṅ	to you
آپ کو	āp ko	آپ کو	āp ko	to you
اِن کو	in ko	اِنہیں	inheṅ	to them
اُن کو	un ko	اُنہیں	unheṅ	to them

Although there is no grammatical difference between the pronoun + کو and the 'extended' counterpart, the extended oblique is used rather more frequently.

معلوم **ma'lūm 'known'**

The adjective معلوم *ma'lūm* literally means 'known'. It is used with کو *ko* in the important construction کو معلوم ہونا *ko ma'lūm honā* 'to be known to', 'to know'. Consider the following sentences and their literal translations:

کیا آپ کو معلوم ہے؟	*kyā āp ko ma'lūm hai?* 'to you is (it) known?' Do you know?
مجھے معلوم نہیں	*mujhe ma'lūm nahīṅ* 'to me (it) is not known' I don't know
ہمیں یہ بات معلوم نہیں ہے	*hameṅ yih bāt ma'lūm nahīṅ hai* 'to us this thing is not known' We don't know this thing

In the last sentence, the subject of the sentence is یہ بات 'this thing' Hence the verb is ہے *hai* 'is'. In English, however, 'this thing' is the *object* of the verb 'to know'.

کہ ***ki* 'that'**

In sentences such as 'I know that he is a doctor', 'that' is translated by the conjunction کہ *ki*. کہ is pronounced *ke*. Note the spelling:

مجھے معلوم ہے کہ وہ اچھے ڈاکٹر ہیں

mujhe ma'lūm hai ki vuh acche ḍākṭar haiṅ

I know that he is a good doctor

In English 'that' is frequently omitted, e.g. 'I know he is a good doctor', but in Urdu the conjunction must always be used. This is also true of questions. In English we say: 'Do you know where Victoria Road is?'. In Urdu you must say 'Do you know *that* where Victoria Road is?':

کیا آپ کو معلوم ہے کہ وکٹوریہ روڈ کہاں ہے؟

kyā āp ko ma'lūm hai ki vikṭorīa roḍ kahāṅ hai?

Similarly کہ *ki* is also used with بتایۓ *batāie* 'tell me':

بتایۓ کہ آپ کا گھر کہاں ہے

batāie ki āp kā ghar kahāṅ hai?

Tell me (that) where is your house?

فرصت *fursat* 'time, leisure'

The word فرصت *fursat* means 'time' in the sense of 'leisure', whereas وقت *vaqt* means 'point of time' 'occasion'. 'Do you have the time (to do something?)' is expressed with فرصت *fursat*:

کیا آپ کو فرصت ہے؟	*kyā āp ko fursat hai?*	'to you is there leisure?' Do you have time?
آج مجھے فرصت نہیں	*āj mujhe fursat nahīṅ*	'today to me there (is) not time' I don't have the time today.

پسند *pasand* 'pleasing', کو پسند ہونا *ko pasand honā* 'to like'

The adjective پسند *pasand* literally means 'pleasing'. It is used in the important expression کو پسند ہونا *ko pasand honā* 'to be pleasing to', 'to like'. Compare the similar construction with معلوم *ma'lūm*.

مجھے پسند ہے	*mujhe pasand hai*	I like
تمہیں پسند نہیں	*tumheṅ pasand nahīṅ*	You don't like
آپ کو پاکستانی کھانا پسند ہے؟	*āp ko pākistānī khānā pasand hai?*	Do you like Pakistani food?

کو ٹیلیفون کرنا *ko ṭelīfon karnā* 'to telephone (to)'

Many verbs and verbal expressions require کو after the object, the word denoting the person or thing who is the recipient of the action. In Urdu you always 'telephone to' someone: رحیم صاحب کو ٹیلیفون کرنا *rahīm sāhib* ***ko*** *ṭelīfon karnā* 'to do a telephone to Rahim':

آپ بیوی کو ٹیلیفون کیجیے	*āp bīvī ko ṭelīfon kījīe*	Phone (to) the wife

Compare the use of کو with بتانا *batānā* 'to tell (to)':

ان کو / انہیں بتائیے کہ آپ یہاں ہیں

un ko/unheṅ batāīe ki āp yahāṅ haiṅ

Tell (to) him that you are here

مشقیں *mašqeṅ* Exercises

3.1 Complete the sentences

Finish off the following sentences by giving the Urdu for the English words in brackets:

1	مجھے معلوم ہے کہ ________ ۔	(you are an engineer)
2	بندر روڈ کہاں ہے؟ مجھے معلوم ________ ۔	(not)
3	کیا آج آپ کو ________ ہے؟	(leisure)
4	مجھے ________ پسند نہیں ہے۔	(English food)
5	کیا آپ کو ________ پسند نہیں؟	(these books)

3.2 Oblique forms

Give both the pronoun + کو and the extended oblique in the following sentences:

1	(to me)	________	معلوم ہے کہ آپ کا گھر لندن میں ہے۔
2	(to you آپ)	________	امریکہ پسند ہے؟
3	(to them وہ)	________	آج ٹیلیفون کیجیے۔
4	(to us)	________	معلوم ہے کہ لاہور پنجاب میں ہے۔
5	(to you تم)	________	میری کتاب پسند نہیں ہے۔
6	(to her یہ)	________	آج بتائیے۔

انناس دال روٹی چاول آم مرغی

مکالمہ دو **mukālima do** **Dialogue 2**

گلشنِ اقبال چلو

John and Rahim take a taxi to a restaurant in Gulshan-e Iqbal.

رحیم : دیکھیے' جان صاحب۔ وہاں ٹیکسی ہے۔ اے بھائی' تم خالی ہو؟

ٹیکسی والا : جی ہاں' صاحب۔ میں خالی ہوں۔ بیٹھیے

رحیم : اچھا' گلشنِ اقبال چلو۔ تم کو معلوم ہے کہ کوہِ نور ریستراں کہاں ہے؟

ٹیکسی والا : جی ہاں' صاحب۔ مجھے معلوم ہے۔ وہاں ایک بڑا اسپتال ہے نا؟

رحیم : جی ہاں اور میٹر سے چلو۔ تو یہ بتائیے جان صاحب' آپ کو کراچی پسند ہے؟ یعنی آپ کو اور آپ کی بیگم کو؟

جان : جی ہاں' ہمیں بہت پسند ہے۔ یہاں سب دلچسپ ہے یعنی ہم لوگ پہلی بار ایشیا میں ہیں نا!

رحیم : اور آپ کی بیگم کو کیا چیزیں پسند ہیں؟

جان : ان کو خاص طور پر بازار پسند ہیں۔ شہر میں بہت شاندار دوکانیں ہیں۔

رحیم : یہ تو سچ ہے۔ لیکن کراچی کافی نیا شہر ہے۔ مجھے لاہور زیادہ پسند ہے۔ وہاں بہت پرانی عمارتیں ہیں اور مجھے تاریخی شہر بہت پسند ہیں۔ دیکھیے' ہمارا ریستراں وہاں ہے۔ بھائی یہاں روکو۔ کتنا کرایہ ہے؟

ٹیکسی والا : اٹھارہ روپے' صاحب۔

رحیم : جی نہیں۔ اٹھارہ روپے بہت زیادہ ہے۔ میٹر پر صرف پندرہ روپے ہیں۔ لو' پندرہ روپے لو۔

gulšan-e iqbāl calo!

rahīm : *dekhīe, jān sāhib. vahāṅ ṭaiksī hai. e bhāī, tum xālī ho?*

ṭaiksīvālā : *jī hāṅ, sāhib. maiṅ xālī hūṅ. baiṭhīe*

rahīm : *acchā. gulšan-e iqbāl calo. tum ko ma'lūm hai ki koh-e nūr resṭarān kahāṅ hai?*

ṭaiksīvālā : *jī hāṅ, sāhib. mujhe ma'lūm hai. vahāṅ ek baṛā aspatāl hai nā?*

rahīm : *jī hāṅ. aur mīṭar se calo. to yih batāīe, jān sāhib. āp ko karācī pasand hai? ya'nī āp aur āp kī begam ko.*

jān : *jī hāṅ, hameṅ bahut pasand hai. yahāṅ sab dilcasp hai. ya'nī ham log pahlī bār ešiyā meṅ haiṅ nā.*

rahīm : *aur āp kī begam ko kyā cīzeṅ pasand hai?*

jān : *un ko xās taur par bāzār pasand haiṅ. šahr meṅ bahut šāndār dūkāneṅ haiṅ.*

rahīm : *yih to sac hai. lekin karācī kāfī nayā šahr hai. mujhe lāhaur ziyāda pasand hai. vahāṅ bahut purānī 'imārateṅ haiṅ. aur mujhe tārīxī šahr bahut pasand haiṅ. dekhīe hamārā restarāṅ vahāṅ hai. bhāī, yahāṅ roko. kitnā kirāya hai?*

taiksīvālā : *aṭhāra rūpīe, sāhib.*

rahīm : *jī nahīṅ. aṭhāra rūpīe bahut ziyāda hai. dekho, mīṭar par sirf pandra rūpīe haiṅ. lo, pandra rūpīe lo.*

Go to Gulshan-e Iqbal!

Rahim : Look, John. There's a taxi. He, driver ('brother')! Are you free?

Driver : Yes, sir. I'm free. Get in ('sit').

Rahim : Right. Go to Gulshan-e Iqbal. Do you know (that) where the Koh-e- Nur Restaurant is?

Driver : Yes, sir. I know. There's a big hospital there, isn't there?

Rahim : Yes. And go by the meter. So, tell me, John. Do you like Karachi? I mean, you and your wife?

John : Yes, we like it very much. Here everything is interesting. I mean, we are in Asia (for) the first time.

Rahim : And what things does your wife like?

John : She especially likes the bazaars. In the city there are (some) very splendid shops.

Rahim : That's true (then). But Karachi is a fairly new city. I like Lahore more. There are many old buildings there. And I like historical cities very (much). Look. Our restaurant is there. Driver! Stop here. How much is the fare?

Driver : Eighteen rupees, sir.

Rahim : No. Eighteen rupees is far too much. Look! There's only fifteen on the meter. There you are! Take fifteen rupees.

ٹیکسی	*ṭaiksī*	taxi (f.)	پہلی بار	*pahlī bār*	for the first time
اے	*e*	oh!, hey!	ایشیا	*ešiyā*	Asia (m.)
اے بھائی	*e bhāī!*	address to a taxi driver, waiter, etc.	خاص طور سے	*xās taur se*	especially
خالی	*xālī*	empty, free	شاندار	*šāndār*	splendid
ٹیکسی والا	*ṭaiksīvālā*	taxi driver (m.)	دوکان	*dūkān*	shop (f.)
صاحب	*sāhib*	Sir	سچ	*sac*	true
ہے نا	*hai nā?*	isn't there?	لاہور	*lāhaur*	Lahore (m.)
میٹر	*mīṭar*	meter (m.)	زیادہ	*ziyāda*	more
میٹر سے چلو	*mīṭar se calo*	'go by the meter'	تاریخی	*tārīxī*	historical
تو	*to*	then, so, however	روکو	*roko*	stop
پہلا	*pahlā*	first	روکنا	*roknā*	to stop
بار	*bār*	time, occasion (f.)	کرایہ	*kirāya*	fare (m.)
			اٹھارہ	*aṭhāra*	eighteen
			روپیہ	*rūpiya*	rupee (m.)
			بہت زیادہ	*bahut ziyāda*	far too much
			پندرہ	*pandra*	fifteen
			لو	*lo*	there you are! take!

قواعد *qavā'id* Grammar

نا *nā* isn't it?

نا is a short form of نہیں *nahīṅ* 'no, not'. Here it is used as a question tag 'isn't it', which can be translated as 'isn't it?', 'aren't you?', 'doesn't it?' according to context:

یہ کھانا اچھا ہے نا؟	*yih khānā acchā hai nā?*	This food is nice, isn't it?

تو *to* 'then, however, so'

The word تو *to*, basically meaning 'then, however, so', has many uses in Urdu. In colloquial speech it is often used to begin a sentence, something like English 'so':

تو یہ بتائیے	*to yih batāīe*	so, tell (me) this

When تو follows a word, it adds emphasis:

میں تو پاکستانی ہوں	*maiṅ to pākistānī hūṅ*	*I am* a Pakistani

بار *bār* 'time, turn' (f.); ایک بار *ek bār* 'once'

We have already met وقت *vaqt* 'point of time' and فرصت *fursat* 'leisure'. The word بار *bār* means 'time' in the sense of 'occasion, turn':

ایک بار	*ek bār*	one time, once
تین بار	*tīn bār*	three times

Note that after numerals بار *bār* remains singular:

پہلی بار	*pahlī bār*	(for) the first time
میں پہلی بار یہاں ہوں	*maiṅ pahlī bār yahāṅ hūṅ*	I'm here for the first time

خاص طور پر *xās taur par/se* 'especially'

The word طور *taur* (m.) means 'way, means', and is used in the adverbial expression خاص طور پر / سے *xās taur par / se* 'on / from a special way', i.e. 'especially'. Note a similar phrase عام طور پر / سے *'ām taur par / se* 'on / from a general way', i.e. 'generally', 'usually'. Either پر or سے may be used in these expressions.

زیادہ ziyāda 'more, most, too, very'

The word زیادہ *ziyāda* may mean 'more, most, too, too much, very'. Compare the following sentences:

یہ زیادہ بڑا ہے

yih ziyāda baṛā hai

This is too big.

میرا گھر یہاں سے زیادہ دور نہیں ہے

merā ghar yahāṅ se ziyāda dūr nahīṅ hai

My house is not very far from here

مجھے لاہور زیادہ پسند ہے

mujhe lāhaur ziyāda pasand hai

I like Lahore more/better

Irregular imperatives

We have already seen that the command or imperative for آپ is formed by adding *-īe* to the stem of the verb, and that for تم by adding و *-o*. Four important verbs لینا *lenā* 'to take', دینا *denā* 'to give', کرنا *karnā* 'to do' and پینا *pīnā* 'to drink' have irregular forms which must be learnt:

تو	**tū**	تم	**tum**	آپ	**āp**	
لے	le	لو	lo	لیجے	*lījīe*	take!
دے	de	دو	do	دیجیے	*dījīe*	give!
کر	kar	کرو	karo	کیجیے	*kījīe*	do!
پی	pī	پیو	pīo	پیجیے	*pījīe*	drink!

پیسے paise 'money'

In both India and Pakistan, the major unit of currency is the روپیہ *rūpīa* rupee. The smallest coin is the پیسہ *paisa*, a hundred of which make one rupee. ایک سو پیسے = ایک روپیہ *ek sau paisa* = *ek rūpīa*. In English 'rupees' is abbreviated to *Rs*.

پانچ روپے *pāṅc rūpīe* Rs. 5

The most common word for 'money' is the plural word پیسے *paise*:

کتنے پیسے؟	*kitne paise?*	How much money?
اسے پیسے دیجیے	*use paise dījīe*	Give him (some) money

مکالمہ ۳ *mukālima tīn* Dialogue 3

Rahim and John choose their meal in the restaurant.

رحیم : آیئے، جان صاحب۔ یہاں تشریف رکھیے۔ یہ میرا پسندیدہ ریستراں ہے۔ بیرا کہاں ہے؟ اے بھائی مینو لاؤ۔

بیرا : بہت اچھا، صاحب۔ مینو لیجیے۔

رحیم : اچھا جان صاحب۔ مینو دیکھیے اُردو میں بھی ہے اور انگریزی میں بھی ہے۔ آپ کو کیا چاہیے؟ آپ کو معلوم ہے کہ یہ سب چیزیں کیا ہیں؟

جان : جی ہاں۔ انگلستان میں بھی بہت ہندوستانی اور پاکستانی ریستراں ہیں نا۔ یہ سب چیزیں مجھے معلوم ہیں۔ مجھے خاص طور سے بھونا گوشت اور نان پسند ہیں۔

رحیم : اچھا مجھے بریانی زیادہ پسند ہے۔ مجھے بریانی اور قورمہ چاہیے اور کیا پینا ہے؟

جان : مجھے صرف پانی چاہیے۔

رحیم : یہاں آپ پانی نہ پیجیے۔ پانی ٹھیک نہیں ہے۔ آپ جوس یا پاک کولا لیجیے۔ وہ زیادہ اچھا ہے۔ بیرا! ادھر آؤ۔ ہمیں کافی چیزیں چاہئیں۔ ایک بھونا گوشت، دو نان، ایک بریانی، ایک قورمہ، ایک جوس اور ایک پاک کولا۔ اور آم بھی ہیں؟

بیرا : جی، آم بھی ہیں اور اناناس بھی ہیں۔

رحیم : جی نہیں، اناناس نہیں چاہیے۔ صرف آم لاؤ، اور جلدی لاؤ!

بیرا : اچھا صاحب

rahīm : *āie jān sāhib. yahāṅ tašrīf rakhīe. yih merā pasandīda restarāṅ hai. berā kahāṅ hai? e bhāī, menyū lāo.*

berā : *bahut acchā sāhib. menyū lījīe.*

rahīm : *acchā, jān sāhib. menyū dekhīe. urdū meṅ bhī hai, aur angrezī meṅ bhī hai. āp ko kyā cāhīe? āp ko ma'lūm hai ki yih sab cīzeṅ kyā haiṅ?*

jān : *jī hāṅ. inglistān meṅ bhī bahut hindustānī aur pākistanī restarāṅ haiṅ nā? yih sab cīzeṅ mujhe ma'lūm haiṅ. mujhe xās taur se bhūnā gošt aur nān pasand haiṅ.*

rahīm : *acchā. mujhe biryānī ziyāda pasand hai. mujhe biryānī aur qorma cāhīe. aur kyā pīnā hai?*

jān : *mujhe sirf pānī cāhīe.*

rahīm : *yahāṅ āp pānī na pījīe. pānī ṭhīk nahīṅ hai. āp jūs yā pāk kolā lījīe. vuh ziyāda acchā hai. berā! idhar āo! hameṅ kāfī cīzeṅ cāhīeṅ. ek bhūnā gošt, do nān, ek biryānī, ek qorma, ek jūs aur ek pāk kolā. aur ām bhī haiṅ?*

berā : *jī, ām haiṅ, aur anānās bhī haiṅ.*

rahīm : *jī nahīṅ, anānās nahīṅ cāhīe. sirf 'ām lāo. aur jaldī lāo.*

berā : *acchā, sāhib.*

Rahim : Come on John. Sit here. This is my favourite restaurant. Where's the waiter? Waiter. Bring the menu.

Waiter : Very well, sir. Here's ('take') the menu.

Rahim : Good, John. Look at the menu. It's in (both) English and Urdu. What do you want? Do you know what all these things are?

John : Yes. In England, there are a lot of Indian and Pakistani restaurants, aren't there? I particularly like 'roast meat' and naan.

Rahim : Good. I like biryani better. I want biryani and korma. And what do you want to drink ('what is to drink')?

John : I only want water.

Rahim : Don't drink the water here. The water's not good. Drink juice or Pak Cola. That's better. Waiter! Come here! We want quite (a lot of) things. One roast meat, two naan, one biryani, one korma, one juice and one Pak Cola. And do you have mangos as well?

Waiter : Yes. There are mangos and pineapple.

Rahim : No. (We) don't want pineapple. Only bring mangos. And bring (it) quickly.

Waiter : Very well, sir.

پسندیدہ	*pasandīda*	favourite	آپ کو ... چاہیے	*āp ko ... cāhīe*	you want...
بیرا	*berā*	waiter (m.)			
مینو	*menyū*	menu (m.)	آپ کو کیا چاہیے؟	*āp ko kyā cāhīe?*	what do you want?
لاؤ	*lāo*	bring			
لیجیے	*lījīe*	take	بھونا	*bhūnā*	roast
اُردو	*urdū*	Urdu (f.)	گوشت	*gošt*	meat (m.)
انگریزی	*angrezī*	English (language) (f.)	نان	*nān*	naan (m.)
			بریانی	*biryānī*	'biryani' rice (f.)

قورمہ	qorma	korma, spiced meat (m.)	نہ پیجیے	na pījīe	don't drink
مجھے ... چاہیے	mujhe ... cāhīe	I want ...	جوس	jūs	juice (m.)
پینا	pīnā	to drink	پاک کولا	pāk kolā	Pak Cola (m.)
کیا پینا ہے؟	kyā pīnā hai?	what (do you want) to drink?	آم	ām	mango (m.)
پانی	pānī	water (m.)	اناس	anānās	pineapple (m.)
			جلدی	jaldī	quickly

قواعد *qavā'id* Grammar

بھی *bhī* 'also'; بھی - بھی *bhī ... bhī* 'both ... and'

بھی *bhī* 'also', 'as well' always follows the word to which it refers:

مجھے پاکستانی کھانا بھی پسند ہے

mujhe pākistānī khānā bhī pasand hai

I like Pakistani food as well (referring to the food)

مجھے بھی پاکستانی کھانا پسند ہے

mujhe bhī pākistānī khānā pasand hai

I also like Pakistani food (referring to 'I')

بھی - بھی *bhī ... bhī* is translated as 'both ... and':

انگریزی میں بھی اُردو میں بھی

angrezī meṅ bhī urdū meṅ bhī

Both in English and in Urdu

کو چاہیے *ko cāhīe* 'to be needed, to want'

'To want, to require' is expressed in Urdu by the phrase کو چاہیے *ko cāhīe*:

آپ کو کیا چاہیے	*āp ko kyā cāhīe?*	'what is needed to you?' What do you want?
مجھے بریانی چاہیے	*mujhe biryānī cāhīe*	'to me biryani is needed' I want biryani

Note that in the last sentence بریانی is the subject.

When the subject is plural, the plural form چاہئیں *cāhīeṅ* 'are needed' is used:

ہمیں بہت چیزیں چاہئیں

hameṅ bahut cīzeṅ cāhīeṅ

We need/want lots of things

آپ کو کیا پینا ہے؟ **āp ko kyā pīnā hai?** 'what do you want to drink?'

When کو is followed by the infinitive + ہے *hai*, the construction may be translated 'you have to', 'you want to', 'you must':

آپ کو کیا پینا ہے؟

āp ko kyā pīnā hai?

What do you want to drink? ('to you what is to drink'?)

رحیم کو کھانا ہے

rahīm ko khānā hai

Rahim has to eat ('to Rahim is to eat')

مجھے ابھی جانا ہے

mujhe abhī jānā hai

I have to go now ('to me now is to go')

نہ پیجیے ***na pījīe*** 'don't drink'

The word نہ *na* (which must be distinguished from نا *nā* which we saw earlier in this unit) is used with the imperative to make a negative command 'don't do!'

انہیں نہ بتائیے	*unheṅ na batāīe*	Don't tell him!
یہاں پانی نہ پیجیے	*yahāṅ pānī na pījīe*	Don't drink the water here!

Numbers 11–20

Here the numerals 11–20 (Appendix 1) should be learnt.

ثقافت *siqāfat* Culture

Most Europeans and Americans are so familiar with Indian and Pakistani food that little commentary is required here. Tastes vary from region to region, but in the north of the subcontinent the favourite combination is meat

(گوشت *gošt* (m.)) and bread (روٹی *roṭī* (f.)), while in Bengal and the south rice (چاول *cāval* (m.)) is preferred. Many of the names of the dishes on the menu of an 'Indian' restaurant are actually Urdu, often derived from Persian. No distinction is made between lunch and dinner. For both the word کھانا *khānā* is used.

Taxis, as well as scooters and rikshaws (رکشا *rikšā* (m.)) are numerous and reliable in India and Pakistan, and are the most convenient form of transport. As in many countries, the fare is usually negotiable, but asking the driver to go by the meter (میٹر سے چلو *mīṭar se calo*) sometimes has the desired effect. Most Urdu speakers, like Mr Rahim in the dialogue, address taxi drivers (ٹیکسی والا *ṭaiksīvālā*) and waiters (بیرا *berā*, from English 'bearer') as اے بھائی *bhāī* 'brother', and use the pronoun تم *tum*. As a foreigner, you would do better always to use آپ *āp*.

مشقیں **mašqeṅ** Exercises

3.3 Dialogue

Give your part in the following dialogue:

Aslam	:	کیا آپ کو پاکستانی کھانا پسند ہے؟
You	:	(say that you like it very much)
Aslam	:	گلشنِ اقبال میں ایک بہت اچھا ریستراں ہے۔
You	:	(say that you know; your hotel is not far from there)
Aslam	:	وہ میرا پسندیدہ ریستراں ہے۔
You	:	(ask him what its name is)
Aslam	:	کوہِ نور ہے۔ چلیں، ساتھ کھانا کھائیں؟
You	:	(say no; at this time you are not free)

3.4 Items on the menu

Look at the menu with the items written in Urdu. Here are some new words:

مصنوعات	*masnū'āt*	dishes (m.p.)
پلاؤ	*pulāo*	pulao, rice cooked with vegetables (m.)

سبزی	*sabzī*	vegetables in general (f.)
ساگ	*sāg*	spinach (m.)
مٹر	*maṭar*	pea(s) (m.)
گوبھی	*gobhī*	cabbage, cauliflower (f.)
تندوری	*tandūrī*	tandoori (baked in an earth oven)
پھل	*phal*	fruit (m.)
کوفی	*kofī*	coffee (f.)

مصنوعات		روپیے
چاول		
پلاؤ	....	۸
بریانی	....	۱۲
سبزی		
ساگ	....	۶
مٹر	....	۵
گوبھی	....	۷
گوشت		
بھونا گوشت	....	۱۵
قورمہ	....	۱۴
مرغی	....	۱۸
تندوری مرغی	....	۶۰
پھل		
آم	....	۱۰
اناناس	....	۸
روٹی		
نان	....	۵
پراٹھا	....	۳
چپاتی	....	۲
چائے	....	۶
کوفی	....	۸

Read the menu and do the following:

1 Call the waiter (address him as آپ) and ask him to come to you.

2 Ask him if the tandoori chicken is good.

3 Tell him you want spinach, *bhūnā gosht* and *pulao*; your friend wants tandoori chicken, naan and lentils (*dāl*).

4 Tell him you do not want fruit today.

5 After the meal you want one coffee and one tea.

6 Work out the price of your meal and write the total in figures.

3.5 Comprehension

Listen to the dialogue and tick the correct answer.

1 Aslam is free today	Yes ( )	No ( )
2 Today there is	A holiday ( )	A meeting ( )
3 Rahim's friend is	American ( )	English ( )
4 Aslam's family is	At home ( )	In town ( )
5 Aslam's house is	Far away ( )	Nearby ( )

4 زندگی بُری نہیں ہے

zindagī burī nahin hai

Life is not so bad!

In this unit you will learn how to:

- express possession
- describe relationships
- give your age
- talk about your origins

اسلم صاحب کی زندگی کا خلاصہ

جیسا کہ آپ کو معلوم ہے اسلم صاحب کا گھر کراچی میں ہے۔ ان کا گھر بندر روڈ پر ہے اور شہر کے مرکز سے صرف ایک میل دور ہے۔ اسلم صاحب کا گھر کافی بڑا ہے۔ ان کے گھر میں سات کمرے ہیں لیکن وہاں بہت لوگ ہیں۔ اسلم صاحب کی بیوی کا نام بلقیس ہے۔ ان کے بچوں کے نام حامد، اقبال، نرگس، اور جمیلہ ہیں۔ یعنی اسلم صاحب کے چار بچے ہیں۔ جان اور ہیلن اسلم صاحب کے انگریز دوست ہیں۔ وہ دونوں ڈاکٹر ہیں اور آج کل پاکستان میں چھٹی پر ہیں۔ ان کے بچے نہیں۔

حامد، یعنی اسلم صاحب کے بڑے بیٹے کا اسکول کلفٹن میں ہے۔ کلفٹن کراچی کے مرکز سے کوئی پانچ میل دور ہے۔ حامد کے اسکول میں صرف لڑکے ہیں۔ وہاں لڑکیاں نہیں ہیں۔ لڑکیوں کا اسکول اسلم صاحب کے گھر سے کافی نزدیک ہے۔ اسلم صاحب کی چھوٹی بیٹی کا نام جمیلہ ہے۔ جمیلہ کی عمر صرف دو سال ہے۔ وہ اسکول میں نہیں۔

اسلم صاحب انجینئر ہیں اور وہ کراچی کے ایک بڑے کارخانے میں ہیں۔ ان کا کارخانہ ان کے گھر سے کافی دور ہے۔ لیکن ان کا کام بہت دلچسپ ہے۔ اسلم اور بلقیس کی زندگی بری نہیں ہے۔ وہ بہت امیر نہیں ہیں لیکن غریب بھی نہیں! وہ کافی خوش ہیں۔

aslam sāhib kī zindagī kā xulāsa

jaisā ki āp ko ma'lūm hai aslam sāhib kā ghar karācī meṅ hai. un kā ghar bandar roḍ par hai aur šahr ke markaz se sirf ek mīl dūr hai. aslam sāhib kā ghar kāfī baṛā hai. in ke ghar meṅ sāt kamre haiṅ lekin vahāṅ bahut log haiṅ. aslam sāhib kī bīvī kā nām bilqīs hai. un ke baccoṅ ke nām hāmid, iqbāl, nargis aur jamīla haiṅ. ya'nī aslam sāhib ke cār bacce haiṅ. jān aur helan aslam sāhib ke angrez dost haiṅ. vuh donoṅ ḍākṭar haiṅ aur āj kal pākistān meṅ chuṭṭī par haiṅ. un ke bacce nahīṅ.

hāmid, ya'nī aslam sāhib ke baṛe beṭe kā iskūl kliftan meṅ hai. kliftan karācī ke markaz se koī pāṅc mīl dūr hai. hāmid ke iskūl meṅ sirf laṛke haiṅ. vahāṅ laṛkīāṅ nahīṅ. laṛkīoṅ kā iskūl aslam sāhib ke ghar se kāfī nazdīk hai. aslam sāhib kī choṭī beṭī kā nām jamīla hai. jamīla kī 'umr sirf do sāl hai. vuh iskūl meṅ nahīṅ.

aslam sāhib injinīr haiṅ. vuh karācī ke ek baṛe kārxāne meṅ haiṅ. un kā kārxāna un ke ghar se kāfī dūr hai. lekin un kā kām bahut dilcasp hai. aslam aur bilqīs kī zindagī burī nahīṅ hai. vuh bahut amīr nahīṅ haiṅ, lekin ğarīb bhī nahīṅ. vuh kāfī xuš haiṅ.

A summary of Aslam's life

As you know, Aslam's house is in Karachi. His house is on Bandar Road and only one mile from the centre of the city. Aslam's house is quite big. In his house there are seven rooms but there are a lot of people there. Aslam's wife's name is Bilqis. His children's names are Hamid, Iqbal, Nargis and Jamila. In other words, Aslam has four children. John and Helen are Aslam's English friends. They are both doctors and these days are on holiday in Pakistan. They have no children.

Hamid, that is Aslam's elder son's school is in Clifton. Clifton is about five miles from the centre of Karachi. In Hamid's school there are only boys. There are no girls. The girls' school is quite near Aslam's house. Aslam's younger daughter's name is Jamila. Jamila is only two. She is not at school.

Aslam is an engineer. He is in a big factory in Karachi. His factory is quite far from his house. But his work is very interesting. Aslam's and Bilqis' life is not (so) bad. They are not very rich, but they are not poor either ('also'). They are quite happy.

زندگی	*zindagī*	life (f.)	کا، کی، کے	*kā, kī, ke*	's, of
برا	*burā*	bad	اسلم صاحب کا گھر	*aslam sāhib kā ghar*	Aslam Sahib's house
اسلم کی زندگی کا	*aslam kī zindagī kā*	of Aslam's life	مرکز	*markaz*	centre (m.)
خلاصہ	*xulāsa*	summary (m.)	شہر کے مرکز سے	*šahr ke markaz se*	from the city centre
جیسا کہ	*jaisā ki*	as			

ان کے گھر میں	*in ke ghar meṅ*	in his house
اسلم صاحب کی بیوی	*aslam sāhib kī bīvī*	Aslam Sahib's wife
بیوی کا نام	*bīvī kā nām*	wife's name
بچوں کے نام	*baccoṅ ke nām*	children's names
اسلم کے چار بچّے ہیں	*aslam ke cār bacce haiṅ*	Aslam has four children
اسلم کے دوست	*aslam ke dost*	Aslam's friends
دونوں	*donoṅ*	both
اسلم صاحب کے بڑے بیٹے کا	*aslam sāhib ke baṛe beṭe kā*	Aslam Sahib's eldest son's
کراچی کے مرکز سے	*karācī ke markaz se*	from the centre of Karachi
کوئی	*koī*	about, roughly
میل	*mīl*	mile (m.)
حامد کے اسکول میں	*hāmid ke iskūl meṅ*	in Hamid's school
لڑکیوں کا اسکول	*larkīoṅ kā iskūl*	the girls' school
اسلم صاحب کے گھر سے	*aslam sāhib ke ghar se*	from Aslam Sahib's house
سے نزدیک	*se nazdīk*	near (from/to)
اسلم صاحب کی بیٹی	*aslam sāhib kī betī*	Aslam Sahib's daughter
بیٹی کا نام	*betī kā nām*	daughter's name
عمر	*'umr*	age (f.)
جمیلہ کی عمر	*jamīla kī 'umr*	Jamila's age
سال	*sāl*	year (m.)
کارخانہ	*kārxāna*	factory (m.)
ایک بڑے کارخانے میں	*ek bare kārxāne meṅ*	in a big factory
زندگی	*zindagī*	life (f.)
اسلم صاحب کی زندگی	*aslam sāhib kī zindagī*	Aslam Sahib's life
امیر	*amīr*	rich
غریب	*ǧarīb*	poor

قواعد qavā'id Grammar

جیسا کہ *jaisā ki* 'as'

جیسا کہ *jaisā ki* is a conjuction consisting of two words meaning 'as':

جیسا کہ آپ کو معلوم ہے، میں پاکستانی ہوں

jaisā ki āp ko ma'lūm hai, maiṅ pākistānī hūṅ

As you know, I am a Pakistani

The oblique case of nouns

Like pronouns, nouns and adjectives also have an oblique case, and change their endings when followed by a postposition.

Masculine nouns ending in ا *-ā* or ہ *-a*, e.g. لڑکا *laṛkā* 'boy' and بچہ *bacca* 'child', form the oblique singular by changing the final vowel ا *-ā* or ہ *-a* to ے *-e*; and the oblique plural by changing the final vowel to وں *-oṅ*. Here are the oblique forms with the postposition سے *se*.

Direct singular	لڑکا	*laṛkā*	the boy
	بچہ	*bacca*	the child
Oblique singular	لڑکے سے	*laṛke se*	from the boy
	بچے سے	*bacce se*	from the child
Direct singular	لڑکے	*laṛke*	the boys
	بچے	*bacce*	the children
Oblique plural	لڑکوں سے	*laṛkoṅ se*	from the boys
	بچوں سے	*bacooṅ se*	from the children

Masculine nouns ending in any other letter, such as گھر *ghar* 'house' and آدمی *ādmī* 'man', make no change for the oblique singular but add وں *-oṅ* for the oblique plural:

Direct singular	گھر	*ghar*	the house
	آدمی	*ādmī*	the man
Oblique singular	گھر سے	*ghar se*	from the house
	آدمی سے	*ādmī se*	from the man
Direct plural	گھر	*ghar*	the houses
	آدمی	*ādmī*	the men
Oblique plural	گھروں سے	*gharoṅ se*	from the houses
	آدمیوں سے	*ādmīoṅ se*	from the men

Feminine nouns ending in ی *-ī*, for example لڑکی *laṛkī* 'girl' make no change for the oblique singular, but add وں *oṅ* for the oblique plural:

Direct singular	لڑکی	*laṛkī*	the girl
Oblique singular	لڑکی سے	*laṛkī se*	from the girl
Direct plural	لڑکیاں	*laṛkīāṅ*	the girls
Oblique plural	لڑکیوں سے	*laṛkīoṅ se*	from the girls

Feminine nouns ending in any other letter, e.g. کتاب *kitāb* 'book', make no change for the oblique singular, but add وں *-oṅ* for the oblique plural:

Direct singular	کتاب	*kitāb*	the book
Oblique singular	کتاب سے	*kitāb se*	from the book
Direct plural	کتابیں	*kitābeṅ*	the books
Oblique plural	کتابوں سے	*kitāboṅ se*	from the books

The oblique case of adjectives

We have already seen that adjectives ending in ا *-ā*, such as اچھا *acchā* 'good' and بڑا *baṛā* 'big', as well as the possessive adjectives such as میرا *merā* 'my', آپ کا *āp kā* 'your', etc., change their endings to agree with the following noun in number (singular, plural) and gender (masculine, feminine). When coming before both singular and plural oblique masculine nouns, adjectives in ا *-ā* change their ending to ے *-e*. When coming before feminine oblique nouns, the ending is ی *-ī*, as for the direct case:

Masculine direct singular	اچھا لڑکا	*acchā laṛkā*	the good boy
Masculine oblique singular	اچھے لڑکے سے	*acche laṛke se*	from the good boy
Masculine direct plural	اچھے لڑکے	*acche laṛke*	the good boys
Masculine oblique plural	اچھے لڑکوں سے	*acche laṛkoṅ se*	from the good boys
Feminine direct singular	اچھی لڑکی	*acchī laṛkī*	the good girl
Feminine oblique singular	اچھی لڑکی سے	*acchī laṛkī se*	from the good girl
Feminine direct plural	اچھی لڑکیاں	*acchī laṛkīāṅ*	the good girls
Feminine oblique plural	اچھی لڑکیوں سے	*acchī laṛkīoṅ se*	from the good girls

Note that even if the noun makes no change in the oblique singular, as is the case with nouns belonging to the second group, it is still regarded as oblique, and the preceding adjective in ا *-ā* must change its form to the oblique accordingly:

اچھا گھر	*acchā ghar*	a good house
اچھے گھر میں	*acche ghar meṅ*	in a good house

Adjectives ending in any other letter, e.g. خوبصورت *xūbsūrat* 'beautiful', مشہور *mašhūr* 'famous' make no change in any circumstances:

خوبصورت بچہ	*xūbsūrat bacca*	a beautiful child
خوبصورت لڑکی سے	*xūbsūrat laṛkī se*	from the beautiful girl
مشہور آدمیوں کو	*mašhūr ādmīoṅ ko*	to famous men

The postposition کا *kā* 's, of'

The postposition کا *kā* which we have already met as the second element of the possessive adjectives ان کا' آپ کا' اس کا is best thought of as the equivalent of the English 's, as in اسلم کا گھر *aslam kā ghar* 'Aslam's house'. کا may also be translated as 'of', i.e. 'the house of Aslam'.

Like other postpositions it must be preceded by the oblique case:

میرے لڑکے کا نام	*mere laṛke kā nām*	my boy's name
لڑکیوں کا اسکول	*laṛkīoṅ kā iskūl*	the girls' school
بڑے شہر کا ہوٹل	*baṛe šahr kā hoṭal*	the big city's hotel

کا also changes for number, gender and case like adjectives in ا *-ā*, having the forms کے' کی' کا *kā, kī, ke*, the same endings as اچھا *acchā*:

اچھا لڑکا	*acchā laṛkā*	a good boy
لڑکے کا اسکول	*laṛke kā iskūl*	the boy's school
اچھے لڑکے	*acche laṛke*	good boys
لڑکے کے دوست	*laṛke ke dost*	the boy's friends
اچھے لڑکوں کو	*acche laṛkoṅ ko*	to the good boys
لڑکے کے دوستوں سے	*laṛke ke dostoṅ se*	from the boy's friends
اچھی لڑکی	*acchī laṛkī*	a good girl
لڑکی کی کتاب	*laṛkī kī kitāb*	the girl's book
اچھی لڑکیوں کو	*acchī laṛkīoṅ ko*	to the good girls
لڑکی کی کتابوں میں	*laṛkī kī kitāboṅ meṅ*	in the girl's books

To sum up, the postposition کا *kā*: must take the oblique case of the word which precedes it; must agree in number, gender and case with the word which comes after it.

میرے بڑے بیٹے کے اسکول کے لڑکوں سے پوچھیے

mere baṛe beṭe ke iskūl ke laṛkoṅ se pūchīe

Ask the boys of my eldest son's school

میری چھوٹی بیٹیوں کی سہیلیوں کے شہروں میں

merī choṭī beṭīoṅ kī sahelīoṅ ke šahroṅ meṅ

In the cities of the friends of my small daughters

سے دور se dūr 'far from'

In Urdu the sentence 'my house is twenty miles (away) from London' is expressed:

میرا گھر لندن سے بیس میل دور ہے

merā ghar landan se bīs mīl dūr hai

My house is twenty miles far from London

In such expressions the word دور must always be included.

دور dūr is regarded as a feminine noun. Thus 'how far?' is کتنی دور *kitnī dūr*? 'how much far?'.

آپ کا گھر یہاں سے کتنی دور ہے؟

āp kā ghar yahāṅ se kitnī dūr hai?

How far is your house from here?

ہونا *honā* 'to have', 'to possess'

We have already noted that Urdu has no verb like the English 'to have, possess'. To have relations or to possess things, which are not actually with you or on you, is expressed by using the postposition کا *kā* with ہونا *honā*:

اسلم کے چار بچے ہیں

aslam ke cār bacce haiṅ

Aslam has four children ('Aslam's four children are')

رحیم صاحب کی گاڑی نہیں ہے

rahīm sāhib kī gāṛī nahīṅ hai

Rahim does not have (own) a car ('Rahim's car is not')

If the noun (i.e. Aslam, Rahim) is replaced by a pronoun (I, you, he, they, etc.), then the possessive adjective (e.g. میرا، اس کا، ہمارا، ان کا etc.) is used:

میرے چار بچے ہیں

mere cār bacce haiṅ

I have four children ('my four children are')

ان کا بہت خوبصورت گھر ہے

un kā bahut xūbsūrat ghar hai

They have a very beautiful house

Expressing your age

There are two ways of expressing age in Urdu. The more straightforward is to use the word عمر *'umr* 'age':

آپ کی عمر کیا ہے؟ میری عمر اٹھارہ سال ہے؟

āp kī 'umr kyā hai? merī 'umr aṭhāra sāl hai

What is your age? My age is eighteen (i.e. I am eighteen)

The other way is to use the postposition کا kā, which must take the gender of the subject:

حامد چودہ سال کا ہے

hāmid cauda sāl kā hai

Hamid is fourteen ('Hamid is of fourteen years')

اس کی بیٹی دو سال کی ہے

us kī beṭī do sāl kī hai

his daughter is two ('of two years')

Note that even though سال *sāl* 'years' is masculine plural and is followed by کی its form does not change to oblique.

مشق *mašq* Exercise

4.1 Correct form of کا *kā*

In the following sentences give the correct form of کا kā. Make sure of the gender, number and case of the word which follows it:

1 رحیم صاحب ______ پرانے گھر میں۔

2 میری بیٹی ______ اسکول اچھا ہے۔

3 اقبال ______ عمر کیا ہے؟

4 اسلم ______ بیٹی کا نام کیا ہے؟

5 پاکستان ______ پرانے شہر دلچسپ ہیں

مکالمہ ایک **mukālima ek Dialogue 1**

Helen and Bilqis go to have some ice cream. Bilqis talks about her origins.

بلقیس : آیئے ہیلن' اس دوکان میں بہت اچھا آئس کریم ہے۔ مجھے آئس کریم بہت پسند ہے۔ آج ہمارے شوہر شہر میں مصروف ہیں۔ چلیں آئس کریم کھائیں۔

ہیلن : آپ کا خیال بہت اچھا ہے۔ لیکن ان لوگوں کو معلوم نہیں ہے کہ ہم کہاں ہیں! کوئی بات نہیں' آیئے بیٹھیے آج واقعی کافی گرمی ہے۔ بلقیس یہ بتایئے' آپ کہاں کی رہنے والی ہیں؟

بلقیس : میں اصل میں دہلی کی ہوں۔ یعنی میرا وطن ہندوستان ہے لیکن میں بچپن سے یہاں کراچی میں ہوں۔ اسلم صاحب کا وطن پنجاب ہے۔ وہ سیالکوٹ کے رہنے والے ہیں۔ لیکن ان کی مادری زبان پنجابی نہیں' اُردو ہے۔

ہیلن : یہ بہت دلچسپ ہے۔ اس شہر میں ہر طرح کے لوگ ہیں۔ بتایئے اس دوکان کا نام کیا ہے؟

بلقیس : اس دوکان کا نام مجھے معلوم نہیں۔ مجھے صرف یہ معلوم ہے کہ اس کا آئس کریم مجھے پسند ہے۔ چلیے' اور کھائیں!

bilqīs : *āīe helan. is dūkān meṅ bahut acchā āis krīm hai. mujhe āis krīm bahut pasand hai. āj hamāre šauhar šahr meṅ masrūf haiṅ. caleṅ, āis krīm khāeṅ.*

helan : *āp kā xayāl bahut acchā hai. lekin un logoṅ ko ma'lūm nahīṅ ki ham kahāṅ haiṅ. koī bāt nahīṅ āīe, baiṭhīe. āj vāqa'ī kāfī garmī hai. bilqīs, yih batāīe. āp kahāṅ kī rahnevālī haiṅ?*

bilqīs : *maiṅ asal meṅ dihlī kī hūṅ. ya'nī merā vatan hindustān hai, lekin maiṅ bacpan se yahāṅ karācī meṅ hūṅ. aslam sāhib kā vatan panjāb hai. vuh sīālkoṭ ke rahnevāle haiṅ. lekin un kī mādrī zabān panjābī nahīṅ. urdū hai.*

helan : *yih bahut dilcasp hai. is šahr meṅ har tarah ke log haiṅ. batāīe is dūkān kā nām kyā hai?*

bilqīs : *is dūkān kā nām mujhe ma'lūm nahīṅ. mujhe sirf yih ma'lūm hai kī is kā āis krīm mujhe bahut pasand hai. calīe. aur khāeṅ.*

Bilqis : Come on, Helen. They have very good ice cream in this shop. I like ice cream very much. Come on, let's have ('eat') some ice cream.

Helen : Your idea is very good. Today our husbands are busy, and they don't know (that) where we are. It doesn't matter. Come on. Sit down. It is really very warm today. Bilqis, tell me. Where are you from?

Bilqis : In fact I am from Delhi, but I have been ('am') here in Karachi since childhood. Aslam's homeland is Panjab. He comes from Sialkot. But his mother tongue is not Panjabi. It's Urdu.

Helen : That's very interesting. In this city there are all sorts of people. Tell me. What's the name of this shop?

Bilqis : I don't know the name of this shop. I only know that I like its ice cream very (much). Come on. Let's have ('eat') some more.

اس دوکان میں	*is dūkān meṅ*	in this shop	دہلی	*dihlī*	Delhi (f.)
دوکان	*dūkān*	shop (f.)	وطن	*vatan*	homeland (m.)
آئس کریم	*āis krīm*	ice cream (m.)	بچپن	*bacpan*	childhood (m.)
شوہر	*šauhar*	husband (m.)	بچپن سے	*bacpan se*	since childhood
چلیں	*caleṅ*	let's go, come on	سیالکوٹ	*sīālkoṭ*	Sialkot (a town in Panjab) (m.)
خیال	*xayāl*	idea, opinion (m.)	کے رہنے والے ہیں	*ke rahnevāle haiṅ*	is from
ان لوگوں کو	*un logoṅ ko*	to them	مادری زبان	*mādrī zabān*	mother tongue (f.)
گرمی	*garmī*	heat (f.)	زبان	*zabān*	tongue (f.)
کافی گرمی ہے	*kāfī garmī hai*	it's quite warm ('there's quite a lot of heat')	ہر طرح کا	*har tarah kā*	all kinds of
کہاں کی رہنے والی ہیں	*kahāṅ kī rahnevālī haiṅ?*	where are you from?	اس دوکان کا	*is dūkān kā*	of this shop
اصل میں	*asal meṅ*	in fact	اور کھائیں	*aur khāeṅ*	let's eat some more

قواعد *qavā'id* Grammar

Oblique forms of یہ and وہ

یہ *yih* 'this, these' and وہ *vuh* 'that, those' have the following oblique forms:

Direct		Oblique singular		Oblique plural	
یہ	*yih*	اِس	*is*	اِن	*in*
وہ	*vuh*	اُس	*us*	اُن	*un*

These forms must be used before nouns in the oblique case; for example.

Direct singular	یہ لڑکا	*yih laṛkā*	this boy
Oblique singular	اِس لڑکے سے	*is laṛke se*	from this boy
Direct plural	یہ لڑکے	*yih laṛke*	these boys
Oblique plural	اِن لڑکوں سے	*in laṛkoṅ se*	from these boys
Direct singular	وہ لڑکی	*vuh laṛkī*	that girl
Oblique singular	اُس لڑکی سے	*us laṛkī se*	from that girl
Direct singular	وہ لڑکیاں	*vuh laṛkīāṅ*	those girls
Oblique plural	اُن لڑکیوں سے	*un laṛkīoṅ se*	from those girls

When Urdu is written without vowel signs, which is usually the case, اس and ان could stand for both *is/us; in/un*. Thus, اس لڑکے کو could be read as *is laṛke ko or us laṛke ko* 'to this boy' or 'to that boy'. Only context can decide which one is which.

Oblique plural pronouns and possessive adjectives

We have seen that the technically plural pronouns ہم *ham* 'we', تم *tum* 'you', آپ *āp* 'you', یہ and وہ *yih/vuh* 'they' can be further pluralised for clarity by adding the word لوگ *log* 'people' to them:

ہم لوگ پاکستانی ہیں

We ('people') are Pakistanis

وہ لوگ کون ہیں

Who are they ('those people')

لوگ is a masculine plural noun, and when it is followed by a postposition it must have the plural oblique form لوگوں *logoṅ*:

ہم لوگوں کو معلوم ہے

ham logoṅ ko ma'lūm hai

We know ('to us people it is known')

تم لوگوں کو یہ کھانا پسند ہے؟

tum logoṅ ko yih khānā pasand hai?

Do you like this food? ('to you people is it pleasing?')

Plural possessive pronouns ('our, your, their') are formed by using لوگ *log*:

ہم لوگوں کا وطن	*ham logoṅ kā vatan*	our homeland ('of us people')
آپ لوگوں کے بچے	*āp logoṅ ke bacce*	your children ('of you people')

کہاں کے رہنے والے ہیں؟ kahāṅ ke rahnevāle haiṅ? 'Where do you come from?'

The word رہنے والا *rahnevālā* (m.) رہنے والی *rahnevālī* (f.), composed of two elements written separately, literally means 'dweller', 'original inhabitant'. When you ask someone آپ کہاں کے رہنے والے ہیں؟ *āp kahāṅ ke rahnevāle haiṅ?* (for a male) or آپ کہاں کی رہنے والی ہیں *āp kahāṅ kī rahnevālī haiṅ?* (for a female), the question usually implies 'where do you and your ancestors originate from?'. The answer will be میں دہلی کا رہنے والا ہوں *maiṅ dihlī kā rahnevālā hūṅ* (for a male) or کی رہنے والی ہوں *kī rahnevālī hūṅ* (for a female) 'I am a dweller of Delhi', even though the person may have been born and brought up in Karachi. In other words, you refer to family origins rather than to where you actually live at present. How to say the latter will be discussed in the next unit.

The emotive word وطن *vatan* 'homeland' again often refers to the ancestoral home:

میرا وطن پنجاب ہے

merā vatan panjāb hai

My (ancestoral) home is Panjab

میں بچپن سے یہاں ہوں maiṅ bacpan se yahāṅ hūṅ

In Urdu, when you say 'I have been here since childhood', 'I have been here for five hours', you say 'I *am* here since ...', 'I *am* here for ...', because you *are* here still. 'Since' and 'for' are expressed by سے *se*:

میں بچپن سے یہاں ہوں

maiṅ bacpan se yahāṅ hūṅ

I have been here since childhood

میں پانچ گھنٹے سے اس ریستراں میں ہوں

maiṅ pāṅc ghanṭe se is restarāṅ meṅ hūṅ

I've been in this restaurant for five hours

گھنٹہ *ghanṭa* means 'hour'. When the word is in the plural and followed by a postposition, the direct plural form is used and not, perhaps unexpectedly, the oblique plural:

پانچ گھنٹے	*pāṅc ghanṭe*	five hours
پانچ گھنٹے سے	*pāṅc ghanṭe se*	for five hours

لاہور یہاں سے کتنی دور ہے؟ بارہ گھنٹے کا راستہ ہے

lāhaur yahāṅ se kitnī dūr hai? bāra ghanṭe kā rāsta hai

How far is Lahore from here? It's twelve hours away ('a road of twelve hours')

اور **aur** 'more', 'some more'

اور as well as meaning 'and', may also mean 'more' or 'some more':

آپ کو اور چائے چاہیے؟	*āp ko aur cāe cāhīe?*	do you want some more tea?
اور کھائیں	*aur khāeṅ*	let's eat some more

مکالمہ دو ***mukālima do*** **Dialogue 2**

Aslam reflects on the size and complexities of his country.

جان : اسلم صاحب، آپ سیالکوٹ کے رہنے والے ہیں نا؟ کیا آپ پنجابی ہیں؟

اسلم : جی نہیں۔ سیالکوٹ میرا وطن ہے لیکن میرے والدین ہندوستان کے ہیں۔ ہماری زبان اُردو ہے۔ جیسا کہ آپ کو معلوم ہے اس ملک میں ہر طرح کے لوگ ہیں لیکن پھر بھی ہم سب لوگ پاکستانی ہیں۔ کافی پیچیدہ بات ہے نا؟

جان : جی نہیں۔ میرے خیال سے بہت زیادہ پیچیدہ نہیں۔ پاکستان اور ہندوستان بہت بڑے ملک ہیں اور ان ملکوں کی تاریخ بہت لمبی ہے۔

اسلم : یہ تو سچ ہے۔ سیالکوٹ کراچی سے کم سے کم ایک ہزار میل دور ہے۔ ریل گاڑی سے بیس پچیس گھنٹے کا سفر ہے۔ وہاں کے موسم اور یہاں کے موسم میں کتنا فرق ہے! ہر طرح کی زبانیں بھی ہیں۔ کیا آپ کو ان باتوں سے دلچسپی ہے؟

جان : ضرور۔ مجھے بہت دلچسپی ہے۔ لیکن، آج بہت گرمی ہے۔ چلیں ایک کپ چائے پیئیں!

اسلم : بالکل ٹھیک، آپ کا خیال اچھا ہے۔ چلیں، اس چائے خانے میں چائے پیئیں۔

jān : *aslam sāhib, āp sīālkoṭ ke rahnevāle haiṅ nā? kyā āp panjābī haiṅ?*

aslam : *jī nahīṅ. sīālkoṭ merā vatan hai lekin mere vālidain hindustān ke haiṅ. hamārī zabān urdū hai. jaisā ki āp ko ma'lūm hai is mulk meṅ har tarah ke log haiṅ, lekin phir bhī ham sab log pākistānī haiṅ. kāfī pecīda bāt hai nā?*

jān : *jī nahīṅ. mere xayāl se behut ziyāda pecīda nahīṅ. pākistān aur hindustān bahut baṛe mulk haiṅ. aur in mulkoṅ kī tārīx bahut lambī hai.*

aslam : *yih to sac hai. sīālkoṭ karācī se kam se kam ek hazār mīl dūr hai. rel gāṛī se bīs paccīs ghanṭe kā safar hai. vahāṅ ke mausam aur yahāṅ ke mausam meṅ kitnā farq hai! har tarah kī zabāneṅ bhī haiṅ. kyā āp ko in bātoṅ se dilcaspī hai?*

jān : *zarūr, mujhe bahut dilcaspī hai. lekin āj bahut garmī hai. caleṅ. ek kap cāe pīeṅ?*

aslam : *bilkul ṭhīk. āp kā xayāl acchā hai. caleṅ, us cāe xāne meṅ cāe pīeṅ.*

John : Aslam Sahib! You come from Sialkot, don't you? Are you a Panjabi?

Aslam : No. Sialkot is my homeland, but my parents are from India. Our language is Urdu. As you know, there are all kinds of people in this country, but even so we are all Pakistanis. It's quite a complicated matter, isn't it?

John : No. In ('from') my opinion it's not all that complicated. Pakistan and India are very big countries. And the history of these countries is very long.

Aslam : That's true. Sialkot is at least a thousand miles from Karachi. By train it's twenty (or) twenty-five hours' journey. What a difference there is in the weather here and the weather there. There are all sorts of languages as well. Are you interested in ('to you is there interest from') these matters?

John : Of course. I am very interested. But it's very warm today. Come on, shall we have a cup of tea?

Aslam : Quite right! That's a good idea of yours. Come on, let's have tea in that tea shop.

ہندوستان کے	hindustān ke	from India	وہاں کا موسم	vahāṅ kā mausam	the weather there
پھر بھی	phir bhī	even so			
پیچیدہ	pecīda	complicated	فرق	farq	difference (m.)
میرے خیال سے	mere xayāl se	in my opinion	علاقہ	'ilāqa	area, region (m.)
ملک	mulk	country (m.)	دلچسپی	dilcaspī	interest (f.)
تاریخ	tārīx	history (f.)	آپ کو دلچسپی ہے	āp ko dilcaspī hai	are you interested
لمبا	lambā	long			
کم سے کم	kam se kam	at least	ان باتوں سے	in bātoṅ se	in these things
ایک ہزار	ek hazār	a thousand			
ریل گاڑی	rel gāṛī	train (f.)	ضرور	zarūr	certainly
پچیس	paccīs	twenty-five	ایک کپ چائے	ek kap cāe	a cup of tea
سفر	safar	journey (m.)			
موسم	mausam	weather, climate (m.)			

قواعد qavā'id Grammar

میں ہندوستان کا ہوں **main hindustān kā hūn**

We have met the phrase میں ہندوستان کا رہنے والا ہوں (کی رہنے والی ہوں) *maiṅ hindustān kā rahnevālā hūṅ (kī rahnevālī hūṅ)* 'I originate from India'. The word رہنے والا' رہنے والی' may be dropped without any difference to the meaning:

میں ہندوستان کا / کی ہوں

maiṅ hindustān kā/kī hūṅ

'I am of India' i.e. I originate from India

آپ کہاں کے ہیں۔ میں اصل میں لندن کا ہوں

āp kahāṅ ke haiṅ? maiṅ asal meṅ landan kā hūṅ

Where are you from? In fact I am from London

ہر har 'every'; سب sab 'all'

ہر *har*, mostly used with singular nouns, means 'every':

ہر ملک	*har mulk*	every country
ہر آدمی	*har ādmī*	every person

When followed by ایک *ek* it means 'every single', ہر ایک چیز *har ek cīz* 'every single thing'.

ہر طرح کا *har tarah kā* means 'all kinds of', 'all sorts of' طرح *tarah* means 'way, method, kind' (f.).

ہر طرح کے لوگ	*har tarah ke log*	all kinds of people
ہر طرح کی کتابیں	*har tarah kī kitābeṅ*	all sorts of books

سب sab 'all' is mostly used with plural nouns:

سب لوگ	*sab log*	all (the) people
سب چیزیں	*sab cīzeṅ*	all (the) things

Note the word order in ہم سب *ham sab* 'all of us' and آپ سب *āp sab* 'all of you'.

میرے خیال سے mere xayāl se 'in my opinion'

خیال *xayāl* 'idea, opinion, thought' (m.) is used in the expression میرے خیال سے *mere xayāl se* 'in (from) my opinion', 'I think that'. Note also the expression آپ کا کیا خیال ہے؟ 'what is your opinion?', 'what do you think?'.

ریل گاڑی سے rel gāṛī se 'by train'

In Urdu, 'by train' is expressed ریل گاڑی سے *rel gāṛī se* or گاڑی سے *gāṛī se*. گاڑی *gāṛī* may be used for any wheeled vehicle. Originally meaning cart, it is now used for car, automobile and train.

دلچسپ dilcasp 'interesting' دلچسپی dilcaspī 'interest'

The adjective دلچسپ means interesting:

دہلی دلچسپ تاریخی شہر ہے

Delhi is an interesting historical city

The noun دلچسپی means interest (f.). The expression مجھے اس سے دلچسپی ہے *mujhe is se dilcaspī hai* 'to me from this is interest' means 'I am interested in this':

کیا آپ کو پاکستان سے دلچسپی ہے؟ جی ہاں مجھے بہت دلچسپی ہے

kyā āp ko pākistān se dilcaspī hai? jī hāṅ mujhe bahut dilcaspī hai

Are you interested in Pakistan? Yes, I am very interested

چلیں *caleṅ* 'let's go', 'shall we go?'

When added to the stem of the verb, the suffix یں *-eṅ* expresses 'let's (do)', 'shall we (do)'. So far we have met the following examples:

چلیں	*caleṅ*	let's go, come on!	(stem چل to go, come)
کھائیں	*khāeṅ*	let's eat	(stem کھا to eat)
پیئیں	*pīeṅ*	let's drink	(stem پی to drink)

The form is discussed in detail later. Note that the verb چلنا *calnā* can mean 'to go, come, walk, depart', and that the exact translation is decided from the context.

گرمی ہے *garmī hai* 'it's hot'; سردی ہے *sardī hai* 'it's cold'

گرمی *garmī* means 'heat' (f); سردی *sardī* means 'cold (ness)' (f.). 'It is hot/cold today' is expressed in Urdu as آج گرمی ہے *āj garmī hai* 'there is heat today' آج سردی ہے *āj sardī hai* 'there is cold today'. موسم *mausam* can mean both 'weather' and 'climate' (m.).

ثقافت *siqāfat* Culture

In India and Pakistan, people are very proud of their origins, and even though they may never have lived in their ancestoral homeland وطن they still feel that they belong to it. The وطن might be a region, for instance Panjab or UP یوپی the former British United Provinces to the east of Delhi, now called Uttar Pradesh (coincidentally with the same initials), or a city like Lahore or Lucknow لکھنؤ *lakhnaū*. After Partition, many Urdu speakers migrated to the newly founded state of Pakistan from Delhi and UP, the homeland of Urdu, and, even when firmly settled, still persisted in describing their وطن as that part of India from which their families and forebears originally came.

In Indian and Pakistani society men and women mix much less freely than they do in the West. In general, women have female friends سہیلی *sahelī* while men prefer the company of their male friends دوست *dost*. Hence the word دوست is generally masculine, and applies to a male friend or friends in general. In exceptional circumstances, especially in Europe, where segregation of the sexes is less rigid, it would be possible to say: وہ میری دوست ہیں *vuh merī dost haiṅ* 'she is my friend', making the word feminine. The word سہیلی can however, only be used by a woman for her female friend.

مشقیں *mašqeṅ* Exercises

4.2 Comprehension

Listen to the conversation between the two ladies, Fahmida (فہمیدہ) and Mumtaz (ممتاز) and tick the correct answer.

1 Fahmida meets Mumtaz	In town ( )	At home ( )
2 The children are	At school ( )	On holiday ( )
3 Mumtaz is asked if she knows	A good shop ( )	A hotel ( )
4 The weather is	Warm ( )	Cold ( )
5 Fahmida proposes they	Have lunch ( )	Have ice cream ( )

4.3 Answer the questions:

Look at the pictures and answer the questions.

1 یہ محمد صاحب اور ان کے بچے ہیں۔ ان کے کتنے بچے ہیں؟
2 آج گرمی ہے یا سردی ہے؟
3 یہ رحیم ہیں۔ ان کو کھانا پسند ہے؟
4 یہ فہمیدہ اور ممتاز ہیں۔ وہ کہاں ہیں؟
5 یہاں دو بینک نوٹ ہیں۔ کتنے روپے ہیں؟

4.4 Translate into Urdu

1 Mr Rahim is in fact a native of Delhi, but his house is in Pakistan.

2 There is much difference in the climate of England and the climate of Asia.

3 Hello, Mumtaz Sāhiba. Let's go and have some ice cream.

4 It's very warm today. Let's go and have a cup of tea.

5 Lahore is at least a thousand miles (far) from Karachi.

5 آپ ہر روز کیا کرتے ہیں؟

āp har roz kyā karte haiṅ?

What do you do every day?

In this unit you will learn how to:

- describe your daily routine
- ask others about their activities
- tell the time
- express the days of the week

مکالمہ ایک *mukālima ek* Dialogue 1

John meets Aslam in his office and asks him about his day.

اسلم : آیئے، جان صاحب! خوش آمدید۔ یہ میرا دفتر ہے۔ عام طور سے میں یہاں کام کرتا ہوں۔ تشریف رکھیے۔ ہم ابھی چائے پیتے ہیں۔

جان : شکریہ، اسلم صاحب۔ آپ کا دفتر واقعی بہت خوبصورت ہے۔ کیا آپ ہر روز یہاں آتے ہیں۔

اسلم : جی ہاں۔ یعنی پیر سے جمعے تک کام پر آتا ہوں۔ ہفتے اور اتوار کو میں گھر پر رہتا ہوں۔

جان : آپ یہاں کتنے بجے پہنچتے ہیں؟

اسلم : میں ہر روز پانچ بجے اٹھتا ہوں، نماز پڑھتا ہوں، اور بیوی اور بچوں کے ساتھ ناشتہ کرتا ہوں۔ اس کے بعد گھر سے کوئی سات بجے نکلتا ہوں۔ خوش قسمتی سے میری گاڑی ہے۔ ڈرائیور اچھا آدمی ہے۔ اور ہمیشہ وقت پر آتا ہے۔ میں دفتر میں کوئی آٹھ بجے پہنچتا ہوں۔

جان : کیا آپ کی بیگم کام کرتی ہیں؟

اسلم : جی نہیں۔ وہ گھر پر رہتی ہیں اور بچوں کی دیکھ بھال کرتی ہیں۔ جیسا کہ آپ کو معلوم ہے، حامد کا اسکول ہمارے گھر سے کافی دور ہے۔ وہ دوسرے بچوں کے ساتھ بس میں اسکول جاتا ہے۔ وہاں نو بجے پہنچتا ہے اور کوئی چار بجے گھر آتا ہے۔ اچھا، پہلے چائے پیجیے۔ اس کے بعد میں آپ کو سب کچھ بتاتا ہوں۔

aslam : *āīe jān sāhib. xuš āmaded. yih merā daftar hai. 'ām taur se maiṅ yahāṅ kām kartā hūṅ. tašrīf rakhīe. ham abhī cāe pīte haiṅ.*

jān : *šukrīa, aslam sāhib. āp kā daftar vāqa'ī bahut xūbsūrat hai. kyā āp har roz yahāṅ āte haiṅ?*

aslam : *jī hāṅ, ya'nī pīr se jum'e tak kām par ātā hūṅ. hafte aur itvār ko maiṅ ghar par rahtā hūṅ.*

jān : *āp yahāṅ kitne baje pahuṅcte haiṅ?*

aslam : *maiṅ har roz pāṅc baje uṭhtā hūṅ, namāz paṛhtā hūṅ, bīvī aur baccoṅ ke sāth nāšta kartā hūṅ. us ke ba'd ghar se koī sāt baje nikaltā hūṅ. xuš qismatī se merī gāṛī hai. ḍrāivar acchā ādmī hai, aur hameša vaqt par ātā hai. maiṅ daftar meṅ koī āṭh baje pahuṅctā hūṅ.*

jān : *kyā āp kī begam kām kartī haiṅ.*

aslam : *jī nahīṅ, vuh ghar par rahtī haiṅ aur baccoṅ kī dekh bhāl kartī haiṅ. jaisā ki āp ko ma'lūm hai, hāmid kā iskūl hamāre ghar se kāfī dūr hai. vuh dūsre baccoṅ ke sāth bas meṅ iskūl jātā hai. vahāṅ nau baje pahuṅctā hai aur koī cār baje ghar ātā hai. acchā pahle cāe pījīe. us ke ba'd maiṅ āp ko sab kuch batātā hūṅ.*

Aslam : Come in, John. Welcome. This is my office. Usually I work here. Take a seat. We'll have ('drink') tea right now.

John : Thank you, Aslam Sahib. Your office is really very beautiful. Do you come here every day?

Aslam : Yes. That is I work from Monday to Friday. On Saturday and Sunday I stay at home.

John : What time do you arrive here?

Aslam : I get up every day at five o'clock. I say (my) prayers; I have ('do') breakfast with the wife and children. After that I leave ('go out from') the house at about seven o'clock. Fortunately, I have a car. The driver is a good man and always come on time. I arrive in the office at about eight.

John : Does your wife work?

Aslam : No, she stays at home and looks after the children. As you know, Hamid's school is quite far from our house. He goes to school by bus with the other children. He arrives there at nine o'clock and comes home at about four. But first drink (your) tea. After that, I'll tell you everything.

ہر روز	*har roz*	everyday	کے ساتھ	*ke sāth*	with
کیا کرتے ہیں	*kyā karte haiṅ?*	what do you do?	ناشتہ کرتا ہوں	*nāšta kartā hūṅ*	(I) have breakfast
خوش آمدید	*xuš āmaded*	welcome!	کوئی	*koī*	about, approximately
دفتر	*daftar*	office (m.)	نکلتا ہوں	*nikaltā hūṅ*	(I) go out
عام طور سے	*'ām taur se*	usually	خوش قسمتی سے	*xuš qismatī se*	fortunately
کام کرتا ہوں	*kām kartā hūṅ*	(I) work	ڈرائیور	*ḍrāivar*	driver (m.)
ابھی	*abhī*	right now	ہمیشہ	*hameša*	always
پیتے ہیں	*pīte haiṅ*	(we'll) drink	وقت پر	*vaqt par*	on time
آتے ہیں	*āte haiṅ*	(you) come	آتا ہے	*ātā hai*	comes
پیر	*pīr*	Monday (m.)	پہنچتا ہے	*pahuṅctā hai*	arrives
جمعے تک	*jum'e tak*	(up) to Friday	کام کرتی ہیں	*kām kartī haiṅ*	(she) works
کام پر	*kām par*	to/at work	رہتی ہیں	*rahtī haiṅ*	(she) stays
آتا ہوں	*ātā hūṅ*	(I) come	بچوں کی دیکھ بھال کرتی ہیں	*baccoṅ kī dekh bhāl kartī haiṅ*	she looks after the children
ہفتے اور اتوار کو	*hafte aur itvār ko*	on Saturday and Sunday	دوسرے	*dūsre*	other
گھر پر	*ghar par*	at home	بس	*bas*	bus (f.)
رہتا ہوں	*rahtā hūṅ*	(I) stay	بس سے	*bas se*	by bus
کتنے بجے	*kitne baje?*	at what time?	اسکول جاتا ہے	*iskūl jātā hai*	goes to school
پہنچتے ہیں	*pahuṅcte haiṅ*	(you) arrive	پہنچتا ہے	*pahuṅctā hai*	(he) arrives
بجے	*baje*	at... o'clock	گھر آتا ہے	*ghar ātā hai*	(he) comes home
پانچ بجے	*pāṅc baje*	at five o'clock	پہلے	*pahle*	first of all
اٹھتا ہوں	*uṭhtā hūṅ*	I get up	اس کے بعد	*us ke ba'd*	after that
نماز پڑھتا ہوں	*namāz paṛhtā hūṅ*	(I) say prayers	بتاتا ہوں	*batātā hūṅ*	I'll tell

قواعد *qavā'id* Grammar

The Urdu verb

A verb is a word which expresses action ('to do, go'), feeling ('to seem, feel'), existence ('to be, live'), etc. A verb is usually referred to by its infinitive, which in English is preceded by 'to': 'to do, go, to be'. Verbs have participles, which in English are often formed by adding -ing (the present participle) and -ed (the past participle) to the verb, e.g. *loving, loved.* English, however, has many irregular forms: '*doing, done; seeing, seen*', etc.) Verbs also have tenses which indicate the time of the action. For example 'I go' is the *present tense*, 'I shall go' is the *future tense*, and 'I went' is the *past tense.* Urdu, being a language from the same family as English, has a similar range of verb forms: infinitive, participles and tense, etc.

The Urdu infinitive always ends in نا *-nā.* So far we have met ہونا *honā* 'to be', بتانا *batānā* 'to tell', آنا *ānā* 'to come' دیکھنا *dekhnā* 'to see' رکھنا *rakhnā* 'to place' کھانا *khānā* 'to eat' and پینا *pīnā* 'to drink'.

The most basic part of the verb, the stem, from which all other parts of the verb are formed, is obtained by dropping the نا *-nā* of the infinitive. In the first dialogue of this unit we met some new verbs. These, with their stems, are as follows:

	Stem		**Infinitive**	
آ	*ā-*	آنا	*ānā*	to come
کر	*kar-*	کرنا	*karnā*	to do
رکھ	*rakh-*	رکھنا	*rakhnā*	to place
پی	*pī-*	پینا	*pīnā*	to drink
رہ	*rah-*	رہنا	*rahnā*	to stay, live
پہنچ	*pahuṅc-*	پہنچنا	*pahuṅcnā*	to arrive
اٹھ	*uṭh-*	اٹھنا	*uṭhnā*	to get up
پڑھ	*paṛh-*	پڑھنا	*paṛhnā*	to read
نکل	*nikal-*	نکلنا	*nikalnā*	to go out
جا	*jā-*	جانا	*jānā*	to go
بتا	*batā-*	بتانا	*batānā*	to tell
سو	*so-*	سونا	*sonā*	to (go to) sleep

The present participle and the present habitual tense

The present participle of the verb, which in some ways corresponds to the English 'going, doing', is formed by adding the suffixes تا *-tā* (m. s.), تی *-tī* (f.), تے *-te* (m. p.) to the stem of the verb. The endings are the same as those of adjectives ending in ا *-ā*, such as اچھا *acchā*:

			Present participle			Stem	Infinitive	
m.p.	کرتے	f.	کرتی	m.s.	کرتا	کر	کرنا	(*karnā*)
m.p.	آتے	f.	آتی	m.s.	آتا	آ	آنا	(*ānā*)
m.p.	پیتے	f.	پیتی	m.s.	پیتا	پی	پینا	(*pīnā*)

The present habitual tense expresses action which is performed regularly and habitually, something which is done always, often or usually. It corresponds to the English tense 'I do (usually), I go (often)', etc.

It is formed with the present participle followed by the relevant part of ہونا *honā*:

میں جاتا ہوں	*maiṅ jātā hūṅ*	'I going am' = I (m.) go
وہ جاتی ہے	*vuh jātī hai*	'she going is' = she goes
وہ جاتے ہیں	*vuh jate haiṅ*	'they going are' = they (m.) go
وہ جاتی ہیں	*vuh jātī haiṅ*	'they going are' = they (f.) go

Gender is indicated by the ending of the participle; number both by the participle and the verb ہونا *honā.*

ہم *ham* 'we', however, is always regarded as masculine plural. Both men and women say ہم جاتے ہیں *ham jāte haiṅ* 'we go'.

Since the verb itself indicates the person to which it refers, the personal pronoun is often omitted:

جاتی ہوں	*jātī hūṅ*	I (f.) go
کرتا ہے	*kartā hai*	he does

The present habitual tense of the verb کرنا *karnā* 'to do' is as follows:

Masculine

maiṅ kartā hūṅ	میں کرتا ہوں	I do
tū kartā hai	تو کرتا ہے	you do
yih, vuh kartā hai	یہ، وہ کرتا ہے	he/it does
ham karte haiṅ	ہم کرتے ہیں	we do

tum karte ho	تم کرتے ہو	you do
āp karte haiṅ	آپ کرتے ہیں	you do
yih, vuh karte haiṅ	یہ' وہ کرتے ہیں	they do

Feminine

maiṅ kartī hūṅ	میں کرتی ہوں	I do
tū kartī hai	تو کرتی ہے	you do
yih, vuh kartī hai	یہ' وہ کرتی ہے	she/it does
ham karte haiṅ	ہم کرتے ہیں	we do
tum kartī ho	تم کرتی ہو	you do
āp kartī haiṅ	آپ کرتی ہیں	you do
yih, vuh kartī haiṅ	یہ' وہ کرتی ہیں	they do

All verbs follow the same patern, without exception:

میں اٹھتا ہوں	I (m.) get up	میرا بیٹا پہنچتا ہے	my son arrives
میں پڑھتی ہوں	I (f.) read	میری بیٹی آتی ہے	my daughter comes
آپ جاتے ہیں	you (m.) go	ہم دیکھتے ہیں	we see
رحیم صاحب بتاتے ہیں	Mr. Rahim tells (plural of respect)	میری بیگم کرتی ہیں	my wife does (plural of respect)

Phrase verbs

Many one-word English verbs are expressed in Urdu by a phrase which usually consists of a noun followed by a verb, for example کام کرنا *kām karnā* 'to do work' = to work; نماز پڑھنا *namāz paṛhnā* 'to read prayer' = to pray; کی دیکھ بھال کرنا *kī dekh bhāl karnā* 'to do the looking after of = to look after; ناشتہ کرنا *nāštā karnā* 'to do breakfast' = to have breakfast. Such verbs are known as phrase verbs.

رحیم صاحب ہر روز کام کرتے ہیں

Rahim works every day ('does work')

اسلم اٹھتے ہیں اور نماز پڑھتے ہیں

Aslam gets up and prays ('reads prayers')

بیگم اسلم بچوں کی دیکھ بھال کرتی ہیں

Mrs Aslam looks after the children ('does the children's looking after')

As well as meaning 'I do something habitually', the present habitual tense can also mean 'I'll do something right away':

ہم ابھی چائے پیتے ہیں
ham abhī cāe pīte haiṅ
We'll have tea right now

Days of the week

The days of the week are:

itvār	اتوار	Sunday
pīr	پیر	Monday
mangal	منگل	Tuesday
budh	بدھ	Wednesday
jumi'rāt	جمعرات	Thursday
jum'a	جمعہ	Friday
hafta	ہفتہ	Saturday

Note that all are masculine except جمعرات 'Thursday'. For پیر 'Monday' there is a common alternative سوموار *somvār*, which is often heard in Panjab. For ہفتہ 'Saturday' some people use سنیچر *sanīcar*. The word literally means 'the planet Saturn', which is regarded as unlucky, and therefore سنیچر is generally avoided.

ہر روز *har roz* means 'every day'. 'On a day' is expressed by کو *ko*. Note that جمعہ and ہفتہ are masculine nouns like بچہ and form their oblique in the normal way:

وہ پیر کو آتا ہے	*vuh pīr ko ātā hai*	He comes on Monday
جمعے کو چھٹی ہے	*jum'e ko chuttī hai*	There is a holiday on Friday
ہفتے کو کام ہے	*hafte ko kām hai*	There is work on Saturday
پیر سے جمعے تک	*pīr se jum'e tak*	From Monday to Friday

The postposition تک *tak* means 'up to, until, as far as'. Note یہ بس کراچی تک جاتی ہے *yih bas karācī tak jātī hai* 'this bus goes as far as Karachi'.

Telling the time

To say 'at ... o'clock' Urdu Uses بجے *baje.*

ایک بجے	*ek baje*	at one o'clock	دو بجے	*do baje*	at two o'clock
دس بجے	*das baje*	at ten o'clock	بارہ بجے	*bāra baje*	at twelve o'clock

Note کتنے بجے *kitne baje*? at what time? 'at how much o'clock?'.

'What is the time' and 'it is ... o'clock' are expressed as follows:

کتنے بجے ہیں	*kitne baje haiṅ*?	What is the time? ('how many are o'clock?)
ایک بجا ہے	*ek bajā hai*	It is one o'clock (singular)
دو بجے ہیں	*do baje haiṅ*	It is two o'clock (plural)

Compound postpositions

So far all the postpositions we have met have consisted of one word: پر on; سے from; میں in; کو to; تک up to. There are many postpositions which consist of two words, the first of which is usually کے *ke*: کے ساتھ *ke sāth* 'with'; کے بعد *ke ba'd* 'after'. These are known as compound postpositions, and take the oblique case in the normal way:

بچوں کے ساتھ	*baccoṅ ke sāth*	with the children
میرے کام کے بعد	*mere kām ke ba'd*	after my work
اس کے بعد	*us ke ba'd*	after that

Selection of clocks ...

(a)

تین بجے

پانچ بجے

سات بجے

گیارہ بجے

(b) کتنے بجے ہیں؟

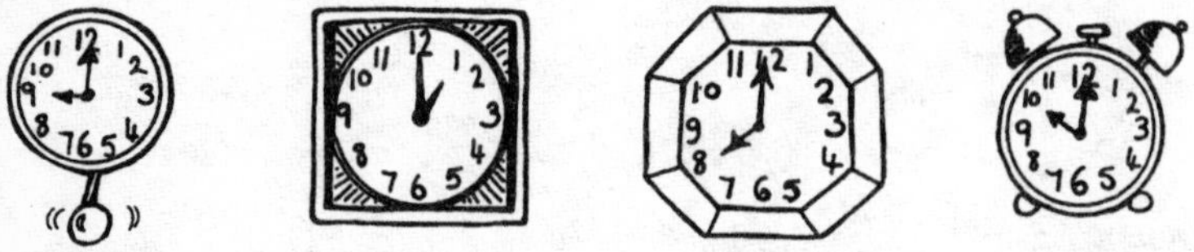

نو بجے ہیں | ایک بجا ہیں | آٹھ بجے ہیں | دس بجے ہیں

کوئی *koī* 'about', 'approximately'

We have met کوئی *koī* in the sense of 'some', 'any':

کوئی بات نہیں

It doesn't matter ('it isn't any thing')

When preceding numerals, کوئی means 'about', 'approximately':

اسلم کوئی سات بجے پہنچتے ہیں

Aslam arrives about seven o'clock

رہنا *rahnā* 'to stay, remain, live'

The verb رہنا *rahnā* has two basic meanings. It can mean to stay:

میری بیگم عام طور سے گھر پر رہتی ہیں

merī begam 'ām taur se ghar par rahtī haiṅ

My wife usually stays at home

Its other meaning is 'to live, reside':

میں کراچی میں رہتا ہوں	*maiṅ karācī meṅ rahtā hūṅ*	I live in Karachi
آپ کہاں رہتے ہیں؟	*āp kahāṅ rahte haiṅ*?	Where do you live?

To go to place

When you say 'I go to school', 'I go to Pakistan' in Urdu, no word for 'to' is required:

میرے بچے نو بجے اسکول جاتے ہیں

mere bacce nau baje iskūl jāte haiṅ

My children go (to) school at nine o'clock

میں ہر سال پاکستان جاتا ہوں

maiṅ har sāl pākistān jatā hūṅ

I go (to) Pakistan every year

The same applies to other verbs of motion such as آنا 'to come' and پہنچنا 'to arrive':

میں آٹھ بجے دفتر آتی ہوں

I (f.) come to the office at eight o'clock

مشق *mašq* Exercise

5.1 Answer the questions in English

In her diary Fahmida records a typical working day. Read her entry and answer in English the questions which follow:

Entries جمعرات ۱۲/مارچ

(۱) پانچ بجے اٹھتی ہوں

(۲) نماز پڑھتی ہوں اور والدین کے ساتھ ناشتہ کرتی ہوں

(۳) گھر سے نکلتی ہوں اور ریل گاڑی سے بینک جاتی ہوں

(۴) ایک چھوٹے ریستوراں میں نرگس کے ساتھ کھانا کھاتی ہوں

(۵) پانچ بجے دفتر سے نکلتی ہوں اور گھر چھ بجے پہنچتی ہوں

(۶) سات بجے کھانا کھاتی ہوں اور ٹیلیویژن دیکھتی ہوں

(۷) گیارہ بجے سوتی ہوں

1 What time does Fahmida get up?
2 What does she do after getting up?
3 With whom does she have her breakfast?
4 How does she get to her bank?
5 Where and with whom does she have lunch?
6 What time does she get home?
7 What does she do in the evening?

مکالمہ-۲ *mukālima do* Dialogue 2

Bilqis discusses her daily life with Helen.

ہیلن : بلقیس، آپ کا گھر واقعی بہت آرامدہ ہے۔

بلقیس : جی ہاں۔ ٹھیک ہے۔ کافی پرانا گھر ہے لیکن ہمیں بہت پسند ہے۔ شہر کے مرکز سے زیادہ دور نہیں۔ اس علاقے میں سب دوکانیں ہیں اور اقبال اور نرگس کے اسکول کافی نزدیک ہیں۔

ہیلن : آپ تو کام نہیں کرتیں!

بلقیس : جی نہیں۔ میں، اکثر عورتوں کی طرح گھر پر رہتی ہوں، بچوں کی دیکھ بھال کرتی ہوں اور کھانا پکاتی ہوں۔ ہمارے دو نوکر ہیں لیکن مجھے کھانا پکانا پسند ہے۔ یہ میری خاص دلچسپی ہے۔

ہیلن : کیا آپ بازار بھی جاتی ہیں۔

بلقیس : جی نہیں، میں زیادہ نہیں جاتی۔ ہمارا نوکر عام طور سے خریداری کرتا ہے اور بازار سے چیزیں لاتا ہے۔ اسلم صاحب کو بازار بالکل پسند نہیں ہے۔ وہ کبھی وہاں نہیں جاتے۔

ہیلن : جی ہاں، مجھے معلوم ہے۔ وہ میرے شوہر کی طرح ہیں۔ وہ دوکانوں میں کبھی نہیں جاتے۔

helan : *bilqīs, āp kā ghar vāqa'ī bahut ārāmdih hai.*

bilqīs : *jī hāṅ, ṭhīk hai. kāfī purānā ghar hai lekin hameṅ bahut pasand hai. šahr ke markaz se ziyāda dūr nahīṅ. is 'ilāqe meṅ sab dūkāneṅ haiṅ, aur iqbāl aur nargis ke iskūl kāfī nazdīk haiṅ.*

helan : *āp to kām nahīṅ kartīṅ?*

bilqīs : *jī nahīṅ. maiṅ aksar 'auratoṅ kī tarah ghar par rahtī hūṅ. baccoṅ kī dekh bhāl kartī hūṅ aur khānā pakātī hūṅ. hamāre do naukar haiṅ, lekin mujhe khānā pakānā pasand hai. yih merī xās dilcaspī hai.*

helan : *kyā āp bāzār bhī jātī haiṅ?*

bilqīs : *jī nahīṅ. maiṅ ziyāda nahīṅ jātī. hamārā naukar 'ām taur se xarīdārī kartā hai, aur bāzār se cīzeṅ lātā hai. aslam sāhib ko bāzār bilkul pasand nahīṅ hai. vuh kabhī vahāṅ nahīṅ jāte.*

helan : *jī hāṅ, mujhe ma'lūm hai. vuh mere šauhar kī tarah haiṅ. vuh dūkānoṅ meṅ kabhī nahīṅ jāte.*

Helen : Bilqis, your home is really very comfortable.

Bilqis : Yes. It's all right. It's quite an old house but we like it very much. It's not very far from the centre of the city. All the shops are in this area, and Iqbal's and Nargis' schools are quite near.

Helen : You don't work?

Bilqis : No. Like most women I stay at home. I look after the children and cook the food. But I like cooking ('to cook'). This is my special interest.

Helen : Do you go to the bazaar as well?

Bilqis : No. I don't go all that much. Our servant usually does the shopping, and brings things from the bazaar. Aslam doesn't like the bazaar at all. He never goes there.

Helen : Yes, I know. He's like my husband. He never goes in the shops.

آرامدہ	*ārāmdih*	comfortable	زیادہ	*ziyāda*	all that much
کام نہیں کرتیں؟	*kām nahīṅ kartīṅ?*	don't you work?	خریداری	*xarīdārī*	shopping
اکثر	*aksar*	most; often	خریداری کرنا	*xarīdārī karnā*	to go shopping
کی طرح	*kī tarah*	like	لانا	*lānā*	to bring
پکانا	*pakānā*	to cook	کبھی نہیں	*kabhī nahīṅ*	not ever, never
خاص	*xās*	special			

قواعد *qavā'id* Grammar

Negative forms of the present habitual tense

The negative of the present habitual tense, 'I do not do', is formed by placing the negative particle نہیں *nahīṅ* immediately before the verb:

میں جاتا ہوں	I go
میں نہیں جاتا ہوں	I do not go
وہ پکاتی ہے	she cooks
وہ نہیں پکاتی ہے	she does not cook

The verb ہونا may be optionally dropped:

میں نہیں جاتا	*maiṅ nahīṅ jātā*	I (m.) don't go
وہ نہیں پکاتی	*vuh nahīṅ pakātī*	she doesn't cook

However when ہونا is dropped from the feminine plural وہ نہیں جاتی ہیں *vuh nahīṅ jātī haiṅ*, 'they (f.) do not go' the participle changes the ending ی -ī to یں -īṅ:

وہ نہیں جاتی ہیں	*vuh nahīṅ jātī haiṅ*	they (f.) don't go
وہ نہیں جاتیں	*vuh nahīṅ jātīṅ*	they (f.) don't go

Similarly وہ نہیں کرتیں *vuh nahīṅ kartīṅ* they do not do, میری بیگم اُردو نہیں بولتیں *merī begam urdū nahīṅ boltīṅ* 'my wife does not speak Urdu'.

اکثر **aksar 'most; often'**

The word اکثر has two functions: as an adjective in the sense of 'most':

اکثر عورتیں کام نہیں کرتیں	Most women do not work
اکثر پاکستانی اُردو بولتے ہیں	Most Pakistanis speak Urdu

and as an adverb meaning 'often', 'mostly':

میری بیگم اکثر گھر پر رہتی ہیں	My wife mostly stays at home
میں اکثر پاکستان جاتا ہوں	I often go to Pakistan

کی طرح **kī tarah 'like'**

کی طرح *kī tarah* 'like' is a compound postposition, of which the first element is کی *kī*:

اکثر عورتوں کی طرح میری بیگم کام نہیں کرتیں

Like most women my wife does not work

آپ کی طرح میں بھی لکھنؤ کا رہنے والا ہوں

Like you, I am also a native of Lucknow

خریداری کرنا **xarīdārī karnā 'to go shopping'**

The verb خریدنا *xarīdnā* means 'to buy':

بازار میں ہم ہر طرح کی چیزیں خریدتے ہیں

bāzār meṅ ham har tarah kī cīzeṅ xarīdte haiṅ

We buy all sorts of things in the bazaar

خریداری *xarīdārī* means 'shopping' (f.) The phrase verb خریداری کرنا *xarīdārī karnā* means 'to shop', 'to go shopping':

ہم اکثر بوہری بازار میں خریداری کرتے ہیں

ham aksar bohrī bāzār meṅ xarīdārī karte haiṅ

We usually go ('do') shopping in Bohri Bazaar

کبھی **kabhī 'ever'; کبھی نہیں kabhī nahīṅ 'not ever, never'**

کبھی *kabhī* means 'ever':

آپ کبھی پاکستان جاتے ہیں؟ Do you ever go to Pakistan?

آپ کبھی فلمیں دیکھتے ہیں؟ Do you ever see films? (فلم *film* 'film' (f.))

In negative sentences کبھی نہیں *kabhī nahīṅ* means 'not ever', 'never':

میرے شوہر بازار کبھی نہیں جاتے

mere šauhar bāzār kabhī nahīṅ jāte

My husband never goes to bazaar

یہاں ہم پانی کبھی نہیں پیتے

yahāṅ ham pānī kabhī nahīṅ pīte

We never drink the water here

مکالمہ ۳ *mukālima tīn* Dialogue 3

Aslam asks John about his routine in England.

اسلم : جان صاحب' انگلستان میں آپ لوگوں کا معمول کیا ہے؟ مجھے اس سے دلچسپی ہے۔

جان : جیسا کہ آپ کو معلوم ہے ہم دونوں ڈاکٹر ہیں۔ اس لئے ہم ہمیشہ مصروف رہتے ہیں۔ آپ کی طرح ہم صبح سویرے اٹھتے ہیں۔ ناشتے کے بعد ہم کلنک پر جاتے ہیں۔ ہمارا کلنک گھر سے زیادہ دور نہیں اور عام طور سے دوپہر کو ہم گھر پر کھانا کھاتے ہیں۔

اسلم : کیا آپ لوگ ہر روز کام کرتے ہیں؟

جان : جی نہیں' عام طور پر ہم منگل کو اور جمعرات کو فارغ رہتے ہیں۔ لیکن ہفتے کو تین بجے تک ہم کام کرتے ہیں۔ شام کو ہم کوئی آٹھ بجے گھر آتے ہیں اور کھانا کھاتے ہیں۔ اس کے بعد ٹیلیویژن پر خبریں دیکھتے ہیں۔

اسلم : اچھا' تو آپ کی زندگی کافی مصروف ہے! خیر کوئی بات نہیں' اب تو آپ کی چھٹی ہے۔ اس سے فائدہ اٹھائیے!

aslam : *jān sāhib inglistān meṅ āp logon kā ma'mūl kyā hai? mujhe is se dilcaspī hai.*

jān : *jaisā ki āp ko ma'lūm hai, ham donoṅ ḍākṭar haiṅ. is lie ham hameša masrūf rahte haiṅ. āp kī tarah ham subh savere uṭhte haiṅ. nāšte ke ba'd ham klinik par jāte haiṅ. hamārā klinik ghar se ziyāda dūr nahīṅ aur 'ām taur se do pahr ko ham ghar par khānā khāte haiṅ.*

aslam : *kyā āp log har roz kām karte haiṅ?*

jān : *jī nahīṅ. 'ām taur par ham mangal aur jumi'rāt ko fāriğ rahte haiṅ. lekin hafte ko tīn baje tak ham kām karte haiṅ. šām ko ham koī āṭh baje ghar āte haiṅ, khānā khāte haiṅ, us ke ba'd ṭelīvižan par xabreṅ dekhte haiṅ.*

aslam : *acchā, to āp kī zindagī kāfī masrūf hai. xair, koī bāt nahīṅ. ab to āp kī chuṭṭī hai. is se fāida uṭhāīe.*

Aslam : John! What's your routine in England?

John : As you know, we are both doctors. Therefore, we are ('remain') always busy. Like you we get up early in the morning. After breakfast we go to the clinic. Our clinic is not far from the house, and usually at midday we have lunch ('eat food') at home.

Aslam : And do you work every day?

John : No. Usually we are ('remain') free on Tuesday and Thursday. But on Saturday we work till three o'clock. In the evening we come home at about eight, have dinner; after that we watch the news on television.

Aslam : I see. So your life is quite busy. Well, never mind. Now you're on holiday. Take advantage of it.

معمول	*ma'mūl*	routine (m.)	صبح سویرے	*subh savere*	early in the morning
ہم دونوں	*ham donoṅ*	both of us	کلنک	*klinik*	clinic (m.)
اس لئے	*is lie*	therefore	کلنک پر	*klinik par*	to the clinic
صبح	*subh*	morning, in the morning (f.)	دوپہر	*do pahr*	midday (f.)
			دوپہر کو	*do pahr ko*	at midday

فارغ	fāriğ	free, at leisure	ٹیلیویژن دیکھنا	ṭelīvižan dekhnā	to watch TV
فارغ رہتے ہیں	fāriğ rahte hain	we are ('remain') free	خبریں	xabreṅ	news (f.p.)
			خیر	xair	well!, so!
شام	šām	evening (f.)	فائدہ	fāida	advantage (m.)
شام کو	šām ko	in the evening	سے فائدہ اٹھانا	se fāida uṭhānā	to take advantage of
ٹیلیویژن	ṭelīvižan	television (m.)			

قواعد qavā'id Grammar

دونوں donoṅ تینوں tīnoṅ 'inclusive numbers'

When the suffix وں *-oṅ* is added to a numeral, it gives the sense of 'all two, all three, all four', so-called 'inclusive numbers'. دو *do* has a slightly irregular form دونوں *donoṅ* which is best translated as 'both':

ہم دونوں ڈاکٹر ہیں *ham donoṅ ḍākṭar haiṅ* We are both doctors

Note the word order ہم دونوں 'we both' which is often rendered in English as 'both of us'. Other numerals add وں *-oṅ* regularly: تینوں *tīnoṅ* 'all three', چاروں *cāroṅ* 'all four', پانچوں *pāṅcoṅ* 'all five':

پاکستان، ہندوستان اور بنگلہ دیش، تینوں ملک جنوبی ایشیا میں ہیں

pākistān, hindustān aur bangla-deš, tīnoṅ mulk janūbī ešiyā meṅ haiṅ

Paistan, India and Bangladesh, all three countries are in South Asia.

رہنا rahnā 'to be somewhere usually'

When you are usually or always somewhere, the verb 'to be' is often translated by رہنا *rahnā* 'to remain':

میں اسٹیشن پر ہوں

maiṅ isṭešan par hūṅ

I am at ('on') the station (now)

میں نو بجے سے پانچ تک دفتر میں رہتا ہوں

maiṅ nau baje se pāṅc tak daftar meṅ rahtā hūṅ

I'm always at the office from 9 till 5

ہم اس وقت مصروف ہیں

ham is vaqt masrūf haiṅ

We are busy at this moment

ہم اکثر مصروف رہتے ہیں

ham aksar masrūf rahte haiṅ

We are usually busy

Times of the day

The most common word for 'day' is دن *din*:

میں دن میں کام کرتا ہوں

maiṅ din meṅ kām kartā hūṅ

I work during ('in') the day

The word روز *roz* is used only in certain expressions like ہر روز *har roz* 'every day', or by itself in the same sense:

میں روز کلنک پر جاتا ہوں

maiṅ roz klinik par jātā hūṅ

I go to ('on') the clinic every day

Divisions of the day are as follows:

صبح	subh	morning / in the morning (f.)
صبح سویرے	subh savere	early in the morning
دوپہر	do pahr	midday (f.)
دوپہر کو	do pahr ko	at midday
دوپہر کے بعد	do pahr ke ba'd	in the afternoon
شام	šām	evening (f.)
شام کو	šām ko	in the evening
رات	rāt	night (f.)
رات کو	rāt ko	at night

These expressions are illustrated in the following passage, which you should practise reading aloud:

میں صبح سویرے اٹھتا ہوں۔ میں صبح نو بجے دفتر پہنچتا ہوں۔ دوپہر کو میں ایک چھوٹے ریستراں میں کھانا کھاتا ہوں۔ دوپہر کے بعد میں دفتر میں کام کرتا ہوں اور عام طور سے میں شام کو کوئی سات بجے گھر پہنچتا ہوں۔ میری بیگم کھانا پکاتی ہیں' اور کھانے کے بعد ہم ٹیلیوژن دیکھتے ہیں۔ رات کو میں صبح تک سوتا ہوں۔

maiṅ subh savere uṭhtā hūṅ. maiṅ subh nau baje daftar pahuṅctā hūṅ. do pahr ko maiṅ ek choṭe restarāṅ meṅ khānā khātā hūṅ. do pahr ke ba'd maiṅ daftar meṅ kām kartā hūṅ aur 'ām taur se maiṅ šām ko koī sāt baje ghar pahuṅctā hūṅ. merī begam khānā pakātī haiṅ, aur khāne ke ba'd ham ṭelīvižan dekhte haiṅ. rāt ko maiṅ subh tak sotā hūṅ.

I get up early in the morning. I arrive at the office at nine o'clock in the morning. At midday I have lunch in a small restaurant. In the afternoon I work in the office and I usually arrive home at about seven in the evening. My wife cooks the dinner. After dinner, we watch the telivision. At night I sleep till morning.

'This morning', 'this afternoon', 'this evening', 'tonight' are expressed:

آج صبح	*āj subh*	today morning
آج دوپہر کے بعد	*āj do pahr ke ba'd*	today afternoon
آج شام کو	*āj šām ko*	today in the evening
آج رات کو	*āj rāt ko*	today at night

Numbers

At this stage the numerals 21–30 (Appendix 1) should be learnt.

ثقافت *siqāfat* Culture

In India and Pakistan, professional people living in cities have a daily routine similar to that of most countries in the world. The British institution of the 'weekend' still aplies and most offices are closed on Saturday and Sunday. Muslims regard Friday as the most important day of worship, and mosques are crowded for midday prayers. Many middle-class women still do not go out to work and fulfil their traditional role of looking after the house and family. Even relatively poor families can afford one or two servants, who often become part of the household, working for little more than their keep. The situation is of course very different in villages, where women play as great a part in agriculture as the men. The amount of freedom women have to go out shopping and enjoy themselves in town with their friends depends upon the traditions of the family and the attitude of their husband.

مشقیں *mašqeṅ* Exercises

5.2 Dialogue

Take your part in the following dialogue. When answering in the first person, make sure you use the appropriate gender for yourself.

Aslam : آپ کہاں کے رہنے والے ہیں / کی رہنے والی ہیں؟

You : (Tell him that you come from England)

Aslam : انگلستان میں آپ کیا کرتے (کرتی) ہیں؟

You : (Tell him that you are a doctor in London)

Aslam : آپ کو پاکستان پسند ہے؟

You : (Tell him you like it very much)

Aslam : کراچی میں آپ کے دوست ہیں؟

You : (Tell him that you have many)

Aslam : آج گرمی ہے۔ چلیں‘ ایک کپ چائے پئیں؟

You : (Tell him that it is a good idea, and agree to go)

5.3 Answer the questions in Urdu

Here is a picture of Aslam and his family. From what you have read about them answer the questions, remembering to use plural of respect for the adults.

1 اسلم صاحب اور بلقیس صاحبہ کہاں رہتے ہیں؟
2 ان کے کتنے بچے ہیں اور بچوں کے نام کیا ہیں؟
3 اسلم صاحب ہر روز کام کرتے ہیں؟
4 گھر پر کھانا کون پکاتی ہیں؟
5 عام طور سے خریداری کون کرتا ہے؟
6 جان اور اسلم کو بازار کی دوکانیں پسند ہیں؟

5.4 True of false?

Here are some statements about our story so far. Tick which are true and which false:

True	False

1 اسلم صاحب بہت امیر ہیں۔ اس لئے وہ کام نہیں کرتے۔
2 بلقیس، بچوں کی دیکھ بھال کرتی ہیں۔
3 اسلم صاحب دہلی کے رہنے والے ہیں۔
4 ہیلن کام نہیں کرتیں اور اکثر گھر پر رہتی ہیں۔
5 حامد ایک بڑے امریکن اسکول میں پڑھتا ہے۔
6 اِس وقت کراچی میں بہت سردی ہے۔

5.5 Tell the time

From the clocks in 1 to 5, state what the time is. Use both words and figures.

a

b

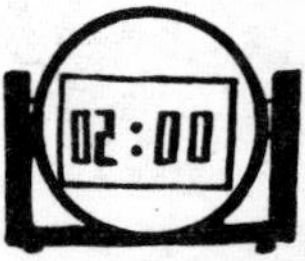

c

d

e

6 ساحلِ سمندر پر By the seaside

In this unit you will learn how to:

- say 'who?, 'whose?'; 'someone', 'someone's'
- state what is usually the case
- say more about the weather
- identify months and dates

Now that you have had plenty of practice in reading the Urdu script, it will no longer be necessary to give the dialogues and reading passages in Roman transcription. All new words, however, will be transcribed in the vocabularies and in the examples given in the grammar sections. Translation of the Urdu texts are given in the Answer key.

مکالمہ ایک ***mukālima ek*** **Dialogue 1**

Aslam and his family take the Smiths to the seaside resort of Clifton for the day. Helen is persuaded to ride a camel along the beach.

جان : اچھا، یہ کلفٹن ہے! یہاں بہت شاندار گھر ہیں۔ میرے خیال سے یہاں کافی امیر لوگ رہتے ہیں۔ دیکھیے، وہ بڑا خوبصورت مکان۔ وہ کس کا گھر ہے؟

اسلم : میرے خیال سے وہ کسی وزیر کا گھر ہے۔ وزیر تو ہر ملک میں امیر ہوتے ہیں نا؟ لیکن وہاں کون رہتا ہے، مجھے معلوم نہیں۔

جان : اور وہاں سمندر ہے۔ بتائیے اسلم صاحب، یہ کون سا سمندر ہے؟

اسلم : یہ بحیرۂ عرب ہے۔ یعنی 'عرب کا سمندر'

ہیلن : لیکن ساحل پر بہت کم لوگ ہیں۔ کیا پاکستان میں لوگ سمندر میں نہیں نہاتے؟

اسلم : جی نہیں۔ پاکستان میں انگلستان کی طرح لوگوں کو ساحل پر بیٹھنے اور سمندر میں تیرنے کی عادت نہیں۔

ہیلن : اور وہ دیکھیے! ساحل پر اونٹ ہے۔ وہ اونٹ کس کا ہے؟

اسلم : میرے خیال سے وہ اس چھوٹے لڑکے کا اونٹ ہے۔ ظاہر ہے کسی کا تو ہے! کبھی کبھی ٹورسٹ یہاں ہوتے ہیں۔ ان کو اونٹ پر بیٹھنا پسند ہے۔

ہیلن : آج کتنا پیارا موسم ہے! نہ گرمی ہے نہ سردی۔

اسلم : جی ہاں۔ نومبر کے مہینے میں موسم عام طور سے اچھا ہوتا ہے۔ چلیے ہیلن صاحبہ۔ اونٹ پر بیٹھیے۔

ساحل سمندر	*sāhil-e samandar*	seashore, seaside
وزیر	*vazīr*	minister (m.)
ہر ایک	*har ek*	every
ہوتے ہیں	*hote haiṅ*	are (usually)
سمندر	*samandar*	sea (m.)
کون سا	*kaun sā*	which?
بحیرۂ عرب	*buhaira-e 'arab*	the Arabian Sea
عرب	*'arab*	Arabia, Arab (m.)
ساحل	*sāhil*	beach, shore (m.)
کم	*kam*	few
نہانا	*nahānā*	to bathe
نہانے کی عادت	*nahāne kī 'ādat*	custom of bathing
عادت	*'ādat*	custom, habit (f.)
بیٹھنا	*baithnā*	to sit
تیرنا	*tairnā*	to swim
اونٹ	*ūṅt*	camel (m.)
کس کا اونٹ	*kis kā ūṅt?*	whose camel?
ظاہر ہے کہ	*zāhir hai ki*	it is obvious that
کسی کا اونٹ	*kisī kā ūṅt*	someone's camel
ٹورسٹ	*tūrisṭ*	tourist (m.)
ہوتے ہیں	*hote haiṅ*	are (often)
پیارا	*piyārā*	lovely
نہ نہ	*na...na*	neither nor
نومبر	*navambar*	November (m.)
مہینہ	*mahīna*	month (m.)
اچھا ہوتا ہے	*acchā hotā hai*	is (usually) good

قواعد **qavā'id Grammar**

ہجے *hijje* Spelling

We have already met the *izāfat* meaning 'of' in the phrases گلشنِ اقبال *gulšan-e iqbāl* 'The Garden of Prosperity' and کوہِ نور *koh-e nūr* 'Mountain of Light'. In the phrase ساحلِ سمندر *sāhil-e samandar* 'the shore of the sea' 'seaside', the *izāfat* is used in the same way.

بحیرۂ عرب *buhaira-e 'arab* is the name for the Arabian Sea by which Karachi and Bombay – بمبئی *bambaī* – stand. It is made up of two Persian words: بحیرہ *buhaira* 'little sea' and عرب *'arab* 'Arabian', linked with the *izāfat*. Note that after a word ending in ہ *choṭī he*, the *izāfat* is written with ء *hamza*.

کون **kaun?** کس کا **kis kā? 'who?, whose?'**

The so-called interrogative pronoun 'who?' is کون *kaun*.

Remember that interrogative words (i.e. words asking questions) which in Urdu mostly begin with ک, such as کون *kaun* 'who', کیا *kya* 'what?', کیسے *kaise* 'how?', کیوں *kyoṅ* 'why?', always come immediately before the verb:

وہ آدمی کون ہے؟	*vuh ādmī kaun hai?*	Who is that man?
آپ کیا کرتے ہیں؟	*āp kyā karte haiṅ?*	What do you do?
وہ کیوں جاتی ہے؟	*vuh kyoṅ jāti hai?*	Why does she go?
آپ لوگ کیسے ہیں؟	*āp log kaise haiṅ?*	How are you (people)?

کون has the oblique form کس *kis*, which is used before postpositions: کس سے from whom? کس پر upon whom? کس کو to whom?.

Note that کس کا *kis kā* 'of whom' = whose.

یہ گھر کس کا ہے؟	*yih ghar kis kā hai?*	Whose house is this?
کس کی بیٹی یہاں ہے؟	*kis kī beṭi yahāṅ hai?*	Whose daughter is here?

کون may be singular or plural, referring to one or more pople:

یہ بچہ کون ہے؟	*yih bacca kaun hai?*	Who is this child?
یہ بچے کون ہیں؟	*yih bacce kaun haiṅ?*	Who are these children?

The plural oblique form, however, is کن *kin*:

یہ کن کے گھر ہیں؟

yih kin ke ghar haiṅ?

Whose houses are these ('of which people?)

یہ کن کا گھر ہے؟ یہ وزیر کا گھر ہے

yih kin kā ghar hai? yih vazīr kā ghar hai

Whose (plural of respect) house is this? It is the minister's house

Like یہ and وہ, کون may be additionally pluralised:

یہ کون لوگ ہیں؟

yih kaun log hain?

Who are these people?

آپ کن لوگوں سے ملتے ہیں؟

āp kin logoṅ se milte haiṅ?

Whom ('which people') do you meet?

یہ کن لوگوں کی کتابیں ہیں؟

yih kin logoṅ kī kitābeṅ haiṅ?

Whose ('of which people') are these books?

کوئی *koī* 'someone' کچھ *kuch* 'something'

The so-called 'indefinite' pronoun کوئی means 'someone', 'anyone': یہاں کوئی ہے؟ *yahāṅ koī hai*? 'is anyone here?'.

In negative sentences کوئی نہیں 'not anyone' can also be translated 'no one': یہاں کوئی نہیں ہے *yahāṅ koī nahīṅ hai* 'there isn't anyone here / there is no one here'.

English overcomplicates the issue with 'someone, anyone, somebody, not anyone, no one, nobody'. In Urdu all these words are expressed simply by کوئی.

The oblique form of کوئی is کسی *kisī*: کسی سے from someone; کسی کو to someone; کسی کا someone's:

کسی سے پوچھیے	Ask someone ('from someone')
میں کسی سے نہیں ملتا	I don't meet anyone
کسی کو دیجیے	Give (it) to someone
یہ کسی کا اونٹ ہے	This is someone's camel

It will be observed that the oblique forms of کون and کوئی are formed similarly to those of یہ and وہ:

Direct singular	یہ	وہ	کون	کوئی
Oblique singular	اِس	اُس	کِس	کسی
Direct plural	یہ	وہ	کون	
Oblique plural	ان	اُن	کن	

کوئی 'someone' can, of course, have no plural forms.

کچھ *kuch* means 'something' or 'some'; کچھ نہیں 'not something' = nothing:

یہاں کچھ ہے؟	*yahāṅ kuch hai?*	Is there something/anything here?
یہاں کچھ نہیں ہے	*yahāṅ kuch nahīṅ hai*	There's nothing here

کون **kaun**, کوئی **koī**, کچھ **kuch**, کون سا **kaun sā** used as adjectives

کون *kaun* may be used as an adjective meaning 'which?':

کون آدمی؟	Which person?	کون لوگ؟	Which people?
کس آدمی سے؟	From which person?	کن کتابوں سے	From which books?

The more common word for 'which', however, is کون سا *kaun sā* (also written as one word کونسا *kaunsā*) which changes for number, gender and case as اچھا does:

Which person?	کون سا آدمی	Which books?	کون سی کتابیں؟
Which people	کون سے لوگ	Which sea is this?	یہ کون سا سمندر ہے؟
From which person?	کون سے آدمی سے	From which people?	کون سے لوگوں سے؟
In which cities?	کون سے شہروں میں	To which girls?	کون سی لڑکیوں کو

کوئی coming before singular nouns means 'some': کوئی کتاب *koī kitāb* 'some book', کسی آدمی سے *kisī ādmī se* from some man.

کچھ coming before plural nouns and nouns which in Urdu can have no plural such as چائے *cāe* 'tea', دودھ *dūdh* 'milk', etc., also means 'some':

کچھ کتابیں	*kuch kitābeṅ*	some books	کچھ لوگ	*kuch log*	some people
کچھ چائے	*kuch cāe*	some tea	کچھ دودھ	*kuch dūdh*	some milk

ہے **hai** 'is', ہوتا ہے **hotā hai** 'is generally'

ہے means 'is' by nature, at a certain time or in a certain place:

وہ انسان ہے	*vuh insān hai*	He/she is a human being (by nature)
وہ آج ٹھیک نہیں ہے	*vuh āj ṭhīk nahīṅ hai*	He/she is not well today
وہ گھر پر ہے	*vuh ghar par hai*	He/she is at home

The regular present habitual tense of ہونا. میں ہوتا ہوں *maiṅ hotā hūṅ*, وہ ہوتا ہے *vuh hotā hai*, تم ہوتے ہو *tum hote ho*, آپ ہوتے ہیں *āp hote haiṅ* and so on means 'I am, he is, you are', habitually, always, generally.

The English sentence 'he is ill' can mean 'he is ill now' or 'he is often ill'. Urdu is much more precise and makes a distinction between the two concepts. Compare the following:

یہ لڑکی خوبصورت ہے

yih laṛkī xūbsūrat hai

This girl is pretty (specific)

لڑکیاں خوبصورت ہوتی ہیں

laṛkīāṅ xūbsūrat hotī haiṅ

Girls are (usually) pretty (general)

آج موسم اچھا ہے

āj mausam acchā hai

Today the weather is good (specific)

نومبر میں موسم اچھا ہوتا ہے

navambar meṅ mausam acchā hotā hai

In November the weather is (usually) good (general)

The infinitive with postpositions

The infinitive of the verb may be used in the same way as a noun such as لڑکا:

لڑکا اچھا ہے	*laṛkā acchā hai*	The boy is good
بولنا اچھا ہے	*bolnā acchā hai*	To talk is good/talking is good

Like nouns in ا -ā it forms its oblique by changing its ending to ے -e.

لڑکے سے	*laṛke se*	from the boy
پڑھنے سے	*paṛhne se*	from reading

The infinitive may often be translated 'reading', 'doing', etc. in such circumstances.

Note carefully the way in which the oblique infinitive is used in the following phrases:

نہانے کی عادت	*nahāne kī 'ādat*	the custom of bathing
جانے کے بعد	*jāne ke ba'd*	after going
کھانے سے پہلے	*khāne se pahle*	before eating

سے پہلے se pahle is a compound postposition meaning 'before'.

کبھی کبھی **kabhī kabhī 'sometimes'**

کبھی کبھی means 'sometimes':

کبھی کبھی بچے اچھے ہوتے ہیں، کبھی کبھی شریر بھی ہوتے ہیں

kabhī kabhī bacce acche hote haiṅ, kabhī kabhī šarīr bhī hote haiṅ

Sometimes children are good; sometimes they are naughty as well

نہ … نہ **na … na 'neither … nor'**

نہ … نہ *na … na* means 'neither … nor':

آج نہ گرمی ہے نہ سردی ہے

āj na garmī hai na sardī hai

Today it is neither hot nor cold

Remember that 'it is hot today', 'it is cold today' is expressed as: آج گرمی ہے *āj garmī hai*, آج سردی ہے *āj sardī hai* 'today there is heat/ coldness'. The adjectives 'hot' and 'cold' are گرم *garm* and ٹھنڈا *ṭhanḍā*: گرم چائے *garm cāe* 'hot tea', ٹھنڈا پانی *ṭhanḍā pānī* 'cold water'.

The names of the months

The word for 'month' is مہینہ *mahīnā*.

For official purposes both India and Pakistan use the 'Christian' calendar, and the names of the months are all adapted from English:

جولائی	*jūlāī* (f.)	جنوری	*janvarī* (f.)
اگست	*agast* (m.)	فروری	*farvarī* (f.)
ستمبر	*sitambar* (m.)	مارچ	*mārc* (m.)
اکتوبر	*aktūbar* (m.)	اپریل	*aprail* (m.)
نومبر	*navambar* (m.)	مئی	*maī* (f.)
دسمبر	*disambar* (m.)	جون	*jūn* (m.)

It is common to add کا مہینہ *kā mahīna* to the name of the month:

نومبر کے مہینے میں بہت پیارا موسم ہوتا ہے

navambar ke mahīne meṅ bahut piyārā mausam hotā hai

In the month of November the weather is quite lovely

بیٹھنا *baiṭhnā* 'to sit, get into transport'

The verb بیٹھنا 'to sit' is used for getting into transport or onto animals:

صبح سویرے میں بس میں بیٹھتا ہوں اور کام پر جاتا ہوں

subh savere main bas men baiṭhtā hūn aur kām par jātā hūn

Early in the morning I get ('sit') in the bus and go to work

مشق *mašq* Exercise

6.1 Complete the sentences

Complete the following sentences with the correct form of ہونا (i.e. ہوں ' ہے ' ہو ' ہیں ' ہوتا ہے ' ہوتے ہیں ' ہوتی ہے etc.):

1 عام طور پر ہندوستان میں کافی گرمی __________

2 آپ کا گھر واقعی بہت خوبصورت __________

3 یہ آم بہت مزے دار __________۔ جی ہاں' آم ہمیشہ مزے دار __________

4 پنجاب کے لوگ مہمان نواز __________

5 وہ آدمی وزیر __________ وزیر عام طور پر امیر __________

مکالمہ ۲ *mukālima do* Dialogue 2

Hamid shows the guests his school; Aslam loses the car keys!

جان : حامد' چونکہ ہم آج کلفٹن میں ہیں' تو ہمیں اسکول دکھاؤ۔ تم یہاں پڑھتے ہو نا؟

حامد : جی ہاں۔ لیکن آج ہفتہ ہے۔ ہمارا اسکول بند ہے۔

جان : کوئی بات نہیں۔ کم سے کم دکھاؤ کہ تم کہاں پڑھتے ہو۔

حامد : اچھا' لیکن کلفٹن کافی بڑا علاقہ ہے۔ میرا اسکول یہاں سے ذرا دور ہے۔

اسلم : ٹھیک ہے۔ خوش قسمتی سے ہمارے پاس آج گاڑی ہے۔ گاڑی میں صرف پانچ منٹ کا راستہ ہے۔ آیئے' گاڑی میں بیٹھیے۔ لیکن ایک منٹ ٹھہریے میرے پاس چابی نہیں ہے۔ چابی کس کے پاس ہے؟ کسی کے پاس ہے۔ بلقیس! چابی تمہارے پاس ہے کیا؟

بلقیس : جی ہاں۔ آپ فکر نہ کیجیے۔ میرے پاس ہے۔

اسلم : تمہارے پاس چابی کیوں ہے؟

بلقیس : میرے پاس اس لئے ہے کہ آپ ہمیشہ سب کچھ بھولتے ہیں۔ کیا آپ کے پاس آج پیسے ہیں؟

اسلم : جی ہاں' میں اب دیکھتا ہوں۔۔۔ جی نہیں میرے پاس پیسے نہیں ہیں

بلقیس : دیکھیے! چابی بھولتے ہیں' پیسے بھولتے ہیں۔ تو اچھا ہے کہ میرے پاس پیسے ہیں۔ چلیے' میرے پاس چابی ہے' تو آج میں گاڑی چلاتی ہوں۔

چلانا	*calānā*	to drive (a car)	کسی کے پاس ہے	*kisī ke pās hai*	is with someone, someone has
چونکہ	*cūṅkī*	since, because	ٹھہرنا	*ṭhahrnā*	to wait, stay
دکھانا	*dikhānā*	to show	میرے پاس ہے	*mere pās hai*	is with me, I have
ہمیں دکھاو	*hameṅ dikhāo*	show (to) us	چابی	*cābī*	key (f.)
پڑھنا	*paṛhnā*	to study	تمہارے پاس ہے	*tumhāre pās hai*	is with you, you have
بند	*band*	closed, shut	فکر	*fikr*	worry, care (m./f.)
ذرا	*zarā*	just, rather	فکر نہ کیجیے	*fikr na kījīe*	don't worry
ہمارے پاس ہے	*hamāre pās hai*	is with us, we have	کیوں	*kyoṅ?*	why?
کے پاس	*ke pās*	with, near, by	اس لئے ہے کہ	*is lie hai ki*	it is because
صرف	*sirf*	only	بھولنا	*bhūlnā*	to forget
پانچ منٹ پہلے	*pāṅc minaṭ kā rāsta*	5 minutes away	آپ کے پاس ہے	*āp ke pās hai*	is with you, you have
منٹ	*minaṭ*	minute (m.)			
کسی کے پاس ہے؟	*kis ke pās hai?*	is with whom? who has?			

قواعد *qavā'id* Grammar

چونکہ *cūṅkī* 'since, because'

چونکہ *cūṅkī* means 'since', in the sense of 'because'. The second part of the sentence (known as the 'main clause') is always introduced by تو *to* 'then'

چونکہ آپ چھٹی پر ہیں تو فائدہ اٹھائیے

cūṅkī āp chuṭṭī par haiṅ, to fāida uṭhāīe

Since you're on holiday, take advantage (of it)

پڑھنا **paṛhnā** 'to read'; 'to study'

پڑھنا can mean both 'to read' and 'to study':

میں ہر روز اخبار پڑھتا ہوں

maiṅ har roz axbār paṛhtā hūṅ

I read a newspaper every day

میرا بیٹا اس بڑے امریکن اسکول میں پڑھتا ہے

merā beṭā us baṛe amrīkan iskūl meṅ paṛhtā hai

My son studies in that big American school

کے پاس **ke pās** 'near, by, with'; 'at the place of'

کے پاس is a compound postposition meaning 'by, near, with, on (you)', 'at the place of':

سمندر کے پاس	By the sea
میرا گھر آپ کے گھر کے پاس ہے	My house is near your house
میں رحیم کے پاس رہتا ہوں	I live at Rahim's place
میں آپ کے پاس آتا ہوں	I'll come to your place

It is also used to express 'to have something with you or on you':

رحیم کے پاس پیسے نہیں ہیں	Rahim has no money ('with/on Rahim there is not money')
آپ کے پاس کتنے پیسے ہیں؟	How much money do you have (on you)?
ان کے پاس گاڑی ہے	He has a car (with him) today

Remember that to have or possess something which is not necessarily with you, and to have relations is expressed with کا or the possessive adjectives میرا ، اُس کا ، ہمارا ، آپ کا etc.:

اسلم کے چار بچے ہیں Aslam has four children

رحیم کی گاڑی ہے لیکن آج ان کے پاس نہیں ہے

Rahim has a car but does not have it with him today

Compound postpositions with pronouns

When a compound postposition, the first element of which is کے or کی (such as کے پاس ‘ کی طرح etc.), is used with one of the pronouns, میں, تو, ہم, تم for example, the oblique form of the possessive adjectives میرے ‘ ہمارے or میری etc. are employed, and the کی / کے elements of the postposition are omitted. In other words we say میرے پاس *mere pās*, میری طرح *merī tarah*, etc. Some examples are as follows:

on/with/after	Rahim	رحیم کے پاس / ساتھ / بعد
,,	me	میرے پاس / ساتھ / بعد
,,	you	تیرے پاس / ساتھ / بعد
,,	him, her, it	اس کے پاس / ساتھ / بعد
,,	him, her, it	اُس کے پاس / ساتھ / بعد
,,	us	ہمارے پاس / ساتھ / بعد
,,	you	تمہارے پاس / ساتھ / بعد
,,	you	آپ کے پاس / ساتھ / بعد
,,	them	ان کے پاس / ساتھ / بعد
,,	them	ان کے پاس / ساتھ / بعد

Similarly:

رحیم کی طرح	like Rahim	میری طرح	like me	اس کی طرح	like him
ہماری طرح	like us	تمہاری طرح	like you	ان کی طرح	like them

اس لئے کہ *is lie ki* ‘because’

The phrase اس لئے کہ *is lie ki means* ‘because’:

میرے پاس اس لئے کہ آپ سب کچھ بھولتے ہیں

mere pās is lie ki āp sab kuch bhūlte haiṅ

(It’s) With me because you forget everything

A verb may come between اس لئے and کہ:

میں آپ سے اس لئے پوچھتا ہوں کہ مجھے معلوم نہیں ہے

maiṅ āp se is lie ***pūchtā hūṅ*** *ki mujhe ma’lūm nahiṅ hai*

I ask you because I don't know

فکر کرنا *fikr karnā* to worry

فکر *fikr* (which may be either masculine or feminine) means 'worry', 'care' and is used in the phrase verb فکر کرنا *fikr karnā* 'to worry':

فکر نہ کیجیے *fikr na kījīe* don't worry

مشق *mašq* Exercise

6.2 صحیح یا غلط؟ *sahīh yā ğalat*? 'True or false'?

Read each of the following statements and tick which answers are true and which are false:

1 رحیم : آج میرے پاس گاڑی ہے۔

2 بلقیس : آپ مجھ سے نہ پوچھیے۔ میرے پاس پیسے نہیں ہیں۔

3 اسلم : حامد، تمہارے پاس چابی ہے؟ حامد: جی ہاں میرے پاس ہے۔

4 جان : آداب عرض ہے، اسلم صاحب۔ آج میرے ساتھ میرے دوست ہیں۔

5 ہیلن : یہ کس کا اونٹ ہے؟ بلقیس: معلوم نہیں۔ کسی کا اونٹ ہے۔

	True	False
1. Rahim has his car with him today.		
2. Bilqis has no money on her.		
3. Aslam has the key.		
4. John has his wife with him.		
5. Bilqis says the camel belongs to the boy.		

مکالمہ ۳ *mukālima tīn* Dialogue 3

The Smiths learn about education in Pakistan.

جان : واہ! واہ! کتنا شاندار اسکول ہے، حامد! یہاں کون سے بچے پڑھتے ہیں۔

اسلم : یہاں زیادہ تر متوسط درجے کے خاندانوں کے بچے پڑھتے ہیں۔ بدقسمتی سے یہاں غریب لوگوں کے بچے نہیں پڑھتے۔ دنیا کے ہر ملک میں غریب لوگ تو ہوتے ہیں نا۔ لیکن کیا کریں، کوئی امیر ہے اور کوئی غریب۔

جان : میرے خیال سے یہاں کی تعلیم اچھی ہے

اسلم : جی ہاں۔ عام طور سے کراچی کے بڑے اسکولوں میں تعلیم بہت اچھی ہوتی ہے۔ حامد' جان صاحب کو بتاؤ کہ تم کیا پڑھتے ہو' اور کون سے مضمون تمھیں پسند ہیں۔

حامد : ہم ہر طرح کے مضمون پڑھتے ہیں' زبانوں میں سے انگریزی' اُردو اور عربی۔ اس کے علاوہ تاریخ' جغرافیہ' سائنس وغیرہ

جان : اور تم کو انگریزی پسند ہے؟

حامد : جی ہاں۔ انگریزی کافی آسان ہے۔ لیکن عربی بہت مشکل ہے۔

واہ ! واہ !	*vāh vāh!*	bravo! wonderful!	یہاں کی تعلیم	*yahāṅ kī ta'līm*	the education (of) here
زیادہ تر	*ziyādatar*	mostly	مضمون	*mazmūn*	subject (m.)
متوسط	*mutavassit*	middle			
متوسط درجہ	*mutavassit darja*	middle class (m.)	میں سے	*meṅ se*	from among
درجہ	*darja*	class (m.)	عربی	*'arabī*	Arabic
خاندان	*xāndān*	family (m.)	اس کے علاوہ	*is ke 'alāva*	in addition
			جغرافیہ	*jugrāfia*	geography (m.)
بدقسمتی سے	*badqismatī se*	unfortunately	سائنس	*sāins*	science (m.)
ہر ایک	*har ek*	every			
کیا کریں؟	*kyā kareṅ?*	what to do?	وغیرہ	*vağaira*	et cetera
			آسان	*āsān*	easy
تعلیم	*ta'līm*	education (f.)			

قواعد *qavā'id* Grammar

خوش قسمتی سے fortunately, بدقسمتی سے unfortunately

قسمت *qismat*, from which the word 'Kismet' comes, means 'fate', 'luck', 'fortune' (f.): میری قسمت اچھی نہیں ہے I don't have good luck.

From it come two phrases:

خوش قسمتی سے	*xuš qismatī se*	fortunately ('from happy fortune')
بدقسمتی سے	*badqismatī se*	unfortunately ('from bad fortune')

میں سے **meṅ se 'from among', 'out of '**

Here the two postpositions میں and سے are used together in the sense of 'from in', 'from among', 'out of':

ان کھانوں میں سے آپ کو کون سا زیادہ پسند ہے

in khānoṅ meṅ se āp ko kaun sā ziyāda pasand hai?
From among these dishes which do you like most?

Dates

There are various ways of expressing dates. The simplest and most common way is to place the numeral before the name of the month:

بیس دسمبر	20 December
پچیس جون	25 June
اٹھارہ جنوری	18 January

'On' a date is expressed by کو ko:

میں پانچ اگست کو پہنچتا ہوں

maiṅ pāṅc agast ko pahuṅctā hūṅ
I arrive on the 5th of August

میری سالگرہ چھبیس فروری کو ہے

merī sālgirah chabbīs farvarī ko hai
My birthday (lit.: year knot) is on the 26th of February

Numbers

Here the numerals 31–40 (Appendix 1) should be learnt.

ثقافت **siqāfat Culture**

Clifton, a smart area of Karachi, about ten minutes' drive from the centre, is on the shore of the Arabian Sea. Its beach is still very under-exploited, and a seaside holiday means little to most Indians and Pakistanis, who would never dream of disrobing themselves to bathe in the water for pleasure. Camel rides are offered to tourists, mainly by small boys who take little money for their services.

Good education is still, unfortunately, the preserve of the middle and upper classes, and in both India and Pakistan the literacy rate is still low. The best schools in the larger cities, however, rank among some of the finest in Asia, and rigidly preserve the former British public school standards and attitudes.

مشقیں *mašqeṅ* Exercises

6.3 Comprehension

Listen to the dialogue on the tape and tick the correct answers to the following questions:

1 Rahim and Khan meet	(a) in a tea shop	(b) at the station
2 The train arrives at	(a) five o'clock	(b) three o'clock
3 Today's date is	(a) the 4th of November	(b) the 8th of November
4 Rahim	(a) is on holiday	(b) is going to work
5 The celebration is for	(a) the minister's birthday	(b) the minister's arrival
6 The minister is a	(a) rich man	(b) great man

6.4 Correct postposition

Complete the following sentences with the correct postposition taken from the following: کو' پر' سے' کی طرح' پاس.

1 آپ ________ میں بھی پاکستانی ہوں۔

2 آیئے میرے دوست' جان صاحب ________ ملیے۔

3 آج میرے ________ پیسے نہیں۔

4 وہ پانچ نومبر ________ پہنچتا ہے۔

5 وہ آج گھر ________ نہیں ہیں۔

6.5 Dates and sums

Write the following using both words and figures. Use the equal sign (=) for 'equals':

On the fifth of November; at twelve o'clock; on the second of January; 9+16 = 25; the thirty first of October; my birthday is on the 27th of April; there are sometimes thirty days in a month and sometimes thirty one days; twenty five rupees; there are a hundred *paisas* in one rupee.

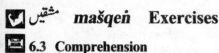

6.6 پاکستان کا نقشہ *pakistān kā naqša* The map of Pakistan

Look at the map of Pakistan, on which approximate distances are given in miles, then answer the questions which follow.

1 نقشے پر کتنے شہر ہیں؟

2 لاہور کہاں ہے؟ پنجاب میں ہے یا سندھ میں؟

3 اسلام آباد لاہور سے کتنی دور ہے؟

4 حیدر آباد ملتان سے کتنی دور ہے؟

5 کراچی کون سے سمندر پر ہے؟

7 ہمارے پاس ریزرویشن نہیں ہے
We don't have a reservation

In this unit you learn how to:

- say what you are doing now
- book tickets and reserve seats
- use the telephone
- express more dates

مکالمہ ایک *mukālima ek* Dialogue 1

John decides to take the train from Karachi to Lahore.

رحیم : آداب عرض ہے' جان صاحب۔ کیسے مزاج ہیں؟ آپ آج کل کیا کر رہے ہیں؟

جان : آپ کی دعا ہے' رحیم صاحب۔ آج کل میں کافی مصروف ہوں۔ ہم لوگ لاہور جانے کی تیاری کر رہے ہیں۔

رحیم : اچھا! کب جا رہے ہیں؟

جان : شاید اگلے ہفتے دس تاریخ کو۔ اب تک ہمیں یقین نہیں ہے۔

رحیم : آپ کیسے جا رہے ہیں؟ ریل گاڑی سے یا ہوائی جہاز سے۔

جان : ریل سے جانے کا ارادہ ہے۔ آپ کا کیا خیال ہے؟

رحیم : یہ اچھا ہے' کیونکہ دس تاریخ کو میری بڑی بہن اور ان کے شوہر ریل سے لاہور جا رہے ہیں۔ ان کے ساتھ جائیے۔

جان : یہ بہت اچھا ہے' لیکن ہمارے پاس ٹکٹ اور ریزرویشن نہیں ہیں۔ ٹکٹ کہاں سے ملتے ہیں؟ کیا اسٹیشن سے ملتے ہیں؟

رحیم : جی نہیں' آپ اسٹیشن پر مت جائیے۔ وہاں ہمیشہ گڑبڑ ہوتی ہے۔ میں ایسا کرتا ہوں۔ میرے ایک دوست یہاں ایک ٹریول ایجنسی میں کام کرتے ہیں۔ آج میں ان کو ٹیلیفون کرتا ہوں۔ آپ فکر نہ کیجئے۔ تو اس کا مطلب یہ ہے۔ کراچی۔ لاہور پہلے درجے کے دو ٹکٹ' دس تاریخ کے لئے۔ ٹھیک ہے؟

جان : رحیم صاحب، آپ کی بڑی مہربانی۔

رحیم : کوئی بات نہیں! آپ مجھے آج شام کو ٹیلیفون کیجیے۔ کیا آپ کے پاس میرا نمبر ہے؟

جان : جی نہیں، میرے پاس نہیں ہے۔

رحیم : اچھا، تو لکھیے: ایک صفر پانچ نو تین۔ اب میں ایک جگہ جا رہا ہوں۔ اجازت۔

جان : بہت شکریہ، رحیم صاحب۔ خدا حافظ۔

ریزرویشن	rezarvešan	reservation (m.)
کیسے مزاج ہیں؟	kaise mizāj haiṅ?	how are you?
کر رہے ہیں؟	kar rahe haiṅ	are you doing?
تیاری	tayyārī	preparation (f.)
جانے کی تیاری	jāne kī tayyārī	preparation for going
کب؟	kab	when?
جا رہے ہیں؟	jā rahe haiṅ?	are you going?
شاید	šāyad	perhaps
ہفتہ	hafta	week (m.)
اگلے ہفتے	agle hafte	next week
دس تاریخ کو	das tārīx ko	on the tenth
تاریخ	tārīx	date (f.)
اب تک	ab tak	up to now, yet
ہمیں یقین ہے	hameṅ yaqīn hai	we are certain
کیسے	kaise	how?
ہوائی جہاز	havaī jahāz	aeroplane (m.)
ہوائی جہاز سے	havaī jahāz se	by air
ارادہ	irāda	intention, plan (m.)
جانے کا ارادہ	jāne kā irāda	intention of going
کیونکہ	kyoṅki	because
بہن	bahin	sister (f.)
جا رہے ہیں	jā rahe haiṅ	are going
ٹکٹ	ṭikaṭ	ticket (m.)
کہاں سے ملتے ہیں؟	kahāṅ se milte haiṅ?	'where are they got?' (where do you get them?)
ملتے ہیں؟	milte haiṅ?	'are they got' (can they be got?)
مت جائیے	mat jāie	don't go!
گڑبڑ	gaṛbaṛ	confusion, trouble (f.)
ایسا	aisā	such, like this
میرے ایک دوست	mere ek dost	a friend of mine
ٹریول ایجنسی	ṭraival ejansī	travel agency (f.)
مطلب	matlab	meaning (m.)
اس کا مطلب یہ ہے	is kā matlab yih hai	this means

پہلے	*pahle*	first (of all)	ایک جگہ	*ek jagah*	'one place', somewhere
درجہ	*darja*	class (m.)			
پہلا درجہ	*pahlā darja*	first class (m.)	جا رہا ہوں	*jā rahā hūṅ*	am going
کے لئے	*ke lie*	for, on behalf of			

قواعد *qavā'id* Grammar

More greetings and politenesses

Urdu has a large stock of greetings and polite phrases, some of which we have already met. 'How are you?' can be expressed in the following ways:

آپ کیسے / کیسی ہیں؟	*āp kaise/kaisī haiṅ?*	how are you?
کیا حال ہے؟	*kyā hāl hai?*	what is (your) condition?
کیسے مزاج ہیں؟	*kaise mizāj haiṅ?*	how are (your) dispositions?

کیسا means 'how?', 'of what sort?', مزاج means 'disposition, temper'.

Typical answers, all meanings 'I am well', 'everything is fine' are:

میں ٹھیک ہوں، شکریہ۔
سب ٹھیک ہے۔
آپ کی دعا ہے۔

In the dialogue we met another common word for 'thank you': مہربانی *mihrbānī*, literally, 'kindness' (f.):

آپ کی اور آپ کے دوستوں کی بڑی مہربانی ہے

āp kī aur āp ke dostoṅ kī baṛī mihrbānī hai

it is the kindness of you and your friends (i.e. thanks to ...)

کیسا *kaisā* 'how', 'what sort of'

کیسا is an adjective meaning 'how?' in the sense of 'of what kind or quality?':

کھانا کیسا ہے؟	How is the food?
وہ کیسا آدمی ہے؟	What sort of man is he?

The adverb کیسے means 'how?' in the sense of 'by what means?'

آپ کیسے جاتے ہیں؟ بس سے؟	How do you go? By bus?

Present continuous tense

The present continuous tense is the equivalent of English 'I am doing (now, at the moment, tomorrow, next week)' and is formed with three elements: the stem of the verb (e.g. کر 'جا 'کھا etc.) + رہا ' رہی ' رہے *rahā* (m.), *rahī* (f.), *rahe* (m.p.) + the relevant part of ہونا: ہوں ' ہے ' ہو ' ہیں. for example:

میں کر رہا ہوں	*maiṅ kar rahā hūṅ*	I am doing (m.)
میں کر رہی ہوں	*maiṅ kar rahī hūṅ*	I am doing (f.)
وہ کر رہے ہیں	*vuh kar rahe haiṅ*	they are doing (m.)
وہ کر رہی ہیں	*vuh kar rahī haiṅ*	they are doing (f.)

As with the present habitual ہم is always regarded as masculine plural, whether said by men or women ہم کر رہے ہیں 'we (m.) are doing'.

The negative ('I am not doing') is formed by placing نہیں directly before the stem:

میں نہیں کر رہا ہوں	*maiṅ nahīṅ kar rahā hūṅ*	I am not doing

The present continuous tense of کرنا is as follows:

Masculine

میں کر رہا ہوں	*maiṅ kar rahā hūṅ*	I am doing
تو کر رہا ہے	*tū kar rahā hai*	you are doing
یہ' وہ کر رہا ہے	*yih/vuh kar rahā hai*	he, it is doing
ہم کر رہے ہیں	*ham kar rahe haiṅ*	we are doing
تم کر رہے ہو	*tum kar rahe ho*	you are doing
آپ کر رہے ہیں	*āp kar rahe haiṅ*	you are doing
یہ' وہ کر رہے ہیں	*yih/vuh kar rahe haiṅ*	they are doing

Feminine

میں کر رہی ہوں	*maiṅ kar rahī hūṅ*	I am doing
تو کر رہی ہے	*tū kar rahī hai*	you are doing
یہ' وہ کر رہی ہے	*yih/vuh kar rahī hai*	she, it is doing
ہم کر رہے ہیں	*ham kar rahe haiṅ*	we are doing
تم کر رہی ہو	*tum kar rahī ho*	you are doing
آپ کر رہی ہیں	*āp kar rahī haiṅ*	you are doing
یہ' وہ کر رہی ہیں	*yih/vuh kar rahī haiṅ*	they are doing

Examples of the present continuous are:

اسلم صاحب' آپ کیا کر رہے ہیں؟	Aslam, Sahib, what are you doing?
ہیلن' آپ کیا کر رہی ہیں؟	Helen, what are you doing?
ہم دس کو کراچی جا رہے ہیں	We are going to Karachi on the tenth
میری بیوی خریداری کر رہی ہیں	My wife is doing the shopping
میں ٹیلیوژن نہیں دیکھ رہا ہوں	I'm not watching TV

Note the difference between the present habitual and the present continuous:

عام طور سے میں صبح نہاتا ہوں

I usually have a bath ('bathe') in the morning

رحیم کہاں ہیں؟ وہ نہا رہے ہیں

Where is Rahim? He's having a bath

تیاری *tayyārī* 'preparation' (f.); کی تیاری کرنا *kī tayyārī karnā* 'to prepare'

We have already had the adjective تیار *tayyār* 'ready, prepared':

کھانا تیار ہے Dinner is ready

The noun تیاری means 'preparation', and the phrase verb کی تیاری کرنا means 'to prepare':

میری بیگم کھانے کی تیاری کر رہی ہیں

merī begam khāne kī tayyārī kar rahī haiṅ

My wife is preparing ('doing the preparation of') the dinner

کرنے کی تیاری کرنا *karne kī tayyārī karnā* means 'to prepare to do':

ہم لاہور جانے کی تیاری کر رہے ہیں We are preparing to go to Lahore

ہفتہ **hafta 'week'**

The word ہفتہ means both 'Saturday' and 'week'. However, no confusion can arise:

ایک ہفتے میں سات دن ہیں

ek hafte meṅ sāt din haiṅ

There are seven days in one week

ہفتہ آخری دن ہے

hafta āxirī din hai

Saturday is the last day

ہفتے کو *hafte ko* means 'on Saturday', ہفتے میں *hafte meṅ* means 'during the week'.

Note also the following expressions:

اس ہفتے	*is hafte*	this week
اگلے ہفتے	*agle hafte*	next week

More on dates

The word for 'date' is تاریخ *tārīx* (f.) (the same as for 'history'). 'On the tenth', without specifying the month, is دس تاریخ کو *das tārīx ko*. We have seen that 'on the tenth of December' is simply دس دسمبر کو and this may also be expressed دسمبر کی دس تاریخ کو *disambar kī das tārīx ko*.

اب 'now', اب تک 'till now, still' ابھی 'right now'

The most usual word for 'now' is اب *ab*:

اب میں تیار ہوں	Now I'm ready

اب تک *ab tak* 'up to now' can be translated as 'so far, still, yet':

اب تک مجھے معلوم نہیں	I don't know yet/so far
ہم اب تک یہاں ہیں	We're still here

ابھی *abhī* is more emphatic 'right now':

میں ابھی آتا ہوں	I'm coming right now

یقین *yaqīn* 'certainty' (m.); مجھے یقین ہے *mujhe yaqīn hai* 'I'm certain'

یقین is a noun meaning 'certainty'. The construction مجھے یقین ہے *mujhe yaqīn hai* 'to me is certainty' means 'I am certain':

مجھے یقین نہیں ہے کہ یہ کیا ہے	I'm not certain (that) what this is

ارادہ *irāda* 'intention, plan'

ارادہ is a noun meaning 'intention, plan' (m.). The construction مجھے کرنے کا ارادہ ہے *mujhe karne kā irāda hai* 'to me is an intention of doing' means 'I intend/plan to do':

اگلے ہفتے ہمیں پاکستان جانے کا ارادہ ہے

Next week we intend to go to Pakistan

These constructions with یقین and ارادہ are similar to مجھے معلوم ہے ، مجھے پسند ہے ، مجھے فرصت ہے.

The imperative expressing 'if'

The imperative (e.g. جایئے ، کیجیے etc.) often has the sense of 'if you do'. The second part of the sentence begins with تو 'then':

ان کے ساتھ جایئے تو کوئی مشکل نہیں

in ke sāth jāie to koī muškil nahīṅ

If you go with them, (then) there is no problem ('go with them, then ...')

The word مشکل 'difficult' is also used as a feminine noun meaning 'problem':

کوئی مشکل نہیں *koī muškil nahīṅ* no problem

ملنا *milnā* 'to be got, to be acquired'

We have already met the verb ملنا in the sense of 'to meet (with)'. But it is also used in the sense of 'to be got, to be acquired', better translated into English as 'one gets':

ریل گاڑی کے ٹکٹ کہاں سے ملتے ہیں؟

rel gāṛī ke ṭikaṭ kahāṅ se milte haiṅ?

'Where are train tickets got?' (i.e. where can you get ...?)

If you want to say 'I get, Mr Rahim gets/acquires', you must say 'to me (مجھے)' to Mr Rahim (رحیم صاحب کو) is got/acquired:

مجھے ریل گاڑی کے ٹکٹ کہاں سے ملتے ہیں؟

mujhe rel gāṛī ke ṭikaṭ kahāṅ se milte haiṅ?

Where do I get train tickets from? ('to me tickets from where are got?')

رحیم صاحب کو دسمبر میں چھٹی ملتی ہے

rahīm sāhib ko disambar meṅ chuṭṭī miltī hai

Rahim gets a holiday in December ('to Rahim is got')

In these sentences the subjects are 'rail tickets' and 'holiday'.

مت جایئے **mat jāīe** 'don't go'

We have seen that when a negative command is given (e.g. 'don't do!') نہ is used for 'not':

فکر نہ کیجیے	don't worry!	نہ جایئے	don't go!
نہ آیئے	don't come!	نہ کیجیے	don't do!

A rather stronger prohibition can be used by using مت in place of نہ:

اسٹیشن پر مت جایئے، وہاں ہمیشہ گڑبڑ ہوتی ہے

isṭešan par mat jāīe; vahāṅ hameša gaṛbaṛ hotī hai

don't go to the station; there's always a mess/confusion there

گڑبڑ *gaṛbaṛ* means 'confusion, mess, disorder, trouble' (f.).

Note the following extremely useful phrase, often to be used in the sub-continent:

میرے پیٹ میں گڑبڑ ہے

mere peṭ meṅ gaṛbaṛ hai

There is confusion in my stomach. (i.e. 'my stomach is upset'):

ایسا **aisā** 'such, like this'

ایسا means 'such' in the sense of 'like this', 'of this quality':

ایسے لوگ	*aise log*	'such people', people like this
ایسی عمارتیں	*aisī 'imārateṅ*	'such buildings', buildings like this

Used as an adverb it means 'like this', 'in this way':

میں ایسا کرتا ہوں۔ میں دس بجے شام کو فون کرتا ہوں

I'll do like this; I'll phone at ten this evening

فون *fon* is, as in English, a common abbreviation for 'telephone' (m.).

مطلب *matlab* 'meaning'

The word مطلب 'meaning' (m.) is used in the following expressions:

اس لفظ کا مطلب کیا ہے؟

is lafz kā matlab kyā hai?

What is the meaning of this word?

اس کا مطلب یہ ہے کہ آپ کو دو ٹکٹ چاہئیں

So that means you need two tickets ('its meaning is that ...')

کے لئے *ke lie* 'for, on behalf of'

کے لئے is a compound postposition meaning 'for' in the 'sense of', 'on behalf of', 'destined for':

میں بیوی اور بچوں کے لئے کام کرتا ہوں

I work for (my) wife and children

میرے لئے ان کو ٹیلیفون کیجیے

Please telephone him for me

یہ گاڑی لاہور کے لئے ہے؟

Is this train for Lahore?

مشق *mašq* Exercise

7.1 وہ لوگ کیا کر رہے ہیں

Look at the pictures and use the present continuous tense to say what each person is doing:

(a)

(b)

(c)

(d)

(e)

مکالمہ دو *mukālima do* Dialogue 2

Rahim succeds in getting John's tickets.

جان : ہیلو، میں جان بول رہا ہوں۔ کیا رحیم صاحب گھر پر تشریف رکھتے ہیں؟

بیگم رحیم : جی ہاں۔ ایک منٹ، میں ابھی بلاتی ہوں۔ وہ آرہے ہیں۔

رحیم : آداب عرض ہے، جان صاحب۔ سنیے۔ ایک خوشخبری ہے۔ آپ کے ٹکٹ میرے پاس ہیں۔ میرے دوست بہت چالاک آدمی ہیں۔ ان کو ٹکٹ ہمیشہ آسانی سے ملتے ہیں۔ مجھے معلوم نہیں کیسے۔ میں کبھی نہیں پوچھتا۔ خیر اس کا مطلب یہ ہے کہ، آپ لوگ اگلے ہفتے یعنی دس تاریخ کو صبح آٹھ بجے جا رہے ہیں۔

جان : شکریہ، رحیم صاحب۔ یہ آپ کی اور آپ کے دوست کی مہربانی ہے۔

رحیم : تو بتائیے جان صاحب، آج شام کو آپ لوگ کیا کر رہے ہیں؟ کہیں باہر جا رہے ہیں؟

جان : جی نہیں، ہم اس وقت ہوٹل میں ہیں۔ عام طور سے ہم شام کا کھانا یہاں کھاتے ہیں۔

رحیم : اچھا آپ وہاں مت کھائیے۔ آپ ادھر آئیے کھانے پر۔ آج شام کو میری بہن اور ان کے شوہر بھی آرہے ہیں۔ آپ ان سے ملیے۔ اب کتنے بجے ہیں، سات بجے ہیں نا؟ تو آپ لوگ آٹھ بجے تک آئیے۔

جان : شکریہ، رحیم صاحب۔ ہم ٹھیک آٹھ بجے پہنچتے ہیں۔

ہیلو	*helo*	hello!	سننا	*sunnā*	to hear, listen
بولنا	*bolnā*	to speak	خوشخبری	*xušxabrī*	good news (f.)
تشریف رکھتے ہیں	*tašrīf rakhte hain?*	is he at home?	چالاک	*cālāk*	clever, cunning
بلانا	*bulānā*	to call			

آسانی	*āsānī*	ease (f.)	ادھر	*idhar*	here, to here
آسانی سے	*āsānī se*	easily			
کہیں	*kahīṅ*	somewhere	آٹھ بجے تک	*āṭh baje tak*	by eight
باہر	*bāhar*	out, outside	ٹھیک آٹھ بجے	*ṭhīk āṭh baje*	at eight precisely
باہر جانا	*bāhar jānā*	to go out			

قواعد *qavā'id* Grammar

ہجّے *hijje* Spelling

As we have seen, the sign ّ *tašdīd* is written above a letter to show that it is doubled: تیّار *tayyār*, بچّہ *bacca*, etc. The infinitive of verbs with a stem ending in ن *nūn*, however, is always written with two separate *nūns*: سُننا *sunnā* (stem سُن *sun-*) 'to hear'.

Making telephone calls

When answering or beginning a telephone call, the universal ہیلو *helo*! 'hello' is also used in Urdu. If a person other than the one you wish to talk to answers, you might ask: رحیم صاحب تشریف رکھتے ہیں؟ 'Is Mr Rahim there?'.

When someone rings you, you can answer by saying:

ہیلو، میں جان بول رہا ہوں / ہیلو، میں ہیلن بول رہی ہوں

helo, maiṅ jān bol rahā hūṅ/helo, maiṅ helan bol rahī hūṅ

Hello! This is John/Helen speaking ('I John am speaking')

If you get a wrong number, you can excuse yourself by saying:

معاف کیجیے *mu'āf kījīe* Excuse me ('do forgiveness')

معاف *mu'āf* is usually pronounced *māf*.

Word order

Urdu is usually strict about the correct order of words in the sentences: the verb always comes at the end of the sentences, and 'question' words, such as 'how?, who?, what?, how much?', etc, always come immediately before the verb. In everyday speech, however, the rules can be broken for various reasons.

In the phrase in the dialogue 'I never ask', the word order should strictly speaking be:

میں کبھی نہیں پوچھتا *maiṅ kabhī nahīṅ pūchtā*

Transferring نہیں to the end of the sentences, i.e. میں کبھی پوچھتا نہیں *maiṅ kabhī pūchtā nahīṅ* puts emphasis on 'never': 'I *never* ask'. The normal word order in the sentence 'come here to dinner' (کھانے پر), would be: آپ ادھر کھانے پر آیئے *āp idhar khāne par āīe*. In the dialogue, however, Rahim says: آپ ادھر آیئے کھانے پر *āp idhar āīe khāne par*, the phrase 'to dinner' being added as an afterthought.

More expressions of time

After بجے the postposition تک 'up to' is used in the sense of 'by':

گاڑی آٹھ بجے تک پہنچتی ہے The car arrives by eight

Before expressions of time ٹھیک has the sense of 'precisely':

وہ ٹھیک آٹھ بجے آرہے ہیں They are coming at eight o'clock precisely
ٹھیک پانچ بجے ہیں It is five o'clock precisely

مکالمہ تین *mukālima tīn* Dialogue 3

Rahim's brother-in-law proposes a hotel for the Smiths in Lahore.

رحیم : آیئے' جان صاحب' آیئے ہیلن صاحبہ۔ تشریف لایئے۔ میری بیگم سے ملیے۔ ان کا نام فاطمہ ہے اور یہ میری بہن کوثر ہیں۔ اور یہ ہیں میرے بہنوئی' قاسم صاحب۔ یہ لاہور کے رہنے والے ہیں۔ یہ لوگ اگلی جمعرات کو آپ کے ساتھ جا رہے ہیں۔ قاسم صاحب لاہور کے بارے میں سب کچھ جانتے ہیں۔ قاسم صاحب' آپ کو معلوم ہے کہ جان اور ہیلن ہمارے انگریز دوست ہیں۔ دونوں انگلستان میں ڈاکٹر ہیں۔ اور دونوں بہت اچھی اُردو بولتے ہیں۔

قاسم : بتایئے' جان صاحب' لاہور میں کہاں ٹھہرنے کا ارادہ ہے؟

جان : اب تک مجھے معلوم نہیں۔ میرے خیال سے کسی ہوٹل میں۔

قاسم : لاہور میں بہت اچھے ہوٹل ہیں لیکن میرا پسندیدہ ہوٹل ایک پرانا انگریزی ہوٹل ہے۔ یہ مال روڈ کے پاس ہے۔ عین مرکز میں۔ آپ کو اس کا ٹیلیفون نمبر دیتا ہوں۔ کل صبح وہاں ٹیلیفون کیجئے اور میرا نام دیجئے۔

ٹھہرنا	*thahrnā*	to stay	بڑی اچھی اُردو	*baṛī acchī*	very good
فاطمہ	*fātima*	Fatima		*urdū*	Urdu
کوثر	*kausar*	Kausar	مال روڈ	*māl roḍ*	Mall Road (Lahore)
بہنوئی	*bahnūī*	brother-in-law (m.)	عین	*'ain*	right, just
			عین مرکز میں	*'ain markaz meṅ*	right in the centre
قاسم	*qāsim*	Qasim			
کے بارے میں	*ke bāre meṅ*	about, concerning	دینا	*denā*	to give
			کل	*kal*	tomorrow
جاننا	*jānnā*	to know	کل صبح	*kal subh*	tomorrow morning

قواعد *qavā'id* Grammar

اگلا *aglā* 'next'

The adjective اگلا *aglā* means 'next' and is used with the names of the days of the week and months:

میں اگلے پیر کو جا رہا ہوں	I am going ('on') next Monday
ہم اگلے جمعے کو پہنچ رہے ہیں	We are arriving next Friday
اگلے ہفتے کو چھٹی ہے	There's a holiday next Saturday
وہ اگلے ہفتے آ رہے ہیں	They are coming next week
اگلے ہفتے میری سالگرہ ہے	Next month I have my birthday

Note that in the last two expressions no postposition is used:

کے بارے میں *ke bāre meṅ* 'about', 'concerning'

کے بارے میں is a compound postposition consisting of three words and means 'about', 'concerning':

لاہور کے بارے میں مجھے بتائیے	Please tell me about Lahore
ہمارے بارے میں آپ کو کیا معلوم ہے؟	What do you know about us?

جاننا *jānnā* 'to know'

جاننا (stem جان *jān-*, i.e. the *infinitive* is written with two *nūns*)
jānnā 'to know' is the equivalent of معلوم ہونا.

جاننا *jānnā* should not be confused with جانا *jānā* (stem جا *jā-*) 'to go'. For example: میں جانتا ہوں *main jāntā hūn* 'I know', but میں جاتا ہوں *main jātā hūn* 'I go'. By and large, جاننا can be used instead of معلوم ہے:

آپ جانتے ہیں کہ بندر روڈ کہاں ہے؟

Do you know (that) where Bandar Road is?

وہ لاہور کے بارے میں بہت جانتا ہے

He knows a lot about Lahore

بڑا *baṛā* 'very'

Coming before other adjectives, بڑا 'very', is the equivalent of بہت:

موسم بڑا اچھا ہے	It is very good weather
آپ بڑی اچھی اردو بولتے ہیں	You speak very good Urdu
وہ بڑے اچھے لوگ ہیں	They are very nice people

ٹھہرنا *ṭhahrnā* 'to wait'; 'to stay/reside'

ٹھہرنا means both 'to wait' and 'to stay' (in a hotel, etc.):

ذرا ٹھہریے، میں ابھی آتا ہوں	Wait a bit. I'm just coming
آپ یہاں کہاں ٹھہر رہے ہیں؟	Where are you staying here?

ثقافت *siqāfat* Culture

In India and Pakistan, trains are efficient, if rather slow, but if you have the time they provide you with one of the best ways of seeing the country and observing its day-to-day life. First-class travel is relatively inexpensive and reasonably comfortable. Second, 'Inter' and Third class can be crowded and chaotic, but for a short journey are worth trying. In India the 'Air-Conditioned Chair Car' between Delhi and Calcutta, Delhi and Bombay is excellent value. This is one way of experiencing what they call the 'real' India or Pakistan. The issue of tickets and reservations is subject to bewildering bureaucracy, a legacy of the British Raj, which has been developed to a fine art. Your chances of acquiring a ticket at the station, especially if you are a stranger to the country, are almost nil. One always seems to be number 529 on the waiting list! The best way is to find a local who knows the system – a friend, a hotel manager, or anyone in a vaguely official position.

مشقیں *mašqeṅ* Exercises

7.2 Take your part in the dialogue

Rahim : آداب عرض ہے' آپ آج کیا کر رہے / رہی ہیں؟

You : Say you are busy and are preparing to go to Islamabad (اسلام آباد)

Rahim : اچھا' کیا آپ ہوائی جہاز سے جا رہے ہیں؟

You : Say no. You are planning to go by train

Rahim : آپ کو معلوم ہے کہ ریل گاڑی یہاں سے آٹھ بجے جاتی ہے؟

You : Say that you know, and ask where you can get a ticket

Rahim : کوئی مشکل نہیں۔ اسٹیشن پر مت جائیے۔ مجھے شام کو فون کیجیے۔

You : Thank Rahim, and say that you will telephone at eight sharp

7.3 Listen to the Urdu dialogue on the tape and tick the correct answer:

1	Kausar is at home :	(a) looking after the children	(b) cooking
2	Fatima asks Kausar if :	(a) she likes cooking	(b) she is free
3	Kausar is :	(a) going out this evening	(b) staying at home
4	Tomorrow morning Kausar :	(a) has time to spare	(b) is busy
5	Fatima ask her to :	(a) come and have ice cream	(b) phone her

7.4 Using the telephone

You ring a number you have been given to find out from Mr Qasim information about going by train to Lahore. Do the following:

1 Say hello and ask is the number is 60495
2 Ask if Mr Qasim is there
3 Tell him you are either Bill Brown (بل براؤن) or Mary Jones (میری جونز) and you are going to Lahore next Thursday. Say you are American
4 Ask if he knows where you can get a first-class reservation
5 Thank him and say that he is very kind. Give him your number and ask him to phone you in the evening.

8 ہمیں حساب دیجیے ؟ Can we have the bill?

In this unit you will learn how to:

- say what you will do in the future
- check out of a hotel
- say what you must do
- hire a porter at the station

مکالمہ ایک *mukālima ek* Dialogue 1

John settles his bill with the hotel manager and prepares for departure.

جان : السلام علیکم ٗ جناب۔

منیجر : وعلیکم السلام ٗ اسمتھ صاحب۔ آپ کیسے ہیں؟ کراچی میں وقت اچھا گزر رہا ہے ؟

جان : جی ہاں ٗ یہاں بہت اچھے دن گزر رہے ہیں۔ ہمیں آپ کا ہوٹل بہت پسند ہے۔ کل صبح ہم لاہور جا رہے ہیں اور وہاں کوئی دس دن کے لئے رہیں گے۔

منیجر : اچھا ٗ آپ کیسے جائیں گے۔ ریل سے یا ہوائی جہاز سے ؟

جان : ہم ریل سے جائیں گے۔ ریل گاڑی صبح آٹھ بجے اسٹیشن سے روانہ ہو گی۔ اس لئے ہمیں سویرے اٹھنا ہے۔ کیا یہاں سے ٹیکسی آسانی سے ملے گی؟

منیجر : جی ہاں ٗ کوئی مشکل نہیں ہو گی۔ میں آپ کے لئے سات بجے ٹیکسی بلاؤں گا۔ جانے سے پہلے یہاں ناشتہ کیجیے۔ کیا آپ کمرے میں ناشتہ کریں گے ؟

جان : یہ بہت اچھا ہو گا۔ اور آج شام تک مجھے حساب دیجیے۔ مجھے ابھی دو تین گھنٹے کے لئے باہر جانا ہے۔ میں کوئی چھے بجے واپس آؤں گا۔

منیجر : ٹھیک ہے ٗ اسمتھ صاحب۔ آپ جائیے۔ چھے بجے تک سب تیار ہو گا۔ کیا آپ لوگ شام کا کھانا یہاں کھائیں گے ؟

جان : جی نہیں۔ ہم دوستوں کے پاس جا رہے ہیں۔ ان کے ساتھ ہم کھانا کھائیں گے۔

منیجر : بہتر ہے ٗ صاحب میں شام کو یہاں رہوں گا۔ اگر آپ کو اور کچھ چاہیئے تو مجھے بتائیے۔

جان : شکریہ۔ ہم شام کو پھر ملیں گے۔

ہم چلیں گے	*ham caleṅge*	we shall leave	ناشتہ کریں گے	*nāšta kareṅge?*	will you have breakfast?
حساب	*hisāb*	bill, account (m.)	اچھا ہوگا	*acchā hogā*	it will be good
مینجر	*mainijar*	manager (m.)	مجھے باہر جانا ہے	*mujhe bāhar jānā hai*	I have to go out
جناب	*janāb!*	Sir!	واپس	*vāpas*	back
گزر رہا ہے	*guzar rahā hai*	is being passed, spent	واپس آؤں گا	*vāpas āūṅgā*	I'll come back
گزرنا	*guzarnā*	to be spent (of time)	تیار ہوگا	*tayyār hogā*	will be ready
جائیں گے	*jāeṅge*	will go	کھائیں گے	*khāeṅge*	we'll eat
روانہ	*ravāna*	departing	بہتر ہے	*bihtar hai*	very well!
روانہ ہوگی	*ravāna hogī*	will depart	رہوں گا	*rahūṅgā*	I shall remain, be
ہمیں اٹھنا ہے	*hameṅ uṭhnā hai*	we have to get up	اگر	*agar*	if
ملے گی	*milegī*	will be got	اور کچھ	*aur kuch*	anything else
نہیں ہوگی	*nahīṅ hogī*	there won't be	ہم ملیں گے	*ham mileṅge*	we shall meet
بلاؤں گا	*bulāūṅgā*	I'll call			

قواعد qavā'id Grammar

گزرنا guzarnā '(of time) to be spent, pass'

گزرنا *guzarnā* means 'to pass, be spent (of time)':

کراچی میں اچھا وقت گزر رہا ہے

karācī meṅ acchā vaqt guzar rahā hai

A good time is being spent in Karachi ('we are having a good time')

عام طور سے چھٹیاں سمندر کے پاس گزرتی ہیں

Holidays are usually spent by the seaside

Note that English usually 'personalises' such expressions: 'we are having a good time; we usually spend ...'.

Future tense 'I shall do'

The future tense, as its name implies, expresses what will happen in the future: 'I shall do, you will be', etc.

The future tense is formed by adding the following endings to the stem of the verb:

Masculine		Feminine	
-وں گا	-ūṅgā	-وں گی	-ūṅgī
-ے گا	-egā	-ے گی	-egī
-یں گے	-eṅge	-یں گی	-eṅgī
-و گے	-oge	-و گی	-ogī

میں کروں گا	*maiṅ karūṅgā*	I shall do	وہ کرے گا	*vuh karegā*	he will do
وہ کرے گی	*vuh karegī*	she will do	آپ کریں گی	*āp kareṅgī*	you (f.) will do
ہم کریں گے	*ham kareṅge*	we will do			

Note that, as usual, ہم is regarded as masculine.

It is made negative by placing the particle نہیں directly before the verb: میں نہیں کروں گا *maiṅ nahīṅ karūṅgā* 'I shall not do'.

The future tense of کرنا *karnā* (stem کر *kar-*) 'to do' is:

Masculine		Feminine		
کروں گا	karūṅgā	کروں گی	karūṅgī	میں
کرے گا	karegā	کرے گی	karegī	تو
کرے گا	karegā	کرے گی	karegī	یہ' وہ
کریں گے	kareṅge	کریں گے	kareṅge	ہم
کرو گے	karoge	کرو گی	karogī	تم
کریں گے	kareṅge	کریں گی	kareṅgī	آپ
کریں گے	kareṅge	کریں گی	kareṅgī	یہ' وہ

The suffixes گا - گی - گے are usually written separately, but may be joined: آپ کرینگے' وہ کریگا' میں کرونگا etc.

The future tense is used in exactly the same way as its English counterpart:

ہم اگلے ہفتے لاہور جائیں گے	We shall go to Lahore next month
رحیم صاحب آج کام نہیں کریں گے	Mr Rahim will not work today
میری بیوی آج باہر نہیں جائیں گی	My wife will not go out today

Future tense of ہونا *honā*

The future tense of ہونا is slightly irregular:

Masculine		Feminine		
ہوں گا	*hūṅgā*	ہوں گی	*hūṅgī*	میں
ہوگا	*hogā*	ہوگی	*hogī*	تو
ہوگا	*hogā*	ہوگی	*hogī*	یہ' وہ
ہوں گے	*hoṅge*	ہوں گے	*hoṅge*	ہم
ہوگے	*hoge*	ہوگی	*hogī*	تم
ہوں گے	*hoṅge*	ہوں گی	*hoṅgī*	آپ
ہوں گے	*hoṅge*	ہوں گی	*hoṅgī*	یہ' وہ

'must', 'have to' obligation

'I must do', 'Mr Rahim has to do' is expressed in Urdu with کو *ko* and the infinitive followed by ہے *hai*:

رحیم کو جانا ہے	*rahīm ko jānā hai*	'to Rahim is to go' Rahim must go
مجھے پڑھنا ہے	*mujhe paṛhnā hai*	'to me is to read' I must read

جلدی کرو۔ ہمیں دوستوں کے ہاں پانچ بجے پہنچنا ہے

jaldī karo! hameṅ dostoṅ ke hāṅ pāṅc baje pahuṅcnā hai

Hurry up! We have to be at (our) friends' place by five ('to us is to arrive')

جلدی *jaldī* means 'hurry' (f.); جلدی کرنا 'to hurry'. Used as an adverb جلدی means 'quickly, soon':

اے بیرا! کھانا لاؤ اور جلدی لاؤ

Waiter! Bring the food, and bring (it) quickly/soon

کے ہاں *ke hāṅ* is a compound postposition meaning 'at the place/ house of':

ہمارے دوست ہمارے ہاں ٹھہریں گے

Our friends will stay at our place

اور کچھ **aur kuch 'something else'**

We have already seen that as well as meaning 'and', اور also means 'more': اور چائے 'more tea', اور کھائیں 'let's eat some more'.

In the phrase اور کچھ it is translated as 'else':

آپ کو اور کچھ چاہیے؟ جی نہیں مجھے اور کچھ نہیں چاہیئے

Do you want something else? No, I don't want anything else

پھر ملیں گے ***phir milenge*** **'we shall meet again'**

When taking leave of each other, people often say: اجازت دیجیے۔ خدا حافظ۔ ہم پھر ملیں گے 'Give me leave. Goodbye. We'll meet again'.

پھر ملیں گے may be better translated as 'see you!':

اچھا رحیم صاحب۔ مجھے اب جانا ہے۔ پھر ملیں گے

Ok, Rahim. I've got to go now. See you!

مکالمہ ۲ *mukālima do* Dialogue 2

John and Helen make their final arrangements for departure.

جان : السلام علیکم، جناب۔ ناشتے کے لیے بہت شکریہ۔ اس کے لئے مجھے آپ کو کتنے پیسے دینے ہیں۔؟

مینیجر : جی نہیں، اسمتھ صاحب۔ کوئی تکلف نہیں ہے۔ یہ ہوٹل کی طرف سے ہے۔ اور سفر کے لئے کچھ پھل ہیں۔ لیجیے۔ یہ بھی ہماری طرف سے ہے۔

جان : ارے، آپ بہت تکلف کر رہے ہیں۔ بہت بہت شکریہ۔ آپ کا ہوٹل ہمیں ہمیشہ یاد رہے گا۔

مینیجر : آپ کا سامان کہاں ہے؟ کمرے میں ہے؟

جان : جی ہاں، تین سوٹ کیس ہیں۔ لیکن وہ کافی بھاری ہیں۔

مینیجر : ٹھیک ہے۔ آپ یہاں تشریف رکھیے۔ میں قلی کو بلاؤں گا۔ وہ سامان لائے گا اور ٹیکسی میں رکھے گا۔ آپ کے پاس بہت وقت ہے۔ کیا جانے سے پہلے چائے یا کوفی پیئیں گے؟

جان : جی نہیں، شکریہ۔ میرے خیال سے ہم ابھی چلیں گے۔ کیونکہ ہمیں اسٹیشن پر دوستوں سے ملنا ہے۔ وہ بھی ہمارے ساتھ لاہور جا رہے ہیں۔

مینیجر : لاہور کے بعد آپ کا کیا ارادہ ہے؟ کیا آپ وہاں سے گھر جائیں گے؟

جان : جی نہیں۔ ہم وہاں سے دہلی جائیں گے اور ہندوستان میں دو ہفتے کے لئے رہیں گے۔

مینیجر : اچھا! آپ کو دہلی بہت پسند آئے گا۔ دہلی میرے خاندان کا وطن ہے۔ یعنی میں دہلی کا رہنے والا ہوں۔ بہت شاندار شہر ہے۔

جان : مجھے یقین ہے کہ دہلی بہت شاندار ہے۔ لیکن ہم پہلے لاہور دیکھیں گے۔ اچھا' یہ ہمارا ٹیکسی والا ہے نا؟ تو ہم چلیں گے۔ ایک بار پھر سے آپ کا بہت بہت شکریہ! ہم پھر ملیں گے۔

مینیجر : پھر کبھی آیئے۔ خدا حافظ۔

جناب	*janāb*	Sir (m.)	سوٹ کیس	*sūt-kes*	suitcase (m.)
مجھے پیسے دینے ہیں	*mujhe paise dene haiṅ*	I have to give money/ pay	بھاری	*bhārī*	heavy
کی طرف سے	*kī taraf se*	from, on	قلی	*qulī*	porter (m.)
سفر	*safar*	journey (m.)	قلی کو بلاؤں گا	*qulī ko bulāūṅgā*	I'll call the porter
پھل	*phal*	fruit (m.)	رکھنا	*rakhnā*	to put
ہماری طرف	*hamārī taraf se*	from us; on us	آپ کے پاس وقت ہے	*āp ke pās vaqt hai*	you have time
ارے	*are!*	oh! well!	کوفی	*kofī*	coffee (f.)
ہمیں یاد رہے گا	*hameṅ yād rahegā*	we'll remember	چلنا	*calnā*	to go, depart, be off
سامان	*sāmān*	luggage (m.)	ایک بار پھر سے	*ek bār phir se*	once more
کمرہ	*kamra*	room (m.)	پھر کبھی آیئے	*phir kabhī āie*	come again some time

قواعد *qavā'id* Grammar

جناب *janāb* 'Sir'

جناب is an Arabic word literally meaning 'courtyard of a noble's palace in which the oppressed might take refuge'. In Persian and Urdu it has come to mean 'My Lord', but in modern Urdu it simply means 'Sir', and may be used when addressing any male.

More rules for obligation 'must'; the object of the verb

In certain circumstances, the infinitive behaves like adjectives in ا -ā, such as اچھا:

	Adjective		**Infinitive**	
Masculine singular	*acchā*	اچھا	*karnā*	کرنا
Masculine singular oblique	*acche*	اچھے	*karne*	کرنے
Masculine plural	*acche*	اچھے	*karne*	کرنے
Feminine	*acchī*	اچھی	*karnī*	کرنی

We have already seen that the masculine singular oblique is used with post-positions: کرنے سے from doing, جانے کے بعد after going, آنے سے پہلے before coming.

We saw earliar that 'I must give, I have to give' is expressed in Urdu as 'to me is to give'. If in such a sentence the verb takes an object, e.g. I must give money, the infinitive (in this case دینا) takes the number and gender of the object. Here the object of the verb is پیسے *paise* 'money', which is masculine plural. Therefore the infinitive also changes to masculine plural دینے in order to 'agree' with its object. The verb also changes to plural (ہیں *haiṅ*):

مجھے پیسے دینے ہیں

mujhe paise dene ***haiṅ***

Compare the following:

مجھے گھر دیکھنا ہے	*mujhe ghar dekhnā* ***hai***	I have to see a house (m.s.)
مجھے کتاب دیکھنی ہے	*mujhe kitāb dekhnī* ***hai***	I have to see a book (f.s.)
مجھے گھر دیکھنے ہیں	*mujhe ghar dekhne* ***haiṅ***	I have to see houses (m.p.)
مجھے کتابیں دیکھنی ہیں	*mujhe kitābeṅ* ***dekhnī haiṅ***	I have to see books (f.p.)

If the object of a verb is a person ('boy', 'Mr Rahim', etc.) or a pronoun ('me, you, him, her, us, them'), the object must be followed by کو *ko*):

میں رحیم کو دیکھتا ہوں	*maiṅ rahīm ko dekhtā hūṅ* I see Rahim
رحیم مجھ کو / مجھے دیکھتے ہیں	*rahīm mujh ko/mujhe dekhte haiṅ* Rahim sees me
ہم لڑکے کو بلاتے ہیں	*ham laṛke ko bulāte haiṅ* We call the boy
قلی کو بلاؤ / اسے بلاؤ	*qulī ko bulāo/use bulāo* Call the porter/call him

Thus مجھے، تجھے، اسے، ہمیں، تمہیں، آپ کو، انہیں coming before a verb as its object are the equivalent of English: 'me, you, him, her, us, them'.

In sentences of obligation, when the verb takes an object followed by کو, the infinitive always remains masculine singular, regardless of the gender or number of the noun or pronoun, and the verb ہے *hai* also remains singular:

مجھے رحیم کو بلانا ہے *mujhe rahīm ko bulānā hai* I must call Rahim
مجھے اس لڑکی کو دیکھنا ہے *mujhe us laṛkī ko dekhnā hai* I must see that girl
ہمیں ان آدمیوں کو بلانا ہے *hameṅ un ādmīoṅ ko bulānā hai* We must call those men

مشق *mašq* Exercise

8.1 Complete the sentences

Complete the following sentences choosing the final two words (infinitive + ہونا) from the following: کرنا ہے۔ جانا ہے۔ دینے ہیں۔ بلانا ہے۔ پڑھنی ہیں۔ کرنی ہے۔

1 اس ہفتے ہمیں کم سے کم پانچ کتابیں ____________
2 آپ کو مجھے پانچ روپئے ____________
3 کیا آپ کو خریداری ____________؟
4 جان کو بیوی کو ٹیلیفون ____________
5 آج شام کو ہمیں باہر ____________
6 کیا آپ کو انہیں ____________؟

کی طرف سے *kī taraf se* 'from' 'on the part of' 'on'

کی طرف سے, literally 'from the side of' can be translated into English as 'on, from', 'on the house':

یہ کھانا میری طرف سے ہے This meal is on me
یہ پھل ہوٹل کی طرف سے ہے The fruit is from the hotel/on the house

یاد *yād* 'memory' مجھے یاد ہے *mujhe yād hai* 'I remember'

یاد *yād* means 'memory' (f.) and مجھے یاد ہے *mujhe yād hai* 'to me a memory is' means 'I remember':

آپ کا نام مجھے یاد نہیں ہے
I don't remember your name ('your name isn't a memory to me')

آپ کا ہوٹل ہمیشہ یاد رہے گا

We shall always remember your hotel ('your hotel will remain a memory')

چلنا *calnā*

We have already met the verb چلنا which expresses the idea of motion in various senses. In English it can be rendered 'to come, go, move, walk, leave, depart, get going', etc. according to the context. Compare the following:

چلیں چائے پئیں	Come on, let's have tea
گاڑی چھ بجے چلتی ہے	The train goes at six
وہ راستے پر چلتے ہیں	They walk along the road
میری گاڑی نہیں چلے گی	My car won't go ('it's broken down)
اے بھائی' چلو! (چلو بھائی)	Get a move on (brother/mate)!
مجھے اب چلنا ہے	I have to leave now

The related verb چلانا *calānā* means 'to drive':

آپ چلاتے ہیں	Do you drive?
بلقیس گاڑی چلاتی ہیں	Bilqis drives a car

پھر *phir* 'then, again'

پھر has two meanings: 'then, afterwards'; 'again':

ہم پہلے لاہور جائیں گے' پھر دہلی جائیں گے	We'll go to Lahore first, then to Delhi
ہم پھر ملیں گے	We'll meet again some time

مکالمہ تین *mukālima tīn* Dialogue 3

John and Helen take a taxi to the station and find a porter.

ٹیکسی والا : کہاں جانا ہے' صاحب' اسٹیشن جانا ہے؟

جان : جی ہاں۔ ہم لاہور جا رہے ہیں۔ گاڑی کس پلیٹ فارم سے چلتی ہے؟ آپ کو معلوم ہو گا؟

ٹیکسی والا : جی ہاں' صاحب۔ کوئی مشکل نہیں۔ میں آپ کے لئے قلی کو بلاؤں گا۔ اسٹیشن یہاں سے زیادہ دور نہیں۔ صرف بیس منٹ کا راستہ ہے۔ آپ لوگ انگریز ہیں نا۔ آپ کو اردو کیسے آتی ہے؟

جان : بس۔ میں اُردو سیکھ رہا ہوں۔ انگلستان میں بہت سے اُردو بولنے والے رہتے ہیں۔

ٹیکسی والا : جی ہاں، مجھے معلوم ہے۔ میرے بڑے بھائی مینچسٹر میں رہتے ہیں۔ میں بھی وہاں جاؤں گا۔

جان : اچھا۔ کب جانے کا ارادہ ہے؟

ٹیکسی والا : ارادے تو ہمیشہ ہوتے ہیں، صاحب۔ لیکن پیسے چاہئیں نا! میں ٹیکسی چلانے والا ہوں۔ میں بہت زیادہ نہیں کماتا۔ لیکن ایک دن میں وہاں ضرور جاؤں گا۔ دیکھیے، اسٹیشن یہاں ہے۔

جان : اوہو! کتنی بڑی بھیڑ ہے۔ ہم پلیٹ فارم تک کیسے پہنچیں گے؟

ٹیکسی والا : کوئی مشکل نہیں، صاحب۔ میں قلی کو بلاؤں گا۔ وہ آپ کو گاڑی میں بٹھائے گا۔ آپ اس کو دس روپئے دیجیے۔ زیادہ نہیں۔

جان : اور مجھے آپ کو کتنے پیسے دینے ہیں؟

ٹیکسی والا : بس۔ پچیس روپئے دیجیے۔ اس آدمی کو دیکھیے۔ وہ آپ کا قلی ہے۔

جان : آپ کی بڑی مہربانی۔ خدا حافظ۔

پلیٹ فارم	*plaiṭfārm*	platform (m.)
آپ کو معلوم ہوگا	*āp ko ma'lūm hogā*	you probably know
آپ کو اردو کیسے آتی ہے؟	*āp ko urdū kaise ātī hai?*	how do you know Urdu?
بس	*bas*	well!, enough
سیکھنا	*sīkhnā*	to learn
اُردو بولنے والے	*urdū bolnevāle*	Urdu speakers
مینچسٹر	*maincesṭar*	Manchester (m.)
چلانے والا	*calānevālā*	driver (m.)
کمانا	*kamānā*	to earn
بھیڑ	*bhīṛ*	crowd (f.)
کتنی بڑی بھیڑ	*kitnī baṛī bhīṛ*	what a huge crowd!
بٹھانا	*biṭhānā*	to seat, show to a seat

قواعد *qavā'id* Grammar

آپ کو معلوم ہوگا *āp ko ma'lūm hogā* 'you probably know'

The future tense can, as in English, have the sense of 'probably', 'must':

آپ کو معلوم ہوگا کہ اسٹیشن کہاں ہے

You probably/must know where the station is ('you will know ...')

میری بہن کراچی میں ہوگی

My sister must be in Karachi ('she will be ...')

مجھے اُردو آتی ہے **mujhe urdū ātī hai** 'I know/speak Urdu'

مجھے اُردو آتی ہے 'Urdu comes to me', i.e. 'I know Urdu'. آنا in the sense of 'to know' is especially common in the context of languages:

حامد کو تین زبانیں آتی ہیں۔ اس کو اُردو، انگریزی اور عربی آتی ہیں

Hamid knows three languages. He knows Urdu, English and Arabic

بس ***bas*! 'well! enough!'**

بس used as an exclamation means 'well!, you see!'.

بس، میں اُردو سیکھ رہا ہوں Well, I'm learning Urdu

When asked کیا حال ہے؟ people often simply reply بس meaning OK. بس can also mean 'enough':

بس! بس! مجھے اور نہ دیجیے Enough! Enough! Don't give me any more

والا **-vālā**

The suffix والا *-vālā* (fem. والی *-vālī*) denotes a person who does, sells or possesses something. In the English of the Raj 'wallah' was often used: 'chaiwallah' a tea vendor = Urdu چائےوالا *cāevālā*; 'boxwallah' someone who carried your boxes = Urdu بکس والا *baksvālā*. Compare ٹیکسی والا a taxi driver, پھل والا a fruit seller.

Added to the oblique infinitive, والا means 'someone who does something':

کام کرنے والا	*kām karnevālā*	a worker
چلانے والا	*calānevālā*	a driver
اُردو بولنے والا	*urdū bolnevālā*	an Urdu speaker

The feminine counterpart والی- would be used by or for a woman:

بلقیس اُردو بولنے والی ہے *bilqīs urdū bolnevālī hai* Bilqis is an Urdu speaker.

بٹھانا biṭhānā 'to seat, show someone to a seat'

بٹھانا (related to بیٹھنا 'to sit') means 'to seat someone'. On Indian and Pakistani stations, the porter, as well as carrying your luggage, will also find your compartment for you, arrange your things, and deal with over-zealous guards and ticket inspectors. All these services are included in بٹھانا.

ثقافت *siqāfat* Culture

In the westernised luxury hotels of large cities in India and Pakistan the system is much the same as anywhere else in the world. The less ostentatious hotels have much more of a 'family' atmosphere. When you speak Urdu, the staff will become extremely friendly and helpful, not to mention curious, and it is not uncommon to find a bowl of fruit placed in your room: ہوٹل کی طرف سے 'on the house'.

According to the code of hospitality, you are the honoured guest, and there will always be porters present to carry your bags and give other services in return for a tip. Tipping بخشش *baxšiš*, from which we have the English words 'buckshee' and 'baksheesh', is customary and expected. In hotels and at stations, many people earn their living almost entirely from tips. If you insist on carrying your own baggage to the train, you will not only be regarded as mean, but definitely as odd!

مشقیں *mašqeṅ* Exercises

8.2 Dialogue

You are at the station. Take your part in the dialogue with the porter:

Porter : آپ اسٹیشن جا رہے / رہی ہیں؟ کہاں جا رہے / رہی ہیں؟

You : Say yes; you are going to Lahore

Porter : آپ کے پاس کتنا سامان ہے؟

You : Say you have only two suitcases

Porter : آپ کا ریزرویشن ہے؟

You : Say you do, and ask at what time the train will depart

Porter : ٹھیک آٹھ بجے چلتی ہے

You : Say thank you, and ask how much you have to give him

8.3 Give the correct form of the infinitive

1 آپ کو سب چیزیں (کھانا) ہیں

2 ہمیں کل صبح چھے بجے (اٹھنا) ہے

3 آپ کو کتنی کتابیں (پڑھنا) ہے

4 مجھے اس لڑکی کو فون (کرنا) ہے

5 رحیم صاحب کو آج اسپتال (جانا) ہے

8.4 Numbers and figures

While staying in Karachi John has made the following accounts (حساب) of his expenditure. Look at his list and then answer the questions that follow.

حساب کتاب

۱۱۰۰	گیارہ سو	ہوٹل کا کرایہ (دس دن)
۷۰۰	سات سو	دوپہر کا کھانا
۹۳۰	نو سو تیس	شام کا کھانا
۱۲۰۰	ایک ہزار دو سو	خریداری
۳۲۰	تین سو بیس	ٹیکسی (پانچ بار)
۶۱۸	چھے سو اٹھارہ	لاہور جانے کا کرایہ (دو ٹکٹ)
۳۰	تیس	تین کتابیں
۲۲	بائیس	بخشش
؟		کل

1 How many days has John stayed in his hotel?

2 How much has he spent altogether on food?

3 How many times has he travelled in a taxi?

4 What is the price of a single ticket to Lahore?

5 How much money has he given in tips?

6 What has been his total expenditure in Karachi.

(The Arabic word کل *kul* means 'total')

9 میری بیوی کہاں ہے؟ Where is my wife?

In this unit you will learn how to:

- say where and how you were
- make comparisons
- identify more of the geography of Pakistan
- say more directions
- use higher numbers

مکالمہ ایک *mukālima ek* Dialogue 1

Qasim meets the Smiths at the station and loses his wife in the crowd.

قاسم : جان صاحب' السلام علیکم۔ آپ لوگ کہاں تھے؟ آپ پلیٹ فارم پر نہیں تھے۔ میں بہت پریشان تھا۔

جان : وعلیکم السلام' قاسم صاحب۔ معاف کیجئے۔ ہم پلیٹ فارم پر تھے لیکن اتنی بڑی بھیڑ تھی۔ مشکل ہے نا! ایسی بھیڑ میں کچھ نظر نہیں آتا۔

قاسم : خیر' کوئی بات نہیں۔ اہم بات تو یہ ہے کہ اب آپ لوگ یہاں ہیں۔ ڈبا کافی آرامدہ ہے نا؟ ہم صرف چار آدمی ہوں گے۔ اور کوئی نہیں ہوگا۔ آپ کو پاکستان پسند آرہا ہے؟

جان : بہت پسند آرہا ہے۔ کراچی میں ہمارا ہوٹل بہت اچھا تھا۔ کھانا اچھا تھا' لوگ اچھے تھے اور ہوٹل کے مینیجر خاص طور سے مہربان تھے۔ کراچی میں اب ہمارے بہت سے دوست ہیں۔

قاسم : لاہور میں اور زیادہ دوست ملیں گے۔ پنجاب کے لوگ بہت مہمان نواز ہوتے ہیں۔ ارے میری بیگم کہاں ہیں! وہ پانچ منٹ پہلے سہیلیوں کے ساتھ پلیٹ فارم پر تھیں' اب وہ کہیں نظر نہیں آتیں۔ آپ لوگ یہاں بیٹھیے میں ان کی تلاش کروں گا۔ گاڑی پانچ منٹ کے بعد روانہ ہوگی۔

جان : قاسم صاحب' آپ پریشان مت ہوئیے۔ دیکھیے وہ آرہی ہیں۔

قاسم : کوثر' آپ کہاں تھیں؟ کیا سہیلیوں کے ساتھ تھیں؟ آیئے ڈبے میں بیٹھیے۔ گاڑی اب چل رہی ہے۔

تھے	*the*	were	اور زیادہ	*aur ziyāda*	even more, many more
پریشان	*parešān*	worried	مہمان نواز	*mihmān navāz*	hospitable
اتنی بڑی بھیڑ	*itnī baṛī bhīṛ*	such a big crowd	پانچ منٹ پہلے	*pāṅc minaṭ pahle*	five minutes ago
نظر نہیں آتا	*nazar nahiṅ ātā*	can't be seen	سہیلی	*sahelī*	woman friend (f.)
خیر	*xair*	well!	تھیں	*thīṅ*	(she) was
اہم	*ahm*	important	کہیں نہیں	*kahīṅ nahīṅ*	nowhere
سب سے اہم	*sab se ahm*	the most important	نظر نہیں آتیں	*nazar nahīṅ ātīṅ*	can't be seen
ڈبا	*ḍibbā*	compartment (m.)	ان کی تلاش کروں گا	*un kī talāš karūṅgā*	I'll look for her
آپ کو پسند آ رہا ہے؟	*āp ko pasand ā rahā hai?*	are you enjoying?			
تھا	*thā*	was			
مہربان	*mirhrbān*	kind, gentle			

قواعد *qavā'id* Grammar

Past tense of ہونا : تھا *thā* 'was'

The past tense refers to what was or happened in the past. First we look at tha past tense of ہونا 'I was, you were, they were', etc. In Urdu the past tense of ہونا shows gender (masculine and feminine) and number (singular and plural), but not does not indicate person ('I, you, he', etc.). It is formed as follows:

Masculine singular

میں تھا	*maiṅ thā*	I was
تو تھا	*tū thā*	you were
یہ، وہ تھا	*yih, vuh thā*	he/it was

Masculine plural

ہم تھے	*ham the*	we were
تم تھے	*tum the*	you were
آپ تھے	*āp the*	you were
یہ، وہ تھے	*yih, vuh the*	they were

Feminine singular

میں تھی	*maiṅ thī*	I was
تو تھی	*tū thī*	you were
یہ، وہ تھی	*yih, vuh thī*	she, it was

Feminine plural

ہم تھے	*ham the*	we were
تم تھیں	*tum thīṅ*	you were
آپ تھیں	*āp thīṅ*	you were
یہ، وہ تھیں	*yih vuh thīṅ*	they were

As usual, ہم is regarded as masculine plural even when used by women. It will be noticed that the past tense of ہونا has only four elements: تھا *thā*, تھی *thī*, تھے *the*, تھیں *thīṅ*:

آپ کل شام کو کہاں تھے؟ میں گھر پر تھا

āp kal šām ko kahāṅ the? maiṅ ghar par thā

Where were you yesterday evening? I was at home

Notice that کل *kal*, as well as meaning 'tomorrow' also means 'yesterday':

میری بیٹیاں کل اسکول میں نہیں تھیں

merī beṭīāṅ kal iskūl meṅ nahīṅ thīṅ

My daughters were not at school yesterday

اتنا *itnā* 'so much (as this)'; 'such'

اتنا means 'so much (as this)', and can sometimes be translated as 'such':

پلیٹ فارم پر اتنی بڑی بھیڑ تھی

plaiṭfārm par itnī baṛī bhīṛ thī

There was such ('so much') a big crowd on the platform

مجھے اتنا نہیں چاہیے

mujhe itnā nahīṅ cāhīe

I don't want so much (as this)

اتنا is often followed by زیادہ meaning the same thing:

میرے پاس اتنے زیادہ پیسے نہیں ہیں

mere pās itne ziyāda paise nahīṅ haiṅ

I don't have so much money

نظر آنا **nazar ānā 'to come into view, be seen'**

نظر *nazar* means 'view, sight' (f.). The phrase verb نظر آنا *nazar ānā* means 'to come into view, be seen':

میری کھڑکی سے پورا لندن نظر آتا ہے

merī khiṛkī se pūrā landan nazar ātā hai

I can see the whole of London from my window ('London comes into view')

یہاں سے کچھ نظر نہیں آتا

yahāṅ se kuch nazar nahīṅ ātā

'from here nothing comes into view' i.e. you can't see anything.

In this sentence the subject is کچھ 'anything'.

Comparison of adjectives

When we make comparisons with adjectives: 'he is bigger than me; he is the biggest', the form 'bigger' is known as the comparative. and the form 'biggest' is known as the superlative. For some English adjectives we have to use 'more, most': 'more beautiful, most beautiful'.

In Urdu 'than' is expressed by the postposition سے. Comparison is effected as follows:

وہ مجھ سے بڑا ہے

vuh mujh se baṛa hai

He is bigger than me ('he than me is big')

وہ سب سے بڑا ہے

vuh sab se baṛā hai

He is the biggest ('he than all is big')

رحیم صاحب اسلم صاحب سے امیر ہے

ṛahīm sāhib aslam sāhib se amīr haiṅ

Mr Rahim is richer than Mr Aslam

لندن انگلستان کا سب سے بڑا شہر ہے

landan inglistān kā sab se baṛā šahr hai

London is th biggest city in ('of') England

Note that 'in' England is انگلستان کا 'of' England in Urdu.

In the comparative, the word زیادہ *ziyāda* 'more' may be placed before the adjective:

میرے بڑے بھائی مجھ سے زیادہ مصروف ہیں

My elder brother is busier ('more busy') than me

کو پسند آنا **ko pasand ānā 'to enjoy'**

The phrase verb کو پسند آنا *ko pasand ānā* 'to come (as) pleasing to' is best translated as 'to enjoy':

مجھے لاہور پسند آ رہا ہے

mujhe lāhaur pasand ā rahā hai

I am enjoying Lahore ('to me Lahore is coming pleasing')

Note the difference between:

مجھے پاکستانی کھانا پسند ہے	I like Pakistani food
مجھے پاکستانی کھانا پسند آتا ہے	I enjoy Pakistani food

پہلے **pahle 'ago'**

In expressions of time, پہلے *pahle* means 'ago':

چالیس منٹ پہلے	*cālīs minaṭ pahle*	forty minutes ago
پینتالیس منٹ پہلے	*paiṅtīs sāl pahle*	thirty-five years ago

The adjective پہلا *pahlā* means 'first':

پہلا درجہ	*pahlā darjā*	first class
پہلی بار	*pahlī bār*	the first time

The adverb پہلے *pahle* or سب سے پہلے means 'first (of all)':

پہلے میں لندن میں تھا۔ اب میں مینچسٹر میں ہوں

First I was in London; now I am in Manchester

آپ سب سے پہلے کہاں تھے؟

Where were you first of all?

کی تلاش کرنا **kī talāš karnā** **'to look for'**

تلاش *talāš* means 'seeking, looking for' (f.). The phrase verb کی تلاش کرنا *kī talāš karnā* 'to do the seeking of' means 'to look for':

میں آپ کی تلاش کر رہا تھا لیکن آپ کہیں نہیں تھے

I was looking for you ('doing your seeking'), but you weren't anywhere

Note کہیں *kahīn* 'somewhere', کہیں نہیں *kahīn nahīn* 'nowhere'.

مشق **mašq** **Exercise**

9.1 Complete the sentences

Complete the sentences with the correct form of the past tense of ہونا (تھا، تھیں، تھے، تھی):

1 آداب عرض اسلم صاحب۔ کل آپ کہاں __________؟

2 قاسم صاحب اور ان کے دوست پلیٹ فارم پر __________۔

3 وہ خاتون بہت مہربان __________۔

4 بلقیس صاحبہ، آپ دہلی میں کب __________؟

5 حامد کہاں ہے؟ پانچ منٹ پہلے وہ یہاں __________۔

مکالمہ ۲ **mukālima do** **Dialogue 2**

While travelling in the train through Sindh, the Smiths hear about Qasim's life.

جان : کیوں، قاسم صاحب۔ آپ لاہور کے رہنے والے ہیں؟

قاسم : جی نہیں، میں اصل میں ملتان کا رہنے والا ہوں۔ ملتان بھی پنجاب میں ہے اور لاہور سے زیادہ دور نہیں۔ میں پہلے فوج میں تھا۔ یعنی دس سال کے لئے میں سپاہی تھا۔ اس کے بعد میں پانچ سال کے لئے حیدر آباد سندھ اور کراچی میں تھا۔ آج کل میں لاہور میں کاروبار کرتا ہوں۔ آج ہماری ریل گاڑی حیدر آباد اور ملتان سے گزرے گی۔ کل صبح آٹھ نو بجے ہم لاہور پہنچیں گے۔

جان : لاہور کراچی سے چھوٹا ہے نا؟

قاسم : جی ہاں۔ لاہور پنجاب کا سب سے بڑا شہر ہے، لیکن کراچی سے بہت چھوٹا ہے۔ میرے خیال سے لاہور کی آبادی کوئی تیس چالیس لاکھ ہے۔ کراچی کی آبادی بہت بڑی ہے۔

پہلے کراچی پاکستان کا دارالحکومت تھا۔ جیسا کہ آپ کو معلوم ہے اب ہمارا دارالحکومت اسلام آباد ہے۔

جان : کیا اسلام آباد لاہور سے دور ہے؟

قاسم : جی نہیں۔ بہت زیادہ دور نہیں ریل سے کوئی پانچ گھنٹے کا راستہ ہے۔ اسلام آباد کافی نیا شہر ہے اور لاہور سے بہت چھوٹا ہے۔ کراچی پاکستان کا سب سے بڑا شہر ہے۔ لیکن میرے خیال سے لاہور سب سے دلچسپ اور خوشگوار ہے۔ اب کتنے بجے ہیں؟ دس بجے ہیں۔ تھوڑی دیر کے بعد ہم حیدر آباد پہنچیں گے۔ وہاں ہم چائے پئیں گے۔

کیوں	*kyoṅ*	why?, well	سے گزرے گی	*se guzregī*	will pass through
ملتان	*multān*	Multan (m.)	آبادی	*ābādī*	population (f.)
پہلے	*pahle*	first (of all)	چالیس	*cālīs*	forty
فوج	*fauj*	army (f.)	لاکھ	*lākh*	100,000
سپاہی	*sipāhī*	soldier, 'sepoy' (m.)	دارالحکومت	*dārul hukūmat*	capital (city) (m.)
حیدر آباد	*haidarābād*	Hyderabad (m.)	اسلام آباد	*islāmābād*	Islamabad (m.)
کاروبار	*kār o bār*	business (m.)	خوشگوار	*xušgavār*	pleasant
سے گزرنا	*se guzarnā*	to pass through	تھوڑی دیر	*thoṛī der*	a little while
			تھوڑا	*thoṛā*	a little/few

قواعد *qavā'id* Grammar

ہجے *hijje* Spelling

Note that when a verb has a stem with two syllables, for example گذرنا *guzarnā* (گذر *guzar-*) and نکلنا *nikalnā* (نکل *nikal-*), if the stem is followed by a vowel, as is the case with the future tense endings وں گا *-ūṅgā*, ے گا *-egā*, etc., the vowel in the second syllable is dropped: گذرے گا *guzregā* 'will pass', نکلے گا *niklegā* 'will go out'.

The Urdu word for 'capital' دار لحکومت *dārul hukūmat* is composed of three Arabic words: دارُ *dāru* 'home', ال *al* 'the' and حکومت *hukūmat* 'government'. After the *u* of *dāru*, the *a* of *al* is elided. Thus *daru al hukūmat* is pronounced *dārul hukūmat*.

The Urdu word for business کاروبار *kār o bār* consists of three Persian words: کار *kār* 'work', و *o* (written simply with the letter *vau*) 'and', and بار *bār* 'activity'. The Persian word و *o* 'and' is used frequently in Urdu to link two Persian words. One of the most common phrases is ہند و پاک *hind o pāk* 'India and Pakistan'.

کیوں **kyoṅ! 'why!, well!'**

کیوں *kyoṅ*? means 'why?' and like all question words immediately precedes the verb:

آپ وہاں کیوں جا رہے ہیں؟ Why are you going there?

As an exclamation at the beginning of the sentence it means 'well!'. In English 'why!' can be used in the same way:

کیوں جان صاحب۔ آپ اکیلے ہیں؟

Well/why!, John! Are you alone?

تھوڑا سا **thoṛā (sā) 'a little'; بہت سا bahut (sā) 'much'**

تھوڑا *thoṛā* means 'a little'; its plural form تھوڑے *thoṛe* means '(a) few'.

After تھوڑا and بہت (in the sense of 'much, many') the word سا *sā* (m.), سی *sī* (f.), سے *se* (m. p. and oblique) may be inserted.

مجھے تھوڑی سی چائے دیجیے	*mujhe thoṛī sī cāe dījīe*	Give me a little tea
مجھے تھوڑے سے پیسے چاہئیں	*thoṛe se paise cāhīeṅ*	(I) need a little money
یہاں بہت سی لڑکیاں ہیں	*yahāṅ bahut sī laṛkīāṅ* haiṅ	There are many girls here

If بہت (in the sense of 'much', 'many') is followed by another adjective, e.g. 'many good films' then the addition of سا 'سی' سے is obligatory:

بہت سا مزے دار کھانا	much tasty food
بہت سی اچھی فلمیں	many good films

This is because بہت مزے دار کھانا would mean 'very good food'.

The word دیر *der* means 'a short space of time', 'a while' (f.):

تھوڑی دیر کے بعد	*thoṛī der ke ba'd*	after a little while

It can also mean 'lateness'. Note the expression:

وہ ہمیشہ دیر سے آتا ہے

vuh hameša der se ātā hai

He always comes late ('with lateness')

Higher numbers 100, 1000 and millions; 'lacs and crores'

We have already met سو *sau* '100' and ہزار *hazār* '1000'. One hundred and a thousand are usually expressed ایک سو *ek sau* and ایک ہزار *ek hazār*.

اس اسکول میں ایک سو لڑکے ہیں

In this school there are a hundred boys

کراچی لندن سے کوئی پانچ ہزار میل دور ہے

Karachi is about five thousand miles from London

The next highest numeral is ایک لاکھ *ek lākh* (often spelt 'lac' in English) which is 100,000 (a hundred thousand) (m.). There is no word for 'million', which would, of course, be دس لاکھ *das lākh* (10 x 100,000). 100 *lākhs* (100 x 100,000) = ایک کروڑ *ek karoṛ* 10,000,000 (ten million). کروڑ is often spelt in English as 'crore'.

The system of lacs and crores operates throughout India and Pakistan, and was widely employed by the British during the time of the Raj. At first, this new concept of counting is rather confusing, and it is difficult for us, who are used to 'millions' to make instant conversions. Useful mnemonics are: On the lottery you can win دس لاکھ پاؤنڈ *das lākh pāūnḍ* 'a million pounds'

لندن کی آبادی کوئی ایک کروڑ ہے

landan kī ābādī koī ek karoṛ hai

The population of London is roughly 10,000,000

مشق *mašq* Exercise

9.2 Karachi to Islamabad

Look at the scheme of the railway line from Karachi to Islamabad (approximate distances are in miles), then answer the questions.

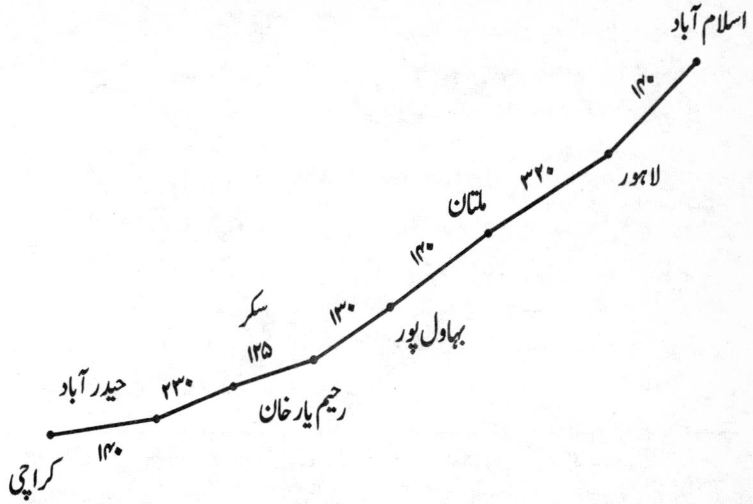

1 کراچی سے لاہور تک ریل گاڑی کن شہروں سے گزرتی ہے؟
2 کراچی کے بعد پہلا اسٹیشن کیا ہے؟
3 حیدر آباد ملتان سے کتنی دور ہے؟
4 نومبر کے مہینے میں لاہور میں کراچی سے زیادہ سردی ہوتی ہے؟
5 پاکستان کا دارالحکومت کیا ہے۔ وہ لاہور سے کتنی دور ہے؟

مکالمہ ۳ *mukālima tīn* Dialogue 3

Arrival in Lahore.

قاسم : بس! آخر ہم لاہور میں ہیں۔ آپ لوگ بہت تھکے ہوں گے، لیکن آپ کا ہوٹل یہاں سے زیادہ دور نہیں۔ ہم ٹیکسی میں بیٹھیں گے اور آپ کو ہوٹل تک پہنچائیں گے۔

جان : شکریہ قاسم صاحب۔ لیکن آپ تکلف نہ کیجیے۔ آپ بھی تھکے ہوں گے۔ آپ سیدھے گھر جائیے۔ ہم آسانی سے ہوٹل پر پہنچیں گے۔

قاسم : کوئی تکلف نہیں۔ آپ کا ہوٹل ہمارے راستے پر ہے۔ آپ دیکھیں گے کہ آپ کا ہوٹل بہت دلچسپ ہے۔ مطلب یہ کہ عمارت دلچسپ ہے۔ پہلے وہ کسی انگریز جرنیل کا

مکان تھا اور وہاں انگریز فوجی تھے۔ اب ہوٹل ہے۔ کمرے بہت بڑے اور آرامدہ ہیں۔ پرانا ہوٹل ہے لیکن میرے خیال سے ان نئے ہوٹلوں سے پرانے ہوٹل زیادہ دلچسپ ہوتے ہیں۔ آئیے، ٹیکسی میں بیٹھیے۔ ہم سیدھے آپ کے ہوٹل جائیں گے۔ وہاں کھانا کھائیے۔ خوب آرام کیجیے۔ کل صبح میں آپ لوگوں کے پاس آؤں گا۔ میں آپ کو لاہور دکھاؤں گا۔

جان : بہت شکریہ قاسم صاحب۔ لیکن آپ کو کل فرصت ہوگی؟

قاسم : جی ہاں، کل دن بھر فرصت ہوگی۔ کل ہفتہ ہے نا۔ میں ہفتے کو کام نہیں کرتا۔ عام طور سے پاکستان میں ہفتے کو چھٹی ہوتی ہے۔ دیکھیے، آپ کا ہوٹل یہاں ہے بائیں ہاتھ پر۔ دائیں ہاتھ پر مال روڈ ہے۔ یہ لاہور کا سب سے بڑا اور سب سے شاندار راستہ ہے اب آپ لوگ جائیے اور آرام کیجیے۔ ہم انشاءاللہ کل صبح ملیں گے۔

جان : شکریہ، قاسم صاحب۔ خدا حافظ۔

آخر	*āxir*	at last	آپ کے ہوٹل جائیں گے	*āp ke hotal jāenge*	we'll go to your hotel
تھکا	*thakā*	tired	خوب	*xūb*	well, fine
تھکے ہوں گے	*thake hoṅge*	you must be tired	آرام کرنا	*ārām karnā*	to rest
پہنچانا	*pahuṅcānā*	to take (someone somewhere)	دن بھر	*din bhar*	all day long
			دایاں	*dāyāṅ*	right
			بایاں	*bāyāṅ*	left
سیدھے	*sīdhe*	straight (there)	ہاتھ	*hāth*	hand (m.)
انگریز	*aṅgrez*	English person (m./f.)	دائیں ہاتھ پر	*dāeṅ hāth par*	on the right (hand side)
جرنیل	*jarnail*	general (in the army) (m.)	بائیں ہاتھ پر	*bāeṅ hāth par*	on the left (hand side)
فوجی	*faujī*	soldier, military person (m.)	انشاءاللہ	*inšallāh*	'if Allah wills'

قواعد *qavā'id* Grammar

ہجے *hijje* Spelling

انشاءاللہ *inšallāh* 'if Allah wills', بسم اللہ *bismillāh* 'in the name of Allah'.

The word اللہ *allāh* 'Allah' is made up of two Arabic words: اَل *al* 'the' and اِلَاہ *ilāh* 'a god'. After اَل *al* the *i* of *ilāh* is elided and the resulting double *lām* is indicated by the sign ّ *tašdīd*. The *alif* which represents the long vowel *ā* is conventionally written above the letter *lām*, and not, as we might expect, after it. In Urdu *allāh* is usually written اللہ with the normal '*choṭī he*'. In Arabic, and sometimes also in Urdu, the final *he* is written with the sign ٰ. اللّٰه is the normal Arabic representation of the divine name.

The phrase انشاءاللہ *inšallāh* 'God willing', very frequently used by Muslims all over the world when stating that something will be done in the future, such as 'we'll meet again', is made up of three Arabic words: اِن *in* 'if', شاءَ *ša-a* 'wished' and اللہ *allāh*. Note that the final *a* of *ša-a* 'wished' is elided before the initial *a-* of *allāh*.

Another very common Arabic expression is بسم اللہ *bismillāh* 'in the name of Allah', which is used before embarking upon any enterprise, even eating. It is composed of three Arabic words: بِ *bi* 'in', اِسم *ismi* 'name' and اللہ 'Allah'. Note how the vowels coalesce: *bi ismi allāh* → *bismillāh* بسم اللہ. Before beginning a meal it is customary to say بسم اللہ کریں *bismillāh kareṅ* 'let's do *bismillāh*'.

See if you can work out the reason for the spelling of the Arabic phrase:

لا الہ الا اللہ

> *lā ilāha illā allāh*

> 'not god except the God' There is no god except Allah

This Islamic profession of faith is found written almost everywhere–over the door of a house, in buses, taxis and so on. It is composed of the following Arabic words:

لا *lā* (also written لا) no, not; الہ *ilāha* 'god' ; الا *illā* (والا) 'except' and اللہ *allāh*. With the Arabic form of *he* it would be: لَا اِلٰهَ اِلَّا اَللّٰه

پہنچانا *pahuṅcānā* 'to take (someone) to'

The verb پہنچانا , related to پہنچنا 'to arrive', literally means 'to cause to arrive', i.e. to take to:

ہم آپ کو اسٹیشن تک پہنچائیں گے

ham āp ko isṭešan tak pahuṅcāeṅge

We'll take you ('cause you to arrive') to the station

دایاں **dāyāṅ 'right'**; بایاں **bāyāṅ 'left'**

The adjectives دایاں *dāyāṅ* 'right' and بایاں *bāyāṅ* 'left' form their plural and oblique in the same way as اچھا *acchā*, but have nasalised final vowels.

Masculine singular	دایاں	*dāyāṅ*	بایاں	*bāyāṅ*
Masculine singular/oblique plural	دائیں	*dāeṅ*	بائیں	*bāeṅ*
Feminine	دائیں	*dāīṅ*	بائیں	*bāīṅ*

The word ہاتھ *hāth* 'hand' is often added to these adjectives:

دایاں ہاتھ	*dāyāṅ hāth*	the right (hand)
دائیں ہاتھ پر	*dāeṅ hāth par*	on the right
بائیں ہاتھ کی طرف	*bāeṅ hāth kī taraf*	towards the left

The compound postposition کی طرف *kī taraf* means 'towards', 'in the direction of':

میں مال روڈ کی طرف جارہا ہوں	I'm going in the direction of Mall Road
میں آپ کی طرف آرہا ہوں	I am coming to you

Going to a place

We know now that when you go to a place, no postposition is required. In such sentences, however, the noun denoting the place is considered to be in the oblique. With a noun such as گھر this does not show, but if the place name ends in ا -ā or ہ -a, e.g. کلکتہ *kalkatta* Calcutta, ڈھاکہ *ḍhāka* Dacca (the capital of Bangladesh) or آگرا *āgrā* Agra (the city of the Taj Mahal), then the ending must change to oblique:

میں کلکتے / ڈھاکے / آگرے جا رہا ہوں

maiṅ kalkatte/ḍhāke/āgre jā rahā hūṅ

I am going to Calcutta/Dacca/Agra

If an adjective such as بڑا *baṛā* or میرا 'اس کا' آپ کا *merā, us kā, āp kā* precedes the noun or place name, then it too must become oblique:

میں کل شام کو آپ کے گھر آؤں گا

maiṅ kal šām ko āp **ke** *ghar āūṅgā*

I shall come to your house tomorrow evening

ثقافت *siqāfat* Culture

Travelling by train is an excellent way to see any country, and the rail system of India and Pakistan, originally constructed by the British, is among the most extensive in the world. The line from Karachi to Lahore follows the course of the River Indus (دریائے سندھ *daryā-e sind*); first crossing the desert via the medieval cities of Hyderabad and Multan and then emerging into the fertile plains of Panjab, the land of the 'five rivers'. 'Panjab' is derived from the two Persian words پنج *panj* 'five' and آب *āb* 'waters'. Refreshment is provided on the train or by the ubiquitous چائے والے at the main stops. The old hotels, which date from the time of the Raj, with their extensive accommodation and carefully tended gardens are always preferable to the bland 'Hiltons' and 'Intercontinentals', and offer a glimpse of how life used to be during the time of the British, who, however far they might have been from home, never neglected their own comfort!

daryā-e sind is the Persian term for the Indus, literally 'River of Sind' (the old name for India). دریا *daryā* 'river' (m.). Note that after ا *-ā*, the *izāfat -e* is written with ے.

مشقیں *mašqeṅ* Exercises

9.3 Match question and answer

The following questions relate to the three dialogues of this unit. Match them with the answers given:

سوالات

1 اسٹیشن کے پلیٹ فارم پر بھیڑ تھی؟
2 جان اور ہیلن کو پاکستان پسند آ رہا ہے؟
3 ہوٹل کے منیجر کیسے آدمی تھے۔ وہ مہربان تھے؟
4 آج کل قاسم صاحب کیا کر رہے ہیں؟
5 لاہور پہنچنے کے بعد جان اور ہیلن بہت تھکے تھے؟
6 عام طور سے پاکستان میں ہفتے کو چھٹی ہوتی ہے؟
7 لاہور کے سب سے بڑے اور شاندار راستے کا نام کیا ہے؟

جواب

1 انہیں پاکستان بہت پسند آ رہا ہے۔

2 جی ہاں، وہ کافی تھکے تھے۔

3 لاہور کے سب سے بڑے راستے کا نام مال روڈ ہے۔

4 جی ہاں، ہفتے کو چھٹی ہوتی ہے۔

5 جی ہاں، بہت بڑی بھیڑ تھی۔

6 وہ بہت مہربان تھے۔

7 لاہور میں کاروبار کر رہے ہیں۔

9.4 Complete the sentences

Complete the following sentences with the correct form of the verb indicated in brackets:

1 آپ فکر نہ کیجیے۔ میں ابھی ____________۔	(am coming)
2 قاسم اور ان کے دوست پہلے فوج میں ____________۔	(were)
3 آج شام کو گھر آیئے۔ میری بیگم قورمہ ____________۔	(will cook)
4 اتوار کو ہم عام طور سے دس بجے ____________۔	(get up)
5 عورتیں سمندر میں کبھی نہیں ____________۔	(bathe)
6 بتایئے، آپ کو کیا ____________ ہے؟	(to read)
7 اے بھائی۔ ادھر آؤ۔ مینو ____________۔	(bring!)
8 آج شام کو میں ٹیلیوژن ____________۔	(shall look at)
9 اکثر پاکستانی اُردو ____________۔	(speak)

9.5 Comparisons

The following sentences suggest comparisons. Complete them by choosing an adjective from the following: پرانا، مزے دار، چھوٹا، بڑا، مشکل، امیر :

1 کراچی لاہور سے __________ ہے۔ لیکن لاہور زیادہ __________ ہے۔

2 حامد اور اقبال اسلم کے بیٹے ہیں۔ اقبال حامد سے __________ ہے۔

3 میرے خیال سے بریانی پلاؤ سے زیادہ __________ ہے۔

4 عربی زبان اُردو سے زیادہ __________ ہے۔

5 رحیم صاحب غریب نہیں ہیں لیکن قاسم صاحب ان سے __________ ہیں۔

10 کتنا شاندار ہوٹل ہے!
What a splendid hotel!

In this unit you will learn how to:

- ask permission and make requests
- say that you are able
- express hunger and thirst
- talk about the city of Lahore and its history

مکالمہ ایک *mukālima ek* Dialogue 1

Qasim and his wife take the Smiths to their hotel.

قاسم : السلام علیکم، جان صاحب۔ کیا میں اندر آسکتا ہوں؟

جان : وعلیکم السلام۔ جی ہاں، قاسم صاحب۔ تشریف لائیے۔ کیا آپ چائے پئیں گے؟ میں چائے منگواؤں؟ یہ ہوٹل کتنا شاندار ہے! ایک کمرہ نہیں بلکہ تین کمرے ہیں۔ یہاں بیٹھنے کا کمرہ ہے اور وہاں سونے کا کمرہ۔ پیچھے ایک بہت بڑا غسل خانہ بھی ہے۔

قاسم : اور بتائیے، کل آپ کا دن کیسا تھا؟ میرے خیال سے سفر کے بعد آپ لوگ بہت تھکے تھے۔

جان : جی ہاں۔ بس ہم دن بھر ہوٹل میں تھے۔ سامنے ایک بہت خوبصورت باغیچہ ہے۔ ہر طرح کا آرام ہے۔ اور موسم کتنا اچھا ہے! لاہور میں کراچی کے مقابلہ میں زیادہ سردی ہے نا؟

قاسم : جی ہاں۔ پنجاب میں نومبر کے مہینے میں زیادہ سردی ہوتی ہے۔ لیکن دن بھر دھوپ ہوتی ہے۔ تو آپ بتائیے۔ ہم آج کیا کریں؟ کیا باہر جائیں؟

جان : اگر آپ کو فرصت ہو تو ہم لاہور کی سیر کر سکیں گے۔ کیا آپ ہمیں سب سے اہم سڑکیں اور عمارتیں دکھا سکیں گے؟

قاسم : جی ہاں۔ بڑی خوشی سے۔ اگر آپ مجھے یہ بتائیں کہ آپ خاص طور پر کیا دیکھنا چاہتے ہیں، تو میں آپ کو دکھاؤں گا۔

جان : میرے خیال سے ہم بادشاہی مسجد سے شروع کریں۔ کہتے ہیں کہ بادشاہی مسجد دنیا کی سب سے بڑی مسجد ہے نا؟

قاسم : مجھے یقین نہیں ہے، لیکن سب سے بڑی مسجدوں میں سے ایک ہو گی۔ کم سے کم دہلی کی جامع مسجد سے بڑی ہے۔ ٹھیک ہے، جلدی چائے پئیں اور چلیں۔

اندر *andar*	inside, in
آسکتا ہوں *ā saktā hūṅ*	can I come?
سکنا *saknā*	to be able
چائے منگواؤں *cāe maṅgvāūṅ*	shall I order tea?
بلکہ *balki*	but, even
بیٹھنے کا کمرہ *baiṭhne kā kamra*	sitting room (m.)
سونا *sonā*	to sleep
سونے کا کمرہ *sone kā kamra*	bedroom (m.)
پیچھے *pīche*	behind
غسل خانہ *ğusal-xāna*	bathroom (m.)
دن بھر *din bhar*	all day long
سامنے *sāmne*	in front
باغیچہ *bāğīca*	garden (m.)
کے مقابلہ میں *ke muqābile meṅ*	compared to
دھوپ *dhūp*	sunshine (f.)
کیا کریں؟ *kyā kareṅ*	what to do?
باہر جائیں؟ *bāhar jāeṅ*	shall we go out?
اگر ۔ ہو *agar ... ho*	if it is
کی سیر کرنا *kī sair karnā*	to go around, visit
سڑک *saṛak*	street (f.)
دکھا سکیں *dikhā sakeṅ*	can you show?
بڑی خوشی سے *baṛī xušī se*	with great pleasure
اگر آپ بتائیں *agar āp batāeṅ*	if you show
چاہنا *cāhnā*	to want, love
دیکھنا چاہتے ہیں *dekhnā cāhte haiṅ*	you want to see
بادشاہی مسجد *bādšāhī masjid*	The Badshahi Mosque (in Lahore)
مسجد *masjid*	mosque (f.)
شروع کرنا *šurū' karnā*	to begin
شروع کریں *šurū' kareṅ*	let's begin
جامع مسجد *jāmi' masjid*	The Jami' Mosque (in Delhi) (f.)

قواعد *qavā'id* Grammar

سکنا *saknā* to be able

The verb سکنا *saknā* 'to be able' is always used with the stem of another verb and can never stand by itself:

میں کر سکتا ہوں	*maiṅ kar saktā hūṅ*	I can/am able to do
ہم آسکتے ہیں	*ham ā sakte haiṅ*	We can come

ہم جا سکیں گے	*ham jā sakeṅge*	We shall be able to go

کیا آپ میرے لئے ایک کام کر سکتے ہیں؟ جی ہاں، میں کر سکتا ہوں

kyā āp mere lie ek kām kar sakte haiṅ? jī hāṅ, maiṅ kar saktā hūṅ

Can you do a job for me? Yes, I can

Subjunctive mood

As well as having tenses (present, past, future), a verb is also said to have 'moods'. For example, the imperative (the form of the verb which makes commands) – go!, be!, do! – is known as a mood. Possibility, probability and doubt – 'I may do, I might do, if I were to do', etc. – are expressed by what is called the subjunctive mood.

The Urdu subjunctive is formed by adding the following endings to the stem:

میں	-وں	*-ūṅ*
تو، یہ وہ	-ے	*-e*
تم	-و	*-o*
ہم آپ، یہ، وہ	-یں	*-eṅ*

It is in fact the same as the future tense without the suffixes.: گے، گی، گا

The subjunctive indicates person and number but makes no distinction for gender:

میں کروں	*maiṅ karūṅ*	I (m./f.) may do
وہ کرے	*vuh kare*	he, she, it may do
تم کرو	*tum karo*	you (m./f.) may do
وہ کریں	*vuh kareṅ*	they (m./f.) may do

The subjunctive of کرنا is as follows:

میں کروں	*maiṅ karūṅ*	I may do
تو کرے	*tū kare*	you may do
یہ، وہ کرے	*yih, vuh kare*	he, she, it may do
ہم کریں	*ham kareṅ*	we may do
تم کرو	*tum karo*	you may do
آپ کریں	*āp kareṅ*	you may do
یہ، وہ کریں	*yih, vuh kareṅ*	they may do

The subjunctive of ہونا is slightly irregular:

میں ہوں	*maiṅ hūṅ*	I may be
تو ہو	*tū ho*	you may be
یہ، وہ ہو	*yih, vuh ho*	he, she, it may be
ہم ہوں	*ham hoṅ*	we may be
تم ہو	*tum ho*	you may be
آپ ہوں	*āp hoṅ*	you may be
یہ، وہ ہوں	*yih, vuh hoṅ*	they may be

Use of the subjunctive

The subjunctive has various uses. Here are some of the most important.

Let us do! Shall/may we do?

چلیں، ہم چائے پیئیں

caleṅ, ham cāe pīeṅ

Come on, let's have tea ('let us go, let us drink tea')

کیا میں اندر آسکوں؟

kyā maiṅ andar ā sakūṅ?

May I come in(side)?

کیا میں آپ کی کتاب پڑھوں؟

kyā maiṅ āp kī kitāb paṛhūṅ?

May I read your book?

آج شام کو ایک فلم دیکھیں؟

āj šām ko ek film dekheṅ?

Shall we see a film this evening?

In 'if' ('conditional') sentences

In the sentence 'if you come with me, I shall show you the city', the condition 'if' is said to be 'open', because it is not certain whether you will come or not. In Urdu, the verb 'come' is put into the subjunctive. The second part of the sentence is introduced by تو *to* 'then':

اگر آپ میرے ساتھ آئیں تو میں آپ کو شہر دکھاؤں گا

agar āp mere sāth āeṅ, to maiṅ āp ko šahr dikhāūṅgā

If you come with me (then) I shall show you the city

اگر آپ کو فرصت ہو تو ہم لاہور کی سیر کریں گے

agar āp ko fursat ho, to ham lāhaur kī sair kareṅge

If you (should) have the time, (then) we'll walk around Lahore

سیر *sair* means 'a stroll, a walk, going around, visit' (f.). The phrase verb کی سیر کرنا *kī sair karnā* can be translated as 'to stroll around, to visit':

ہم آج کل پاکستان کی سیر کر رہے ہیں

ham āj kal pākistān kī sair kar rahe haiṅ

These days we're visiting/touring Pakistan

کل صبح ہم بادشاہی مسجد کی سیر کریں گے

kal subh ham bādšāhī masjid kī sair kareṅge

Tomorrow morning we'll visit/take a trip to the Badshahi Mosque

Negative of the subjunctive

The subjunctive always forms its negative with نہ *na*:

اگر سردی نہ ہو تو ہم سمندر کے پاس جائیں گے

agar sardī na ho, to ham samandar ke pās jāeṅge

If it's not cold, then we'll go to the seaside

بلکہ *balki* 'but'; نہ صرف بلکہ *na sirf ... balki* 'not only but also'

بلکہ *balki* means 'but' in the sense of 'even', 'not only but also':

ہمارے ہوٹل میں ایک کمرہ نہیں بلکہ تین کمرے ہیں

hamāre hotal meṅ ek kamra nahīṅ balki tīn kamre haiṅ

In our hotel there is not just one (but) there are three rooms

بھر *bhar* 'all through, all over'

بھر *bhar* following the word to which it refers, means 'all through, all over':

رات بھر	all through the night	دن بھر	all day long
دنیا بھر	all over the world	شہر بھر	all over the city

کے مقابلے میں *ke muqābile meṅ* 'in comparison with'

کے مقابلے میں like سے 'than' can also be used to make comparisons:

کراچی کے مقابلے میں دہلی میں زیادہ گرمی ہوتی ہے

karācī ke muqābile meṅ dihlī meṅ ziyāda garmī hotī hai

In comparison with Karachi it is (usually) hotter in Delhi

سورج sūraj 'the sun' (m.) دھوپ dhūp 'sunshine' (f.). (سورج is the sun itself; دھوپ is 'sunshine'):

سورج پانچ بجے اٹھتا ہے اور چھے بجے ڈوبتا ہے

sūraj pāṅc baje uṭhtā hai aur che baje ḍūbtā hai

The sun rises at five and sets at six

نومبر میں دن بھر دھوپ ہوتی ہے

navambar meṅ din bhar dhūp hotī hai

In November it's sunny (there's sunshine) all day long

'To sunbathe' is دھوپ کھانا 'to eat (!) sun':

پاکستان میں عام طور پر لوگ ساحل سمندر پر دھوپ نہیں کھاتے

pākistān meṅ 'ām taur par log sāhil-e samandar par dhūp nahīṅ khāte

In Pakistan people do not usually sunbathe on the beach

چاہنا cāhnā 'to want, wish, love'

The verb چاہنا, to which چاہیے is related, means 'to want': آپ کیا چاہتے ہیں؟ 'what do you want' (the equivalent of آپ کو کیا چاہیے؟).

It may be used with the infinitive meaning 'to want/wish to do':

میں لاہور جانا چاہتا ہوں	I want to go to Lahore
میری بیٹی سونا چاہتی ہے	My daughter wishes to sleep

شروع کرنا، شروع ہونا šurū' karnā, šurū' honā 'to begin'

شروع *šurū'* is a noun meaning 'beginning' (m.). The phrase verb شروع کرنا *šurū' karnā* means 'to begin (something)'; with the infinitive it means 'to begin to do, start doing':

ہم اب کام شروع کریں گے

ham ab kām šurū' kareṅge

we'll begin work now

بادشاہی مسجد سے شروع کریں

bādšāhī masjid se šurū' kareṅ

Let's start with the Badshahi Mosque

شروع ہونا *šurū' honā* means 'to begin/start' (as in 'my work begins at nine'):

میرا کام نو بجے شروع ہوتا ہے
merā kām nau baje šurū' hotā hai
My work begins (usually) at nine o'clock

جلدی کرو۔ فلم ابھی شروع ہو رہی ہے
jaldī karo! film abhī šurū' ho rahī hai
Hurry up! The film's starting

مکالمہ دو **mukālima do Dialogue 2**

Qasim shows John and Helen around the old city of Lahore.

جان : اچھا تو یہ بادشاہی مسجد ہے۔ واقعی بہت وسیع مسجد ہے۔ قاسم صاحب بتائیے۔ یہ کس کی مسجد ہے؟

قاسم : یہ اورنگ زیب کی مسجد ہے۔ آپ کو یاد ہوگا کہ اورنگ زیب شاہ جہاں کے صاحب زادے تھے۔ اور شاہ جہاں کی سب سے مشہور عمارت تاج محل ہے۔ تاج محل آگرے میں ہے۔ وہ دونوں مغل بادشاہ تھے اور مغلوں کے زمانے میں تین شہر، یعنی لاہور، دہلی اور آگرہ، سب سے اہم پائے تخت تھے۔

جان : کیا ہم اندر جا سکتے ہیں؟

قاسم : ضرور۔ کوئی مشکل نہیں۔ اگر آپ کی بیگم سر پر چادر یا اسکارف پہنیں تو اچھا ہوگا۔

جان : اس کا مطلب یہ ہے کہ خواتین مسجد میں داخل ہو سکتی ہیں؟

قاسم : کیوں نہیں؟ اسلام کے اعتبار سے سب انسان برابر ہیں۔ دیکھیے دروازہ وہاں ہے۔ چلیں۔ اندر جائیں؟

ہیلن : کتنی شاندار مسجد ہے! وہاں آٹھ اونچے مینار ہیں اور تین سفید گمبد۔ دیواروں کا رنگ لال ہے۔ اور کتنا صاف ستھرا ہے! لیکن یہاں بہت کم لوگ ہیں۔

قاسم : جی ہاں، لیکن نماز کے وقت بہت بڑی بھیڑ ہوگی۔ یہاں ایک لاکھ آدمی نماز پڑھ سکتے ہیں۔

ہیلن : کیا میں ایک تصویر کھینچ سکتی ہوں؟

قاسم : ضرور۔ لیکن یہاں سے مت کھینچیے۔ سورج آپ کے سامنے ہے۔ اگر آپ اُس طرف جائیں تو اچھی تصویر نکلے گی۔

وسیع	*vasī'*	vast
اورنگ زیب	*aurangzeb*	Emperor Aurangzeb
آپ کو یاد ہوگا	*āp ko yād hogā*	you probably recall
شاہجہاں	*šāhjahān*	Emperor Shahjahan
صاحبزادہ	*sāhibzāda*	son (m.)
تاج محل	*tāj mahal*	Taj Mahal (m.)
آگرا	*āgrā*	Agra (m.)
مغل	*muğal*	Mughal (dynasty) (m.)
پائے تخت	*pāe taxt*	(imperial) capital (m.)
سر	*sar*	head (m.)
چادر	*cādar*	shawl (m.)
اسکارف	*iskārf*	scarf (m.)
پہننا	*pahinnā*	to put on (clothes)
خواتین	*xavātīn*	ladies (f.p.)
میں داخل ہونا	*meṅ dāxil honā*	to enter
اسلام	*islām*	Islam (m.)
کے اعتبار سے	*ke i'tibār se*	from the point of view of
اعتبار	*i'tibār*	point of view (m.)
انسان	*insān*	human being (m.)
برابر	*barābar*	equal
دروازہ	*darvāza*	door (m.)
اونچا	*ūṅcā*	high
مینار	*mīnār*	minaret (m.)
سفید	*safed*	white
گنبد	*gumbad*	dome (m.)
رنگ	*rang*	colour (m.)
دیوار	*dīvār*	wall (f.)
صاف	*sāf*	clean
صاف ستھرا	*sāf-suthrā*	spotlessly clean
کے وقت	*ke vaqt*	at the time of
تصویر	*tasvīr*	picture, photo (f.)
تصویر کھینچنا	*tasvīr khaiṅcnā*	to take a photo
سورج	*sūraj*	sun (m.)
کے سامنے	*ke sāmne*	in front of
اُس طرف	*us taraf*	over there
تصویر نکلے گی	*tasvīr niklegī*	the photo will come out

قواعد *qavā'id* Grammar

ہجے *hijje* Spelling

Note the spelling of پائے تخت *pāe taxt* 'capital', which is composed of two Persian words: پائے *pāe* 'foot' and تخت *taxt* 'throne'. پائے تخت is a much grander word than دارالحکومت as it has royal (rather than mere government) connotations.

صاحبزادہ **sāhibzāda 'son'**; صاحبزادی **sāhibzādī 'daughter'**

The Persian suffix زادہ *zāda* (f. زادی *zādī*) means 'born of'. صاحبزادہ literally means 'born of a *sāhib*', hence 'son'; its feminine counterpart is صاحبزادی 'daughter'. These words are frequently used in polite conversation:

• کیا آپ کے صاحبزادے بھی تشریف لائیں گے؟

kyā āp ke sāhibzāde bhī tašrīf lāeṅge?

Will your son (plural of respect) be coming as well?

خواتین **xavātīn 'ladies'; broken 'Arabic' plurals**

We have already met the word خاتون *xātūn*, a polite word for 'lady'. The plural is خواتین *xavātīn*, which is its normal Arabic plural form.

Arabic forms plurals by altering the internal structure of the word. These are known as 'broken plurals', many of which have been taken into Urdu from Arabic.

The main letters of the word *xātūn* are خ *x*, ت *t*, ن *n*. The plural is formed by keeping the main letters in their original order, but by changing the vowels:

XāTūN; XavāTīN. Another common example is مضمون *mazmūn* 'subject'; مضامین *mazāmīn* 'subjects' (main letters MZMN). Broken plurals are best learnt separately as they are encountered. Broken plurals do not take case endings:

خواتین کو بتائیے *xavātīn ko batāīe* 'tell the ladies'

میں داخل ہونا **meṅ dāxil honā 'to enter'**

داخل *dāxil* means 'entering'. The phrase verb میں داخل ہونا *meṅ dāxil honā* means 'to enter (into)' ('to be entering'):

خواتین مسجد میں داخل ہو سکتی ہیں

xavātīn masjid meṅ dāxil ho saktī haiṅ

Ladies can enter a mosque

مکالمہ ۳ **mukālima tīn Dialogue 3**

Qasim takes the Smiths to Anarkali Bazaar, and starts feeling hungry.

ہیلن : بادشاہی مسجد واقعی بہت خوبصورت تھی اور اس علاقے کی سڑکیں کتنی دلچسپ ہیں!
معلوم ہوتا ہے کہ ہم الف لیلا کی کہانیاں دیکھ رہے ہیں۔ اگر میں آنکھیں بند کروں تو پرانا
بغداد نظر آتا ہے۔

قاسم : کیا آپ کو لاہور کراچی سے زیادہ پسند ہے؟

ہیلن : یہ میں نہیں کہوں گی۔ اتنا میں کہہ سکتی ہوں کہ بالکل مختلف ہے۔

قاسم : اچھا تو آگے چلیں اور دوپہر کے کھانے سے پہلے میں آپ کو پرانا شہر دکھاؤں گا۔ ایک بہت مشہور بازار ہے۔ اس کا نام انار کلی ہے۔ انار کلی مغلوں کے زمانے میں ایک بچاری لڑکی تھی۔ وہ بہت مشہور گانے والی اور ناچنے والی تھی لیکن اس کی زندگی اُداس تھی۔ اس کی قبر پرانے قلعے میں ہے۔ اگر آپ انار کلی تک پیدل جانا چاہیں تو ہم پرانے شہر کو پار کریں گے۔ آپ کو سب کچھ نظر آئے گا۔

ہیلن : جی ہاں۔ پیدل چلیں۔ موسم بہت پیارا ہے اور مجھے نہ بھوک ہے نہ پیاس۔ مجھے صرف اِس قدیم اور خوبصورت شہر سے محبت ہے۔

قاسم : ٹھیک ہے۔ پیدل چلیں، لیکن ایک گھنٹے کے بعد بھوک ضرور ہو گی۔ انار کلی میں ایک بہت اچھا ریستراں جانتا ہوں۔ معاف کیجئے۔ مجھے بھی پُرانی عمارتوں سے شوق ہے لیکن اس دنیا میں روٹی بھی اہم چیز ہوتی ہے۔

انار کلی	*anārkalī*	Anarkali Bazaar (f.)	گانا	*gānā*	to sing
معلوم ہوتا ہے	*ma'lūm hotā hai*	it seems	گانے والا	*gānevālā, -vālī*	singer (m./f.)
الف لیلا	*alf lailā*	the Arabian Nights (m.)	ناچنا	*nācnā*	to dance
کہانی	*kahānī*	story (f.)	ناچنے والا / والی	*nācnevālā, -vālī*	dancer (m./f.)
آنکھ	*āṅkh*	eye (f.)	اداس	*udās*	sad
بند کرنا	*band karnā*	to close, shut	قبر	*qabr*	grave, tomb (f.)
بغداد	*baǧdād*	Baghdad (m.)	قلعہ	*qil'a*	fort (m.)
کہنا	*kahnā*	to say	پیدل	*paidal*	on foot
مختلف	*muxtalif*	different	کو پار کرنا	*ko pār karnā*	to cross
آگے	*āge*	forward, on(wards)	بھوک	*bhūk*	hunger (f.)
آگے چلیں	*āge caleṅ*	let's go on	پیاس	*piyās*	thirst (f.)
بچارا	*bicārā*	poor, miserable	مجھے بھوک / پیاس ہے	*mujhe bhūk/piyās hai*	I feel hungry/thirsty
			قدیم	*qadīm*	ancient
			محبت	*muhabbat*	love (f.)

سے محبت کرنا	*se muhabbat honā*	to be in love with	شوق	*šauq*	fondness, interest (m.)

قواعد qavā'id Grammar

مجھے معلوم ہوتا ہے (mujhe) ma'lūm hotā hai 'it seems (to me)'

مجھے معلوم ہوتا ہے *mujhe ma'lūm hotā hai* 'it seems to me' must not be confused with مجھے معلوم *mujhe ma'lūm hai* 'I know':

مجھے معلوم ہوتا ہے کہ کل موسم اچھا ہوگا

mujhe ma'lūm hotā hai ki kal mausam acchā hogā

It seems to me that the weather will be fine tomorrow

The phrase can be translated into English as 'I think that':

مجھے معلوم ہوتا ہے کہ وہ ہمارے ہاں نہیں آئیں گے

I think that he will not come to our place

الف لیلا alf lailā The Arabian Nights

The Arabic word الف *alf* means 'one thousand'; لیلا *lailā* means 'night (s)'. The full Arabic title of the famous work, composed in Baghdad in the 14th and 15th centuries, is الف لیلا و لیلا *alf lailā va lailā* 'One Thousand Nights and (one) Night'.

More uses of the suffix والا -vālā

Added to the oblique infinitive, the suffix والا *vālā* (f. والی *vālī*) expresses someone who performs the action:

ناچنا	*nācnā* 'to dance'	ناچنے والی	*nācnevālī* 'dancer/dancing girl'
گانا	*gānā* 'to sing'	گانے والا	*gānevālā* 'singer'

It can also mean 'about to do, going to do' something:

میں لاہور جانے والا ہوں

maiṅ lāhaur jānevālā hūṅ

I'm about to go Lahore

بلقیس صاحبہ، آپ کیا کرنے والی ہیں؟

bilqīs sāhiba, āp kyā karnevālī haiṅ?

What are you going to do, Bilqis?

لاہور جانے والی گاڑی

lāhaur jānevālī gāṛī

A train bound for Lahore

کو پار کرنا **ko pār karnā** 'to cross over'

The object of the phrase verb پار کرنا *pār karnā* 'to cross' takes کو ko:

شہر کو پار کریں گے	*šahr ko pār kareṅge*	We shall cross the city
سڑک کو پار کیجیے	*saṛak ko pār kījie*	Cross the street!

Note راستہ is a (main) road; سڑک is a street in a town.

محبت *muhabbat* 'love'

The word محبت *muhabbat* (more correctly pronounced *mahabbat*) means 'love' (f.). The phrase verb سے محبت کرنا *se muhabbat karnā* ('to do love from') means 'to be in love with', 'to love'. The words میں تجھ سے محبت کرتا ہوں *maiṅ tujh se muhabbat kartā hūṅ* 'I am in love with you' form a favourite cliché of Hindi film songs. Note that in this phrase the familiar pronoun تو / تجھ *tū/tujh* is used.

محبت may also be used with ہونا:

مجھے تجھ سے محبت ہے

mujhe tujh se muhabbat hai

I love you ('to me from you is love')

مجھے اس خوبصورت شہر سے محبت ہے

mujhe is xūbsūrat šahr se muhabbat hai

I love this beautiful city

بھوک **bhūk** 'hunger' (f.); پیاس **piyās** 'thirst' (f.)

'I am hungry/thirsty' is expressed in Urdu as:

مجھے بھوک ہے	*mujhe bhūk hai*	'to me hunger is'
مجھے پیاس ہے	*mujhe piyās hai*	'to me thirst is'

شوق šauq 'fondness', 'great interest'

شوق *šauq* means 'fondness for', 'great interest in' (m.). The construction in which it is used is the same as that of دلچسپی *dilcaspī*.

آپ کو موسیقی سے شوق ہے؟

āp ko mūsīqī se šauq hai?

Are you fond of music? (to you is there fondness...?)

موسیقی *mūsīqī* 'music' (f.)

انارکلی anārklī

انارکلی (انار *anār* 'pomegranate' (m.), کلی *kalī* 'bud' (f.) is the name of one of Lahore's most famous bazaars. It is called after Anarkali, who was a dancing girl in the Emperor Akbar's harem (حرم *haram* 'private enclosure'). When Akbar's son, Jahangir fell in love with her, the poor girl was walled up alive in the Lahore Fort.

ثقافت siqāfat Culture

Lahore, the favourite residence of Emperor Jahangir, is one of the most impressive cities of Pakistan. In the 17th century, along with Delhi and Agra, it had great political and cultural importance, a reputation which it still enjoys. Its finest building is undoubtedly the Badshahi Mosque, built by Aurangzeb in 1674, one of the largest and grandest mosques in the world. But its old bazaars and modern thoroughfares, like the British-built Mall, offer many attractions to visitors. In Pakistan, mosques may be visited by anyone. All that is required is a certain sobriety in dress, and ladies are asked to wear a headscarf. There is usually no restriction on photography, but it is always polite to ask. The language of Lahore is Panjabi, but, as almost everywhere in Pakistan, everyone speaks Urdu as well as their mother tongue.

The rulers of the Mughal (مغل *muğal*) dynasty of India, whose presence you can hardly escape when visiting the subcontinent, ruled mainly from Delhi between 1525 and 1857. Lahore and Agra, the city of the Taj Mahal, also served as their capitals at various times, They claimed their descent from the Mongol dynasties of Genghis Khan (چنگیز خان *cingīz xān*) and Tamberlane (تیمور *taimur*), and chose grand Persian titles for themselves.

The first six Mughals, whose names you will repeatedly hear, were بابر Bābur (1526–30), the founder of the dynasty; ہمایوں Humāyūn (1530–56) (tomb in Delhi); اکبر Akbar 'Greatest' (1556–1605) (tomb neaar Agra); جہانگیر Jahāngīr 'World Conqueror' (1605–26) (tomb near Lahore); شاہجہاں Shāhjahān 'King of the World' (1626–66) (tomb in the Taj Mahal at Agra) and اورنگ زیب Aurangzeb 'Adorning the Crown' (1666–1707) (grave near Aurangabad, Central India).

مشقیں *mašqeṅ* Exercises

10.1 Dialogue

You go to travel agency in Lahore. Take your part in the following dialogue:

Say that you want to go by train to Islamabad next Thursday : You

اچھا' آپ صبح یا دوپہر کے بعد جانا چاہتے ہیں!

Ask at what time the train departs from Lahore and arrives in Islamabad : You

صبح کی گاڑی لاہور سے ۹ بجے روانہ ہوتی ہے اور ۱۱ بجے پہنچتی ہے

Ask if you can easily get a hotel, and how much it will be for one night : You

جی ہاں۔ کوئی مشکل نہیں۔ ایک رات ۳۰۰ روپے ہوں گے

Ask what the most intersting things in Islamabad are : You

وہاں دنیا کی سب سے بڑی مسجد ہے۔ آپ وہاں سے کب واپس آئیں گے ؟

Say that you have to come back to Lahore on Sunday, because next week you are going by air to Delhi : You

10.2 Complete the sentences

Complete the sentences with one of the verbs or verbal phrases given in the list:

آتی ہے کھائیں ہوتی ہے ٹھہریں گے رہتے ہیں منگواؤں سکتے ہیں

1 کیا آپ میرے لئے ایک کام کر __________ ؟

2 حامد کو عربی __________

3 مجھے بھوک ہے۔ چلیں کھانا __________ ؟

4 عام طور سے نومبر میں دھوپ ________

5 کراچی میں آپ ہوٹل میں ________؟

6 آیئے' بیٹھئے۔ کیا میں چائے ________؟

7 ہم لوگ ایک خوبصورت گھر میں ________

10.3 آپ کو پاکستان کے بارے میں کیا معلوم ہے؟ What do you know about Pakistan?

During their stay in Pakistan, John and Helen have learnt a lot about the country. Read the questions out loud and say whether their anwers are true or false:

سوالات

1 پاکستان کا دارالحکومت کیا ہے؟

2 پاکستان میں لوگوں کو ساحلِ سمندر پر دھوپ کھانا پسند ہے؟

3 لاہور کہاں ہے؟

4 خواتین مسجد میں داخل ہوسکتی ہیں؟

5 جہانگیر اکثر پنجاب میں تھے

6 عام طور سے پاکستانی اردو بول سکتے ہیں؟

7 لاہور کراچی سے بہت پرانا شہر ہے؟

جواب

1 پاکستان کا دارالحکومت لاہور ہے

2 جی ہاں' ان کو دھوپ کھانا بہت پسند ہے

3 لاہور پنجاب میں ہے۔

4 خواتین مسجد میں داخل نہیں ہوسکتی ہیں

5 جی ہاں وہ اکثر پنجاب میں تھے

6 پاکستانی صرف پنجابی بول سکتے ہیں

7 جی ہاں لاہور کراچی سے پرانا ہے

11 میں آپ کو اپنا گاؤں دکھاؤں گا
I'll show you my village

In this unit you will learn how to:

- say what you used to do and were doing
- talk about the weather
- say the points of the compass
- express dates in other ways

مکالمہ ایک *mukalīma ek* Dialogue 1

Qasim proposes a visit to his village in the Panjab countryside.

قاسم : کیوں جان صاحب۔ آپ یہاں اکیلے ہیں؟ ہیلن صاحبہ نہیں ہیں کیا؟

جان : جی ہاں۔ میں سوچ رہا تھا کہ میں دو تین خط لکھوں گا۔ آج صبح میری بیگم انار کلی میں گھوم رہی ہیں۔ وہ ہوٹل کے مینیجر کی بیگم کے ساتھ کپڑے خرید رہی ہیں۔ یہ کمرہ اتنا آرامدہ ہے کہ میں سوچ رہا تھا کہ میں اپنی بیوی کی غیر موجودگی سے پورا فائدہ اٹھاؤں گا۔ میں بازاروں سے بہت ڈرتا ہوں۔

قاسم : جی ہاں۔ ہیلن صاحبہ مجھ سے کہہ رہی تھیں کہ آپ کو دُکانوں میں گھومنا پسند نہیں ہے۔

جان : یہ سچ ہے۔ کیا میں چائے منگواؤں؟

قاسم : بہت اچھا خیال ہے۔ چائے پیئں اور باتیں کریں۔ جان صاحب میں سوچ رہا تھا کہ چونکہ آپ لوگ لاہور میں ہیں، تو میں آپ کو اپنا گاؤں دکھاؤں گا۔ میرا گاؤں شیخوپورہ کی طرف ہے۔ بچپن میں میں وہاں رہتا تھا۔ مجھے بچپن ہمیشہ یاد آتا ہے۔

جان : اچھا۔ آپ گاؤں کے رہنے والے ہیں؟

قاسم : جی ہاں، اکثر پاکستانی گاؤں میں رہتے ہیں اور ہمارا بچپن کتنا اچھا تھا۔ ہم کھیتوں میں کھیلتے تھے، اچھے سے اچھا کھانا کھاتے تھے۔ اُس زمانے میں سب کچھ اچھا ہوتا تھا۔ ممکن ہے کہ ہم پرسوں چلیں۔ ہمارا گاؤں زیادہ دور نہیں ہے۔

جان : اچھا، ہم جانے کا انتظام ضرور کریں گے۔ بتایئے، قاسم صاحب، آپ لوگ کل شام کو کیا کر رہے تھے؟ آپ کا ٹیلیفون بج رہا تھا۔ معلوم ہوتا تھا کہ آپ گھر پر نہیں تھے۔

قاسم : جی ہاں۔ ہم ایک محفل میں تھے۔ میری بیگم وہاں گا رہی تھیں۔

جان : اچھا۔ آپ کی بیگم گاتی ہیں؟

قاسم : جی ہاں۔ کبھی گھر پر آیئے اور سنیئے۔

اپنا	apnā	my own	رہتا تھا	rahtā thā	I used to live
گاؤں	gāoṅ	village (m.)	کھیت	khet	field (m.)
اکیلا	akelā	alone	کھیلتے تھے	khelte the	we used to play
سوچ رہا تھا	soc rahā thā	I was thinking	اچھے سے اچھا	acche se achhā	the very best
خط	xat	letter (m.)	کھاتے تھے	khāte the	we used to eat
گھومنا	ghūmnā	to stroll, go round	ممکن ہے کہ	mumkin hai ki	it's possible that
کپڑے	kapṛe	clothes (m.p.)	پرسوں	parsoṅ	the day before yesterday
خریدنا	xarīdnā	to buy	کا انتظام کرنا	kā intizām karnā	to arrange
اپنی بیوی	apnī bīvī	my own wife	کر رہے تھے	kar rahe the	were you doing?
غیر موجودگی	ğair maujūdagī	absence (f.)	بجنا	bajnā	to ring
ڈرنا	ḍarnā	to fear, be afraid of	بج رہا تھا	baj rahā thā	was ringing
سے ڈرتے ہیں	se ḍarte haiṅ	you are afraid of	معلوم ہوتا تھا	ma'lūm hotā thā	it seemed
سے باتیں کرنا	se bāteṅ karnā	to chat to	محفل	mahfil	party (f.)
شیخوپورا	šaixūpūra	Shaikhpura (town near Lahore)	گا رہی تھیں	gā rahī thīṅ	she was singing

قواعد *qavā'id* Grammar

Past habitual and past continuous tenses: 'I used to do, I was doing'

The past tense counterparts of the present habitual and present continuous are known as the past habitual 'I used to do (once upon a time)' and the past continuous 'I was doing'. They are formed by substituting the past tense of ہونا for the present:

میں کرتا ہوں	*maiṅ kartā hūṅ*	I (m.) do
میں کرتا تھا	*maiṅ kartā thā*	I (m.) used to do
میں کر رہا ہوں	*maiṅ kar rahā hūṅ*	I (m.) am doing
میں کر رہا تھا	*maiṅ kar rahā thā*	I (m.) was doing

The past habitual and past continuous of کرنا are, respectively, as follows:

	Masculine		**Feminine**	
میں کرتا تھا	*maiṅ kartā thā*	کرتی تھی	*kartī thī*	I used to do
تو کرتا تھا	*tū kartā thā*	کرتی تھی	*kartī thī*	you used to do
یہ' وہ کرتا تھا	*yih, vuh kartā thā*	کرتی تھی	*kartī thī*	he, she, it used to do
ہم کرتے تھے	*ham karte the*	کرتے تھے	*karte the*	we used to do
تم کرتے تھے	*tum karte the*	کرتی تھیں	*kartī thīṅ*	you used to do
آپ کرتے تھے	*āp karte the*	کرتی تھیں	*kartī thīṅ*	you used to do
یہ' وہ کرتے تھے	*yih, vuh karte the*	کرتی تھیں	*kartī thīṅ*	they used to do

Masculine

میں کر رہا تھا	*maiṅ kar rahā thā*	I was doing
تو کر رہا تھا	*tū kar rahā thā*	you were doing
یہ' وہ کر رہا تھا	*yih, vuh kar rahā thā*	he, it was doing
ہم کر رہے تھے	*ham kar rahe the*	we were doing
تم کر رہے تھے	*tum kar rahe the*	you were doing
آپ کر رہے تھے	*āp kar rahe the*	you were doing
یہ' وہ کر رہے تھے	*yih, vuh kar rahe the*	they were doing

Feminine

میں کر رہی تھی	*maiṅ kar rahī thī*	I was doing
تو کر رہی تھی	*tū kar rahī thī*	you were doing
یہ' وہ کر رہی تھی	*yih, vuh kar rahī thī*	she, it was doing
ہم کر رہے تھے	*ham kar rahe the*	we were doing
تم کر رہی تھیں	*tum kar rahī thīṅ*	you were doing
آپ کر رہی تھیں	*āp kar rahī thīṅ*	you were doing
یہ' وہ کر رہی تھیں	*yih, vuh kar rahī thīṅ*	they were doing

The negative is formed by placing نہیں *nahīṅ* before the verb:

میں نہیں کرتا تھا	*maiṅ nahīṅ kartā thā*	I used not to do
وہ نہیں کر رہی تھی	*vuh nahīṅ kar rahī thī*	she was not doing

English tends to be rather imprecise in the use of its tenses, and 'I didn't work' can mean either 'I did not work at one particular time' or 'I used not to work'. Urdu is very precise, and when English 'I did' implies I 'used to do', the past habitual must always be used.

The past habitual and past continuous are used in much the same way as their English counterparts:

بچپن میں میں گاؤں میں رہتا تھا' لیکن اب میں لاہور میں رہتا ہوں

In my childhood I used to live in a village, but now I live in Lahore

میری بیگم ہر روز پکاتی تھیں لیکن اب انہیں پکانے سے کوئی دلچسپی نہیں

My wife used to cook every day, but now she has no interest in cooking

بلقیس اور ہیلن بازار میں کپڑے خرید رہی تھیں

Bilqis and Helen were buying clothes in the bazaar

میں سوچ رہا تھا کہ میں دو تین خط لکھوں گا

maiṅ soc rahā thā ki maiṅ do tīn xat likhūṅgā

I thought ('was thinking') that I would write a couple of letters

In the last sentence note the use of the future tense in the second part of the sentence, where the words are reported in the form in which they were originally expressed. In Urdu you say: 'I was thinking that 'I will write a couple of letters''. In English, however 'will' changes to 'would' to match the past tense used in the first part of the sentence:

وہ کہہ رہے تھے کہ وہ دو بجے آئیں گے

vuh kah rahe the ki vuh do baje āeṅge

He was saying that he would ('will') come at two

کہنا **kahnā** 'to say, tell'

The verb کہنا *kahnā* means 'to say'. In Urdu when you say something to someone, 'to' is expressed by سے. Note 'to say to' is usually 'to tell' in English:

وہ مجھ سے کہہ رہی تھیں کہ آپ کو بازار پسند نہیں ہے

She was telling ('saying to') me that you don't like the bazaar

آپ مجھ سے کہہ رہے تھے کہ آپ لاہور جائیں گے

You were telling me that you would ('will') go to Lahore

اپنا *apnā* 'one's own'

In English 'he was going out with his wife' can mean with his own wife, or with someone else's wife. In Urdu, when the possessive adjective ('my, you, his, their', etc.) refers to the subject of the sentence : '*I* read *my* book; *she* combs *her* hair' where *I* and *my*, *she* and *her* are the same person, the possessive adjective اپنا *apnā* 'one's own' must be used for all persons:

میں اپنی کتاب پڑھ رہا تھا

maiṅ apnī kitāb paṛh rahā thā

I was reading my (own) book

وہ اپنی بیوی کے ساتھ پاکستان جا رہا تھا

He was going to Pakistan with his (own) wife

The sentence وہ اس کی بیوی کے ساتھ جا رہا تھا would mean he was going with his (i.e. someone else's) wife.

بات *bāt* 'matter'; سے باتیں کرنا *se bāteṅ karnā* 'to chat to'

بات means 'thing' in the sense of 'matter, affair'. چیز *cīz* is a tangible thing.

کیا بات ہے؟	What is the matter?
کوئی بات نہیں	It's no matter/it doesn't matter
اچھی بات ہے	Very well ('it's good thing')

میں ابھی چلتا ہوں۔ پانچ بجے واپس آؤں گا۔ اچھی بات ہے

I'm going now. I'll be back at five. Very well

بچوں کی چیزیں ہر جگہ بکھری پڑی ہیں

The children's things are scattered everywhere

بات may also mean 'something said', 'a word':

اُس آدمی کی بات سچ نہیں معلوم ہوتی ہے

That person doesn't seem to be telling the truth ('his word does not seem true')

The phrase verb سے باتیں کرنا means 'converse/chat with':

وہ مجھ سے باتیں کر رہا تھا	He was chatting with me
آیئے، تشریف رکھیے۔ ہم باتیں کریں گے	Come and sit down; we'll have a chat

اچھے سے اچھا **acche se acchā** 'the very best'

The phrase اچھے سے اچھا 'better than good' means 'the very best':

گاؤں میں اچھے سے اچھا کھانا کھاتے تھے

In the village we used to get the very best of food

ممکن ہے کہ ***mumkin hai ki*** 'it is possible that'

We have seen that the subjunctive mainly expresses probability, possibility and doubt: 'I may/might do'. Therefore it is used after the phrase ممکن ہے کہ 'it is possible that':

ممکن ہے کہ کل موسم اچھا ہو

It is possible that the weather will ('may') be fine tomorrow

ممکن ہے کہ وہ آج نہ آئے

It is possible that he might not come today

کل ***kal*** and پرسوں ***parsoṅ***

کل means both 'yesterday' and 'tomorrow'. Similarly پرسوں can mean 'the day before yesterday' and 'the day after tomorrow'. The tense of the verb decides the meaning:

میں کل / پرسوں آپ کے ہاں آؤں گا

I'll come to your place tomorrow/the day after tomorrow

میں کل / پرسوں ان سے باتیں کر رہا تھا

I was chatting to him yesterday/the day before yesterday

انتظام **intizām 'arrangement'**; انتظام کرنا **intizām karnā 'to arrange'**

انتظام *intizām* means 'arrangement' (m.) It has a special Arabic plural form انتظامات *intizāmāt* 'arrangements':

آپ فکر نہ کریں۔ میں سب انتظامات کروں گا

āp fikr no kareṅ; maiṅ sab intizāmāt karūṅgā

Don't worry; I'll make all arrangements

The phrase verb کا انتظام کرنا *kā intizām karnā* means 'to arrange':

ہم سفر کا انتظام کریں گے

We shall arrange the journey

It may also be used with the oblique infinitive:

ہمیں آج پاکستان جانے کا انتظام کرنا ہے

hameṅ āj pākistān jāne kā intizām karnā hai

We have to arrange to go to Pakistan today

مکالمہ دو **mukālima do** Dialogue 2

John and Helen drive with Qasim to his village.

قاسم : السلام علیکم' جان صاحب۔ میں بے وقت تو نہیں ہوں،

جان : جی نہیں' قاسم صاحب' ہم لوگ تیار ہیں۔ آج موسم بہت اچھا ہے۔ کل رات کو بارش ہو رہی تھی' ہے نا؟

قاسم : جی ہاں' عام طور سے نومبر میں بارش نہیں ہوتی۔ خیر آج اچھی دھوپ کھل رہی ہے۔ آیئے' ہم چلیں۔ گاڑی میں بیٹھیے۔

جان : شیخوپورہ یہاں سے زیادہ دور نہیں۔ ہے نا؟

قاسم : جی نہیں۔ کوئی چونتیس (۳۴) میل دور ہے۔ شمال کی طرف۔ اگر آپ یہاں سے مشرق کی طرف جائیں' تو ہندوستان کی سرحد آئے گی۔ اگر شیخوپورہ سے اگے جائیں' تو آپ اسلام آباد پہنچیں گے۔ اُس سے آگے پیشاور اور شمال مغرب کی سرحد ہے۔ لیکن وہ کافی دور ہے۔ اسلام آباد لاہور سے کوئی ایک سو ساٹھ میل دور ہے۔

جان : شیخوپورہ پرانا شہر ہے؟

قاسم : جی ہاں۔ سترہویں صدی میں جہانگیر وہاں رہتے تھے۔ اور آس پاس کے جنگل میں شکار کھیلتے تھے۔ اُن کا قلعہ اب تک وہاں ہے۔

جان : اور آپ کا گاؤں بڑا ہے؟

قاسم : کافی بڑا گاؤں ہے۔ میرے رشتےدار اب تک وہاں کھیتی باڑی کرتے ہیں۔ جیسا کہ آپ کو معلوم ہے' پنجاب کا مطلب "پانچ دریاؤں کا ملک" ہے۔ زمین بہت زرخیز ہے۔ میرا خاندان اٹھارہویں صدی سے وہاں مقیم ہے۔ تقسیم سے پہلے وہاں مسلمان' ہندو اور سکھ سب ساتھ رہتے تھے۔ لیکن اب صرف مسلمان ہیں۔ جیسا کہ میں آپ سے پرسوں

کہہ رہا تھا‘ دنیا بہت تیزی سے بدلتی ہے۔ انشاءاللہ آنے والی صدی میں ہم زیادہ خوش رہ سکیں گے۔ دیکھیے۔ ہمارا گاوں یہاں سے نظر آ رہا ہے۔ چلیں۔ میں آپ کو اپنے گھر والوں سے ملاؤں گا اور ہم خوب کھانا کھائیں گے۔

بے وقت	*be vaqt*	at the wrong time
بارش	*bāriš*	rain (f.)
بارش ہو رہی تھی	*bāriš ho rahī thī*	it was raining
شمال	*šimāl*	north (m.)
مشرق	*mašriq*	east (m.)
سرحد	*sarhad*	border, frontier(f.)
آگے	*āge*	further on
پیشاور	*pešāvar*	Peshawar (town in North Pakistan)
سرحد شمال مغرب	*sarhad-e šimāl mağrib*	North West Frontier
مغرب	*mağrib*	west (m.)
ساٹھ	*sāṭh*	sixty
سترہواں	*satravāṅ*	seventeenth
صدی	*sadī*	century (f.)
آس پاس کا	*ās pās kā*	surrounding, nearby
جنگل	*jangal*	jungle, forest (m.)
شکار	*šikār*	hunting (m.)
شکار کھیلنا	*šikār khelnā*	to hunt
قلعہ	*qil'a*	fort (m.)
رشتےدار	*rište dār*	relation (m.)
کھیتی باڑی	*khetī bāṛī*	agriculture (f.)
دریا	*daryā*	river (m.)
زرخیز	*zarxez*	fertile
اٹھارہواں	*aṭhāravāṅ*	eighteenth
مقیم	*muqīm*	resident, settled
تقسیم	*taqsīm*	partition (f.)
ہندو	*hindū*	Hindu (m.)
سکھ	*sikh*	Sikh (m.)
تیز	*tez*	quick, fast, strong
تیزی سے	*tezī se*	quickly
بدلنا	*badalnā*	to change
آنےوالا	*ānevālā*	the coming, future
گھروالا	*gharvālā*	relation (m.)
سے ملانا	*se milānā*	to introduce to
کھلنا	*khulnā*	to open, come open

قواعد *qavā'id* Grammar

ہجے *hijje* Spelling

The word رشتے دار *rište dār* 'relation' is composed of two Persian words: رشتے *rište* 'connections' (m.p.) and دار *dār* 'having'. The two elements are written separately. The Hindi synonym is گھروالا *gharvālā* 'person of the house', and it means exactly the same thing: میرے گھروالوں سے ملیے 'meet my relations'.

بارش ہونا *bāriš honā* 'to rain'

بارش *bāriš* means 'rain' (f.). بارش ہو رہی ہے *bāriš ho rahī hai* 'rain is being' means 'it is raining'.

The present and past continuous tenses of ہونا ہو رہا ہے *ho rahā hai* and ہو رہا تھا *ho rahā thā* 'is was/being' can usually be translated into Enlish as 'is/was happening, coming about, going on':

وہاں کیا ہو رہا ہے / تھا؟

vahāṅ kyā ho rahā hai/thā?

What is/was happening/going on there?

Note the following expressions with بارش :

دیکھیے، بارش ہو رہی ہے، جلدی گھر چلیں

dekhīe, bāriš ho rahī hai; jaldī ghar caleṅ

Look, it's raining; let's go home quickly

ریڈیو پر کہتے ہیں کہ بارش ہونے والی ہے

reḍio par kahte haiṅ ki bāriš honevālī hai

They say on the radio that it is likely to rain ('rain is about to be')

برِ صغیر میں جون سے اگست تک خوب بارش ہوتی ہے

barr-e sagīr meṅ jūn se agast tak xūb bāriš hotī hai

In the subcontinent from June until August it rains heavily ('well'):

برِّ صغیر *barr-e sagīr* 'continent (*izāfat*) small' is 'the subcontinent' (m.).

بے وقت *be vaqt* 'out of time', 'at the wrong time'

بے is a Persian suffix, widely used in Urdu, meaning 'un-, dis-', 'without'. بے وقت *be vaqt* means 'untimely, at the wrong time, at an inconvenient moment':

میں بے وقت تو نہیں ہوں؟

maiṅ be vaqt to nahīṅ hūṅ?

Have I come at an inconvenient moment? ('I'm not then at the wrong time?')

The points of the compass

The most common words in Urdu for the points of the compass are:

شمال	*šimāl*	north	جنوب	*janūb*	south
مشرق	*mašriq*	east	مغرب	*mağrib*	west

'North east', 'south west' are expressed as in English: شمال مشرق, جنوب مغرب etc.

'Northern, southern, eastern, western' are شمالی *šimālī*, جنوبی *janūbī*, مشرقی *mašriqī*, مغربی *mağribī*:

شمالی پاکستان	northern Pakistan
جنوبی ہندوستان	southern India

The 'Hindi' equivalents, which are commonly used in Urdu, especially in villages and rural areas, are:

اُتر	*uttar*	north (as in اتر پردیش *uttar pradeš* UP 'North Province')
دکھن	*dakkhin*	south (in English Southern India is referred to as the 'Deccan')
پورب	*pūrab*	east (the eastern dialects of Urdu/Hindi are called پوربی *pūrabī* 'eastern')
پچھم	*pacchim*	west

The North West Frontier Province of Pakistan (NWFP), the capital of which is پیشاور *pešāvar* Peshawar, is known as صوبۂ سرحد شمال مغرب *sūba- e sarhad-e šimāl-mağrib* 'Province of (*izāfat*) frontier of (*izāfat*) North West. صوبہ *sūba* means 'province', especially one of the four provinces of Pakistan. (Note that after ہ the *izāfat* is written with ء *hamza*):

صوبۂ سندھ	*sūba-e sindh*	Sindh Province
صوبۂ بلوچستان	*sūba-e balocistān*	Balochistan Province
صوبۂ پنجاب	*sūba-e panjāb*	Panjab Province
صوبۂ سرحدِ شمال مغرب	*sūba-e sarhad-e šimāl mağrib*	NWFP

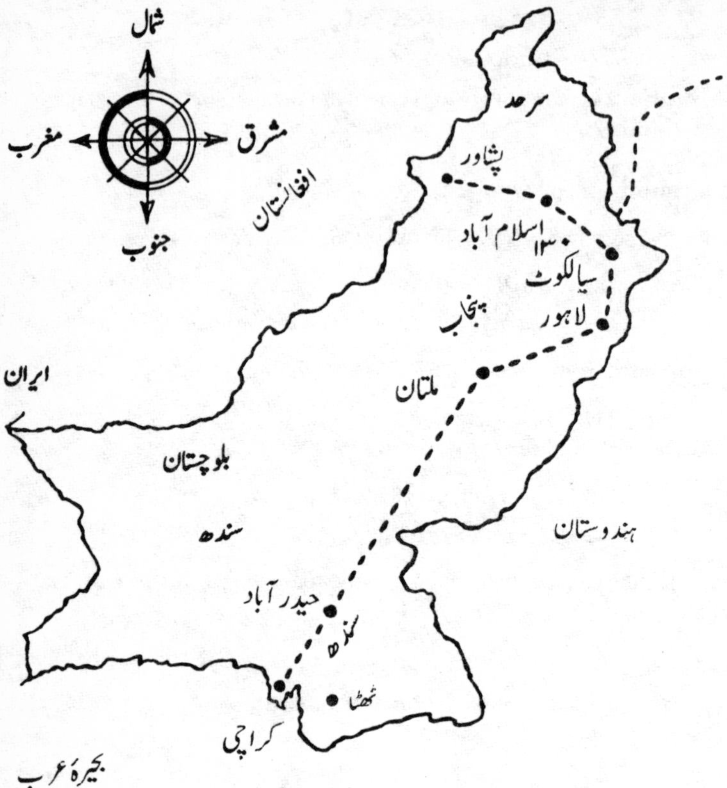

پاکستان کا نقشہ

Ordinal numerals; more on dates

The simple numerals 'one, two, three', etc. are known as the cardinal numerals. 'First, second, third', etc. are known as ordinal numerals. The Urdu ordinal numerals: 'first, second', etc. are as follows:

پہلا	*pahlā*	first
دوسرا	*dūsrā*	second
تیسرا	*tīsrā*	third
چوتھا	*cauthā*	fourth
پانچواں	*pāṅcvāṅ*	fifth

چھٹا	*chaṭṭā*	sixth
ساتواں	*sātvāṅ*	seventh

Thereafter the suffix واں *-vāṅ* (f. ویں *-vīṅ*; m. oblique ویں *-veṅ*, which can be compared with دایاں، بایاں 'right, left') are added to the cardinal numeral. In numbers such as بارہ، سترہ which end in ہ *choṭī he*, either ہ *choṭī he* or ھ *do-cašmī he* is written before the suffix واں :

آٹھواں	*āṭhvāṅ*	eighth
نواں	*navvāṅ*	ninth
دسواں	*dasvāṅ*	tenth
گیارہواں / گیارھواں	*giyāravāṅ*	eleventh
سولہواں / سولھواں	*solavāṅ*	sixteenth
پچیسواں	*paccīsvāṅ*	twenty-fifth
چالیسواں	*cālīsvāṅ*	fortieth

The feminine and masculine oblique forms ویں، ویں *-vīṅ/-veṅ* are spelt in the same way, but, of course, pronounced differently:

سترہویں صدی	*satravīṅ sadī*	the 17th century (f.)
آٹھویں دن سے	*āṭhveṅ din se*	from the eighth day (m. oblique)

The ordinal numerals are frequently used to express the date of the month. We have already seen that '(on) the third of October' can be expressed simply as دو اکتوبر کو *do aktūbar (ko)*. A more 'official' (and some would say more correct) version would be:

اکتوبر کی تیسری تاریخ کو

aktūbar kī tīsrī tārīx ko

on the third date of October

نومبر کی پندرہویں تاریخ کو

navambar kī pandravīṅ tārīx ko

on the 15th of November

آس پاس کا **ās pās kā 'nearby', 'surrounding'**

آس پاس کا is an adjectival phrase meaning 'surrounding, nearby'

اُردو دہلی اور دہلی کے آس پاس کے علاقوں کی زبان ہے

Urdu is the language of Delhi and the nearby areas of Delhi

جہانگیر آس پاس کے جنگل میں شکار کھیلتے تھے

Jahangir used to hunt in the surrounding jungle

شکار کھیلنا *šikār khelnā* 'to play hunting' means 'to hunt'.

کھیتی باڑی **khetī bāṛī 'agriculture'**

کھیتی باڑی *khetī bāṛī* (literally 'field and garden work') means 'agriculture' (f.). The phrase verb کھیتی باڑی کرنا means 'to practise agriculture'.

دریا **daryā 'river' and words for relations**

دریا forms its plural and oblique cases as follows:

Masculine singular direct	دریا	*daryā*
Masculine plural direct	دریا	*daryā*
Masculine singular oblique	دریا	*daryā*
Masculine plural oblique	دریاوں	*daryāoṅ*

The word راجا *rājā* 'king, Raja' and the relationship terms چچا 'uncle' (father's brother), دادا *dādā* 'grandfather' (father's father), and نانا *nānā* 'grandfather' (mother's father), follow the same pattern:

راجا کا محل	the king's palace
میرے چچاؤں کے گھر	my uncles' houses
میرے دادا کا نام	my (paternal) grandfather's name
ان کے نانا کی زمین	his (maternal) grandfather's land
پانچ دریاوں کا ملک	the land of five rivers

تیز **tez 'quick',** تیزی **tezī 'quickness, speed'**

The adjective تیز can mean fast, quick (speed or intelligence), smart (in a good or bad sense), strong (of tea), hot or spicy (of food):

تیز گاڑی	a fast train	تیز آدمی	a smart/devious man
تیز چائے	strong tea	تیز کھانا	hot/spicy food

The noun تیزی means 'quickness' and تیزی سے means 'quickly, speedily, fast':

گاڑی تیزی سے چلتی ہے	The train moves fast
زمانہ تیزی سے بدلتا ہے	Time(s) change quickly

آنے والا **ānevālā 'the coming, future'**

آنے والا 'about to come' means 'the coming, the next':

آنے والی صدی میں کیا ہوگا؟

What will happen ('be') in the next/coming century?

سے ملانا **se milānā 'to introduce to'**

ملانا (related to ملنا 'to meet') means 'to introduce to':

میں آپ کو اپنے رشتے داروں سے ملاؤں گا

I shall introduce you to my (own) relations

مجھے اپنی بیگم سے ملایئے

Please introduce me to your wife

Numbers

At this stage the numerals 41–60 should be learnt (Appendix 1).

ثقافت *siqāfat* Culture

Although India and Pakistan have some of the largest cities in the world, the majority of the population lives in villages, and most people spend their life engaged in agriculture. Indeed, many people who have settled in towns still maintain close links with their native village. Indian and Pakistani villages bear little resemblance to those in England or America, and are often quite remote. Villagers are noted for their hospitality, and one rarely escapes without being plied with local delicacies. Many Muslim families proudly claim descent from Afghan and Central Asian forebears who migrated to the subcontinent during the Middle Ages. Such origins are reflected in names and titles such as Khan (a Mongol title), Bukhari (from Bukhara in Uzbekistan), Chishti (from Chisht in Afghanistan) and Tabrizi (from Tabriz in Iran).

مشقیں *mašqeṅ* Exercises

11.1 The subcontinent

Look at the map of the subcontinent. The names of the major cities are written in Urdu. On the basis of what you have learnt in the last two units, answer the questions:

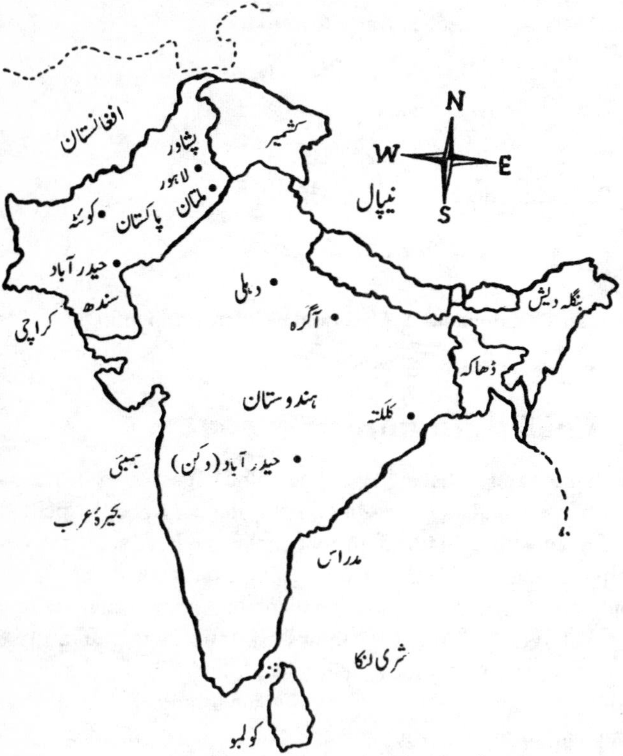

1 پاکستان کے شمال مغرب میں کون سا ملک ہے؟

2 پاکستان میں کتنے صوبے ہیں؟ ان کے دارالحکومت کیا ہیں؟

3 اگر آپ ریل گاڑی میں کراچی سے لاہور جائیں تو کون سے شہروں سے گزریں گے۔

4 دہلی شمالی ہندوستان یا جنوبی ہندوستان میں ہے؟

5 مدراس کہاں ہے۔ جنوب یا شمال میں؟

6 ہندوستان کا سب سے بڑا شہر کیا ہے؟

7 نقشے پر دو حیدر آباد ہیں۔ ایک ہندوستان کے دکن میں ہے۔ دوسرا حیدر آباد کہاں ہے؟

8 بادشاہی مسجد کہاں ہے۔ کیا وہ دہلی کی جامع مسجد سے بڑی ہے؟

9 بمبئی کون سے سمندر کے پاس ہے؟

10 ڈھاکہ کس ملک میں ہے؟

11.2 Subjunctive mood

All the following sentences require the verb to be in the subjunctive. Complete the sentences with the correct form of the verb given in brackets:

1 ممکن ہے کہ ہمارے دوست آج نہ (پہنچنا)۔

2 اگر آپ اس طرح کی باتیں (کرنا) تو لوگ خوش ہوں گے۔

3 آج رحیم صاحب نہیں آئیں گے۔ کیا میں ان کو فون (کرنا)؟

4 آپ فکر نہ (کرنا)۔ بارش نہیں ہو گی۔

5 اگر آپ پاکستان (جانا) تو گاؤں ضرور دیکھیے۔

6 اگر تم عربی (پڑھنا) تو بہت اچھا ہو گا۔

7 کیا میں آپ کے لئے چائے (منگوانا؟)

12 ہم دہلی جا رہے ہیں We're off to Delhi

In this unit you will learn how to:

- say what you did
- say you are going to do something
- excuse yourself

مکالمہ ایک *mukālima ek* Dialogue 1

John phones Aslam in Karachi and reports on his time in Lahore.

جان : ہیلو، بلقیس صاحبہ۔ فرمائیے۔ آپ کیسی ہیں؟

بلقیس : اچھا، جان صاحب ہیں؟ آپ لوگ کیسے ہیں؟ لاہور خیریت سے پہنچے؟

جان : جی ہاں، شکریہ۔ یہاں سب خیریت ہے۔ لاہور واقعی بہت شاندار جگہ ہے۔ کیا اسلم صاحب تشریف رکھتے ہیں؟

بلقیس : جی ہاں۔ میں ابھی اُنہیں بلاتی ہوں۔ لیجیے وہ آ رہے ہیں۔

اسلم : جان صاحب! بڑی خوشی ہوئی۔ آج کل آپ لوگ کیا کر رہے ہیں؟

جان : ہم بہت مصروف ہیں۔ پرسوں ہم قاسم صاحب کا گاؤں دیکھنے شیخوپورہ گئے۔ وہ واقعی بہت دلچسپ تھا۔ کل ہم جہانگیر کے مقبرے کی سیر کرنے گئے۔

اسلم : اور موسم کیسا ہے؟

جان : کراچی سے یہاں زیادہ سردی ہے۔ کہتے ہیں کہ جاڑوں میں پنجاب میں کافی سردی ہوتی ہے۔ پرسوں تھوڑی دیر کے لئے بارش ہوئی۔ اس کے بعد سورج نکلا اور دن بھر دھوپ رہی۔

اسلم : اور اب آپ کا کیا ارادہ ہے؟

جان : تین دن کے بعد، یعنی منگل کو، ہم لوگ دہلی جا رہے ہیں۔ ہم ہوائی جہاز سے جائیں گے کیونکہ ہمارے پاس زیادہ وقت نہیں ہے۔

اسلم : اچھا' میں دہلی کبھی نہیں گیا۔ آپ کو معلوم ہے کہ دہلی بلقیس کا وطن ہے۔ کیا آپ میرے لئے ایک کام کر سکیں گے؟ ہمارے ایک پرانے دوست چاندنی چوک کے پاس رہتے ہیں۔ آپ ان سے ملنے جائیے۔ اور ہماری طرف سے سلام کہیے۔ ان کا نام شریف احمد ہے اور وہ کوچۂ رحمٰن میں رہتے ہیں۔ گھر کا نمبر ایک ہزار پینتالیس (۱۰۴۵) ہے' کوئی بھی رکشے والا آپ کو راستہ دکھائے گا۔

جان : جی ہاں' اسلم صاحب۔ وہ کام میں ضرور کر سکوں گا۔

اسلم : اور آج آپ لوگوں کا کیا پروگرام ہے؟

جان : ہم کچھ دوستوں کے ہاں کھانا کھانے جا رہے ہیں۔ کل ان سے ایک چائے خانے میں ملاقات ہوئی۔ اس کے بعد وہ ہمیں راوی کے کنارے لے گئے۔

اسلم : اچھا' جان صاحب۔ خوب سیر کیجیے اور ہمیں دہلی سے لکھیے۔ سفر مبارک ہو۔

فرمائیے	farmāīe	tell (me)	جاڑے	jāṛe	winter (m.p.)
پہنچے	pahuṅce	(you) arrived	جاڑوں میں	jāṛoṅ meṅ	in the winter
خیریت	xairīat	safety (f.)	نکلا	niklā	came out
خیریت سے	xairīat se	safely	دھوپ رہی	dhūp rahī	it was sunny ('sunshine remained')
سب خیریت ہے	sab xairīat hai	all's well	کبھی نہیں گیا	kabhī nahīṅ gayā	I have never gone
لیجیے	lījīe	here you are	چاندنی چوک	cāndanī cauk	Chandni Chowk (a street in Ḍelhi) (m.)
ہوئی	hūī	has come about, happened	ملنے جائیے	milne jāīe	go to meet
بڑی خوشی ہوئی	baṛī xušī hūī	I'm very glad ('happiness has come about')	ہماری طرف سے	hamārī taraf se	from us
گاؤں دیکھنے	gāoṅ dekhne	(in order) to see	سلام	salām	greeting, 'salaam' (m.)
گئے	gae	(we) went	سلام کہنا	salām kahnā	to greet
مقبرہ	maqbara	tomb, shrine (m.)			
کی سیر کرنے گئے	kī sair karne gae	went to visit			

شریف احمد	*šarīf ahmad*	Sharif Ahmad	سے ملاقات ہوئی	*se mulāqāt hūī*	we met ('meeting happened with')
کوچہ	*kūca*	lane, small street (m.)	راوی	*rāvī*	River Ravi (Lahore) (m.)
کوچۂ رحمٰن	*kūca-e rahmān*	Rahman Lane	کنارہ	*kināra*	river bank (m.)
کوئی بھی	*koī bhī*	any (at all)	کے کنارے	*ke kināre*	to the banks of
رکشےوالا	*rikševālā*	rickshaw driver (m.)	لے گئے	*le gae*	will take
پروگرام	*progrām*	programme (m.)	مبارک	*mubārak*	congratulations (m.)
کھانا کھانے جائیں گے	*khānā khāne jāeṅge*	we'll go for a meal	سفر مبارک	*safar mubārak*	have a good journey
ملاقات	*mulāqāt*	a meeting (f.)			

قواعد *qavā'id* Grammar

ہجے *hijje* Spelling

کوچۂ رحمٰن *kūca-e rahmān* 'Rahman Lane' – notice in the word رحمٰن *rahmān* 'Merciful' (one of the names of Allah), the *alif* is written over the last syllable of the word.

کوچہ is a narrow lane, many of which can be found in old Delhi, known as شاہجہاں آباد Shajahanabad (since it was built by Shahjahan). The main thoroughfare of the old city is called چاندنی چوک *cāndanī cauk* 'Moonlight Square'.

فرمانا *farmānā* 'to do, say'

The Urdu فرمانا *farmānā* literally means 'to order', but in polite speech it can mean 'to say' or 'to tell', i.e. کہنا, or 'to do', i.e. کرنا. Since it is employed for respect, you can never use it for yourself:

رحیم صاحب' فرمایئے۔ مزاج شریف ہیں

rahīm sāhib farmāie; mizāj šarīf haiṅ?

Tell me, Rahim. Are you well?

آپ کیا فرما رہے تھے؟

āp kyā farmā rahe the?

What were you saying?

آرام فرمائیے (= کیجیے)

āram farmāīe (=kījīe)

Please take a rest

The past participle

We have already seen that the present participle of the Urdu verb (roughly corresponding to the English 'coming', 'seeing', 'going', etc.) is formed by adding to the stem the suffixes تا *-tā* (m.s.), تی *-tī* (f.s.), تے *-te* (m.p.), تیں *-tīṅ* (f.p.)

The past participle, which roughly corresponds to the English '(having) come', '(having) seen', '(having) gone', etc. is formed by adding to stems that end in a consonant the suffixes: ا *-ā* (m.s.), ی *-ī* (f.s.), ے *-e* (m.p.), یں *-īṅ* (f.p.)

Singular		Plural		
Masculine	Feminine	Masculine	Feminine	
دیکھا *dekhā*	دیکھی *dekhī*	دیکھے *dekhe*	دیکھیں *dekhīṅ*	'seen'
پہنچا *pahuṅcā*	پہنچی *pahuṅcī*	پہنچے *pahuṅce*	پہنچیں *pahuṅcīṅ*	'arrived'

Verbs whose stem ends in either the vowel ا *-ā* or و *-o* take the suffixes یا *-yā* (m.s.), ئی *-ī* (f.s.), ئے *-e* (m.p.), ئیں *-īṅ* (f.p.):

Singular		Plural		
Masculine	Feminine	Masculine	Feminine	
آیا *āyā*	آئی *āī*	آئے *āe*	آئیں *āīṅ*	'(having) come'
سویا *soyā*	سوئی *soī*	سوئے *soe*	سوئیں *soīṅ*	'(having) slept'

سونا *sonā* means 'to sleep'.

Note that the vowel junctions آئی آئے ائیں are marked with ء *hamza*. Here are a few examples of past participles of verbs with which you are familiar:

Consonant stem

پہنچا	پہنچی	پہنچے	پہنچیں	arrived
پڑھا	پڑھی	پڑھے	پڑھیں	read
لکھا	لکھی	لکھے	لکھیں	written

Vowel stem

کھایا	کھائی	کھائے	کھائیں	eaten
بتایا	بتائی	بتائے	بتائیں	told
سویا	سوئی	سوئے	سوئیں	slept

If the stem consists of two syllables, e.g. نکلنا *nikalnā* (stem نکل *nikal-*) 'to go out', گزرنا *guzarnā* (stem گزر *guzar-*) 'to pass by', the vowel of the second syllable (*-a*) is dropped when the past participle suffixes are added:

نکلا	*niklā*	نکلی	*niklī*	نکلے	*nikle*	نکلیں	*niklīṅ*	gone out
گزرا	*guzrā*	گزری	*guzrī*	گزرے	*guzre*	گزریں	*guzrīṅ*	changed

The following five verbs have slightly irregular forms:

جانا	گیا	*gayā*	گئی	*gaī*	گئے	*gae*	گئیں	*gaīṅ*	gone
دینا	دیا	*diyā*	دی	*dī*	دیے	*dīe*	دیں	*dīṅ*	given
لینا	لیا	*liyā*	لی	*lī*	لیے	*līe*	لیں	*līṅ*	taken
پینا	پیا	*piyā*	پی	*pī*	پیے	*pīe*	پیں	*pīṅ*	drunk
کرنا	کیا	*kiyā*	کی	*kī*	کیے	*kīe*	کیں	*kīṅ*	done

Transitive and intransitive verbs

Urdu verbs, like those of English, fall into two major groups: transitive and intransitive.

Transitive verbs are those which take a direct object, e.g. to *see* him; to *love* the girl; to *eat* food (*him, girl, food* are the objects of the verb).

Intransitive verbs are those which do not take an object, e.g. 'to go, to come, to arrive, to sleep'.

The distinction between transitive and intransitive is very important in Urdu in the formation of the past tenses: simple past 'I went'; *perfect* 'I have gone' and *pluperfect* 'I had gone', all three of which we shall meet in this unit.

Simple past tense of intransitive verbs

The Urdu simple past tense is the equivalent of English 'I went, I arrived,

I slept' etc. The simple past of intransitive verbs consists merely of the past participle:

میں پہنچا	*maiṅ pahuṅcā*	I (m.) arrived
میں آئی	*maiṅ āī*	I (f.) came
لڑکی گئی	*laṛkī gaī*	the girl went
میرے بیٹے سوئے	*mere beṭe soe*	my sons slept
خواتین پہنچیں	*xavātīn pahuṅcīṅ*	the ladies arrived

The negative is usually formed by placing نہیں *nahīṅ* directly before the verb:

میں نہیں گیا	*maiṅ nahīṅ gayā*	I did not go
عورتیں نہیں آئیں	*'auratеṅ nahīṅ āīṅ*	the women did not come

Sometimes نہ *na* may be used instead of نہیں making no difference to the sense, e.g. وہ نہ آیا *vuh na āyā* 'he did not come'.

The simple past tense of پہنچنا *pahuṅcnā* 'to arrive' and آنا *ānā* 'to come' is as follows:

Masculine		**Feminine**		
پہنچنا	**pahuṅcnā**			**to arrive**
میں پہنچا	*maiṅ pahuṅcā*	پہنچی	*pahuṅcī*	I arrived
تو پہنچا	*tū pahuṅcā*	پہنچی	*pahuṅcī*	you arrived
یہ، وہ پہنچا	*yih, vuh pahuṅcā*	پہنچی	*pahuṅcī*	he, she, it arrived
ہم پہنچے	*ham pahuṅce*	پہنچے	*pahuṅce*	we arrived
تم پہنچے	*tum pahuṅce*	پہنچیں	*pahuṅcīṅ*	you arrived
آپ پہنچے	*āp pahuṅce*	پہنچیں	*pahuṅcīṅ*	you arrived
یہ، وہ پہنچے	*yih, vuh pahuṅce*	پہنچیں	*pahuṅcīṅ*	they arrived
آنا	**ānā**			**to come**
میں آیا	*maiṅ āyā*	آئی	*āi*	I came
تو آیا	*tū āyā*	آئی	*āi*	you came
یہ، وہ آیا	*yih, vuh āyā*	آئی	*āi*	he, she, it came
ہم آئے	*ham āe*	آئے	*āe*	we came
تم آئے	*tum āe*	آئیں	*āīṅ*	you came
آپ آئے	*āp āe*	آئیں	*āīṅ*	you came
یہ، وہ آئے	*yih, vuh āe*	آئیں	*āīṅ*	they came

As always ہم is registered as masculine plural for both sexes.

ہوا **hūā 'became, came about, happened'**

ہوا *hūā* is the simple past tense of ہونا, but has the sense of 'became, came about, happened'. The past tense تھا *thā*, however, means 'was'. Compare the following sentences:

کیا ہوا؟	*kyā hūā?*	What's happened? What's the matter?
آپ کو کیا ہوا؟	*āp ko kyā hūā?*	What's happened to you?
وہاں کیا تھا	*vahāṅ kyā thā ?*	What was there?
وہ بیمار ہوئی	*vuh bīmār hūī*	She became/fell ill
وہ بیمار تھی	*vuh bīmār thī*	She was ill
دوکان بند ہوئی	*dūkān band hūī*	The shop closed ('became closed')
دوکان بند تھی	*dūkān band thī*	The shop was closed
وہ لوگ خوش ہوئے	*vuh log xuš hūe*	They became happy
وہ لوگ خوش تھے	*vuh log xuš the*	They were happy

The phrase مجھے بڑی خوشی ہوئی *mujhe baṛī xušī hūī* 'to me great happiness came about' is best translated 'I'm so glad, pleased'. Note پرسوں بارش ہوئی *parsoṅ bāriš hūī* 'it rained the day before yesterday' ('rain came about').

خیریت **xairīat 'well-being, safety'**

The noun خیریت *xairīat* means 'safety, well-being'. It is used in two common phrases:

یہاں سب خیریت ہے

yahāṅ sab xairīat hai

All is well here ('all well-being is')

آپ خیریت سے پہنچے؟

āp xairīat se pahuṅce?

Did you arrive safely? ('with safety')

دیکھنے جانا **dekhne jānā 'to go to see'**

The masculine oblique infinitive دیکھنے ' کھانے ' پینے etc. used with verbs expressing motion, 'to go, come' has the sense of 'in order to do':

ہم قاسم صاحب کا گاؤں دیکھنے گئے

ham qāsim sāhib kā gāoṅ dekhne gae

We went to see Qasim's village

میں اب کھانا کھانے جا رہا ہوں

maiṅ ab khānā khāne jā rahā hūṅ

I'm going to have dinner

پرانا **purānā** بوڑھا **būṛhā** 'old'

پرانا is usually only used for things:

ہم پرانے شہر کی سیر کرنے گئے

We went to visit the old city

When used with people it has the sense of 'long-standing':

احمد میرے ایک پرانے دوست ہیں

Ahmad is an old friend of mine ('my one old friend')

بوڑھا refers only to the age of people:

میرے چچا بہت بوڑھے ہیں

My uncle is very old

ملنا **milnā** as an intransitive verb

In English 'to meet' is transitive and takes a direct object; ملنا *milnā* (because it is used with سے) is regarded as intransitive:

وہ مجھ سے کراچی میں ملے

vuh mujh se karācī meṅ mile

He met me (from me) in Karachi

آپ کو کتنے پیسے ملے؟

āp ko kitne paise mile?

How much money did you get? ('were acquired to you?')

کسی سے میری ملاقات ہوئی *kisī se merī mulāqāt hūī* 'my meeting came about with ('from') someone' is the equivalent of میں کسی سے ملا *maiṅ kisī se milā* 'I met someone'.

سلام **salām** 'greetings', 'regards'

سلام 'peace' is, as we have seen, the universal Muslim greeting. کو سلام کہنا 'to say to someone *salām*' means to greet someone/to give one's regards to':

رحیم صاحب کو میرا سلام کہیے۔

Give Rahim Sahib my regards ('from my side')

کوئی بھی *koī bhī* 'any ... at all'

In this phrase بھی *bhī* has the sense of 'at all':

کوئی بھی رکشے والا آپ کو راستہ دکھائے گا

Any rickshaw driver (at all) will show you the way ('road')

لے جانا *le jānā* 'to take'

The verbal phrase لے جانا 'to take (away)' is formed with the root of لینا 'to take' and جانا 'to go' ('to take-go'):

وہ ہمیں راوی کے کنارے لے جائیں گے

They will take us to the bank(s) of the Ravi (the river on which Lahore stands)

مبارک ہو *mubārak ho* 'congratulations'

مبارک literally means 'lucky, auspicious', and can often be translated as 'congratulations'. Note the following phrases:

سفر مبارک ہو!

Have a good journey! Bon voyage!

Here the subjunctive ہو *ho* means 'may it be!':

سالگرہ، نیا سال، عید مبارک ہو

sālgirah/nayā sāl/īd mubārak ho

Happy birthday, New Year, Eid (an important Muslim festival)

مشق *mašq* Exercise

12.1 Answer in Urdu

Read the following statements then answer the questions:

1 اسلم صاحب کل شام کو پانچ بجے میرے گھر آئے۔
2 پرسوں ہم بادشاہی مسجد کی سیر کرنے گئے۔
3 ہمارے دوست ہمیں راوی کے کنارے لے گئے۔
4 جہانگیر شیخوپورے کے آس پاس کے جنگل میں شکار کھیلتے تھے۔
5 رحیم صاحب آگرے جانے کا انتظام کریں گے۔

6 ریل گاڑی دیر سے پہنچے گی۔ چار بجے آئے گی۔

7 بچپن میں قاسم صاحب گاؤں میں رہتے تھے۔

سوالات

a اسلم صاحب کتنے بجے آئے؟

b پرسوں وہ کیا کرنے گئے؟

c ان کے دوست انہیں کہاں لے گئے؟

d جہانگیر شکار کہاں کھیلتے تھے؟

e رحیم صاحب کہاں جانے کا انتظام کریں گے؟

f ریل گاڑی کتنے بجے آئے گی؟

g قاسم صاحب کا بچپن کہاں گزرا؟

مکالمہ دو ***mukālima do*** **Dialogue 2**

Qasim calls at the hotel and finds no one at home.

قاسم : السلام علیکم۔ آخر آپ لوگ موجود ہیں۔ میں کوئی پانچ بجے یہاں سے گزرا، لیکن آپ کمرے میں نہیں تھے۔

جان : میں معافی چاہتا ہوں، قاسم صاحب۔ ہم لوگ باہر گئے تھے۔ میں ابھی آیا ہوں۔ پانچ منٹ پہلے ہیلن منیجر کی بیوی سے باتیں کر رہی تھیں۔ معلوم ہوتا ہے کہ وہ کہیں گئی ہیں۔ تھوڑی دیر کے بعد آئیں گی۔

قاسم : آج آپ کہاں گئے تھے؟

جان : کل شام کو ہم ایک چائے خانے میں بیٹھے تھے اور وہاں ایک شخص سے ملاقات ہوئی تھی۔ وہ یہاں کی عدالت میں وکیل ہیں۔ وہ فوراً پوچھنے لگے کہ ہمیں اُردو کیسے آتی ہے۔ اس کے بعد ہم ان کے گھر گئے اور ان کے گھر والوں سے ملے۔ ان کی بیگم کھانے کی تیاری کر رہی تھیں، تو ہم بھی کھانے میں شامل ہوئے۔ ہم کوئی بارہ بجے رات کو ہوٹل پہنچے۔ جیسا کہ آپ فرما رہے تھے، پنجابی لوگ بہت مہمان نواز ہوتے ہیں۔ آج دوپہر کے بعد ہم لوگ پھر ملے اور راوی کے کنارے سیر کرنے گئے۔ میں معافی چاہتا ہوں کہ میں آپ کو فون نہ کر سکا۔

قاسم : اوہو! نئے دوست، نئی عادتیں۔ ہمیں آپ فون نہیں کر سکتے تھے! میں سوچنے لگا کہ آپ لوگ میری اجازت کے بغیر ہندوستان گئے۔

جان : معاف کیجیے، قاسم صاحب۔ یہ ہماری غلطی تھی۔

قاسم : جی نہیں، جان صاحب۔ یہ صرف مذاق تھا۔ بڑی خوشی کی بات ہے کہ آپ کو ہمارے پنجابی بھائی پسند آئے۔ اچھا ہندوستان جانے کی سب تیاریاں مکمل ہیں؟

جان : ہم تقریباً تیار ہیں۔ ہمارے پاس کافی وقت ہوگا۔ ہوائی جہاز کل کوئی گیارہ بجے چلتا ہے۔

قاسم : ٹھیک ہے۔ میں کل صبح آٹھ بجے یہاں آؤں گا اور آپ کو ہوائی اڈے تک پہنچاؤں گا۔ خداحافظ۔

موجود	*maujūd*	present	پوچھنے لگے	*pūchne lage*	began to ask
گزرا	*guzrā*	(I) passed by	شامل	*šāmil*	included
معافی چاہتا ہوں	*mu'āfī cāhtā hūṅ*	I'm sorry	شامل ہوئے	*šāmil hūe*	we joined in
گئے تھے	*gae the*	had gone, went	سوچنے لگا	*socne lagā*	I began to think
آیا ہوں	*āyā hūṅ*	have come	اجازت	*ijāzat*	permission (f.)
گئی ہیں	*gaī haiṅ*	has gone	کے بغیر	*ke bağair*	without
بیٹھے تھے	*baiṭhe the*	were sitting	غلطی	*ğalatī*	fault, mistake (f.)
ہوئی تھی	*hūī thī*	had come about, came about	مذاق	*mazāq*	joke (m.)
عدالت	*'adālat*	court (f.)	مکمل	*mukammal*	completed
وکیل	*vakīl*	lawyer (m.)	مکمل ہوئے	*mukammal hūe*	have been completed
فوراً	*fauran*	at once	تقریباً	*taqrīban*	approximately, nearly

قواعد *qavā'id* Grammar

ہجے *hijje* spelling

اً*-an*, *tanvīn* – Urdu has many adverbs, taken from Arabic, ending with the sign اً, which is pronounced *-an*. This sign is known as تنوین *tanvīn* 'adding a *nūn*'. In the dialogue we had فوراً *fauran* 'immediately, at once' and تقریباً *taqrīban* 'almost, about, nearly'.

Excusing oneself

We have already met the word معاف *mu'āf* (often pronounced *māf*) in the phrase معاف کیجیے 'please excuse me'. This may also be expressed with the subjunctive معاف کریں *mu'āf kareṅ* 'may you excuse me'. Here, as often, the subjunctive is used in place of the imperative کریں, being considered more polite. The noun معافی *mu'āfī* means 'forgiveness' (f.):

میں معافی چاہتا ہوں

maiṅ mu'āfī cāhtā hūṅ

I'm sorry ('I want your forgiveness')

Perfect and pluperfect tenses

The perfect tense means roughly the same as English 'I have gone'. It is formed with the past participle followed by ہوں، ہے، ہو، ہیں *hūṅ, hai, ho, haiṅ*:

میں آیا ہوں	*maiṅ āyā hūṅ*	I (m.) have come
وہ گئی ہے	*vuh gaī hai*	she has gone
تم پہنچے ہو	*tum pahuṅce ho*	you (m.) have arrived

The feminine plural participle گئیں، آئیں etc. cannot be used before the following verb 'to be'. The feminine singular form is used instead:

آپ گئی ہیں	*āp gaī haiṅ*	you (f.) have gone
لڑکیاں سوئی ہیں	*laṛkīāṅ soī haiṅ*	the girls have slept/gone to sleep

The perfect tense of پہنچنا ('I have arrived, you have arrived', etc.) is as follows:

Masculine		**Feminine**	
میں پہنچا ہوں	*maiṅ pahuṅcā hūṅ*	پہنچی ہوں	*pahuṅcī hūṅ*
تو پہنچا ہے	*tū pahuṅcā hai*	پہنچی ہے	*pahuṅcī hai*
یہ، وہ پہنچا ہے	*yih/vuh pahuṅcā hai*	پہنچی ہے	*pahuṅcī hai*
ہم پہنچے ہیں	*ham pahuṅce haiṅ*	پہنچے ہیں	*pahuṅce haiṅ*
تم پہنچے ہو	*tum pahuṅce ho*	پہنچی ہو	*pahuṅcī ho*
آپ پہنچے ہیں	*āp pahuṅce haiṅ*	پہنچی ہیں	*pahuṅcī haiṅ*
یہ، وہ پہنچے ہیں	*yih/vuh pahuṅce haiṅ*	پہنچی ہیں	*pahuṅcī haiṅ*

Some examples are:

آپ خیریت سے پہنچے ہیں؟

Have you arrived safely?

میں ابھی گھر آیا ہوں

I have just come home

آپ مجھ سے ملنے آئے ہیں؟

Have you come to meet me?

The pluperfect tense means roughly the same as the English 'I had gone'. It is formed with the past participle followed by تھا ، تھی ، تھے ، تھیں *thā, thī, the, thīṅ*:

میں آیا تھا	*maiṅ āyā thā*	I had gone
گاڑی پہنچی تھی	*gāṛī pahuṅcī thī*	The train had arrived
ہم سوئے تھے	*ham soe the*	We had slept

As was the case with the perfect, the plural feminine past participle cannot be used before تھیں – the singular form is used instead:

لڑکیاں نکلی تھیں	*laṛkīāṅ niklī thīṅ*	The girls had gone out
میری بیگم آئی تھیں	*merī begam āī thīṅ*	My wife had come

The pluperfect of پہنچنا ('I had arrived, you had arrived', etc.) is as follows:

Masculine		**Feminine**	
میں پہنچا تھا	*maiṅ pahuṅcā thā*	پہنچی تھی	*pahuṅcī thī*
تو پہنچا تھا	*tū pahuṅcā thā*	پہنچی تھی	*pahuṅcī thī*
یہ، وہ پہنچا تھا	*yih/vuh pahuṅcā thā*	پہنچی تھی	*pahuṅcī thī*
ہم پہنچے تھے	*ham pahuṅce the*	پہنچے تھے	*pahuṅce the*
تم پہنچے تھے	*tum pahuṅce the*	پہنچی تھیں	*pahuṅcī thīṅ*
آپ پہنچے تھے	*āp pahuṅce the*	پہنچی تھیں	*pahuṅcī thīṅ*
یہ، وہ پہنچے تھے	*yih/vuh pahuṅce the*	پہنچی تھیں	*pahuṅcī thīṅ*

The pluperfect has two major functions. It corresponds to English 'had gone', etc.:

ہم اسٹیشن گئے اور گاڑی آئی تھی

We went to the station and the train had arrived

لڑکیاں گاؤں سے آئی تھیں

The girls had come from the village

It can also be used in place of the simple past, especially when the time of the action is stated:

میں پانچ بجے آیا تھا

maiṅ pāṅc baje āyā thā

I came ('had come') at five o'clock

کل شام کو بارش ہوئی تھی

kal šām ko bāriš hūī thī

Yesterday evening it rained ('rain had come about')

پچھلے سال ہم پاکستان گئے تھے

pichle sāl ham pākistān gae the

Last year we went ('had gone') to Pakistan

پچھلے سال *pichle sāl* 'last year'; پچھلے ہفتے *pichle hafte* 'last week'.

In the last three sentences, the simple past could also have been used. When time is stated, however, it is more common for the pluperfect to be used.

The perfect and pluperfect in the negative

The perfect and pluperfect tenses cannot be used in negative sentences. When نہیں or نہ is used before the verb, the tense reverts to the simple past:

کیا آپ لاہور پہنچے ہیں؟ جی نہیں، اب تک میں نہیں پہنچا

kyā āp lāhaur pahuṅce haiṅ? jī nahīṅ. ab tak maiṅ nahīṅ pahuṅcā

Have you arrived at Lahore? No, I have not arrived yet

میں دہلی کبھی نہیں گیا

I have never been to Delhi ('gone to')

آپ پچھلے ہفتے آئے تھے۔ جی نہیں، میں نہیں آیا

Did you come last week? No, I did not come

چکنا **cuknā** 'to finish doing'

The intransitive verb چکنا 'to finish' doing something, like سکنا, is used with the stem of another verb: کر چکنا *kar cuknā* 'to finish doing', کھا چکنا *khā cuknā* 'to finish eating', etc. It is mainly used in the past tenses:

میں کام کر چکا	*maiṅ kām kar cukā*	I finished working
وہ کھانا کھا چکی ہے	*vuh khānā khā cukī hai*	She has finished eating dinner
رحیم صاحب خط لکھ چکے تھے	*rahīm sāhib xat likh cuke the*	Rahim had finished writing the letter

The perfect and pluperfect tenses of چکنا may be translated into English as 'I have already done':

ریل گاڑی آچکی ہے

rel gāṛī ā cukī hai

The train has already come ('has finished coming')

میں گھر پہنچا اور بلقیس کھانا پکا چکی تھیں

maiṅ ghar pahuṅcā aur bilqīs khānā pakā cukī thīṅ

I arrived home and Bilqis had already cooked dinner

بیٹھنا **baiṭhnā** 'to sit'; تھکنا **thaknā** 'to be tired'

The present habitual tense of بیٹھنا : میں بیٹھتا ہوں means 'I (usually) sit', while the perfect tense میں بیٹھا ہوں means 'I am (actually) sitting somewhere'. The pluperfect tense means 'I was sitting/seated':

میں ہمیشہ اس کرسی پر بیٹھتا ہوں

maiṅ hameša is kursī par baiṭhtā hūṅ

I always sit on this chair

ہم ایک چائے خانے میں بیٹھے تھے

ham ek cāe xāne meṅ baiṭhte the

We were sitting in a tea shop

The same applies to the verb تھکنا *thaknā* 'to be/get tired':

میری بیگم رات کو تھکتی ہیں

merī begam rāt ko thaktī haiṅ

My wife gets tired at night

آج ہم بہت تھکے ہیں

āj ham bahut thake haiṅ

Today we are very tired

وہ پوچھنے لگے **vuh pūchne lage 'they began to ask'**

The intransitive verb لگنا *lagnā* has a wide range of meanings and uses. With the masculine oblique infinitive it has the sense of 'to begin to do', and it is used most frequently in the future and past tenses:

رحیم صاحب کہنے لگے کہ وہ پاکستان جائیں گے

rahīm sāhib kahne lage ki vuh pākistān jāeṅge

Rahim began to say that he would ('will') go to Pakistan

وہ پوچھنے لگے کہ ہمیں اُردو کہاں سے آتی ہے

vuh pūchne lage ki hameṅ urdū kahāṅ se ātī hai

They began to ask (that) how we knew Urdu ('from where does Urdu come to us')

In novels, the formula وہ کہنے لگے 'he began to say' is often used in the sense of 'he said':

بارش ہونے لگی / لگے گی

bāriš hone lagī/lagegī

It started/will start to rain ('began/will begin')

ثقافت siqāfat Culture

In India and Pakistan hospitality is almost an article of faith. It is not uncommon for perfect strangers to entertain you to tea, to spend a whole afternoon accompanying you around the town, and even invite you to their home after a brief chance meeting. The entertaining of guests also adds to the honour of the host, and sometimes people can become a bit too possessive. In the second dialogue of this unit, Qasim is not too pleased when the Smiths find another friend. If you are staying with someone, you might find it difficult to go about as you please, or to accept invitations from others. The usual formula would be: 'Well, of course, you are my guest, and if you feel you must go to have dinner with somone else, it is your right.' This often puts you in an awkward situation, from which, unfortunately, there is no escape.

مشقیں mašqeṅ Exercises

12.2 Answer in Urdu

Listen to the passage on the tape, then answer the questions in Urdu:

1 اقبال احمد کہاں کے رہنے والے ہیں؟

2 پچھلے ہفتے وہ کہاں گئے تھے؟

3 لاہور میں سردی تھی یا گرمی تھی؟

4 جمعرات کو اقبال کن کے ہاں گئے تھے؟
5 وہاں کن سے ملاقات ہوئی؟
6 وکیل کیا کہنے لگے؟

12.3 Telephone conversation

Take your part in the telephone conversation, using the appropriate gender for yourself:

قاسم کیا یہ نو دو پانچ چھے صفر ہے؟ (۹۲۵۶۰)
You Say it is and ask who is speaking.
قاسم آپ آج کہاں تھے / تھیں؟ میں آپ کے پاس پانچ بجے آیا تھا۔
You Say you are sorry, but you were shopping in the bazaar.
قاسم اور آپ کتنے بجے آئے تھے / آئی تھیں؟
You Say that you arrived at about six.
قاسم اچھا، تو آپ میرے ہاں شام کو کھانے پر آ سکتے / آ سکتی ہیں؟
You Ask at what time you have to come.
قاسم آٹھ بجے تک آیئے۔ میرے بھائی محمد آئے ہیں۔
You Say that you will certainly come, and will be very pleased.

12.4 Use the correct tense

You have now learnt a wide range of Urdu tenses. Complete the sentences using the tense indicated:

1 اسلم کے بیٹے کون سے مضامین (پڑھنا)؟ (Present habitual)
2 ہم اِس وقت دہلی جانے کی تیاری (کرنا)؟ (Present continuous)
3 وہ لڑکا ہر روز سمندر میں (نہانا)؟ (Past habitual)
4 اس کمرے میں مت جاؤ۔ والد صاحب نماز (پڑھنا)؟ (Past continuous)
5 مجھے معلوم نہیں کہ آپ کی والدہ کیا (کہنا)؟ (Future)
6 آج صبح بلقیس صاحبہ آٹھ بجے گھر سے (نکلنا)؟ (Simple past)
7 کیوں، جان صاحب آپ میرے دوست سے (ملنا)؟ (Perfect)
8 ہم اسٹیشن دیر سے پہنچے اور گاڑی جا (چکنا)؟ (Pluperfect)

13 آپ نے خود سامان باندھا؟ Did you pack the luggage yourself?

In this unit you will learn how to:

- check in at the airport
- express more in the past
- tell the time in more detail
- take leave formally

مکالمہ ایک *mukālima ek* Dialogue 1

John and Helen check in at Lahore airport on their way to Delhi.

جان : معاف کیجیے۔ یہ قطار دہلی کے لئے ہے؟

افسر : جی ہاں۔ آپ قطار میں انتظار کیجیے۔ آپ کی پرواز گیارہ بج کر پچیس منٹ پر ہے۔ یہ آپ کا سامان ہے؟

جان : جی ہاں۔ دو سوٹ کیس اور ایک بیگ۔

افسر : آپ نے خود سامان باندھا؟ اور کسی کے لیے چیزیں لے جا رہے ہیں؟

جان : جی نہیں، ہم نے خود باندھا۔ سب چیزیں ہماری ہی چیزیں ہیں۔

افسر : اچھا۔ آیئے۔ ٹکٹ اور پاسپورٹ دکھایئے۔ اس کے بعد آپ سیدھے لاؤنج میں جا سکیں گے۔ یہ بتایئے، آپ نے اردو کہاں سے سیکھی؟

جان : میں نے سب سے پہلے لندن میں دوستوں کے ساتھ اردو سیکھی۔ ہم آج کل برِ صغیر کی سیر کر رہے ہیں۔ کراچی اور لاہور میں اردو بولنے کی کافی مشق ہوئی۔

افسر : اچھا، اسمتھ صاحب۔ مجھے آپ سے مل کر بڑی خوشی ہوئی۔ بہت کم غیر ملکی اتنی اچھی اردو بول سکتے ہیں۔ آپ جایئے۔ آپ کے پاس کافی وقت ہے۔

جان : اب کتنے بجے ہیں؟ میری گھڑی رک گئی ہے۔

افسر : اب گیارہ بجنے میں بیس منٹ باقی ہیں۔ جی نہیں، معاف کیجیے۔ پونے گیارہ بجے ہیں۔

جان : اور ہم دہلی کتنے بجے پہنچتے ہیں؟

افسر : زیادہ لمبی پرواز نہیں ہے۔ آپ کوئی سوا بارہ' ساڑھے بارہ' بجے پہنچیں گے۔ کیا' آپ کو لاہور پسند آیا۔

جان : بہت پسند آیا۔ میرے خیال سے ہم نے تقریباً سبھی کچھ دیکھا۔ ہمیں پاکستان ہمیشہ یاد رہے گا۔ بس یہ ہماری پرواز کا اعلان ہے۔ خدا حافظ۔ انشاء اللہ ہم پھر ملیں گے۔

قطار	qatār	queue (f.)
انتظار کرنا	intizār karnā	to wait
پرواز	parvāz	flight (f.)
بجکر پچیس منٹ پر	bajkar paccīs minaṭ par	at twenty-five past
بیگ	baig	bag (m.)
آپ نے باندھا	āp ne ... bāndhā	did you pack?
باندھنا	bāndhnā	to pack
خود	xud	(one)self, yourself
ہماری ہی	hamārī hī	just ours
ہی	hī	just, only
پاسپورٹ	pāsporṭ	passport (m.)
لاؤنج	lāūnj	lounge (m.)
آپ نے سیکھی	āp ne ... sīkhī	did you learn?
میں نے سیکھی	maiṅ ne ... sīkhī	I learnt
مشق	mašq	practice (f.)
آپ سے ملکر	āp se milkar	having met you
کم	kam	few
غیر ملکی	ğair mulkī	foreigner (m.)
گھڑی	ghaṛī	watch (f.)
رک گئی	ruk gaī	has stopped
بجنے میں بیس منٹ باقی	bajne meṅ bīs minaṭ bāqī	twenty to
پونے گیارہ بجے	paune giyāra baje	quarter to twelve
سوا بارہ بجے	savā bāra baje	quarter past twelve
ساڑھے بارہ بجے	sāṛhe bāra baje	half past twelve
سبھی کچھ	sabhī kuch	absolutely everything
ہم نے ... دیکھا	ham ne ... dekhā	we saw
اعلان	i'lān	announcement (m.)

قواعد qavā'id Grammar

کا انتظار کرنا *kā intizār karnā* 'to wait for'

The phrase verb کا انتظار کرنا *kā intizār karnā* 'to do the waiting of' means 'to wait for':

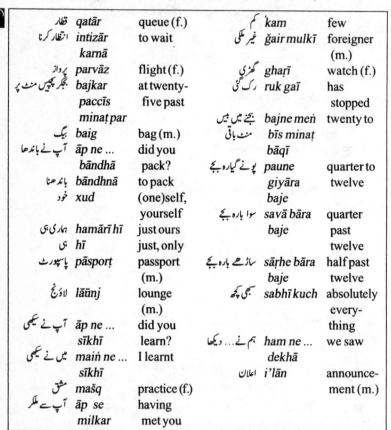

ہم آپ کا انتظار کر رہے تھے

ham āp kā intizār kar rahe the

We were waiting for you

Past tenses of transitive verbs

The simple past tense of transitive verbs 'I saw (someone)', 'I did (some thing)', is formed with the past participle, but in Urdu you say: 'by me someone seen', 'by me something done'. The object of the English sentence 'someone', 'something' becomes the subject in Urdu.

In this construction the word for 'by' is the postposition نے *ne*, which takes the oblique case of nouns in the usual way: لڑکے نے *laṛke ne* 'by the boy', لڑکیوں نے *laṛkīoṅ ne* 'by the girls', etc. The personal pronouns and interrogative pronoun before نے *ne*, however, have special forms:

میں نے	*maiṅ ne*	by me
تو نے	*tū ne*	by you
اِس نے	*is ne*	by him, her, it
اُس نے	*us ne*	by him, her, it
ہم نے	*ham ne*	by us
تم نے	*tum ne*	by you
آپ نے	*āp ne*	by you
اِنہوں نے	*inhoṅ ne*	by them
اُنہوں نے	*unhoṅ ne*	by them
کس نے	*kis ne?*	by whom? (singular)
کنہوں نے	*kinhoṅ ne?*	by whom? (plural)
کسی نے	*kisī ne*	by someone

The simple past of transitive verbs

In Urdu 'I saw' is simply میں نے دیکھا *maiṅ ne dekhā* 'by me seen'. Similarly: میں نے کہا *maiṅ ne kahā* I said ('by me said'); اس نے پوچھا *us ne pūchā* he/she asked ('by him/her asked'); ہم نے کیا *ham ne kiyā* we did ('by us done'); انہوں نے کھایا *unhoṅ ne khāyā* they ate ('by them eaten'); لڑکے نے بتایا *laṛke ne batāyā* the boy told ('by the boy told'); لڑکیوں نے بلایا *laṛkīoṅ ne bulāyā* the girls called ('by the girls called') etc.

Note that the participle remains masculine singular whatever the gender or number of the person by whom the action is carried out.

When the object in the English sentence 'I read a book' is expressed this is rendered in Urdu as: 'by me book read'. Since کتاب is feminine, the participle changes its gender to feminine in order to match کتاب. Thus: میں نے کتاب پڑھی *maiṅ ne kitāb (f.s.) paṛhī* (f.s.) ('by me book read') 'I read a book'.

Similarly:

ہم نے اچھا گھر دیکھا

ham ne acchā ghar (m.s.) dekhā (m.s.)

('by us house seen') We saw a good house

آپ نے دو اچھے گھر دیکھے

āp ne do acche ghar (m.p.) dekhe (m.p.)

('by us houses seen') You saw two good houses

انہوں نے کتابیں دیکھیں

unhoṅ ne kitābeṅ (f.p.) dekhīṅ (f.p.)

('by them books seen') They saw the books

Here are some more examples of the past tense of transitive verbs. Read them aloud noting the way in which the participles agree with the noun they follow:

میں نے آپ کا گھر دیکھا	I saw your house (m.s.)
رحیم نے دو خط لکھے	Rahim wrote two letters (m.p.)
اسلم نے چائے منگوائی	Aslam ordered tea (f.s.)
آپ نے وہ نئی فلم دیکھی؟	Did you see that new film? (f.s.)
کس نے کہا؟	Who said (so)? (m.s.)
ہم نے مسجد کی سیر کی	We walked around the mosque (f.s.)
کسی نے یہ کتاب دیکھی	Someone wrote this book (f.s.)
بچوں نے کیا کیا؟	What did the children do? (m.s.)
لڑکیوں نے روٹی بنائی	The girls made the bread (f.s.)

The simple past with a person or pronoun as its object

We have seen that if the object of a transitive verb is a noun referring to a person, or is a pronoun, the object is followed by the postposition کو *ko*:

میں رحیم کو دیکھتا ہوں	*maiṅ rahīm ko dekhtā hūṅ*	I see Rahim
ہم اس کو بلاتے ہیں	*ham us ko bulāte haiṅ*	We call him

When this happens in the simple past construction, the past participle after کو *ko* is always masculine singular, regardless of the gender or number of its logical object. In other words, you say: 'by me to Rahim seen', 'by us to him called':

میں نے رحیم کو دیکھا — I saw Rahim
maiṅ ne rahīm ko dekhā

ہم نے اس کو (اسے) بلایا — We called him
ham ne us ko (use) bulāyā

The perfect and pluperfect tenses of transitive verbs

The perfect and pluperfect tenses of transitive verbs ('I have seen', 'I had seen') are formed wth the past participle followed by ہے (perfect), and تھا (pluperfect). The 'logical' subject of the sentence takes نے *ne*:

Perfect

میں نے دیکھا ہے — I have seen ('by me seen is')
maiṅ ne dekhā hai

انہوں نے بتایا ہے — they have told ('by them told is')
unhoṅ ne batāyā hai

When an object is expressed, the participle agrees with the 'object' in gender and number, and the verb 'to be' in number:

میں نے گھر دیکھا ہے
maiṅ ne ghar dekhā hai — I have seen the house
'by me house (m.s.) seen (m.s.) is (s.)'

ہم نے کتاب پڑھی ہے
ham ne kitāb paṛhī hai — I have read the book
'by us book (f.s.) read (f.s.) is (s.)'

آپ نے یہ کمرے دیکھے ہیں؟
āp ne yih kamre dekhe haiṅ? — Have you seen these rooms?
'by you these rooms (m.p.) seen (m.p.) are (p.)?'

The feminine plural past participle cannot be used before ہیں: the feminine singular form is used instead:

انہوں نے وہ عمارتیں دیکھی ہیں

unhoṅ ne vuh 'imārateṅ dekhī haiṅ They have seen those buildings
'by them those buildings (f.p.) seen (f.s.) are (p.)'

Pluperfect

The construction is the same as that of the perfect, except that تھا follows the participle, agreeing with the 'object' in both number and gender:

میں نے دیکھا تھا

maiṅ ne dekhā thā I had seen
'by me seen was'

رحیم نے کام کیا تھا

rahīm ne kām kiyā thā Rahim had worked
'by Rahim work (m.s.) done (m.s.) was (m.s.)'

فہمیدہ نے چھٹی لی تھی

fahmīda ne chuṭṭī lī thī Fahmida had taken a holiday
'by Fahmida holiday (f.s.) taken (f.s.) was (f.s.)'

آپ کے دوست نے خط لکھے تھے

āp ke dost ne xat likhe the Your friend had written the letters
'by your friend letters (m.p.) written (m.p.) were (m.p.)'

جان نے مسجدیں دیکھی تھیں

jān ne masjideṅ dekhī thīṅ John had seen the mosques
'by John mosques (f.p.) seen (f.s.) were (f.p.)'

With the perfect and the pluperfect, as with the simple past, if کو *ko* stands between the object and the participle, the participle 'reverts' to masculine singular, and the verb 'to be' also remains singular, i.e. ہے *hai* (perfect) تھا *thā* (pluperfect):

میری بیگم نے رحیم کو دیکھا ہے

merī begam ne rahīm ko dekhā hai My wife has seen Rahim
'by my wife Rahim seen (m.s.) is (s.)'

عورتوں نے آپ کو بلایا تھا

'auratoṅ ne āp ko bulāyā thā The women called you

'by women you called (m.s.) was (m.s.)'

The perfect and pluperfect tenses may not be used with نہیں *nahīṅ* or نہ *na.* As with intransitive verbs, only the simple past is used in negative sentences:

آپ نے وہ نئی فلم دیکھی ہے؟ جی نہیں، میں نے اس کو نہیں دیکھا۔

āp ne vuh naī film dekhī hai? jī, nahīṅ, maiṅ ne us ko nahīṅ dekhā

Have you seen that new film? No, I haven't seen (it)

Finally, the verbs سکنا *saknā* and چکنا *cuknā* are always intransitive, regardless of the verb with which they are used:

میں وہ کتاب نہ پڑھ سکا	I could not read that book
میری بیگم بریانی نہیں پکا سکیں	My wife could not cook *biryani*
وہ اپنا کام کر چکا ہے	He has already done his work
جمیلہ روٹی پکا چکی تھی	Jamila had already cooked the bread

Fractions and minutes to the hour

It was once remarked that 'Arabic numerals are the nightmare of a bankrupt financier' and you may be forgiven for thinking that the Urdu numerical system is equally troublesome. You will now find that it also possesses separate words for fractions as well. All you can do is learn them.

The most important fractions (half, three-quarters, one and a quarter, etc.) are as follows:

آدھا	*ādhā*	half
پون	*paun*	three-quarters
سوا	*savā*	one and a quarter
ڈیڑھ	*ḍeṛh*	one and a half
ڈھائی	*ḍhāī*	two and a half

These are used like adjectives, آدھا *ādhā* behaving like اچھا *acchā*:

آدھا گھنٹہ	*ādhā ghanṭa*	half an hour
آدھی دنیا	*ādhī dunyā*	half the world
سوا روپیہ	*savā rūpīa*	one and a quarter rupees (singular)

ڈیڑھ گھنٹہ	*ḍeṛh ghanṭa*	one and a half hours
ڈھائی روپے	*ḍhāī rūpīe*	two and a half rupees (plural)

You can count up to three using fractions:

آدھا	ایک	سوا	ڈیڑھ	دو	ڈھائی	تین
½	1	1¼	1½	2	2½	3

1¾, 2¼ and fractions after 2½ are expressed with the following words, which come before the numeral:

پونے	*paune*	minus a quarter
سوا	*savā*	plus a quarter
ساڑھے	*sāṛhe*	plus a half

Thus:

پونے دو	*paune do*	2 minus a quarter = 1¾
سوادو	*savā do*	2 plus a quarter = 2¼
پونے تین	*paune tin*	3 minus a quarter = 2¾
تین	*tīn*	3
سوا تین	*savā tīn*	3 plus a quarter = 3¼
ساڑھے تین	*sāṛhe tīn*	3 plus a half = 3½
پونے چار	*paune cār*	4 minus a quarter = 3¾
چار	*cār*	4

Thereafter: سواچار 4¼, ساڑھے چار 4½, پونے پانچ 4¾, پانچ 5, etc.

Telling time: divisions of the hour

Quarter to, quarter past, half past

The fractions we have just seen are used with بجے to express divisions of the hour:

پون بجے	*paun baje*	quarter to one (¾ o'clock)
سوا بجے	*savā baje*	quarter past one (1¼ o'clock)
ڈیڑھ بجے	*ḍeṛh baje*	half past one (1½ o'clock)
پونے دو بجے	*paune do baje*	quarter to two (2 minus ¼ o'clock)
سوا دو بجے	*savā do baje*	quarter past two (2¼ o' clock)

ڈھائی بجے	*dhāī baje*	half past two (2½ o'clock)
پونے تین بجے	*paune tīn baje*	quarter to three (3 minus ¼ o'clock)

Thereafter: سوا تین بجے *savā tīn baje* 3.15, ساڑھے تین بجے *sāṛhe tīn baje* 3.30, پونے چار بجے *paune cār baje* 3.45, چار بجے *cār baje* 4.00, etc.

Minutes to, minutes past

We have met the verb بجنا *bajnā* used in the sense of 'to ring', but it can also mean 'to strike (of a clock)', and بجنے میں *bajne meṅ* 'in striking' and بجکر bajkar, the conjunctive participle 'having' struck' are used to express minutes to and past the hour.

Minutes to the hour are expressed with the phrases:

X بجنے میں Y منٹ پر

X bajne meṅ Y minaṭ par

At Y (minutes) to X ('X in striking on Y minutes')

X بجنے میں Y منٹ باقی ہیں

X bajne meṅ Y minaṭ bāqī haiṅ

It is Y (minutes) to X ('X in striking Y minutes are remaining')

باقی *bāqī* means 'remaining, left over'.

چھ بجنے میں دس منٹ پر
At ten to six

بارہ بجنے میں بیس منٹ پر
At twenty to twelve

نو بجنے میں پانچ منٹ باقی ہیں
It is five to nine

سات بجنے میں تیئیس منٹ باقی ہیں
It is twenty three to seven

Minutes past the hour are expressed by the phrases:

X بجکر Y منٹ پر

X bajkar Y minaṭ par

At Y (minutes) past X ('X having struck on Y minutes')

X بجکر Y منٹ ہیں

X bajkar Y minaṭ haiṅ

It is Y (minutes) past X ('X having struck Y minutes are')

آٹھ بجکر پچیس منٹ پر

At twenty–five past eight

دس بجکر پانچ منٹ پر

At five past ten

گیارہ بجکر سات منٹ ہیں

It is seven minutes past elveen

تین بجکر دس منٹ ہیں

It is ten past three

An easier way of expressing minutes to and past the hour is, as often in English:

سات دس	پانچ چالیس
'seven ten'	'five forty'

This shorthand method is much less common in Urdu than in English, and is largely restricted to westernised, English- speaking circles.

کی مشق کرنا *kī mašq karnā* 'to practise'

As well as meaning 'exercise', مشق also means 'practice'. The phrase verb کی مشق کرنا means 'to practise':

میں ہر روز اردو بولنے کی مشق کرتا ہوں
I practise speaking Urdu every day
('do the practice of speaking')

پاکستان میں اردو بولنے کی بہت مشق ہوئی
In Pakistan we had a lot of practice in talking Urdu
('practice came about')

مشق *mašq* Exercise

13.1 Correct form of the past participle

All the verbs in this exercise are transitive. Give the correct form of the past participle of the verb in brackets, making it agree with its 'logical' object. Remember that if the object is followed by کو the partciple remains masculine singular.

1 ۱ کل شام کو میں نے رحیم صاحب سے باتیں (کرنا)
2 ۲ پرسوں انہوں نے پرانے شہر کی سیر (کرنا)
3 ۳ حامد کہاں ہے۔ کیا آپ نے اس کو (دیکھنا) ہے؟
4 ۴ بلقیس نے اپنی سہیلی کے ساتھ آئس کریم (کھانا)
5 ۵ پچھلے سال ہم نے بہت زیادہ کام (کرنا) تھا
6 ۶ میں اب نکل نہیں سکتا۔ میں نے نماز نہیں (پڑھنا)
7 ۷ آپ نے خود اپنا سامان (باندھنا)

مکالمہ دو *mukālima do* Dialogue 2

John and Helen find themselves in conversation with an unhappy fellow passenger.

ایرہوسٹس : السلام علیکم۔ مہربانی کر کے اپنا بورڈنگ پاس دکھائیے۔ آپ کی نشستیں وہاں ہیں دائیں ہاتھ پر۔

جان : شکریہ میں سمجھا۔ اٹھارہ اور اُنیس کھڑکی کے پاس۔ لیکن دیکھیے ہماری نشستوں میں دو آدمی بیٹھے ہیں۔ کیا ہوا؟ میں جا کے ان سے بات کروں گا۔ معاف کیجیے۔ لگتا ہے کہ آپ ہماری نشستوں میں بیٹھے ہیں۔ اٹھارہ اور انیس۔

ایک آدمی : اچھا! معاف کریں۔ آپ کا کہنا بالکل درست ہے۔ ایک منٹ ہم یہاں سے ہٹیں گے۔ کیا آپ دہلی جا رہے ہیں؟

جان : جی ہاں۔ میرے خیال سے ہم سب لوگ دہلی جا رہے ہیں، ورنہ ہم غلط ہوائی جہاز میں بیٹھے ہیں۔

آدمی : یہ تو سچ ہے۔ آج میرا دماغ ٹھیک سے کام نہیں کر رہا ہے۔ میں رات بھر نہیں سویا۔ کل شام کو میں دوستوں سے ملنے گیا اور ہم چار بجے صبح تک باتیں کر رہے تھے۔ گھر جا کر میں نے جلدی سامان باندھا اور سیدھے ہوائی اڈے آیا۔ کوئی بات نہیں، دہلی پہنچ کر میں خوب آرام کروں گا۔ لیکن گھر پر بیوی ہے، بچے ہیں، رشتے دار ہیں، وہ کبھی مجھے آرام کرنے نہیں دیتے۔ آرام حرام ہے گھر پر! مجھے بہت بھوک لگی ہے۔ کل شام کو میں نے کچھ نہیں کھایا۔ آج صبح چائے بھی نہیں پی۔ آپ کو معلوم ہے، زندگی کبھی کبھی بہت مشکل ہوتی ہے۔ میں ہر روز صبح سویرے اٹھکر کام پر جاتا ہوں۔ شام کو گھر پہنچ کر میں کھانا چاہتا ہوں۔ کھانا ملتا ہے؟ کچھ نہیں ملتا۔ میری بیوی دن بھر اپنی سہیلیوں کے ساتھ بیٹھتی ہے۔ گھر آکر کہتی ہے "میں تھکی ہوں آپ ہی کھانا بنائیے"۔ میں بھی تھکتا ہوں۔ مجھے پیاس بھی لگی ہے۔ کیا اس پرواز میں چائے نہیں دیتے؟ میں غریب آدمی ہوں، بھائی۔ کبھی کبھی میں سوچتا ہوں کہ میں انگلستان جا کر کام کروں گا۔ ایک بار میں نے جانے کی کوشش کی، لیکن انہوں نے مجھے ویزا نہیں دیا۔ بھائی، میں آپ سے کیا کہوں؟ دیکھیے۔ وہ لڑکی چائے لا رہی ہے۔ اللہ کا شکر ہے! لیکن وہ واپس جا رہی ہے۔ کیا ہمیں چائے نہیں ملے گی۔ ہائے ہائے!

مہربانی کرکے	*mihrbānī karke*	please	جاکر	*jākar*	having gone
بورڈنگ پاس	*borḍing pās*	boarding pass (m.)	ہوائی اڈا	*havāī aḍḍā*	airport (m.)
نشست	*nišist*	seat (f.)	پہنچ کر	*pahun̆ckar*	having arrived
سمجھنا	*samajhnā*	to understand	کرنے نہیں دیتے	*karne nahīn̆ dete*	don't let me rest
میں سمجھا	*main̆ samjhā*	I understand	حرام	*harām*	forbidden
کھڑکی	*khiṛkī*	window (f.)	مجھے بھوک لگی ہے	*mujhe bhūk lagī hai*	I feel hungry
جاکے	*jāke*	having gone	اٹھکر	*uṭhkar*	having got up
بات کرنا	*bāt karnā*	to have a word	طریقہ	*tarīqā*	way, method (m.)
لگتا ہے	*lagtā hai*	it seems	پیاس لگی ہے	*piyās lagī hai*	I feel thirsty
آپ کا کہنا	*āp kā kahnā*	what you say	جانے کی کوشش کی	*jāne kī košiš kī*	I tried to go
درست	*durust*	correct	ویزا	*vīzā*	visa (m.)
ہٹنا	*haṭnā*	to shift, move off	اللہ کا شکر	*allāh kā šukr*	thank God!
ورنہ	*varna*	otherwise, if not	ہائے ہائے	*hāe hāe!*	alas!
غلط	*ğalat*	the wrong			
دماغ	*dimāğ*	brain (m.)			

قواعد *qavā'id* Grammar

The conjunctive participle 'having done'

The conjunctive participle of the verb, which can be literally translated into English as 'having done' (in the sense of 'when I did'), is used in Urdu to join together ('conjunct') two or more separate ideas.

In English we might say: 'I went home and had dinner'; Urdu prefers 'Having gone home, I had dinner'-'subordinating' the first idea to the second. This is effected with the conjunctive participle.

The conjunctive participle is formed by adding either کر *-kar* or کے *-ke* to the stem of the verb:

جاکے	*jāke*	or	جاکر	*jākar*	'having gone'
آکے	*āke*	or	آکر	*ākar*	'having come'
کھاکے	*khāke*	or	کھاکر	*khākar*	'having eaten'

Both forms are equally common. کرنا has only the form کرکے *karke* 'having done'. Compare the following sentences with the English translation:

گھر جاکر کھانا کھاؤں گا

I shall go home and have dinner ('having gone')

مہربانی کرکے اپنا بورڈنگ پاس دکھایئے

Please show your boarding pass ('having done kindness')

صبح اٹھکر وہ نماز پڑھتے ہیں

He gets up in the morning and says prayers ('having got up')

آپ سے ملکر بڑی خوشی ہوئی

I'm very pleased to meet you ('having met you')

سمجھنا *samajhnā* 'to understand'

سمجھنا can be both transitive or intransitive. میں نے سمجھا *maiṅ ne samjhā* and میں سمجھا *maiṅ samjhā* are both correct.

The present habitual tense میں سمجھتا ہوں means 'I usually understand'. The past tense میں (نے) سمجھا means either 'I understood' or 'I understand now'.

| عام طور سے میں اردو سمجھتا ہوں | I (usually) understand Urdu |
| معاف کریں' میں (نے) نہیں سمجھا | I'm sorry, I don't understand |

More uses of لگنا *lagnā*

We have seen لگنا used with the oblique infinitive in the sense of 'to begin to do', but it may best be understood if it is translated very literally into English as 'to be applied to'. A more appropriate English rendering is often: 'to seem, feel, be felt', etc. Compare the following:

مجھے لگتا ہے کہ آپ ہماری نشستوں میں ہیں

mujhe lagtā hai ki āp hamārī nišistoṅ meṅ haiṅ

It seems to me that you are in our seats ('it is applied to me')

لگتا ہے کہ بارش ہوگی

lagtā hai ki bāriš hogī

It looks as if it will rain ('it is applied that')

مجھے بارہ بجے ہمیشہ بھوک لگتی ہے

mujhe bāra baje hameša bhūk lagtī hai

I always get/feel hungry at twelve ('hunger is applied to me always')

مجھے اب بھوک لگی ہے

mujhe ab bhūk lagī hai

I feel hungry now ('hunger has been applied')

In such expressions the present habitual tense expresses what is usually the case; the perfect tense expresses what is the actual case now.

گرمیوں میں عام طور سے پیاس لگتی ہے

garmīoṅ meṅ 'ām taur par piyās lagtī hai

(One) usually gets thirsty in the hot season

کیا آپ کو پیاس لگی ہے؟

kyā āp ko piyās lagī hai?

Do you feel thirsty (now)?

Note the feminine plural word گرمیاں *garmīāṅ* 'the hot season'. Compare جاڑے *jāṛe* 'the cold season' (m.p.).

آپ کا کہنا **āp kā kahnā 'what you say'**

We have seen that the infinitive can often be used as a noun: بولنا اچھا ہے to talk/talking is good.

کہنا as a noun can be translated into English as 'what (one) says'

آپ کا کہنا درست ہے

āp kā kahnā durust hai

What you say is right ('your saying')

میرے دوست کا کہنا غلط ہے

mere dost kā kahnā ğalat hai

What my friend says is wrong

حرام **harām 'forbidden'**; حلال ***halāl* 'approved'**

In Islam anything which is approved of or pure is termed حلال *halāl*. حلال گوشت, is meat from an animal which has been slaughtered according to the method prescribed in the Holy Quran.

حرام is anything which is forbidden by the precepts of Islam. The rhyming phrase آرام حرام ہے *ārām harām hai* 'rest is forbidden' jokingly means 'I get no peace!'.

کی کوشش کرنا ***kī košiš karnā* 'to try'**

کوشش *košiš* (f.) means 'a try, a attempt'. The phrase verb کرنے کی کوشش کرنا *(karne) kī košiš karnā* 'to do an attempt (of doing)' means 'to try to do':

میں آپ سے ملنے کی کوشش کروں گا	I'll try to meet you
میں نے ولایت جانے کی کوشش کی	I tried to go to Britain

کرنے دینا ***karne denā* 'to allow to do, to let do'**

With the oblique infinitive دینا *denā* 'to give' has the sense of 'to allow':

اس نے ہم کو وہاں جانے نہیں دیا

us ne ham ko vahāṅ jāne nahīṅ diyā

He did not allow us to go there ('did not give us to go')

بچے مجھے آرام کرنے نہیں دیتے

bacce mujhe ārām karne nahīṅ dete

The children don't allow me to rest

خود ***xud* 'oneself'**

خود *xud* (note the *u* is pronounced short after خ *xe*) coming after a noun or pronoun means (one)self:

میں خود	*maiṅ xud*	I myself
آپ خود	*āp xud*	you yourself
آپ نے خود سامان باندھا؟	*āp ne xud sāmān bāṅdhā*	Did you pack the luggage yourself?

ہی *hī* 'only, just'

ہی coming after the word it refers to, often has the sense of 'only, just':

یہ ہماری ہی چیزیں ہیں	These are only our things
میں کراچی ہی جاؤں گا	I shall go just to Karachi

Sometimes it can be rendered in English merely by stress: میں ہی کہہ رہا تھا *I* was saying/it was *I* who was saying.

Numbers

At this stage the numerals 61–80 (Appendix 1) should be learnt.

ثقافت *siqāfat* Culture

In the subcontinent ritual purity is regarded as extremely important. What is حلال *halāl* and حرام *harām* for Muslims is carefully defined in the Holy Quran (قرآن شریف *qurān šarīf*). Meat may only be taken from an animal which has been slaughtered by a Muslim butcher, who will drain off all the blood and pronounce a prayer over the carcass. In the west, Muslim butchers' shops usually bear a sign with the Urdu words حلال گوشت *halāl gošt*, followed by the Arabic equivalent لحم حلال *lahm halāl* 'Halal Meat'.

مشقیں *mašqeṅ* Exercises

13.2 Using the conjunctive participle

The following sentences consist of two separate statements. Link them by using the conjunctive participle:

1 میں اب گھر جاؤں گا۔ کھانا کھاؤں گا
2 فہمیدہ کراچی گئی۔ سب رشتے داروں سے ملی
3 حامد نے کتاب پڑھی۔ آرام کیا
4 ہم نے سامان باندھا۔ ہوائی اڈے گئے
5 وہ ٹیکسی میں بیٹھے۔ ڈرائیور سے باتیں کرنے لگے

13.3 Match question and answer

The following questions relate to the two dialogues in this unit. Can you match the answers to the questions?

سوالات

1 ہوائی اڈے میں جان کے پاس کتنا سامان تھا؟

2 جان اور ہیلن چھٹی پر کیا کر رہے تھے؟

3 وہ دہلی کتنے بجے پہنچیں گے؟

4 ان کی نشستوں میں کون بیٹھے تھے؟

5 کیا اُس آدمی نے ناشتہ کیا تھا؟

6 دہلی پہنچکر وہ آدمی آرام کرے گا؟

7 اس کو ولایت جانے کا ویزا ملا؟

جواب

1 وہ کوئی سوا بارہ' ساڑھے بارہ بجے پہنچیں گے۔

2 جی نہیں۔ اس کو بہت بھوک لگ رہی تھی۔

3 جی نہیں۔ اس کے لئے آرام حرام ہے۔

4 ان کے پاس دو سوٹ کیس اور ایک بیگ تھا۔

5 جی نہیں۔ اس کو ویزا نہیں ملا۔

6 وہ برِ صغیر کی سیر کر رہے تھے۔

7 دو آدمی بیٹھے تھے۔

13.4 Translate into Urdu

Yesterday we got up ('having got up') early and arrived at the airport at half past eight in the morning. The aeroplane was due to go ('about to go') at twenty to ten. 'Come on', I said to my wife. 'We have lots of time. Let's first go and have ('go to drink') a cup of tea.' We went ('having gone') straight to the restaurant and ordered tea. Since we had not had breakfast, I said to my wife: 'I feel hungry. Shall I order some food as well?' 'What's the time?', she asked. 'It's quarter to nine', I said. 'We can sit here for half an hour. After that we can take our luggage and go towards the lounge'. The queue was not very long. We showed our passports and went into the lounge. It was half past nine. 'Our flight will depart after fifty minutes', I said. 'This evening we shall be in Delhi. Bon voyage!'

14 اُردو ہی میں باتیں کریں
Let's talk only in Urdu

In this unit you will learn how to:

- express action performed on your own behalf
- express action performed for others
- give your date of birth
- talk to a doctor

مکالمہ ایک *mukālima ek* Dialogue 1

John and Helen arrive in India and talk to a Sikh taxi driver about Delhi.

جان : آخر ہم دہلی پہنچ گئے ہیں۔ چلیں، ہم ٹیکسی ڈھونڈلیں اور سیدھے ہوٹل جائیں۔ ہوٹل کا پتہ میرے پاس ہے۔ وہ راج پتھ پر ہے۔ وہاں تھوڑا سا کھانا کھالیں۔ اس کے بعد لال قلعے اور جامع مسجد کی سیر کریں گے۔

ہیلن : جان صاحب! آپ مجھ سے اردو میں باتیں کیوں کر رہے ہیں؟ آپ انگریزی بھول گئے ہیں کیا؟

جان : جی نہیں، میں سوچ رہا تھا کہ چونکہ ہم اردو کے وطن آگئے ہیں تو اردو ہی میں باتیں کرنی چاہئیں۔ اردو دہلی کی گلیوں اور کوچوں میں پیدا ہوئی تھی۔ ہے نا؟

ہیلن : آپ واقعی پاگل ہوگئے ہیں۔ خیر، کوئی بات نہیں۔ اردو ہی میں باتیں کریں۔ مجھے کوئی اعتراض نہیں ہے۔ میری اردو آپ کی اردو سے زیادہ اچھی ہے۔

جان : وہ ٹیکی کھڑی ہے۔ اے سردار جی۔ ٹیکسی خالی ہے؟

سردار : جی ہاں صاحب۔ بیٹھیے۔ کہاں جانا ہے؟

جان راج پتھ جانا ہے۔ آپ کو معلوم ہے کہ امپیریل ہوٹل کہاں ہے؟

سردار : جی ہاں، صاحب۔ بیٹھیے۔ آپ کہاں سے آرہے ہیں؟

جان لاہور سے آرہے ہیں۔

سردار : اچھا، لاہور میرا وطن ہے۔ تقسیم کے بعد سن سیتالیس میں (۱۹۴۷ء) میرا خاندان

یہاں منتقل ہوا۔ میرا بچپن وہاں گذرا۔

جان : دہلی میں بہت سکھ رہتے ہیں نا؟

سردار : جی ہاں، صاحب۔ دہلی میں ہر طرح کے لوگ رہتے ہیں۔ ہندو بھی ہیں اور مسلمان زیادہ تر پرانے شہر میں، یعنی چاندنی چوک کی طرف، رہتے ہیں۔ آپ اچھی اردو بول لیتے ہیں۔ آپ پاکستانی تو نہیں ہیں۔

جان : جی نہیں، ہم انگلستان کے ہیں۔ وہاں ہمارے بہت ہندوستانی اور پاکستانی دوست ہیں۔ اس لئے میں نے اردو سیکھ لی۔

سردار : خوب۔ آپ کا ہوٹل آگیا ہے۔

جان : میں آپ کو کتنے پیسے دوں؟

سردار : بس، ساٹھ روپے دے دیجیے۔

جان : اچھا، لیجیے۔ شکریہ آپ کا۔ انشاء اللہ ہم پھر ملیں گے۔

پہنچ گئے ہیں	*pahuṅc gae haiṅ*	have arrived
ڈھونڈنا	*ḍhūṅḍnā*	to look for
ڈھونڈ لیں	*ḍhūṅḍl leṅ*	let's look for
پتہ	*pata*	address (m.)
راج پتھ	*rāj path*	Raj Path (street in Delhi) (m.)
کھالیں	*khā leṅ*	let us eat
لال قلعہ	*lāl qil'a*	the Red Fort
بھول گئے ہیں	*bhūl gae haiṅ*	have you forgotten?
آگئے ہیں	*ā gae haiṅ*	have come
باتیں کرنی چاہئیں	*bāteṅ karnī cāhīeṅ*	we should chat
گلی	*galī*	alley (f.)
کوچہ	*kūca*	lane (m.)
پیدا ہوئی تھی	*paidā hūī thī*	was born
پاگل	*pāgal*	mad
ہو گئے ہیں	*ho gae haiṅ*	have become
اعتراض	*i'tirāz*	objection (m.)
مجھے اعتراض نہیں	*mujhe i'tirāz nahīṅ*	I have no objection
کھڑا	*kharā*	standing
سردار جی	*sardār jī*	a term of address for a Sikh
امپیریل ہوٹل	*impīrīal hoṭal*	Imperial Hotel (m.)
تقسیم	*taqsīm*	Partition (f.)
سن	*san*	in the year (m.)

منتقل	*muntaqil*	shifted, trans-ferred	آ گیا ہے	*ā gayā hai*	has come
			دوں	*dūṅ*	shall/may I give?
سکھ	*sikh*	Sikh (m.)	ساٹھ	*sāṭh*	sixty
سیکھ لی	*sīkh lī*	learnt	دے دیجیے	*de dījīe*	give!

قواعد *qavā'id* Grammar

ہجے *hijje* Spelling

Since the Urdu alphabet has no capital letters, it is not always easy to spot a proper name in the text. For this reason the sign ˜ is often written over the name in order to identify it:

امپیریل ہوٹل *impīrīal hoṭal* the Imperial Hotel

The word سن *san* 'in the year of' comes before the numerals expressing the year: سن انیس سو پینتالیس *san unnīs sau paiṅtālīs* (year) nineteen hundred (and) forty-seven. When the year is written in figures, the numerals are written over the sign ‿ which is pronounced *san*: ۱۹۴۷ء

You may have noticed that it is sometimes difficult to read certain numerals when they are written only with letters. For example, the words for 23 and 33 تیئیس تینتیس *teīs* and *taiṅtīs* are confusable. For this reason the figures are often written over the words in order to avoid confusion:

تیئیس۲۳ تینتیس۳۳.

Compound verbs with جانا *jānā*

In colloquial English, we often use the verb 'to go' in conjunction with another verb: 'I've gone and eaten my dinner'; 'you've really gone and done it'. The addition of 'gone' makes hardly any difference to the sense. Urdu has a similar construction (in the case of Urdu, however, it is not considered colloquial or slang), and such combinations are known as compound verbs.

Many compound verbs consist of the stem of the main verb followed by جانا *jānā* 'to go'. Most intransitive verbs, e.g. آنا 'to come', پہنچنا 'to arrive', بیٹھنا 'to sit', سونا 'to sleep', etc. may form such componds:

Simple form		Compound form		
آنا	*ānā*	آ جانا	*ā jānā*	to come
پہنچنا	*pahuṅcnā*	پہنچ جانا	*pahuṅc jānā*	to arrive

بیٹھنا	*baiṭhnā*	بیٹھ جانا	*baiṭh jānā*	to sit (down)
سونا	*sonā*	سو جانا	*so jānā*	to sleep

The verb جانا *jānā* 'to go' cannot form a compound with itself. For fairly obvious reasons, you cannot say جا جانا *jā jānā.*

With verbs expressing motion 'to come, arrive, go out', etc. there is little difference, if any, between the simple and compound forms:

وہ دس بجے آ جاتا ہے	=	وہ دس بجے آتا ہے
vuh das baje ā jātā hai		*vuh das baje ātā hai*
He comes at ten o'clock		
ہم دہلی پہنچ گئے ہیں	=	ہم دہلی پہنچے ہیں
ham dihlī pahuṅc gae haiṅ		*ham dihlī pahuṅce haiṅ*
We have arrived at Delhi		
وہ گھر سے نکل جائے گا	=	وہ گھر سے نکلے گا
vuh ghar se nikal jāegā		*vuh ghar se niklegā*
He will go out of the house		

Note that the present and past continuous tenses cannot be used in a compound with, nor can a compound verb be used with, نہیں *nahīṅ*:

میں آٹھ بجے آ گیا	*maiṅ āṭh baje ā gaya*	I came at eight
میں آٹھ بجے نہیں آیا	*maiṅ āṭh baje nahīṅ āyā*	I did not come at eight

بیٹھ جانا baiṭh jānā, سو جانا so jānā, اٹھ جانا uṭh jānā

Some intransitive verbs express the transition of one state to another, e.g. بیٹھنا *baiṭhnā* 'to sit (from standing)'; سونا *sonā* 'to sleep (from being awake)'; اٹھنا *uṭhnā* 'to get up (from lying down)', etc. With such verbs the compound with جانا expresses that transition. This is especially the case in the past tenses. Compare the following:

وہ ہمیشہ اس کرسی پر بیٹھتا ہے

vuh hameša is kursī par baiṭhtā hai

He always sits on this chair

وہ آ جاتا ہے اور فوراً بیٹھ جاتا ہے

vuh ā jātā hai aur fauran baiṭh jātā hai

He comes and immediately sits down

احمد عام طور سے سویرے اٹھتا ہے

ahmad 'ām taur se savere uṭhtā hai

Ahmad usually gets up early

کیا احمد اٹھ گیا ہے؟

kyā ahmad uṭh gayā hai?

Has Ahmad got up?

وہ رات بھر سوتی ہے

vuh rāt bhar sotī hai

She sleeps all night long

وہ اب سو گئی ہے

vuh ab so gaī hai

She has now gone to sleep

The verbs لینا *lenā* 'to take' and دینا *denā* 'to give'

The verbs لینا and دینا have slightly irregular forms in some of their tenses. The present and past habitual and the present and past continuous tenses are completely regular but the subjunctive and future tenses are irregular:

Subjunctive

لینا	**lenā**	دینا	**denā**	
میں لوں	main lūṅ	دوں	dūṅ	'I may take/give'
تو لے	tū le	دے	de	
یہ، وہ لے	yih/vuh le	دے	de	
ہم لیں	ham leṅ	دیں	deṅ	
تم لو	tum lo	دو	do	
آپ لیں	āp leṅ	دیں	deṅ	
یہ، وہ لیں	yih/vuh leṅ	دیں	deṅ	

The future is formed by adding the suffixes گا گی گے *-gā, -gī, -ge,* to the subjunctive in the normal way:

میں لوں گا، لوں گی	*maiṅ lūṅgā, lūṅgī*	I (m./f.) shall take
میں دوں گا، دوں گی	*maiṅ dūṅgā, dūṅgī*	I (m./f.) shall give
وہ لے گا، لے گی	*vuh legā, legī*	he, she, it will take
وہ دے گا، دے گی	*vuh degā. degī*	he, she, it will give

آپ لیں گے، لیں گی	*āp leṅge, leṅgī*	you (m./f.) wll take
آپ دیں گے، دیں گی	*āp deṅge, deṅgī*	you will give

Compound verbs with لینا and دینا

Many transitive verbs form compounds which consist of the stem of the main verb + لینا or دینا. For example:

Simple verb		Compound + لینا		
کھانا	*khānā*	کھا لینا	*khā lenā*	to eat
ڈھونڈنا	*ḍhūṅḍnā*	ڈھونڈ لینا	*ḍhūṅd lenā*	to look for
سیکھنا	*sīkhnā*	سیکھ لینا	*sīkh lenā*	to learn
کرنا	*karnā*	کر لینا	*kar lenā*	to do

Simple verb		Compound + دینا		
دینا	*denā*	دے دینا	*de denā*	to give
پہنچانا	*pahuṅcānā*	پہنچا دینا	*pahuṅcā denā*	to take to
بھیجنا	*bhejnā*	بھیج دینا	*bhej denā*	to send
کرنا	*karnā*	کر دینا	*kar denā*	to do

The main function of the compound with لینا is to express action performed on behalf of oneself or towards oneself. For example, when you eat something, you naturally eat 'for yourself', taking the food 'into yourself':

میں کھانا کھا لیتا ہوں

maiṅ khānā khā letā hūṅ

I eat dinner (for myself)

میں ٹیکسی ڈھونڈ لوں گا

maiṅ ṭaiksī ḍhūṅḍ lūṅgā

I shall look for a taxi (on my own behalf)

اس نے بہت کام کر لیا ہے

us ne bahut kām kar liyā hai

He has done a lot of work (for himself)

The compound with دینا expresses action performed on someone else's behalf or away from oneself:

میں آپ کو پیسے دے دیتا ہوں

maiṅ āp ko paise de detā hūṅ

I give you money (for yourself)

ہم آپ کو اسٹیشن تک پہنچا دیں گے

ham āp ko isṭešan tak pahuṅcā deṅge

We'll take you as far as the station (doing you the favour)

میں نے آپ کے لئے یہ کام کر دیا تھا

maiṅ ne āp ke lie yih kām kar diyā thā

I had done/did this work for you

In the examples the compound underlines the direction of the action. The simple verb could also be used without making a vast difference to the sense.

Note that these compounds cannot be used with the continuous tenses, nor in the negative:

میں آپ کو پیسے دے دوں گا

maiṅ āp ko paise de dūṅgā

میں آپ کو پیسے نہیں دوں گا

maiṅ āp ko paise nahīṅ dūṅgā

Further observations on compound verbs

The rules hold true in the vast majority of cases, but as you proceed, you will find that certain verbs 'prefer' one or other of the compound forms, while some 'prefer' to remain simple. There are no hard and fast rules which determine correct usage, which is best learnt as and when encountered.

The verb بھولنا *bhūlnā* 'to forget' is almost always compounded wth جانا especially in its past tenses, and is regarded as intransitive, even though it can take an object:

میں بھول گیا/ بھول گیا ہوں/ بھول گیا تھا

maiṅ bhūl gayā/bhūl gayā hūṅ/bhūl gayā thā

I forgot/have/had forgotten

معاف کیجیے میں آپ کا نام بھول گیا ہوں

I'm sorry, I have forgotten your name

With some verbs, the لینا compound has the sense of 'managing to do, doing something reasonably well':

وہ کافی اچھی اردو بول لیتا ہے

vuh kāfī acchī urdū bol letā hai

He speaks Urdu quite well

میں نے انگریزی فوج میں سیکھ لی

maiṅ ne angrezī fauj meṅ sīkh lī

I managed to learn English in the army

Sometimes دینا gives the verb a sense of completion :

میں نے یہ کام کر دیا

maiṅ ne yih kām kar diyā

I've done (and completed) the work

لے جانا **le jānā** 'to take away'; لے آنا **le ānā** 'to bring'

The compound لے جانا (لینا + جانا) means 'to take (away)' ('to take and go'). The compound لے آنا (لینا + آنا) means 'to bring' ('to take and come'). The verb لانا 'to bring' is a contracted one-word form of لے آنا.

Since the 'operative' parts of these verbs are جانا and آنا they are regarded as intransitive (even though 'to take away' and 'to bring' are transitive in English).

میں آپ کو پاکستان لے جاؤں گا

maiṅ āp ko pākistān le jāūṅgā

I shall take you (away) to Pakistan

بھائی یہ روٹی یہاں سے لے جائیے۔ باسی ہے

bhāī, yih roṭī yahāṅ se le jāīe. bāsī hai

Waiter! Take this bread away from here. It's stale

میرے لئے چائے اور بسکوٹ لے آیئے / لائیے

mere lie cāe aur biskūṭ le āīe/lāīe

Bring tea and biscuits for me

ہم آپ کے لئے اُس کی نئی کتاب لے آئے ہیں / لائے ہیں

ham āp ke lie us kī naī kitāb le āe haiṅ/lāe haiṅ

We have brought (for) you his new book

Both لے آنا and لے جانا may be used with تشریف:

یہاں سے تشریف لے جایئے

yahāṅ se tašrīf le jāīe

Go away ('take your honour away') from here (a polite dismissal)

آیئے' تشریف لے آیئے / لایئے

āīe, tašrīf le āīe/ lāīe

Please come in

کرنا چاہیے **karnā cāhīe 'ought to do'**

Used with the infinitive چاہیے *cāhīe* expresses 'moral' obligation: کرنا چاہیے 'ought to do'. The past form کرنا چاہیے تھا *karnā cāhīe thā* means 'ought to have done'. Compare the following sentences:

مجھے اب جانا ہے	*mujhe ab jānā hai*	I have to go now
مجھے اب جانا چاہیے	*mujhe ab jānā cāhīe*	I ought to go now
مجھے جانا تھا	*mujhe jānā thā*	I had to go
مجھے جانا چاہیے تھا	*mujhe jānā cāhīe thā*	I ought to have gone

If there is an object, the infinitive must 'agree' with the object in gender and number, and چاہیے must agree in number having its plural form چاہئیں *cāhīeṅ*. چاہیے تھا *cāhīe thā* has the masculine plural form چاہئے تھے *cāhīe the;* the feminine singular is چاہیے تھی *cāhīe thī* and the feminine plural is چاہیے تھیں *cāhīe thīṅ*. For this agreement compare the rules given in Unit 8. Thus:

مجھے خط لکھنا ہے — *mujhe xat likhnā hai*
I must write a letter

مجھے خط لکھنا چاہیے — *mujhe xat likhnā cāhīe*
I ought to write a letter

مجھے دو کتابیں پڑھنی چاہیں — *mujhe do kitābeṅ paṛhnī cāhieṅ*
I ought to read two books

مجھے کتاب پڑھنی تھی — *mujhe kitāb paṛhnī thī*
I had to read a book

مجھے دو خط لکھنے چاہیے تھے — *mujhe do xat likhne cāhīe the*
I ought to have written two letters

Note that the plural form چاہیں cannot be used before ہیں and تھے.

If the object is followed by کو only the singular forms چاہیے and چاہیے تھا are used:

مجھے رحیم صاحب کو اسٹیشن پہنچانا چاہیے

mujhe rahīm sāhib ko isṭešan pahuṅcānā cāhīe

I ought to take Rahim to the station

مجھے اپنی بیٹیوں کو کلکتے بھیجنا چاہیے تھا

mujhe apnī beṭīoṅ ko kalkatte bhejnā cāhīe thā

I ought to have sent my daughters to Calcutta

ہو جانا **ho jānā** 'to become'

The compound verb ہو جانا ('go and be') means 'to become', and may often be rendered into English as 'to get, go, happen, be', etc.

مغرب میں لوگ جلدی امیر ہو جاتے ہیں

maǧrib meṅ log jaldī amīr ho jāte haiṅ

In the West people quickly become/get rich

میں ناراض ہو جاؤں گا

maiṅ nārāz ho jāūṅgā

I shall become/get angry

In the past tenses ہو گیا (ہے تھا) coincide with ہوا (ہے' تھا) 'became, has become, had become':

آپ پاگل ہو گئے ہیں / ہوئے ہیں

āp pāgal ho gae haiṅ/hūe haiṅ

You've gone mad

کیا ہو گیا تھا/ ہوا تھا؟

kyā ho gayā thā/kyā hūā thā?

What (had) happened?

Like other compounds ہو جانا cannot be used in negative sentences. In the habitual and future tenses it is replaced by ہوتا ہے' ہوتا تھا and ہوگا ; in the past tenses it is replaced by ہوا:

وہ اکثر ناراض ہو جاتا ہے	he often gets angry
وہ اکثر ناراض نہیں ہوتا ہے	he doesn't often get angry
ہم امیر ہو جائیں گے	we shall become rich

ہم کبھی امیر نہیں ہوں گے	we shall never become/be rich
وہ بالکل پاگل ہو گیا ہے	he's gone completely mad
وہ بالکل پاگل نہیں ہوا	he hasn't gone completely mad

پیدا ہونا **paidā honā** 'to be born'

پیدا ہونا means 'to be born'

بچے ہر ایک منٹ پیدا ہوتے ہیں

bacce har ek minaṭ paidā hote haiṅ

Children are born every minute

میں پیدا ہوا *maiṅ paidā hūā* (f. میں پیدا ہوئی *maiṅ paidā hūī*) means 'I was ('became') born':

میں ۱۹۵۰ء میں پیدا ہوا تھا / ہوئی تھی

maiṅ san unnīs sau paccās meṅ paidā hūā thā/hūī thī

I was born in nineteen hundred (and) fifty

Here the pluperfect is used because the date is stated.

کھڑا ہونا **khaṛā honā** 'to stand'

کھڑا *khaṛā* is an adjective meaning 'standing'. The name for the medieval language from which Urdu and Hindi came was کھڑی بولی *khaṛī bolī* 'the standing (i.e. 'established') speech'.

سردار جی **sardār jī**

In medieval times the Sikhs were given the honorific title سردار *sardār* 'headman, leader'. Sikhs are still addressed as سردار جی *sardār jī*.

مکالمہ دو *mukālima do* Dialogue 2

Helen feels unwell and John calls the doctor.

جان : آخر ہم ہوٹل آگئے ہیں۔ میں بہت تھکا ہوں، آج ہم نے بہت زیادہ کیا۔ صبح لاہور سے دہلی آگئے۔ دوپہر کے بعد ہم نے لال قلعہ اور جامع مسجد کی سیر کی۔ اب ساڑھے سات بجے ہیں۔ چلیں کھانا وانا کھائیں۔

ہیلن : معاف کیجیے، جان۔ میں ذرا بیمار ہوں۔ میں تھوڑی دیر کے لئے لیٹوں گی۔

جان : میں سوچ رہا تھا کہ تم بہت خاموش تھیں۔ تھکی سی نظر آتی ہو۔ تم کو کیا ہوا؟

ہیلن : میں کچھ نہیں سمجھتی ہوں۔ سر میں درد ہے۔ تھوڑا سا بخار ہے اور پیچش بھی ہونے لگی۔

جان : میرے خیال سے میں ڈاکٹر کو بلانے کی کوشش کروں گا۔ تم لیٹو' میں ریسپشن میں جاکر کسی سے پوچھ لوں گا۔

(تھوڑی دیر کے بعد جان واپس آتے ہیں)

جان : بس۔ ہو گیا۔ ڈاکٹر فوراً آئیں گے۔ انھوں نے یہاں سے فون کیا۔ سنو۔ دروازے پر کوئی ہے۔ میرے خیال سے ڈاکٹر ہوں گے۔

ڈاکٹر : نمستے۔ میں نے سنا ہے کہ آپ لوگ اردو بولتے ہیں۔ میرا نام ڈاکٹر شرما ہے۔ بتائیے۔ کیا بات ہے؟

ہیلن : نمستے' ڈاکٹر صاحب۔ میں بیمار سی ہو گئی ہوں۔ پیٹ میں گڑبڑ ہے۔ پیچش ہے اور سر میں سخت درد ہے۔ معلوم ہوتا ہے کہ بخار بھی ہے۔

ڈاکٹر : میں سمجھا۔ آپ بستر پر لیٹیے' اور میں دیکھ لوں گا۔ ہاں آپ کا درجۂ حرارت ایک سو چار (۱۰۴) ہے۔ ذرا زبان دکھائیے۔ آپ تھکی سی معلوم ہوتی ہیں۔ ممکن ہے کہ یہ آب و ہوا کی تبدیلی کی وجہ سے ہو۔ میں آپ کو کچھ اینٹی بایوٹک دوں گا۔ اور کھانے پینے میں احتیاط برتیے۔

ہیلن : دھنیاواد' ڈاکٹر صاحب۔ ہمیں آپ کو کتنا دینا چاہیے؟

ڈاکٹر : بس' ٹھیک ہے۔ آپ ہمارے مہمان ہیں۔ ایک دن آرام فرمائیے اور جب آپ کی صحت ٹھیک ہو جائے گی تو خوب سیر کیجیے۔ میں ابھی چلتا ہوں۔ نمستے۔

کھانا وانا	*khānā vānā*	food and stuff	پیچش	*peciš*	diarrhoea, dysentery (f.)
بیمار	*bīmār*	ill	ریسپشن	*rīsepšan*	reception (m.)
لیٹنا	*leṭnā*	to lie down	ہو گیا	*ho gayā*	it's OK ('it's become')
خاموش	*xāmoš*	quiet, silent	دروازہ	*darvāza*	door (m.)
تھکی سی	*thakī sī*	a bit tired	دروازے پر	*darvāze par*	at the door
نظر آتی ہو	*nazar ātī ho*	you look	نمستے	*namaste*	hello (Hindu greeting)
درد	*dard*	pain (m.)			
سر میں درد ہے	*sar meṅ dard hai*	I have a headache			
بخار	*buxār*	fever (m.)			

شرما	*šarmā*	Sharma	احتیاط	*ihtīāt*	caution (f.)
بیمار سی	*bīmār sī*	a bit ill	برتنا	*baratnā*	to use, exercise
سخت	*saxt*	hard, harsh, terrible	احتیاط برتنا	*ihtīāt baratnā*	to take care
بستر	*bistar*	bed (m.)	دھنیاواد	*dhanyāvād*	thank you (to Hindus)
درجۂ حرارت	*darja-e harārat*	temperature (m.)	مہمان	*mihmān*	guest (m.)
زبان	*zabān*	tongue (f.)	جب	*jab*	when
آب و ہوا	*āb o havā*	climate (f.)	صحت	*sihat*	health (f.)
تبدیلی	*tabdīlī*	change			
کی وجہ سے	*kī vajah se*	because of			
اینٹی بایوٹک	*ainṭī bāyoṭik*	antibiotic (m.)			

قواعد **qavā'id Grammar**

ہجے **hijje Spelling**

درجۂ حرارت *darja-e harārat* 'temperature' is formed from two Persian words درجہ 'class, degree' and حرارت *harārat* 'heat'. Notice that the *izāfat* is written over final ہ (*choṭī he*) with ء *hamza*.

کھانا وانا **khānā vānā 'food and stuff'**

A word is often followed by its rhyme beginning with و *vāū*, giving the sense 'X and stuff, X and things'. Compare پیسے ویسے *paise vaise* 'money and things' چائے وائے *cāe vāe* 'tea and stuff'.

سا **sā '-ish'**

We have met the word سا ‘ سی ‘ سے *sā, sī, se* used after the adjectives تھوڑا and بہت : بہت سے لوگ 'many people', بہت سا کھانا 'a lot of food'.

Used after adjectives it has the sense of '-ish', 'sort of', 'a bit':

وہ اچھا سا آدمی ہے	He's a good sort of man
آپ بیمار سے نظر آتے ہیں	You look a bit ill
وہ تھکی سی ہے	She's a bit tired
لال سا رنگ	a reddish colour

Illness

Unfortunately, the subcontinent is not without its perils for the intrepid traveller, and minor ailments, especially stomach complaints, are all too common. The usual way of saying you 'have' something is: مجھے × ہے / ہو گیا ہے *mujhe X hai* or *ho gayā hai* 'I have/have got X (to me is/has become)':

مجھے زکام ہے	*mujhe zukām hai*	I have a cold
مجھے بخار ہے	*mujhe buxār hai*	I have a fever
مجھے پیچش ہے	*mujhe peciš hai*	I have diarrhoea
میرے سر میں درد ہے	*mere sar meṅ dard hai*	I have a headache
میرے پیٹ میں گڑبڑ ہے	*mere peṭ meṅ gaṛbaṛ hai*	I have an upset (stomach)
میرے گلے میں خراش ہے	*mere gale meṅ xarrāš hai*	I have a sore throat

The most common ailments you are likely to suffer are:

زکام	*zukām*	head cold (m.)	پیلیا	*pīliā*	jaundice (m.)
بخار	*buxār*	fever (m.)	کھجلی	*khujlī*	itching, rash (f.)
پیچش	*peciš*	diarrhoea (f.)	تھکاوٹ	*thakāvaṭ*	tiredness (f.)
الٹی	*ulṭī*	vomiting (f.)			

Serious illnesses are:

ہیضہ	*haizā*	cholera (m.)	ملیریا	*maleriā*	malaria (m.)
چیچک	*cecak*	smallpox (m.)	سوزاک	*sozāk*	venereal disease (m.)

The word for 'broken' is ٹوٹا *ṭūṭā*:

میرا بازو ٹوٹا ہے	*merā bāzū ṭūṭā hai*	My arm is broken
میری ٹانگ ٹوٹی ہے	*merī ṭāṅg ṭūṭī hai*	My leg is broken

The principal parts of the body are:

سر	*sar*	head (m.)	چھاتی	*chātī*	breast, chest (f.)
بال	*bāl*	hair (m.p.)	دل	*dil*	heart (m.)
آنکھ	*āṅkh*	eye (f.)	کلیجی	*kalejī*	liver (f.)
کان	*kān*	ear (m.)	پیٹ	*peṭ*	stomach (m.)
ناک	*nāk*	nose (f.)	کمر	*kamar*	waist (f.)
گلا	*galā*	throat (m.)	ٹانگ	*ṭāṅg*	leg (f.)
گردن	*gardan*	neck (f.)	پاؤں	*paoṅ*	foot (m.)
کاندھا	*kāndhā*	shoulder (m.)	بازو	*bāzū*	arm (m.)

مشق *mašq* Exercise

14.1 Diagnose the illnesses

Look at the illustrations of a man with various ailments. Can you provide the diagnosis?

(1)

(2)

(3)

(4)

(5)

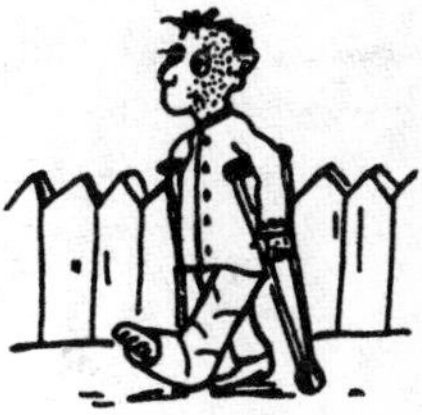

(6)

namaste 'hello'; *dhanyāvād* 'thank you'

نمستے is the usual greeting for Hindus, and is used in the sense of both 'hello' and 'goodbye'. The usual word for 'thank you' to Hindus is دھنیاواد although شکریہ is just as common.

Numbers

At this stage you should learn the numerals 81–100 (Appendix 1).

ثقافت *siqāfat* Culture

When travelling in Pakistan and India, so long as you have had all the required injections and take sensible precautions, you stand little risk of becoming seriously ill. Minor stomach ailments are, however, very common. In both countries there is no shortage of well-trained doctors who can be called out on a fee-paying basis. Hotels can usually make such arrangements. Surgeries and hospitals are run very much as in Britain, and a pharmacy (دواخانہ *davā xanā* m.) will usually be able to provide you with what you need. Traditional homoeopathic medicine can be very effective for common upsets. The Muslim system is known as یونانی *yūnānī* 'Greek', transmitted by the Arabs from Ancient Greek sources. The Hindu آیورویدک *āyurvedik* system depends upon Sanskrit medical texts.

The word for 'injection' is ٹیکا *ṭīkā* (m.) 'To have an injection done' ٹیکا لگوانا *ṭīkā lagvānā*:

مجھے ہیضے' پیلیے / ٹی. بی / مینجائٹس کا ٹیکا لگوانا ہے

mujhe haize/pīlīe/ṭī bī/meninjāiṭis kā ṭīkā lagvāna hai

I have to have an injection for cholera/hepatitis/T.B./meningitis

The most common way of saying 'I don't feel well' is میری طبیعت ٹھیک / اچھی نہیں ہے *merī tabī'at ṭhīk/acchī nahīn hai* 'my state (of health) is not good'.

In India and Pakistan you should always insist on having boiled water اُبلا ہوا پانی *ublā hūā pānī* (ابلنا *ubalnā* 'to come to the boil)' if bottled water is not available.

مشقیں *mašqeṅ* Exercises

14.2 Answer the questions

Mr Khan is not feeling well and calls a doctor. Listen to the dialogue and answer the questions:

1 What are Mr Khan's two main symptoms?

2 What two further questions does the doctor ask?

3 How high is Mr Khan's temperature?

4 What seems to be the main cause of the indisposition?

5 What does the doctor prescribe?

6 What should Mr Khan do if things do not improve?

14.3 Write using both words and figures

1 I was born in 1960. 2 It is quarter past ten. 3 The plane leaves at about half past twelve. 4 We ought to arrive there at quarter to five. 5 What's the time? It's sixteen minutes to five. 6 It is now eighteen minutes past eleven.

14.4 Compound verbs

Replace the verbs underlined in the following sentences with their corresponding compound:

1 میں کل شام کو آپ کے پاس آیا (آ جانا)
2 ہوائی جہاز ڈھائی بجے پہنچا تھا۔ (پہنچ جانا)
3 رحیم صاحب اپنے گھر سے نو بجے نکلے۔ (نکل جانا)
4 میری بیگم کھانا پکا کے سوئیں۔ (سو جانا)
5 کیا ریل گاڑی پہنچی ہے؟ (پہنچ جانا)

14.5 Compounds with *lenā* and *denā*

Replace the verbs underlined in the following sentences with their corresponding لینا or دینا compound, as indicated:

1 سردار جی۔ میں آپ کو کتنے پیسے دوں؟ (دے دینا)
2 انہوں نے سب کھانا کھایا۔ (کھا لینا)
3 میں آپ کو اپنی کتابیں بھیجوں گا۔ (بھیج دینا)
4 آپ نے میری کتاب پڑھی تھی؟ (پڑھ لینا)
5 انہوں نے دہلی میں اردو سیکھی تھی۔ (سیکھ لینا)

15 آپ کو دہلی آئے ہوئے کتنے دن ہو گئے ہیں؟
How long have you been in Delhi?

In this unit you will learn how to:

- say 'while doing' and 'as soon as I do'
- say how long you have been somewhere
- announce yourself to total strangers
- start to use the postal system

مکالمہ ایک *mukālima ek* Dialogue 1

John finds Aslam's friend, Sharif Ahmad, and introduces himself.

جان : آداب عرض ہے۔ آپ شریف احمد صاحب ہیں؟

شریف احمد : جی ہاں۔ اور آپ کا اسم شریف؟

جان : میرا نام جان اسمتھ ہے۔ آپ مجھے نہیں جانتے۔ مجھے امید ہے کہ بے وقت نہیں ہوں۔ بات یہ ہے کہ دو تین ہفتے پہلے میں کراچی میں تھا اور وہاں محمد اسلم خان صاحب سے میری ملاقات ہوئی تھی۔ انہوں نے مجھے آپ کا پتہ دے دیا اور مجھ سے کہا کہ مجھے دہلی میں ہوتے ہوئے آپ سے ملنا چاہیے۔ مجھے آپ کو ٹیلیفون کرنا چاہیے تھا لیکن میرے پاس آپ کا نمبر نہیں تھا۔

شریف احمد : اچھا، آپ اسلم صاحب کو جانتے ہیں؟ میں ان کی بیگم کے خاندان سے خوب واقف ہوں۔ آیئے، تشریف لایئے اور مجھے سب کچھ تفصیل سے سنایئے۔ اور آپ کہاں کے رہنے والے ہیں۔ دہلی آئے ہوئے کتنے دن ہو گئے ہیں؟ یہاں آپ کی کیا مصروفیات ہیں؟

جان : آپ شاید اندازہ لگا سکتے ہیں کہ میں انگریز ہوں۔ انگلستان میں میرے بہت ہندوستانی اور پاکستانی دوست ہیں۔ ان کے ساتھ رہتے رہتے میں نے تھوڑی بہت اردو سیکھ لی۔

شریف احمد : آپ کی اردو بہت اچھی ہے۔ ماشاء اللہ۔ اور اسلم صاحب سے کب ملاقات ہوئی تھی؟

جان : کراچی پہنچتے ہی میں ان سے ملا۔ شہر میں چلتے چلتے میں نے ان کو روک لیا اور ان سے دریافت کیا کہ وکٹوریہ روڈ کہاں ہے۔ انہوں نے فوراً گھر پر آنے کی دعوت دی۔ بہت شریف آدمی ہیں۔

شریف احمد : میں بھی شریف ہوں۔ یعنی شریف میرا نام ہے۔ آئیے میں آپ کو چائے پلاؤں گا۔ میری ایک چھوٹی سی گزارش ہے۔ آپ کو معلوم ہوگا کہ ہندوستان اور پاکستان کے درمیان تعلقات عموماً اچھے نہیں ہوتے۔ میں آپ کو اپنی نئی کتاب دوں گا۔ اگر آپ انگلستان پہنچتے ہی اسلم صاحب کو ہوائی ڈاک سے بھیج سکیں، تو میں آپ کا بے حد ممنون ہوں گا۔ مجھے پتہ نہیں کہ کتنا خرچ ہوگا، لیکن میں آپ کو دو سو روپے دوں گا۔

جان : جی نہیں شریف صاحب۔ مجھے کتاب دے دیجیے اور لندن میں اترتے ہی میں اس کو فوراً ڈاک میں ڈالوں گا۔

آئے ہوئے کتنے دن ہو گئے	āe hūe kitne din ho gae	how long have you been here?
اسم شریف	ism šarīf	name (formal) (m.)
مجھے امید ہے	mujhe ummīd hai	I hope
امید	ummīd	hope (f.)
بات یہ ہے	bāt yih hai	the matter is that
مجھے ... ہوتے ہوئے	mujhe ... hote hūe	while I was
سے واقف	se vāqif	acquainted with
تفصیل	tafsīl	detail (f.)
سنانا	sunānā	to tell, relate
مصروفیات	masrūfīāt	activities (f.p.)
اندازہ	andāza	guess, estimate (m.)
اندازہ لگانا	andāza lagānā	to guess
رہتے رہتے	rahte rahte	while staying
تھوڑا بہت	thoṛā bahut	a little
ماشاءاللہ	māšāllāh	praise be to God
پہنچتے ہی	pahuṅcte hī	as soon as I arrived
چلتے چلتے	calte calte	while walking
روکنا، روک لینا	roknā, rok lenā	to stop (someone)
سے دریافت کرنا	se daryāft karnā	to enquire from
دعوت	da'vat	invitation (f.)
شریف	šarīf	honourable, kind
پلانا	pilānā	to give to drink
گزارش	guzāriš	request (f.)

کے درمیان	*ke darmiyāṅ*	between	ہوں گا	*mamnūn hūṅgā*	grateful to you
تعلقات	*ta'luqāt*	relations, connections (m.p.)	بے حد	*be had*	extremely
عموماً	*'umūman*	generally	مجھے پتہ نہیں	*mujhe pata nahīṅ*	I don't know
پہنچتے ہی	*pahuṅcte hī*	as soon as you arrive	خرچ	*xarc*	expense (m.)
ڈاک	*ḍāk*	post, mail (f.)	اترنا	*utarnā*	to come down, land
ہوائی ڈاک	*havāī ḍāk*	air mail (f.)	اترتے ہی	*utarte hī*	as soon as I land
ممنون	*mamnūn*	indebted, grateful	ڈالنا	*ḍālnā*	to put in
آپ کا ممنون	*āp kā*	I shall be	ڈاک میں ڈالنا	*ḍāk meṅ ḍālnā*	to post

قواعد *qavā'id* Grammar

ہجے *hijje* Spelling

ماشاء اللہ *māsāllāh* 'Praise be to Allah!' is composed of three Arabic words: ما *mā* 'which, as'; شاء *šā-a* 'wished'; اللہ *allāh* : i.e. 'as Allah wished'. Note the way in which the final -*a* of شاء and the initial -*a* of اللہ are elided. The phrase is often used to express praise, and may be rendered in English as 'Praise be to God!'.

عموماً *'umūman* 'usually' is another example of an Arabic adverb ending in ً *tanvīn*. Compare the examples given in Unit 11.

اسم شریف **ism šarīf 'your good name'**

This formal phrase, used when politely enquiring someone's name (something like the rather old-fashioned English: 'What is your good name, sir?'), is composed of two Arabic words: اسم *ism* 'name' and شریف *šarīf* 'noble, honourable'. شریف is also a common Muslim name (e.g. the Egyptian film star Omar Shareef عمر شریف *'umar šarīf*). A شریف آدمی *šarīf ādmī* is someone who observes high moral standards, and it can be rendered in English as 'a decent fellow'. In the dialogue Sharif Ahmad makes a weak pun on his name.

امید *ummīd* 'hope'

The phrase verb مجھے امید ہے کہ *mujhe ummīd hai (ki)* 'to me there is hope (that) means 'I hope that ...':

ہمیں امید ہے کہ کل بارش نہیں ہوگی

We hope that it will not rain tomorrow

Some uses of the present and past participles

We have seen that the present participle ('doing, going') is formed by adding the suffixes: تا 'تی 'تے to the stem of the verb: کرتا 'کرتی 'کرتے etc. The past participle ('gone, done') is formed by adding the suffixes: ا 'ی - ے 'یں to the consonant stems, and یا 'ئی 'ئے 'ئیں to the vowel stems: پڑھا 'پڑھی 'پڑھے آیا 'آئی 'آئے etc.

The Urdu participles are in fact adjectives and to some extent function like any other adjectives, as they do in English, e.g. 'a loving mother; a burning house; a desired child; a dead man'. It should be noted that in both Urdu and English not every participle can be used in this way. For example we cannot say 'an arrived bus' or 'a doing person'.

We may illustrate the adjectival use of the participles in Urdu by using the two verbs جلنا *jalnā* 'to burn/to be burnt' and مرنا *marnā* 'to die'.

The participles form their feminine, masculine plural and oblique like اچھا *acchā*:

Present participle

	جلتا	*jaltā*	'burning'	مرتا	*martā*	'dying'
Masculine singular direct	جلتا	*jaltā*		مرتا	*martā*	
Masculine singular oblique	جلتے	*jalte*		مرتے	*marte*	
Masculine plural	جلتے	*jalte*		مرتے	*marte*	
Feminine	جلتی	*jaltī*		مرتی	*martī*	

Past participle

	جلا	*jalā*	'burnt'	مرا	*marā*	'dead'
Masculine singular direct	جلا	*jalā*		مرا	*marā*	
Masculine singular oblique	جلے	*jale*		مرے	*mare*	
Masculine plural	جلے	*jale*		مرے	*mare*	
Feminine	جلی	*jalī*		مری	*marī*	

These participles may be used simply as adjectives:

جلتا مکان	'a burning house'	جلتے مکان میں	'in a burning house'
مرتے لوگ	'dying people'	مرتی عورت	'a dying woman'
جلا مکان	'a burnt house'	جلے مکان میں	'in a burnt house'
مری عورت	'a dead woman'		

These phrases may be compared to: اچھے لوگ ' اچھی عورت ' اچھے مکان میں ' اچھا مکان .

The past participle of ہونا : ہوا , ہوئے ' ہوئی *hūā, hūī, hūe*, is often placed directly after the present and past participles of the main verb:

جلتا ہوا	*jaltā hūā*	جلا ہوا	*jalā hūā*
مرتا ہوا	*martā hūā*	مرا ہوا	*marā hūā*

Both elements change for gender, number and case:

جلتی ہوئی روٹی	'burning bread'	مرتے ہوئے لوگ	'dying people'
جلے ہوئے مکان میں	'in a burnt house'	مری ہوئی عورت	'a dead woman'

This is by far the most common form of the participles, especially when used as adjectives.

When the participle is used as an adjective, it can often be translated into English by a clause beginning with 'who' or 'which':

یہ آپ کی لکھی ہوئی کتاب ہے

yih āp kī likhī hūī kitāb hai?

Is this the book which you wrote ('your written book')

The masculine oblique participle in adverbial phrases

In English typical adverbial phrases' are: 'while going', 'since coming', 'as soon as arriving'. In the following examples the English translation of the participle phrases should be carefully noted:

دہلی میں ہوتے ہوئے میں ان سے ملا

dihlī meṅ hote hūe maiṅ un se milā

While (being) in Delhi, I met him

دوستوں کے ساتھ رہتے ہوئے میں نے اردو سیکھ لی

dostoṅ ke sāth rahte hūe maiṅ ne urdū sīkh lī

While staying with friends, I learnt Urdu

آپ کو کراچی آئے ہوئے کتنے دن ہو گئے؟

āp ko karācī āe hūe kitne din ho gae haiṅ?

How long have you been in Karachi ('to you having come to Karachi how many days have come about')?

When it is implied that the action took place gradually, the oblique present participle, without the addition of ہوئے , is repeated:

ان کے ساتھ رہتے رہتے میں نے اردو سیکھ لی

un ke sāth rahte rahte maiṅ ne urdū sīkh lī

While staying with them I gradually learnt Urdu

راستے پر چلتے چلتے میں گر گیا

rāste par calte calte maiṅ gir gayā

While walking (gradually) along the road, I fell down

گرنا *girnā/gir jānā* means 'to fall down'

Followed by ہی the masculine oblique present participle has the sense of 'as soon as':

لندن پہنچتے ہی میں آپ کو فون کروں گا

landan pahuṅcte hī maiṅ āp ko fon karūṅgā

As soon as I arrive in London, I'll phone you ('as soon as arriving')

ہیتھرو اترتے ہی میری چھٹی بھیج دیجیے

hīthro utarte hī merī ciṭṭhi bhej dījīe

Send my letter as soon as you land at Heathrow ('as soon as landing')

The past participle of چلنا : چلا ' چلی ' چلے *calā, calī, cale* followed by جانا means 'to go away':

میں ابھی چلا جاتا ہوں	*maiṅ abhī calā jātā hūṅ*	I'm going away now
لڑکی چلی گئی ہے	*laṛkī calī gaī hai*	The girl's gone away
ہم یہاں سے چلے جائیں گے	*ham yahāṅ se cale jāeṅge*	We'll go away from here
چلے جاؤ	*cale jāo*	Go away

How long?

When you ask how long a person has been/will be somewhere, in Urdu you have to specify what you mean by 'long' – 'a little while', 'so many days/months/years'?

آپ کتنی دیر کے لئے یہاں رہیں گے؟

āp kitnī der ke lie yahāṅ raheṅge?

For how long will you stay here?

Here دیر means 'short space of time'. Its use in the last question implies that the person is not expected to stay very long.

آپ کو یہاں آئے ہوئے کتنے دن ہو گئے؟

āp ko yahāṅ āe hūe kitne din ho gae?

How long ('for how many days') have you been here? کتنے دن could be substituted by کتنے مہینے 'how many months?' کتنے سال 'how many years?', etc.

تھوڑا بہت **thoṛā bahut 'a little'**

The rather curious combination تھوڑا بہت 'little much' means 'a little (bit of)'

آپ کو اردو آتی ہے! جی ہاں، تھوڑی بہت اردو آتی ہے

Do you know Urdu? Yes I know a little Urdu

Pairs of verbs

In past units we have had a number of examples of pairs of related verbs. The second of the pair is often distinguished from the first by having ا *-ā* added to the stem. The addition of ا usually has the literal sense of 'to cause to', 'to make', although in English we often employ a completely different verb to convey this 'causal' meaning. Examples are:

پہنچنا	to arrive	پہنچانا	'to cause to arrive' = to take to
پڑھنا	to read	پڑھانا	'to cause to read' = to teach
لگنا	to be applied	لگانا	'to cause to be applied' = to apply
سننا	to hear	سنانا	'to cause to hear' = to relate, tell

In this unit we met the phrase verb اندازہ لگانا *andāza lagānā* 'to apply a guess' = 'to guess'.

The verb سنانا *sunānā* 'to tell' means more or less the same as بتانا : مجھے سب کچھ تفصیل سے سنائیے ('tell me everything in detail') and is frequently used in the context of story telling:

میں آپ کو کہانی سناؤں گا   I'll tell you a story

There are also some slightly irregular formations such as:

پینا	*pīnā*	'to drink'	پلانا	*pilānā*	'to cause/give to drink'
کھانا	*khānā*	'to eat'	کھلانا	*khilānā*	'to cause/give to eat'./ 'to feed'

آیئے تشریف رکھیے اور میں آپ کو چائے پلاؤں گا

Come and sit down and I'll give you some tea (to drink)

گاؤں میں وہ آپ کو خوب کھلائیں گے

In the village they will feed you well

No hard and fast rules can be given for the formation of one of the pairs from the other, and individual verbs are best learnt as separate items of vocabulary.

مجھے پتہ نہیں **mujhe pata nahīṅ 'I don't know'**

The word پتہ literally means 'trace', and is also used in the sense of 'address'

میرے پاس آپ کا پتہ نہیں تھا

I didn't have your address

The phrase مجھے پتہ نہیں 'to me is/not a trace' is the exact equivalent of معلوم نہیں.

مجھے پتہ نہیں کہ خرچ کتنا ہوگا

I don't know how much the cost will be

ڈاک **ḍāk 'the post', 'mail'**

The word ڈاک *ḍāk* is used throughout the subcontinent for 'post', 'mail'. Common words and expressions in which it occurs are:

ڈاک خانہ	*ḍāk xāna*	post office (m.)
ہوائی ڈاک سے	*havāī ḍāk se*	by air mail
ڈاک سے بھیجنا	*ḍāk se bhejnā*	to send by post
ڈاک میں ڈالنا	*ḍāk meṅ ḍālnā*	to post' ('to put into the post')

مشق *mašq* Exercise

15.1 Complete the sentences

Complete the verb in brackets:

(burnt bread) مجھے ____ ____ نہیں چاہیے۔ اُس کو یہاں سے لے جاؤ۔ 1

(as soon as arriving) ہوائی اڈے ____ ____ میں آپ کو فون کروں گا۔ 2

3 پاکستان میں _____ _____ بچارہ احمد بیمار ہو گیا۔ (while staying)

4 راستے پر _____ _____ وہ گانا گارہا تھا۔ (while walking gradually)

5 لندن میں _____ _____ میں شریف سے ملوں گا۔ (while being)

مکالمہ دو *mukālima do* Dialogue 2

Sharif Ahmad invites John to give a talk on the Indians and Pakistanis of Britain.

جان : شریف صاحب۔ آپ مجھے اپنے بارے میں اور اپنی زندگی کے بارے میں کچھ بتائیے۔ کیا آپ دہلی کے رہنے والے ہیں۔

شریف احمد : جی نہیں۔ میں مراد آباد میں پیدا ہوا تھا۔ وہ جگہ عموماً اردو کی جائے پیدائش کہلاتی ہے۔ جب میں سب سے پہلے دہلی آیا تھا۔ تو میں ایک کالج میں داخل ہوا اور وہاں ابتدائی تعلیم حاصل کی۔ بی۔ اے کرنے کے بعد میں دہلی یونیورسٹی کے شعبۂ اردو میں داخل ہوا اور وہاں میں نے ایم۔ اے حاصل کی۔ ۱۹۷۰ء (انیس سو ستر) میں مجھے شعبۂ اردو میں ملازمت ملی اور تب سے میں اس شعبے میں اردو ادب پڑھا رہا ہوں۔ یعنی وہاں اردو پڑھاتے ہوئے تیس (۳۰) سال ہو گئے ہیں۔

جان : ظاہر ہے کہ اردو کے بہت طالب علم ہوں گے۔

شریف احمد : جی ہاں۔ نہ صرف ہندوستانی بلکہ کافی غیر ملکی طلبہ بھی ہیں۔ جاپانی ہیں، امریکن ہیں، روسی ہیں وغیرہ۔ جب آپ کو فرصت ہوگی تو آپ شعبے میں تشریف لائیے۔ کیا کل شام کو آپ کو فرصت ہوگی؟

جان : جی ہاں۔ کیا میں اپنی بیگم کو بھی لے آسکتا ہوں؟

شریف احمد : ضرور۔ غیر ملکی طلبہ میں سے ایک امریکن ہیں جو اتنی اچھی اردو بولتے ہیں جتنی آپ بولتے ہیں۔ ایک جاپانی طالب علم ہیں جن سے ملکے آپ کو بڑی خوشی ہوگی۔ جس وقت آپ آنا چاہیں آئیے۔ کل شام کو پانچ بجے تارکین وطن کے بارے میں بحث ہوگی۔ یعنی جو ہندوستانی اور پاکستانی تارکین وطن یورپ اور امریکہ میں آباد ہیں، ان کے مسائل پر گفتگو ہوگی۔ کیا آپ ایک چھوٹی سی تقریر کر سکیں گے۔

جان : احمد صاحب، میں نے کبھی اردو میں تقریر نہیں کی، لیکن میں کوشش کروں گا۔

اپنے بارے میں	*apne bāre meṅ*	about yourself
مرادآباد	*murādābād*	Muradabad (town near Delhi)
جائے پیدائش	*jā-e paidāiš*	birthplace (f.)
کہلانا	*kahlānā*	to be called
کالج	*kālij*	college (m.)
داخل ہوا	*dāxil hūā*	I entered, was enrolled
ابتدائی	*ibtidāī*	initial
تعلیم	*ta'līm*	education (f.)
حاصل کرنا	*hāsil karnā*	to acquire, receive
تعلیم حاصل کی	*ta'līm hāsil kī*	I was educated
بی اے	*bī e*	BA (f.)
یونیورسٹی	*yūnīvarsiṭī*	university (f.)
شعبہ	*šu'ba*	department (m.)
شعبۂ اردو	*šu'ba-e urdū*	Department of Urdu (m.)
ستر	*sattar*	seventy
ملازمت	*mulāzimat*	employment (f.)
تب سے	*tab se*	from then on
ادب	*adab*	literature (m.)
پڑھانا	*paṛhānā*	to teach
طالب علم	*tālib 'ilm*	student (m.)
طلبہ	*talaba*	students (m.p.)
جاپانی	*jāpānī*	Japanese
روسی	*rūsī*	Russian
جب	*jab*	when
جو	*jo*	who, which
اتنی ... جتنی	*itnī ... jitnī*	as ... as
جن سے ملکے	*jin se milke*	meeting whom
جس وقت	*jis vaqt*	at the time when
آنا چاہیں	*ānā cāheṅ*	you may wish to come
تارکین وطن	*tārikīn-e vatan*	emigrants (m.p.)
بحث	*bahs*	discussion (f.)
جو ہندوستانی تارکین وطن	*jo hindustānī tārikīn-e vatan*	the Indian emigrants who ...
یورپ	*yūrap*	Europe (m.)
آباد	*ābād*	settled, living
مسائل	*masāil*	problems (m.p.)
گفتگو	*guftagū*	conversation (f.)
گفتگو کرنا	*guftagū karnā*	to converse
تقریر	*taqrīr*	speech (f.)
تقریر کرنا	*taqrīr karnā*	to make a speech

قواعد *qavā'id* Grammar

ہجے *hijje* Spelling

More on the *izāfat*

After ا *(alif)*, the izāfat is written ے:

جائے پیدائش *jā-e paidāiš* place of birth, birthplace

Note the expression تارکینِ وطن *tārikīn-e vatan* 'emigrants' (literally 'abandoners of the native land'). The Arabic word تارک *tārik* means 'one who abandons/gives up'. Its special Arabic plural is تارکین *tārikīn*.

Abbreviations

Many English abbreviations are employed in Urdu. These are written by spelling out the English sounds in the Urdu script:

بی اے	*bī e*	BA
ایم اے	*em e*	MA
ٹی وی	*ṭī vī*	TV

اپنے بارے میں *apne bāre meṅ* 'about oneself'

We have seen that when a compound postposition such as کی طرف' کے ساتھ' کے بارے میں is used in conjunction with one of the personal pronouns then the corresponding possessive adjective must be used as the equivalent of the pronoun + کے or کی: میرے ساتھ 'with me', ہمارے بارے میں 'about us', اس کی طرف سے 'on his/ her behalf'.

In sentences like 'tell me about yourself'; 'I'll take it with me'; 'she'll give the money on her own behalf', where both pronouns refer to the same person, the second pronoun in the English sentence is expressed by اپنے or اپنی:

اپنے بارے میں بتائیے	Tell me about yourself
میں اپنے ساتھ لوں گا	I'll take it with me
وہ اپنی طرف سے پیسے دے گی	She'll give the money on her own behalf

کو کہنا 'to call'; کہلانا 'to be called'

The English sentence 'what is this called?' can be expressed with the personal phrase کو کہنا *ko kahnā* 'to say for':

اس کو (اسے) اردو میں کیا کہتے ہیں؟ اسے کتاب کہتے ہیں

us ko/use urdū meṅ kyā kahte haiṅ? use kitāb kahte haiṅ

What do they call ('say for') this in Urdu? They call ('say for') it *kitāb*.

ہم دہلی کو اردو کی جائے پیدائش کہتے ہیں

We call Delhi the birthplace of Urdu

It can also be expressed with the verb کہلانا *kahlānā* (related to کہنا) 'to be called':

اردو میں یہ کتاب کہلاتی ہے

urdū meṅ yih kitāb kahlātī hai

In Urdu this is called *kitāb*

دہلی اردو کی جائے پیدائش کہلاتی ہے

Delhi is called the birthplace of Urdu

مشق *mašq* Exercise

15.2 اردو میں اسے کیا کہتے ہیں؟

(a)

(b)

(c)

(d)

(e)

جب *jab* 'when', تب *tab* 'then'

In sentences such as 'When I was in Karachi, the weather was fine'; 'When you go to Bombay, meet my friends', the word 'when', is expressed in Urdu by جب *jab* which is used in much the same way as its English counterpart. There are, however, two important points to remember:

- if the 'when' half of the sentence refers to a future event, then the verb must be in the future tense:
- the second half of the sentence is introduced by تو to 'then'.

Note the following examples carefully:

جب میں اردو بولتا ہوں تو مجھے خوشی ہوتی ہے
When I speak Urdu (then) I am happy

جب آپ بمبئی جائیں گے تو میرے دوست سے ملیے
When you (will) go to Bombay (then) meet my friends

جب میں کراچی گیا تو موسم اچھا تھا
When I went to Karachi (then) the weather was fine

The phrase جب سے *jab se* (literally) 'from when' means 'since' in the sense of 'from the time when'. If we say: 'Since I have been working here I have been very happy', the second half of the sentence usually begins with تب سے *tab se* 'since then'. The verb in the first half of the sentence 'have been working' is present continuous in Urdu, logically enough since you are *still working*; similarly the verb in the second half of the sentence is also in the present:

جب سے میں یہاں کام کر رہا ہوں تب سے میں بہت خوش ہوں
Since I have been working ('am working') here, (since then) I have been ('am') very happy

حاصل کرنا **hāsil karnā** 'to acquire', 'to receive'

حاصل کرنا is a phrase verb meaning 'to acquire, receive, get'. It is often used in the context of education تعلیم *ta'līm* (f.)

آپ نے تعلیم کہاں سے حاصل کی؟ میں نے دہلی یونیورسٹی سے تعلیم حاصل کی
Where did you acquire (your) education? I acquired (my) education from Delhi University

جو *jo* 'who', 'which'

In sentences such as 'The man who came ...' 'The film which is running ...' 'who' and 'which' are both expressed in Urdu by the so-called relative pronoun جو *jo*:

آدمی جو آیا	The man who came
فلم جو چل رہی ہے	The film which is running/showing

Note the use of چلنا *calnā* in the last sentence.

جو frequently precedes the noun to which it refers. In other words you can also say: 'which man came...'; 'which film is running....'. The second half of the sentence begins with یہ or وہ. For 'who was the man who came yesterday', in Urdu you have to say: 'the man who came' or 'which man came yesterday, who was he?':

آدمی جو کل آیا وہ کون تھا؟

جو آدمی کل آیا وہ کون تھا؟

In such sentences either construction may be used, but the second pattern with جو preceding the noun to which it refers is rather more common.

Oblique forms of جو

Like the pronouns یہ and وہ, جو also has plural and oblique forms, but makes no change for gender:

Singular direct	جو	*jo*
Singular oblique	جس	*jis*
Plural direct	جو	*jo*
Plural oblique	جن	*jin*

As always, the oblique forms are mainly used with postpositions. Compare the following sentences, paying attention to the English translation:

Singular direct

وہ خاتون جو یہاں تھیں' وہ پاکستانی ہیں؟

جو خاتون یہاں تھیں وہ پاکستانی ہیں؟

Is the lady who was here a Pakistani?

Singular oblique

آدمی جس سے آپ باتیں کر رہے تھے' وہ انگریز ہے

جس آدمی سے آپ باتیں کر رہے تھے' وہ انگریز ہے

The man to whom you were speaking is English

Plural direct

تاریکین وطن جو یورپ میں مقیم ہیں' ان کے مسائل بہت بڑے ہیں

جو تارکین وطن یورپ میں مقیم ہیں' ان کے مسائل بہت بڑے ہیں

The problems of emigrants who are settled in Europe.are very great

Plural oblique

لوگ جن کے پاس پیسے ہیں' وہ ہمیشہ خوش رہتے ہیں

جن لوگوں کے پاس پیسے ہیں' وہ ہمیشہ خوش رہتے ہیں

People who have money always remain happy

Note the oblique phrase جس وقت *jis vaqt* 'at which time' i.e. 'when(ever)': جس وقت آپ آنا چاہیں' آئیے Come whenever you wish ('at which time you may want, come').

اتنا جتنا *itnā ... jitnā* 'as ... as'

We have seen that اتنا means 'so much'. The corresponding جتنا means 'as much'. They 'echo' each other in sentences like the following and may be translated into English as, 'so much as', 'as ... as':

لندن میں اتنی گرمی نہیں ہوتی جتنی کراچی میں ہوتی ہے

It's not as warm in London as it is in Karachi ('in London there is not so much heat as much as there is in Karachi')

وہ اتنی اچھی اردو بولتے ہیں جتنی آپ بولتے ہیں

He speaks Urdu as well as you ('he speaks so much good Urdu as much as you speak')

More Arabic plurals

The following Arabic plural forms are very commonly used in Urdu: مصروفیات *masrūfīāt* 'occupations' (f.p.) (there is no singular). Note the phrase: آپ کی کیا مصروفیات ہیں؟ 'What are you up to?' (literally 'What are your occupations?'); مسائل *masāil* 'problems' (m.p.). The singular is مسئلہ *masala*, written with *hamza* between the *sīn* and the *lām*. طلبہ *talaba* 'students' (m.p.). The singular is طالب علم *tālib 'ilm* which literally means 'seeker (of) knowledge'.

Regarded as a masculine Urdu noun طالب علم can also be used as a plural:

میرے کالج میں بہت سے غیر ملکی طالب علم / طلبہ ہیں

There are many foreign students in my college

ثقافت *siqāfat* Culture

Even during the 19th century, Indians began to migrate to other parts of the world, especially to East Africa, to take up employment. After Independence and the Partition of India and Pakistan in 1947, many people from both countries sought opportunities in Britain, and to a certain extent in the USA. The presence of these communities, especially in Britain, can hardly be ignored, and their culture has always made a significant impact upon the societies in which they have come to dwell. Language and the preservation of its traditions have always been burning issues. The younger generation, born outside the subcontinent, however, unfortunately shows increasingly less interest in the 'mother tongue'. For this reason, much effort is spent in fostering its study in schools and elsewhere. Time will tell how successful these efforts will be.

مشقیں *mašq* Exercises

15.3 صحیح یا غلط True or false?

The following statements relate to the two dialogues in this unit. Say whether they are true or false:

1 جان نے شریف احمد کو ٹیلیفون نہیں کیا کیونکہ ان کے پاس ان کا نمبر نہیں تھا
2 جان نے ہندوستان میں رہتے ہوئے اُردو سیکھ لی
3 شریف احمد بلقیس کے خاندان سے خوب واقف ہیں
4 ہندوستان اور پاکستان کے درمیان تعلقات اچھے ہیں
5 جان شریف احمد کی کتاب بھیج نہیں سکیں گے

15.4 At the post office

John is at the post office. Listen to his conversation with the clerk, then answer the questions:

1 How many letters does John want to post?
2 To which countries are they to be sent?
3 How much does it cost to send a letter by air to America?
4 What has John done with his parcel?

5 Where is the parcel being sent to?

6 Has he filled in the form?

7 What other services does John require?

15.5 Complete the sentences

Complete the sentences with the correct form of the pronouns کون، کوئی، جو:

1 دہلی میں آپ (کون) کے پاس ٹھہریں گے؟

2 (جو) لوگ کل شام کو آئے تھے، وہ کون تھے؟

3 میں لاہور گیا لیکن (کوئی) سے نہیں ملا۔

4 (جو) وقت آپ آنا چاہیں، آئیے۔

5 وہ آدمی (جو) سے آپ باتیں کر رہے تھے، وہ انگریز تھے؟

6 وہ (کون) کا سوٹ کیس ہے؟ میرا ہے۔

7 ہم یہاں (کوئی) سے واقف نہیں ہیں۔

8 (جو) لوگوں کے پاس آپ رہتے ہیں، وہ بہت مہربان ہیں۔

15.6 Dialogue

Take your part in the dialogue:

خان صاحب	آپ بڑی اچھی اردو بولتے ہیں / بولتی ہیں۔ آپ نے اردو کہاں سیکھی!
You	Say that you learnt it while staying with friends in London
خان صاحب	کیا لندن میں بہت اردو بولنے والے رہتے ہیں؟
You	Say that there are many Indian and Pakistani emigrants in England
خان صاحب	وہ لوگ عام طور سے کیا کام کرتے ہیں؟
You	Say that many of them work in offices and factories
خان صاحب	میرے ایک دوست وہاں رہتے ہیں۔ کیا آپ انہیں یہ چٹھی دے سکیں گے / سکیں گی؟
You	Ask for his address and say you will gladly give it to him

Urdu – English Vocabulary

آ alif madd

آج	*āj*	today
آج کل	*ājkal*	nowadays
آخر	*āxir*	at last
آداب عرض	*ādāb 'arz*	'my respects', hello, how do you do?
آدمی	*ādmī*	man, person (m.)
آدھا	*ādhā*	half
آرام	*ārām*	rest, ease (m.)
آرام کرنا	*ārām karnā*	to rest
آرام دہ	*ārāmdih*	comfortable
آسان	*āsān*	easy
آسانی سے	*āsānī se*	easily
آس پاس کا	*ās pās kā*	nearby, surrounding
آگے	*āge*	forward, before, in front
آگے چلنا	*āge calnā*	to go forward, advance
کے آگے	*ke āge*	in front of
آم	*ām*	mango (m.)
آنا	*ānā*	to come
آنکھ	*āṅkh*	eye (f.)
آنے والا	*ānevālā*	the coming, next
آہستہ	*āhista*	slowly, quietly
آئس کریم	*āis krīm*	ice cream (m.)

ا alif

اب	*ab*	now, from now on
اب تک	*ab tak*	still, till now
ابھی	*abhī*	now, right now
اُبلنا	*ubalnā*	to come to the boil
اُبلا ہوا	*ublā hūā*	boiled
اپریل	*aprail*	April (m.)
اپنا	*apnā*	one's own
اُترنا	*utarnā*	to come down, land
اتنا	*itnā*	so much
اتنا زیادہ	*itnā ziyāda*	so much, all this much
اتنے میں	*itne meṅ*	meanwhile

اتوار	*itvār*	Sunday (m.)
اٹھنا	*uṭhnā*	to rise, get up
اجازت	*ijāzat*	leave, may I take my leave? (f.)
اجازت دینا	*ijāzat denā*	to give leave
اچھا	*acchā*	good; well; really
اخبار	*axbār*	newspaper (m.)
ادھر	*idhar*	to here, here
اردو	*urdū*	Urdu (f.)
اسپتال	*aspatāl*	hospital (m.)
استاد	*ustād*	teacher (m.)
اسٹیشن	*isṭešan*	station (m.)
اسکول	*iskūl*	school (m.)
اضافت	*izāfat*	the *izāfat* (f.)
اعتراض	*i'tirāz*	objection (m.)
اعتراض کرنا	*i'tirāz karnā*	to object
افسوس	*afsos*	sorrow (m.)
مجھے افسوس ہے	*mujhe afsos hai*	I'm sorry
اکتوبر	*aktūbar*	October (m.)
اکثر	*aksar*	most, mostly, often
اکیلا	*akelā*	alone, lonely
اگر	*agar*	if
اگرچہ	*agarce*	although
اگست	*agast*	August (m.)
اگلا	*aglā*	next
اگلے سال	*agle sāl*	next year
اگلے ہفتے	*agle hafte*	next week
السلام علیکم	*assalāmu 'alaikum*	Muslim greeting 'peace be upon you'
اللہ	*allāh*	Allah, God (m.)
امید	*ummīd*	hope (f.)
امید ہے کہ	*ummīd hai ki*	(I) hope that
امیر	*amīr*	rich
انتظار	*intizār*	waiting (m.)
(کا) انتظار کرنا	*(kā) intizār karnā*	to wait for
انتظام	*intizām*	arrangement (m.)
(کا) انتظام کرنا	*(kā) intizām karnā*	to arrange
انجینئر	*injinīr*	engineer (m.)
انشاءاللہ	*inšāllāh*	God willing
اناناس	*ananās*	pineapple (m.)
اوپر	*ūpar*	above, upstairs

اور	aur	and; more; else
اور کچھ	aur kuch	something else
اور کوئی	aur koī	someone else
اور بھی	aur bhī	even more
اونٹ	ūṅṭ	camel (m.)
اونچا	ūṅcā	high, tall
اہم	ahm	important
ایسا	aisā	such
ایک	ek	one, a
ایک بار	ek bār	one time, once
ایک ہی	ek hī	the same

ب be

بات	bāt	thing, matter, word (f.)
سے باتیں کرنا	se bāteṅ karnā	to converse with
کوئی بات نہیں	koī bāt nahīṅ	it doesn't matter
بار	bār	time, occasion (f.)
ایک بار	ek bār	once
ایک بار پھر سے	ek bār phir se	once again
بارش	bāriš	rain (f.)
بارش ہونا	bāriš honā	to rain
کے بارے میں	ke bāre meṅ	about, concerning
بازار	bāzār	bazaar, market (m.)
باغیچہ	bāğīca	garden (m.)
باقی	bāqī	remaining, left over
بال	bāl	hair (m.p)
بالکل	bilkul	quite, absolutely
باندھنا	bāṅdhnā	to tie, tie up, pack
ساری باندھنا	sāṛī bāṅdhnā	to put on a saree
باورچی خانہ	bāvarcīxānā	kitchen (m.)
باہر	bāhar	out, outside
بایاں	bāyāṅ	left
بائیں ہاتھ پر	bāyeṅ hāth par	on the left
بتانا	batānā	to tell
بٹھانا	biṭhānā	to seat, show to a seat
بجنا	bajnā	to ring, strike, be played
بجے	baje	o'clock
ایک بجے	ek baje	at one o'clock
کتنے بجے	kitne baje?	at what time?

بچارہ	*bicāra*	poor, wretched
بچپن	*bacpan*	childhood (m.)
بچہ	*bacca*	child
بخار	*buxār*	fever (m.)
بد قسمتی سے	*bad qismatī se*	unfortunately
بدلنا	*badalnā*	to change
بدھ	*budh*	Wednesday (m.)
بُرا	*burā*	bad
بڑا	*baṛā*	big, great, elder; very
بڑے بھائی	*baṛe bhāī*	elder brother
بس	*bas*	bus (f.)
بس	*bas*	well, enough
(کے) بعد	*(ke) ba'd*	after
بعد میں	*ba'd meṅ*	afterwards
بعض	*ba'z*	some
بکھرا پڑا	*bikhrā paṛā*	scattered about
بُلانا	*bulānā*	to call
بلکہ	*balki*	but, indeed
بنانا	*banānā*	to make
بند	*band*	shut, closed
بند کرنا	*band karnā*	to shut, turn off
بولنا	*bolnā*	to speak
بھاری	*bhārī*	heavy
بھائی	*bhāī*	brother (m.)
بہت	*bahut*	much, many, very
بہت سا / سے	*bahut sā/se*	much, many
بھر	*bhar*	all through, all over
دن بھر	*din bhar*	all day long
بہتر	*bihtar*	good, better, fine
بہن	*bahin*	sister (f.)
بھوک	*bhūk*	hunger (f.)
(کو) بھوک لگنا	*(ko) bhūk lagnā*	to feel hungry
(کو) بھوک ہونا	*(ko) bhūk honā*	to be hungry
بھولنا	*bhūlnā*	to forget
بھونا گوشت	*bhūnā gošt*	'roast meat' (m.)
بھی	*bhī*	also, as well, even
بھیجنا	*bhejnā*	to send
بھیڑ	*bhīṛ*	crowd (f.)
بیٹا	*beṭā*	son (m.)

بیٹی	*beṭī*	daughter (f.)
بیٹھنا	*baiṭhnā*	to sit
بس میں بیٹھنا	*bas meṅ baiṭhnā*	to get onto a bus
بے حد	*be-had*	extremely
بیرا	*berā*	waiter (m.)
بیچنا	*becnā*	to sell
بیگم	*begam*	lady, wife (f.)
بیمار	*bīmār*	ill
بینک	*baiṅk*	bank (m.)
بے وقت	*be-vaqt*	untimely, out of time
بیوی	*bīvī*	wife (f.)

پ pe

پار کرنا	*pār karnā*	to cross
کے پاس	*ke pās*	near, by, with
پاسپورٹ	*pāsporṭ*	passport (m.)
پاگل	*pāgal*	mad
پانا	*pānā*	to find, manage to
پانی	*pānī*	water (m.)
پتہ	*pata*	address, sign (m.)
پتہ نہیں	*pata nahīṅ*	don't know
پتلون	*patlūn*	trousers (m.)
پچھلا	*pichlā*	last, previous
پچھلے ہفتے / سال	*pichle hafte/sāl*	last week/ year
پر	*par*	on, at
کام پر	*kām par*	at work
گھر پر	*ghar par*	at home
پرانا	*purānā*	old (of things)
پریشان	*parešān*	worried, anxious
پڑنا	*paṛnā*	to fall, to have to, must
پڑھنا	*paṛhnā*	to read, study
پسند	*pasand*	pleasing
(کو) پسند آنا	*(ko) pasand ānā*	to enjoy
پسند کرنا	*pasand karnā*	to choose
(کو) پسند ہونا	*(ko) pasand honā*	to like
پسندیدہ	*pasandīda*	favourite
پکانا	*pakānā*	to cook
(سے) پوچھنا	*(se) pūchnā*	to ask
پورا	*pūrā*	full, whole

پوشاک	*pošāk*	dress (f.)
پونے	*paune*	less one quarter
پونے تین	*paune tīn*	two and three quarters
پھر	*phir*	once more, then, again
پھر بھی	*phir bhī*	even so
پھر سے	*phir se*	again
پھل	*phal*	fruit (m.)
پہلا	*pahlā*	first
پہلے	*pahle*	at first, ago, before
دو سال پہلے	*do sāl pahle*	two years ago
سے پہلے	*se pahle*	before
پہنچانا	*pahuṅcānā*	to deliver, take (to)
پہنچنا	*pahuṅcnā*	to arrive
پہننا	*pahinnā*	to put on (clothes), wear
پھول	*phūl*	flower (m.)
پیاس	*pyās*	thirst (f.)
(کو) پیاس لگنا	*(ko) pyās lagnā*	to feel thirsty
(کو) پیاس ہونا	*(ko) pyās honā*	to be thirsty
پیٹ	*peṭ*	stomach (m.)
پیچھے	*pīche*	behind
(کے) پیچھے	*(ke) pīche*	behind
پیدل	*paidal*	on foot
پیدل جانا / چلنا	*paidal jānā/calnā*	to go on foot, walk
پیر	*pīr*	Monday (m.)
پیسہ	*paisā*	paisa, money (m.)
پیسے	*paise*	money (m.p.)
پینا	*pīnā*	to drink

ت te

تاریخ	*tārīx*	history, date (f.)
تب	*tab*	then
تب سے	*tab se*	since then
تجربہ کار	*tajruba-kār*	experienced
تشریف	*tašrīf*	honour (f.)
تشریف رکھنا	*tašrīf rakhnā*	to sit down, be (at home)
تشریف لانا	*tašrīf lānā*	to come (in)
تصویر	*tasvīr*	picture; photograph (f.)
تصویر کھینچنا	*tasvīr khaiṅcnā*	to take a photograph
تعلیم	*ta'līm*	education (f.)
تعلیم پانا	*ta'līm pānā*	to be educated

تفصیل	*tafsīl*	detail (f.)
تفصیل سے	*tafsīl se*	in detail
تفصیلات	*tafsīlāt*	details (f.p.)
تقریباً	*taqrīban*	almost, about
تقسیم	*taqsīm*	division, partition (f.)
تک	*tak*	up to, as far as, even
تکلف	*takalluf*	trouble, formality (m.)
کوئی تکلف نہیں	*koī takalluf nahīṅ*	it's no trouble
(کی) تلاش کرنا	*(kī) talāš karnā*	to look for
تمام	*tamām*	all, every, whole, complete
تو	*to*	then, so, well
تھا، تھی، تھے، تھیں	*thā, thī, the, thīṅ*	was, were
تھکا (ہوا)	*thakā (hūā)*	tired
تھکنا	*thaknā*	to become tired
تھوڑا (سا)	*thoṛā (sā)*	a little, some
تھوڑے (سے)	*thoṛe (se)*	a few
تھوڑی دیر کے بعد	*thoṛī der ke ba'd*	in a little while
تیار	*tayyār*	ready
تیار کرنا	*tayyār karnā*	to prepare
تیاری	*tayyārī*	preparation (f.)
(کی) تیاری کرنا	*(kī) tayyārī karnā*	to prepare
تیز	*tez*	quick, smart, spicy, strong
تیزی سے	*tezī se*	quickly
تیسرا	*tīsrā*	third

ٹ ṭe

ٹکٹ	*ṭikaṭ*	ticket; (postage) stamp (m.)
ٹوپی	*ṭopī*	hat (f.)
ٹھنڈا	*ṭhanḍā*	cold, cool
ٹھہرنا	*ṭhahrnā*	to stay, reside
ٹھیک	*ṭhīk*	all right, precisely
ٹھیک چار بجے	*ṭhīk cār baje*	at four o'clock precisely
ٹیکسی	*ṭaiksī*	taxi (f.)
ٹیکسی والا	*ṭaiksīvālā*	taxi driver (m.)
ٹیلی فون	*ṭelīfon*	telephone (m.)
ٹیلی وژن	*ṭelīvižan*	television (m.)

ج jīm

جاگنا	*jāgnā*	to wake up
جان	*jān*	darling (f.)

جانا	*jānā*	to go
جاننا	*jānnā*	to know
جب	*jab*	when
جتنا	*jitnā*	as much as, as
جتنی جلدی ہو سکے	*jitnī jaldī ho sake*	as quickly as possible
جگہ	*jagah*	place (f.)
ہر جگہ	*har jagah*	all over the place
جلد	*jald*	quickly, soon
جلد ہی	*jald hī*	very soon
جلدی	*jaldī*	speed, haste, hurry; quickly (f.)
جلدی سے	*jaldī se*	quickly
جلدی کرنا	*jaldī karnā*	to hurry
جمع کرنا	*jam' karnā*	to collect
جمع ہونا	*jam' honā*	to be collected, gather
جمعہ	*jum'a*	Friday (m.)
جمعرات	*jumi'rāt*	Thursday (f.)
جناب	*janāb*	sir (m.)
جنوب	*janūb*	south (m.)
جنوری	*janvarī*	January (f.)
جو (جس، جن)	*jo (jis, jin)*	who, which
جواب	*javāb*	answer (m.)
جواب دینا	*javāb denā*	to answer
جوتا	*jūtā*	shoe (m.)
جولائی	*jūlāī*	July (f.)
جون	*jūn*	June (m.)
جہاز	*jahāz*	ship, aeroplane (m.)
جہاں	*jahāṅ*	where
جی	*jī*	life, soul; Mr, sir; yes (m.)
جی ہاں	*jī hāṅ*	yes
جی نہیں	*jī nahīṅ*	no
جیسا	*jaisā*	as, like
جیسا کہ	*jaisā ki*	as
جیسے	*jaise*	as, like, for example

چ ce

چابی	*cābī*	key (f.)
چادر	*cādar*	scarf, wrap; 'chadur' (f.)
چاول	*cāval*	rice (m.)
چاہنا	*cāhnā*	to want, wish; to love

(کو) چاہیے	*(ko) cāhīe*	is needed; ought to
مجھے چاہیے	*mujhe cāhīe*	I need, want
مجھے جانا چاہیے	*mujhe jānā cāhīe*	I ought to go
چاہیے تھا	*cāhīe thā*	ought to have
چائے	*cāe*	tea (f.)
چائے خانہ	*cāe xānā*	tea shop (m.)
چچا	*cacā*	uncle, father's brother (m.)
(کر) چکنا	*(kar) cuknā*	to finish (doing)
چلانا	*calānā*	to drive
چلنا	*calnā*	to walk, move, go, depart
پیدل چلنا	*paidal calnā*	to go on foot
چوتھا	*cauthā*	fourth
چونکہ	*cūṅki*	since, because
چھٹا	*chaṭṭā*	sixth
چھٹی	*chuṭṭī*	holiday (f.)
چھوٹا	*choṭā*	small, little, short; younger
چھوٹا بھائی	*choṭā bhāī*	younger brother (m.)
چھوڑنا	*choṛnā*	to leave, abandon, give up
چیز	*cīz*	thing (f.)

ح **baṛī he**

حال	*hāl*	condition, state; the present (m.)
کیا حال ہے؟	*kyā hāl hai?*	how are you?
حال ہی میں	*hāl hī meṅ*	recently
حالانکہ	*hālāṅki*	although
حساب	*hisāb*	account, bill (m.)

خ **xe**

خاتون	*xātūn*	lady (f.)
خاص	*xās*	special
خاص طور پر / سے	*xās taur par/se*	especially
خاص کر	*xāskar*	especially
خالی	*xālī*	empty
خاموش	*xāmoš*	silent, quiet
خاندان	*xāndān*	family (m.)
خبر	*xabar*	news, information (f.)
خبریں	*xabreṅ*	the news (f.p.)
ختم	*xatam*	end, finish (m.)
ختم کرنا	*xatam karnā*	to finish

ختم ہونا	*xatam honā*	to be finished
خدا	*xudā*	God (m.)
خدا حافظ	*xudā hāfiz*	goodbye
خدمت	*xidmat*	service (f.)
خوراک	*xarc*	expense, spending (m.)
خرچ کرنا	*xarc karnā*	to spend (money)
خرچ ہونا	*xarc honā*	to be spent
خریداری	*xarīdārī*	shopping (f.)
خریدنا	*xarīdnā*	to buy
خط	*xat*	letter (m.)
خواتین	*xavātīn*	ladies (f.p.)
خوب	*xūb*	good, excellent, well
خوبصورت	*xūbsūrat*	beautiful
خود	*xud*	self
میں خود	*maiṅ xud*	(I) myself
خوش	*xuš*	happy
خوش آمدید	*xuš āmaded*	welcome!
خوش خبری	*xuš xabarī*	good news (f.)
خوش قسمتی سے	*xuš qismatī se*	fortunately
خوشگوار	*xušgavār*	pleasant
خوشی	*xušī*	happiness, pleasure (f.)
آپ سے ملکر بڑی خوشی ہوئی	*āp se milkar baṛī xušī hūī*	very pleased to meet you
خیال	*xayāl*	idea, thought, opinion (m.)
میرے خیال سے	*mere xayāl se*	in my opinion, I think
خیر	*xair*	well, all right

د **dāl**

داخل ہونا	*dāxil honā*	to enter, be enrolled
دادا	*dādā*	grandfather, father's father (m.)
دادی	*dādī*	grandmother, father's mother (f.)
دارالحکومت	*dārul-hukūmat*	capital (m.)
دال	*dāl*	lentils (f.)
دایاں	*dāyāṅ*	right
دائیں ہاتھ پر	*dāeṅ hāth par*	on the right
درجہ	*darja*	class, rank (m.)
پہلا درجہ	*pahlā darja*	first class
درد	*dard*	pain (m.)
کے درمیان	*ke darmiyān*	between, among

دروازہ	*darvāzā*	door (m.)
دریا	*daryā*	river (m.)
دسمبر	*disambar*	December (m.)
دعا	*du'ā*	a prayer (f.)
آپ کی دعا ہے	*āp kī du'ā hai*	polite answer to an enquiry after one's health
دعوت	*da'vat*	invitation, party (f.)
دعوت دینا	*da'vat denā*	to invite
دفتر	*daftar*	office (m.)
دکھانا	*dikhānā*	to show
دل	*dil*	heart (m.)
دلچسپ	*dilcasp*	interesting
دلچسپی	*dilcaspī*	interest (f.)
مجھے اس سے دلچسپی ہے	*mujhe is se dilcaspī hai*	I am interested in this
دلہن	*dulhan*	bride (f.)
دن	*din*	day (m.)
دن بھر	*din bhar*	all day long
دنیا	*dunyā*	world (f.)
دوپہر	*dopahr*	midday (m.)
دوپہر کا کھانا	*dopahr kā khānā*	lunch (m.)
دوپہر کے بعد	*do pahr ke ba'd*	in the afternoon, pm
دودھ	*dūdh*	milk (m.)
(سے) دور	*(se) dūr*	far (from)
کتنی دور	*kitnī dūr?*	how far?
دوست	*dost*	friend (m.)
دوسرا	*dūsrā*	second; other; next
دوسرے دن	*dūsre din*	the next day
دولھا	*dūlhā*	bridegroom (m.)
دونوں	*donoṅ*	both
دھوپ	*dhūp*	sunshine (f.)
دھونا	*dhonā*	to wash
دیر	*der*	lateness, delay (f.)
دیر سے (آنا)	*der se (ānā)*	to come late
دیر کرنا	*der karnā*	to be late, delay
تھوڑی دیر کے بعد	*thoṛī der ke ba'd*	in a little while
(کی) دیکھ بھال کرنا	*(kī) dekh bhāl karnā*	to look after
دیکھنا	*dekhnā*	to see, watch
دینا	*denā*	to give
دیوار	*dīvār*	wall (f.)

ڈ **ḍāl**

ڈاک	*ḍāk*	post (f.)
ڈاک خانہ	*ḍāk xāna*	post office (m.)
ڈاکٹر	*ḍākṭar*	doctor (m.)
ڈالنا	*ḍālnā*	to pour, put in
ڈبا	*ḍibbā*	compartment, carriage (m.)
ڈھائی	*ḍhāī*	two and a half
ڈھائی بجے	*ḍhāī baje*	at half past two
ڈیڑھ	*ḍeṛh*	ane and a half
ڈیڑھ بجے	*ḍeṛh baje*	at half past one

ذ **zāl**

ذرا	*zarā*	just, rather, a bit
ذریعہ	*zarī'a*	way, method
کے ذریعے	*ke zarī'e*	through, by means of

ر **re**

رات	*rāt*	night (f.)
رات کو	*rāt ko*	at night
راجا/راجہ	*rājā/rāja*	king, Rajah (m.)
راستہ	*rāsta*	road, way (m.)
پانچ منٹ کا راستہ	*pāṅc minaṭ kā rāsta*	five minutes away
رسم	*rasm*	custom, ceremony (f.)
رشتے دار	*rištedār*	relation (m.)
رکشا	*rikšā*	rickshaw (m.)
رکھنا	*rakhnā*	to put, place, keep
رنگ	*rang*	colour (m.)
رنگین	*rangīn*	colourful
روانگی	*ravānagī*	departure
روانہ	*ravāna*	going, departing
روانہ ہونا	*ravānā honā*	to depart, be under way
روپیہ	*rūpiya*	rupee (m.)
روٹی	*roṭī*	bread, food (f.)
روز	*roz*	day (m.)
ہر روز	*har roz*	every day
روکنا	*roknā*	to stop (something)
یہاں روکو	*yahāṅ roko*	stop here!
رونا	*ronā*	to weep, cry
رہنا	*rahnā*	to remain, live, stay, be, keep on (doing)

رہنے والا	rahnevālā	native (of), inhabitant (m.)
ریشمی	rešamī	silk (en)
ریل (گاڑی)	rel (gāṛī)	train (f.)
ریل (گاڑی) سے	rel (gāṛī) se	by train

ز ze

زبان	zabān	tongue, language (f.)
زمانہ	zamānā	age, time, period (m.)
زندگی	zindagī	life (f.)
زیادہ	ziyāda	more, most, very
بہت زیادہ	bahut ziyāda	much more, too much
سے زیادہ	se ziyāda	more than
زیادہ تر	ziyādatar	more, usually, mostly
زورات	zevarāt	jewels (m.p.)

س se

سا، سی، سے	sā, sī, se	-ish
بہت / تھوڑا سا	bahut/thoṛā sā	much/a little
اچھا سا	acchā sā	'goodish', quite good
ساتھ	sāth	along with, together
کے ساتھ	ke sāth	with
ساتھی	sāthī	companion, friend (m.)
ساحل	sāhil	beach, shore (m.)
سارا	sārā	all, whole
ساڑی	sāṛī	saree (f.)
ساڑھے	sāṛhe	plus one half
ساڑھے تین	sāṛhe tīn	three and a half
سال	sāl	year (m,)
سالگرہ	sālgirah	birthday (f.)
سامان	sāmān	luggage (m.)
سامنے	sāmne	in front, before
کے سامنے	ke sāmne	in front of
سب	sab	all, every
سب سے اچھا	sab se acchā	best (of all)
سب سے پہلے	sab se pahle	first of all
سب کچھ	sab kuch	everything
سبزی	sabzī	vegetables, greens (f.)
سبق	sabaq	lesson (m.)
سبھی کچھ	sabhī kuch	every single thing

سپاہی	*sipāhī*	soldier (m.)
ستمبر	*sitambar*	September (m.)
سجانا	*sajānā*	to decorate
سچ	*sac*	true
یہ تو سچ ہے	*yih to sac hai*	this is true
سخت	*saxt*	hard; extremely
سر	*sar*	head (m.)
سر میں درد ہونا	*sar meṅ dard honā*	to have a headache
سردی	*sardī*	cold (ness) (m.)
(کو) سردی لگنا	*(ko) sardī lagnā*	to feel cold
سردی ہونا	*sardī honā*	to be cold
آج سردی ہے	*āj sardī hai*	it's cold today
سردیاں	*sardīāṅ*	winter, cold season (f. p.)
سڑک	*saṛak*	street (f.)
سستا	*sastā*	cheap
سفر	*safar*	journey, travel (m.)
سفر کرنا	*safar karnā*	to travel
سفید	*safed*	white
سکنا	*saknā*	to be able, can
جا سکتا ہوں	*jā saktā hūṅ*	I can go
سلام	*salām*	greeting, peace (m.)
(کو) سلام کرنا	*(ko) salām karnā*	to greet
سمجھ	*samajh*	understanding (f.)
سمجھ میں آنا	*samajh meṅ ānā*	to understand
سمجھنا	*samajhnā*	to understand
سمندر	*samandar*	sea (m.)
سن	*san*	year (m.)
سن ۱۹۴۷	*san 1947*	in (the year) 1947
سننا	*sunnā*	to hear, listen to
سو	*sau*	hundred
سوا	*savā*	plus one quarter
سوا تین	*savā tīn*	three and a quarter
کے سوا	*ke sivā*	except
سوال	*savāl*	question (m.)
سوٹ کیس	*sūṭ kes*	suitcase
سوچنا	*socnā*	to think
سورج	*sūraj*	sun (m.)
سونا	*sonā*	to sleep
سہیلی	*sahelī*	(female) friend (f.)

سے	se	from, by, than
اس سے اچھا	is se acchā	better than this
سے پہلے	se pahle	before
سے دور	se dūr	far from
سے زیادہ	se ziyāda	more than
سے نزدیک	se nazdīk	near (to)
سیاح	sayyāh	tourist (m.)
سیر	sair	going/looking around, travelling (f.)
لاہور کی سیر کرنا	lāhaur kī sair karnā	to look around Lahore
سیکھنا	sīkhnā	to learn

ش šīn

شادی	šādī	wedding (f.)
شادی کرنا	šādī karnā	to get married
شادی شدہ	šādī šuda	married
شام	šām	evening (f.)
شام کا کھانا	šām kā khānā	'evening meal', dinner
شام کو	šām ko	in the evening
شاندار	šāndār	splendid, fabulous
شاہ	šāh	king, Shah (m.)
شخص	šaxs	person (m.)
شروع	šurū'	beginning (m.)
شروع کرنا	šurū karnā	to begin (something)
شروع ہونا	šurū' honā	(something) to begin
شکار	šikār	hunting (m.)
شکار کھیلنا	šikār khelnā	to hunt
شکر	šakar	sugar (f.)
شکریہ	šukriya	thank you
شلوار قمیض	šalvār qamīz	'shalwar qameez' (f.)
شمال	šimāl	north (m.)
شمالی	šimālī	north(ern)
شوہر	šauhar	husband (m,)
شہر	šahr	town, city (m.)

ص svād

صاحب	sāhib	gentleman, sir, Mr, (m.)
صاحبزادہ	sāhibzāda	son (m.)
صاحبہ	sāhiba	lady, Mrs (f.)
صاف	sāf	clean

صاف ستھرا	*sāf suthrā*	clean and tidy
صبح	*subh*	morning; in the morning (f.)
صبح سویرے	*subh savere*	early in the morning
صحت	*siht*	health (f.)
صحیح	*sahīh*	correct
صدی	*sadī*	century (f.)
صرف	*sirf*	only
صفر	*sifr*	zero (m.)
صوبہ	*sūba*	province (m.)

ض **zvād**

ضرور	*zarūr*	certainly, of course
ضرورت	*zarūrat*	necessity, need (f.)
مجھے اس کی ضرورت ہے	*mujhe is kī zarūrat hai*	I need this
ضروری	*zarūrī*	necessary

ط **toe**

طالب علم	*tālib-'ilm*	student (m.)
طبیعت	*tabī'at*	health (f.)
طرح	*tarah*	way, means, sort, kind (f.)
ہر طرح کا	*har tarah kā*	all sorts of
اس طرح	*is tarah*	in this way
کی طرح	*kī tarah*	like, as
طرف	*taraf*	direction, way (f.)
اس طرف	*is taraf*	in this direction
کس طرف؟	*kis taraf?*	in which direction
طور	*taur*	way, method, means (m.)
خاص طور سے	*xās taur se*	especially
عام طور سے	*'ām taur se*	usually

ع **'ain**

عادت	*'ādat*	custom, habit (f.)
عام	*'ām*	general, common, usual
عام طور سے / پر	*'ām taur se/par*	generally, usually
عربی	*'arabī*	Arabic
علاقہ	*'ilāqa*	area, region (m.)
علم	*'ilm*	knowledge (m.)
عمارت	*'imārat*	building (f.)
عمر	*'umr*	age (f.)

میری عمر بیس سال ہے	*merī 'umr bīs sāl hai*	I am twenty years old
آپ کی عمر کیا ہے؟	*āp kī 'umr kyā hai?*	how old are you?
عورت	*'aurat*	woman (f.)

غ ğain

غریب	*ğarīb*	poor
غسل خانہ	*ğusal xāna*	bathroom (m.)
غلط	*ğalat*	mistaken, wrong
غلطی	*ğalatī*	mistake (f.)
غیر ملکی	*ğair mulkī*	foreigner; foreign (m.)

ف fe

فارغ	*fāriğ*	free, at leisure
فائدہ	*fāida*	advantage, opportunity
(سے) فائدہ اٹھانا	*(se) fāida uṭhānā*	to take advantage (of)
فرصت	*fursat*	leisure, time off (f.)
مجھے فرصت ہے	*mujhe fursat hai*	I have time/leisure
فرق	*farq*	difference (m.)
فرمائیے	*farmāīe*	say, tell; do
فکر	*fikr*	worry, anxiety (m.)
فکر کرنا	*fikr karnā*	to worry
فوج	*fauj*	army (f.)
فون کرنا	*fon karnā*	to 'phone
فی صد	*fī sad*	per cent

ق qāf

قریب	*qarīb*	nearby, almost
کے قریب	*ke qarīb*	near
قریب قریب	*qarīb qarīb*	almost, approximately
قسمت	*qismat*	fate (f.)
قطار	*qatār*	queue (f.)
قلعہ	*qil'a*	fort, castle (m.)
قمیض	*qamīz*	shirt (f.)
قلی	*qulī*	porter (m.)
قیمت	*qīmat*	price (f.)
قیمتی	*qīmatī*	expensive

ک kāf

کا' کی' کے	*kā, kī, ke*	of, 's
کارخانہ	*kārxāna*	factory (m.)

کاروبار	*kār o bār*	business (m.)
کافی	*kāfī*	quite, very, enough
کالج	*kālij*	college (m.)
کام	*kām*	work, job (m.)
کام پر	*kām par*	at work
کام کرنا	*kām karnā*	to work
کان	*kān*	ear (m.)
کاندھا	*kāndhā*	shoulder (m.)
کب؟	*kab?*	when?
کب تک؟	*kab tak?*	how long?
کب سے؟	*kab se*	since when? for how long?
کبھی	*kabhī*	ever, sometimes
کبھی کبھی	*kabhī kabhī*	sometimes
کبھی نہیں	*kabhī...nahīṅ*	never
کپڑا	*kapṛā*	cloth (m.)
کپڑے	*kapṛe*	clothes (m.f.)
کتاب	*kitāb*	book (f.)
کتنا؟	*kitnā?*	how much; how?
کتنے بجے؟	*kitne baje?*	at what time?
کتنے بجے ہیں؟	*kitne baje haiṅ?*	what time is it?
کچھ	*kuch*	some; something; a little
کچھ نہیں	*kuch...nahīṅ*	nothing
کرایہ	*kirāya*	fare, rent (m.)
کرنا	*karnā*	to do
کل	*kal*	yesterday; tomorrow
کل ملاکر	*kul milākar*	in total
کلو	*kilo*	kilo (m.)
کلومیٹر	*kilomīṭar*	kilometer (m.)
کم	*kam*	less, few
کم سے کم	*kam se kam*	at least
کو	*ko*	to, for, at, on
کوچہ	*kūca*	narrow lane (m.)
کون (کس)	*kaun (kis)?*	who? what? which?
کس وقت	*kis vaqt?*	at what time?
کس طرف	*kis taraf?*	in what direction?
کون سا	*kaun sā?*	which?
کوئی (کسی)	*koī (kisī)*	some; someone; approximately
کوئی بات نہیں	*koī bāt nahīṅ*	it doesn't matter
کوئی دو بجے	*koī do baje*	at about two o'clock

کوئی نہیں	*koī nahīṅ*	no one
کہ	*ki*	(he said) that; or
کہ نہیں	*ki nahīṅ?*	or not?
کہاں	*kahāṅ?*	where?
کھانا	*khānā*	food, dinner (m.)
کھانا	*khānā*	to eat
کھڑا ہونا	*khaṛā honā*	to stand, be standing
کہلانا	*kahlānā*	to be called
(سے) کہنا	*(se) kahnā*	to say, tell
کھولنا	*kholnā*	to open
کھیت	*khet*	field (m.)
کھیتی باڑی	*khetī bāṛī*	agriculture (f.)
کھیلنا	*khelnā*	to play
کہیں	*kahīṅ*	somewhere; somehow
کہیں نہیں	*kahīṅ nahīṅ*	nowhere
کھینچنا	*khaiṅcnā*	to pull, drag
تصویر کھینچنا	*tasvīr khaiṅcnā*	to take a photograph
کئی	*kaī*	several
کیا؟	*kyā?*	what? which?
اور کیا؟	*aur kyā!*	so what!
کیا بات ہے؟	*kyā bāt hai?*	what's the matter?
کیا حال ہے؟	*kyā hāl hai?*	how are you?
کیسا؟	*kaisā?*	how? of what kind?
کیسے؟	*kaise?*	how? in what way?
کیوں؟	*kyoṅ?*	why? well
کیونکہ	*kyoṅki*	because

گ **gāf**

گاڑی	*gāṛī*	car, train (f.)
گانا	*gānā*	to sing
گانے والا	*gānevālā*	singer (m.)
گرم	*garm*	hot, warm
گرمی	*garmī*	heat, warmth, summer (f.)
گرمی ہونا	*garmī honā*	to be hot, warm
آج گرمی ہے	*āj garmī hai*	it's warm today
گرمیاں	*garmīāṅ*	summer, the hot season (f.p)
گڑبڑ	*gaṛbaṛ*	confusion, upset, mess (m.)
پیٹ میں گڑبڑ ہے	*peṭ meṅ gaṛbaṛ hai*	I have an upset stomach
گزرنا	*guzarnā*	to pass (of time); to go/pass through

گلا	*galā*	throat, neck (m.)
گلے میں خراش ہے	*gale meṅ xarrāš hai*	I have a sore throat
گوشت	*gošt*	meat (m.)
گھر	*ghar*	house, home (m.)
گھر پر	*ghar par*	at home
گھنٹہ	*ghanṭa*	hour (m.)

ل lām

لاکھ	*lākh*	one hundred thousand (m.)
دس لاکھ	*das lākh*	one million
لال	*lāl*	red
لانا	*lānā*	to bring
لڑکا	*laṛkā*	boy (m.)
لڑکی	*laṛkī*	girl (f.)
لفافہ	*lifāfa*	envelope (m.)
لکھنا	*likhnā*	to write
لگنا	*lagnā*	to be applied; seem; feel; begin to
لگتا ہے کہ	*lagtā hai ki*	it seems that
(کو) اچھا لگتا ہے	*(ko) acchā lagtā hai*	it seems good to; one likes
کرنے لگا	*karne lagā*	he began to do
بھوک لگتی ہے	*bhūk lagtī hai*	one feels hungry
لمبا	*lambā*	long; tall
لوٹنا	*lauṭnā*	to come back, return
لوگ	*log*	people (m.p.)
لے آنا	*le ānā*	to bring
لے جانا	*le jānā*	to take away
کے لئے	*ke lie*	for (the sake of)
دو دن کے لئے	*do din ke lie*	for two days
لیکن	*lekin*	but
لینا	*lenā*	to take

م mīm

ماتھا	*māthā*	forehead (m.)
مارچ	*mārc*	March (m.)
ماں	*māṅ*	mother (f.)
مبارک	*mubārak*	congratulations (m.)
عید، سالگرہ مبارک	*'īd, sālgirah mubārak*	Happy Eid, Birthday
سفر مبارک ہو	*safar mubārak ho*	bon voyage!
مبارک باد دینا	*mubārakbād denā*	to congratulate

مت	mat	do not (+ imperative)
مٹر	maṭaṛ	pea (s) (m.)
مٹھائی (آں)	miṭhāī (āṅ)	sweet (s) (f.)
محبت	mahabbat/muhabbat	love (f.)
تم سے محبت ہے	tum se mahabbat hai	I love you
مدد	madad	help (f.)
(کی) مدد کرنا	(kī) madad karnā	to help
مذاق	mazāq	joke (m.)
کا مذاق اڑانا	kā mazāq uṛāna	to make fun of
مرد	mard	man (m.)
مرغی	murğī	chicken (f.)
مرکز	markaz	centre (m.)
مرنا	marnā	to die
مزا	mazā	pleasure (m.)
مزاج شریف	mizāj šarīf?	how are you?
کیسے مزاج؟	kaise mizāj?	how are you?
مزے دار	mazedār	tasty, pleasurable, funny
مسائل	masāil	problems (m.p.)
مسجد	masjid	mosque (f.)
مسلم	muslim	Muslim (m.)
مسئلہ	masala	problem (m.)
مشرق	mašriq	east (m.)
مشق	mašq	practice (f.)
مشق کرنا	mašq karnā	to practise
مشکل	muškil	difficult
مشکل	muškil	problem (f.)
کوئی مشکل نہیں	koī muškil nahīṅ	no problem
مشہور	mašhūr	famous
مصروف	masrūf	busy
مصروفیات	masrūfīāt	activities (f.p.)
مضامین	mazāmīn	subjects (m.p.)
مضمون	mazmūn	subject (m.)
مطلب	matlab	meaning (m.)
مطلب یہ ہے کہ	matlab yih hai ki	this means that
معاف	m'uāf (māf)	excused
معاف کرنا	mu'āf karnā	to excuse
معاف کیجیے	mu'āf kījīe	excuse me. I'm sorry
معلوم	ma'lūm	known
کو معلوم ہونا	ko ma'lūm honā	to know

مجھے معلوم ہے	*mujhe ma'lūm hai*	I know
معلوم ہوتا ہے کہ	*ma'lūm hotā hai ki*	it seems that
مجھے معلوم ہوا	*mujhe ma'lūm hūā*	I found out
معلومات	*ma'lūmāt*	information (m.p.)
مغرب	*mağrib*	west (m.)
کے مقابلے میں	*ke muqābile meṅ*	compared to, than
مقبرہ	*maqbara*	tomb, shrine (m.)
مکان	*makān*	house, building (m.)
ملازمت	*mulāzimat*	work, employment (f.)
ملانا	*milānā*	to introduce; to mix
ملاقات	*mulāqāt*	meeting (f.)
سے ملاقات ہونا	*se mulāqāt honā*	to meet (with)
ملک	*mulk*	country (m.)
ملنا	*milnā*	to be acquired, meet
مجھے ملتا ہے	*mujhe miltā hai*	I get, acquire
سے ملنا	*se milnā*	to meet with
پھر ملیں گے	*phir mileṅge*	'we'll meet again', see you!
ممکن	*mumkin*	possible
ممکن ہے کہ	*mumkin hai ki*	it's possible that
مناسب	*munāsib*	appropriate
منتظر	*muntazir*	waiting, looking forward
میں اس کا منتظر ہوں	*maiṅ is kā muntazir hūṅ*	I'm looking forward to it
منٹ	*minaṭ*	minute (m.)
ایک منٹ ٹھہریے	*ek minaṭ ṭhahrīe*	wait a mimute!
منگل	*mangal*	Tuesday (m.)
منگنی	*maṅganī*	engagement (for marriage) (f.)
میری منگنی ہوئی	*merī maṅganī hūī*	I'm engaged
منگوانا	*maṅgvānā*	to order (meals, etc.)
منہ	*muṅh*	face, mouth (m.)
منہ ہاتھ دھونا	*muṅh hāth dhonā*	'to wash face and hands', have a wash
موسم	*mausam*	weather (m.)
موزہ (موزے)	*moza (moze)*	sock (s) (m.)
مہربان	*mihrbān*	kind, pleasant
مہربانی	*mihrbānī*	kindness; thank you (f.)
مہربانی کرکے	*mihrbānī karke*	please
مہمان	*mihmān*	guest (m.)
مہمان نواز	*mihmān navāz*	hospitable

مہمان نوازی	*mihmān navāzī*	hospitality (f.)
مہنگا	*mahaṅgā*	expensive, dear
مہینہ	*mahīna*	month (m.)
مئی	*maī*	May (f.)
میٹر	*mīṭar*	meter (in a taxi) (m.)
میز	*mez*	table (f.)
میل	*mīl*	mile (m.)
میں	*meṅ*	in, among
میں سے	*meṅ se*	from among, among, out of
مینار	*mīnār*	minaret (m.)

ن nūn

نا	*nā*	isn't it?
ناپ	*nāp*	measurement, size (f.)
ناچنا	*nācnā*	to dance
ناچنے والی	*nācnevālī*	dancing girl (f.)
ناراض	*nārāz*	angry
ناشتہ	*nāšta*	breakfast (m.)
ناشتہ کرنا	*nāšta karnā*	to have breakfast
نام	*nām*	name (m.)
نان	*nān*	naan, oven-baked bread (m.)
نانا	*nānā*	grandfather, mother's father (m.)
نانی	*nānī*	grandmother, mother's mother (f.)
نزدیک	*nazdīk*	near, nearby
سے نزدیک	*se nazdīk*	near
نسخہ	*nusxa*	copy (of a book); prescription (m.)
نظر آنا	*nazar ānā*	to come into view, be seen
مجھے نظر آتا ہے	*mujhe nazar atā hai*	I can see
نقشہ	*naqša*	map (m.)
نکاح	*nikāh*	wedding ceremony (m.)
نکالنا	*nikālnā*	to take out, extract
نکلنا	*nikalnā*	to go out
نکل آنا	*nikal ānā*	to come out
نماز	*namāz*	prayer (s) (f.)
نماز پڑھنا	*namāz paṛhnā*	to pray
نمستے	*namaste*	hello, goodbye (Hindu greeting)
نوکر	*naukar*	servant (m.)
نوکری	*naukarī*	(manual) work (f.)
نومبر	*navambar*	November (m.)

نہ	*na*	not, nor
نہ... نہ	*na... na*	neither... nor
نہ جائیے	*na jāīe*	don't go
ہے نہ	*hai na?*	isn't it?
نہانا	*nahānā*	to bathe, have a bath/shower
نہیں	*nahīṅ*	not; no
نے	*ne*	postposition used with past transitive verbs
نیا (نئی، نئے)	*nayā (naī, nae)*	new
نیلا	*nīlā*	blue
نیند	*nīnd*	sleep (f.)
(کو) نیند آنا	*(ko) nīnd ānā*	to feel sleepy

و vāū

واپس	*vāpas*	back
واپس آنا	*vāpas ānā*	to come back, return
واقعی	*vāqa'ī*	really, indeed
سے واقف ہونا	*se vāqif*	acquainted with
والد	*vālid*	father (m.)
والدہ	*vālida*	mother (f.)
والدین	*vālidain*	parents (m.p.)
وجہ	*vajah*	reason (f.)
اس وجہ سے	*is vajah se*	for this reason
کی وجہ سے	*kī vajah se*	because of
وزن	*vazan*	weight (m.)
وطن	*vatan*	homeland (m.)
وغیرہ	*vağaira*	etcetera, and so on
وقت	*vaqt*	time (m.)
اس وقت	*is vaqt*	at this time
وقت پر	*vaqt par*	on time
وکیل	*vakīl*	lawyer (m.)
وہاں	*vahāṅ*	there
وہیں	*vahīṅ*	right there

ہ choṭī he

ہاتھ	*hāth*	hand (m.)
ہاتھی	*hāthī*	elephant (m.)
ہار	*hār*	necklace, garland (m.)
ہاں	*hāṅ*	yes, indeed

ہر	*har*	every
ہر ایک	*har ek*	every one, every single
ہر روز	*har roz*	every day
ہر طرح کا	*har tarah kā*	all kinds of
ہر طرف	*har taraf*	everywhere
ہر قسم کا	*har qism kā*	of every kind
ہزار	*hazār*	thousand
ہفتہ	*hafta*	week; Saturday (m.)
اس ہفتے	*is hafte*	this week
ہفتے کو	*hafte ko*	on Saturday
ہمیشہ	*hameša*	always
ہنسنا	*hańsnā*	to laugh
ہوائی اڈا	*havāī aḍḍā*	airport (m.)
ہوائی جہاز	*havāī jahāz*	aeroplane (m.)
ہوٹل	*hoṭal*	hotel (m.)
ہو جانا	*ho jānā*	to become
ہونا	*honā*	to be
ہی	*hī*	only, just
ہیلو	*helo!*	hello! (answering the telephone)

ی ye

یا	*yā*	or
یاد	*yād*	memory (f.)
(کو) یاد آنا	*(ko) yād ānā*	to be recalled, come to mind
یاد رہنا	*yād rahnā*	to remain in the memory
یاد ہونا	*yād honā*	to be remembered
مجھے یاد ہے	*mujhe yād hai*	I remember
یعنی	*ya'nī*	that is, namely
یقین	*yaqīn*	certainty (m.)
کو یقین ہونا	*ko yaqīn honā*	to be certain
مجھے یقین ہے	*mujhe yaqīn hai*	I am certain
یونیورسٹی	*yūnīvarsiṭī*	university (f.)
یہاں	*yahāń*	here
یہیں	*yahīń*	right here

Answer key

Unit 1

Exercise 1.1

1 اچھی 2 دلچسپ 3 نئی 4 بڑا 5 ہندوستانی

Exercise 1.2

1 السلام علیکم ' خان صاحب۔ کیا حال ہے؟

2 بندر روڈ کہاں ہے؟

3 میرا نام .... ہے۔

4 میرا ہوٹل دور نہیں ہے۔

5 اچھا' اجازت۔ خدا حافظ۔

Exercise 1.3

1 وعلیکم السلام میں بالکل ٹھیک ہوں۔ 2 جی ہاں میں انگریز ہوں۔ 3 جی ہاں' میں ہوٹل میں ہوں۔ 4 جی نہیں۔ دور نہیں ہے۔ 5 خدا حافظ۔

Exercise 1.4

1 سات 2 نو 3 دس 4 آٹھ 5 چھے

Exercise 1.5

ا. السلام علیکم ' خان صاحب۔ آپ کا گھر کہاں ہے؟

ب. میرا گھر لندن میں ہے۔

ا. آپ پاکستانی ہیں یا ہندوستانی؟

ب. میں پاکستانی ہوں۔

ا. آپ کا گھر یہاں سے دور ہے؟

ب. جی نہیں' بہت دور نہیں ہے۔

ا. اور آپ کا گھر اچھا ہے۔

ب. جی ہاں' اچھا ہے' لیکن پرانا ہے۔

A Hello, Khan Sahib. Where is your house?

B My house is in London.

A Are you a Pakistani or an Indian?

B I'm a Pakistani.

A Is your house far from here?

B No, it's not very far.

A Is your house nice?

B Yes, it's nice, but it's old.

Answers: 1 In London 2 Pakistan 3 No 4 Old

Exercise 1.6

1 Pakistan 2 False 3 False 4 Ten 5 False

Unit 2

Exercise 2.1

پانچ بیٹیاں *pāṅc beṭīāṅ* — سات بچے *sāt bacce* — آٹھ کتابیں *āṭh kitābeṅ*

چھے گھر *che ghar* — دس آدمی *das ādmī*

Exercise 2.2

1 اچھے، ہیں 2 انگریز، ہیں 3 ہیں، ہیں 4 آپ کے، ہیں 5 ان کے، بڑے، اچھے، ہیں

Exercise 2.3

1 ہو 2 ہیں، ہیں 3 ہیں 4 ہیں، ہیں 5 ہے، ہے۔

Exercise 2.4

1 آؤ 2 لائیے، رکھیے 3 دیکھیے 4 چلیے 5 بتاؤ

Exercise 2.5

جان : رحیم صاحب، یہ بتائیے۔ آپ کے کتنے بچے ہیں؟

رحیم : ہمارے دو بیٹے ہیں اور ایک چھوٹی بیٹی۔

جان : کیا وہ سب اسکول میں ہیں؟

رحیم : میرے دو بیٹے اسکول میں ہیں۔ چھوٹی لڑکی، یعنی بلقیس، اسکول میں نہیں۔ وہ گھر پر ہے۔

جان : اور ان کا اسکول اچھا ہے؟

رحیم : جی ہاں۔ وہ بڑا امریکن اسکول ہے۔
جان : اور آپ کا گھر بڑا ہے؟
رحیم : جی نہیں۔ صرف پانچ کمرے ہیں۔ لیکن وہاں بہت لوگ ہیں۔ یعنی میں ہوں اور میری بیگم ہیں۔ میرے والدین اور میرے چچا بھی ہیں۔
جان : اور یہ مشکل ہے؟
رحیم : جی نہیں، بہت مشکل نہیں۔ ہم پاکستانی ہیں اور کیا!

John : Rahim Sahib, tell me. How many children do you have?
Rahim : We have two sons and one small daughter.
John : Are they all at school?
Rahim : My two sons are at school. The little girl, namely Bilqis, is not at school. She is at home.
John : And is their school good?
Rahim : Yes. It's the big American school.
John : And is your house big?
Rahim : No. There are only five rooms. But they are lots of people there. Namely, I and my wife, my parents and my uncle.
John : Is that difficult?
Rahim : No. It's not very difficult. We are Pakistanis. So what!

Answers : 1 Three 2 No 3 American 4 Five 5 Yes

Unit 3

Exercise 3.1

1 آپ انجنیر ہیں؟ 2 نہیں 3 فرصت 4 انگریزی کھانا 5 یہ کتابیں

Exercise 3.2

1 مجھے / مجھ کو 2 آپ کو 3 انہیں، ان کو 4 ہمیں، ہم کو 5 تمہیں، تم کو
6 اسے، اس کو

Exercise 3.3

1 جی ہاں۔ مجھے بہت پسند ہے۔
2 مجھے معلوم ہے۔ میرا ہوٹل وہاں سے زیادہ دور نہیں۔
3 اس کا نام کیا ہے؟

4 جی نہیں، اس وقت مجھے فرصت نہیں ہے۔

Exercise 3.4

1 اے بیرا۔ ادھر آیئے۔
2 تندوری مرغی اچھی ہے؟
3 مجھے ساگ، بھونا گوشت اور پلاؤ چاہیے۔ میرے دوست کو تندوری مرغی، نان اور دال چاہیے۔
4 ہمیں آج پھل نہیں چاہیے۔
5 ہمیں ایک کوفی اور ایک چائے چاہیے۔
6 ۷۳ روپے۔

Exercise 3.5

رحیم : آداب عرض ہے، اسلم صاحب۔ کیا حال ہے؟
اسلم : ٹھیک ہوں، شکریہ۔ اور آپ؟
رحیم : میں بالکل ٹھیک ہوں۔ کیا آج آپ کو فرصت ہے؟
اسلم : جی ہاں، آج چھٹی ہے۔
رحیم : میرے دوست سے ملیے۔ ان کا نام بل ہے۔ وہ امریکن ہیں۔
اسلم : اچھا۔ یہ بہت دلچسپ ہے۔ چلیں، چائے پئیں۔ میرے گھر میں۔ آج میری بیوی اور بچے شہر میں ہیں۔ لیکن گھر میں اچھی چائے ہے۔
رحیم : آپ کا گھر یہاں سے دور ہے؟
اسلم : جی نہیں۔ نزدیک ہے۔ بندر روڈ پر۔

Rahim : Hello, Aslam. How are you?
Aslam : I'm well, thanks. And you?
Rahim : I'm extremely well. Are you free today?
Aslam : Yes. It's a holiday today.
Rahim : Meet my friend. His name is Bill. He's an American.
Aslam : Really? That's very interesting. Come on, let's have tea. In my house. Today my wife and children are in town, but I have some good tea in the house.
Rahim : Is your house far from here?
Aslam : No, it's nearby. On Bandar Road.

Answers : 1 Yes 2 A holiday 3 American 4 In town 5 Nearby

Unit 4

Exercise 4.1

1 کے   2 کا   3 کی   4 کی   5 کے

Exercise 4.2

فہمیدہ : السلام علیکم، ممتاز، کیا حال ہے؟

ممتاز : میں ٹھیک ہوں، شکریہ۔ کیا تم شہر میں ہو؟

فہمیدہ : جی ہاں بچے اسکول میں ہیں۔ مجھے فرصت ہے۔

ممتاز : مجھے بھی فرصت ہے۔ چلیں، ایک کپ چائے پیئیں؟

فہمیدہ : ضرور۔ کیا یہاں کوئی ہوٹل ہے؟ تمہیں معلوم ہے کہاں؟

ممتاز : جی ہاں۔ وہاں ہے۔ چائے بھی ہے اور مزے دار کھانا بھی ہے۔

فہمیدہ : مجھے صرف چائے چاہیے۔ آج کافی گرمی ہے نا؟

ممتاز : جی ہاں، بہت گرمی ہے۔ تو چلیں، چائے پیئیں، ایک گھنٹے کی فرصت ہے۔

فہمیدہ : کیا وہاں آئس کریم بھی ہے؟

ممتاز : ضرور۔ چلیں، آئس کریم کھائیں۔ بہت اچھا خیال ہے۔

F : Hello, Mumtaz. How are things?

M : I'm well, thank you. What, are you in town?

F : Yes, the children are at school. I've got some free time.

M : I'm also free. Come on, let's have a cup of tea.

F : Of course. Is there some hotel here? Do you know where?

M : Yes. There's (one) there. They have both tea and also delicious food.

F : I only want tea. It's quite warm today, isn't it?

M : Yes, it's very warm. Come on then, let's go and have tea. I've got an hour.

F : Do they have ice cream there as well?

M : Of course. Let's go and have ice cream. It's a good idea.

Answers: 1 In town 2 At school 3 A hotel 4 Warm 5 Have ice cream

Exercise 4.3

1 محمد صاحب کے دو بچے ہیں۔

2 آج بہت گرمی ہے۔
3 جی ہاں۔ ان کو کھانا پسند ہے۔
4 وہ آئس کریم کی دوکان میں ہیں۔
5 بیس روپے ہیں۔

Exercise 4.4

1 رحیم صاحب اصل میں دہلی کے رہنے والے ہیں' لیکن ان کا گھر پاکستان میں ہے۔
2 انگلستان کے موسم اور ایشیا کے موسم میں بہت فرق ہے۔
3 السلام علیکم' ممتاز صاحبہ۔ چلیں۔ آئس کریم کھائیں۔
4 آج بہت گرمی ہے۔ چلیں' ایک کپ چائے پیئیں۔
5 لاہور کراچی سے کم سے کم ایک ہزار میل دور ہے۔

Unit 5

Exercise 5.1

1 At 5 am 2 Says prayers and has breakfast 3 With her parents 4 By train 5 In a little restaurant with Nargis 6 At 6 o'clock 7 Eats and watches TV

Exercise 5.2

1 میں انگلستان کا رہنے والا ہوں / کی رہنے والی ہوں۔
2 میں لندن میں ڈاکٹر ہوں۔
3 جی ہاں۔ مجھے پاکستان بہت پسند ہے۔
4 جی ہاں۔ کراچی میں میرے بہت دوست ہیں۔
5 یہ بہت اچھا خیال ہے۔ چلیں۔

Exercise 5.3

1 وہ کراچی میں رہتے ہیں
2 ان کے چار بچے ہیں۔ بچوں کے نام حامد' اقبال' نرگس اور جمیلہ ہیں۔
3 جی نہیں' وہ پیر سے جمعے تک کام کرتے ہیں۔
4 گھر پر بلقیس کھانا پکاتی ہیں۔
5 عام طور سے نوکر خریداری کرتا ہے۔
6 جی نہیں۔ ان کو دوکانیں پسند نہیں۔

Exercise 5.4

1 False 2 True 3 False 4 False 5 True 6 False

Exercise 5.5

1 پانچ بجے' پانچ بجے ہیں ۵
2 نو بجے' نو بجے ہیں ۹
3 دو بجے' دو بجے ہیں ۲
4 گیارہ بجے' گیارہ بجے ہیں ۱۱
5 چھے بجے' چھے بجے ہیں ۶

Unit 6

Dialogue 1 At the seaside

John : So, this is Clifton. There are (some) very splendid houses here. I think quite rich people live here. Look, that big, beautiful house. Whose house is that?

Aslam : I think it is some minister's house. Ministers in every country are rich, aren't they? But who lives there, I don't know.

John : And there is the sea. Tell me, Aslam Sahib. Which sea is this?

Aslam : This is the *Buhaira-e Arab*, that is ‘the Arabian Sea’.

Helen : But there are very few people on the beach. In Pakistan don’t people bathe in the sea?

Aslam : No. In Pakistan there is no custom, like in England, of sitting on the beach and swimming in the sea.

Helen : And look. There's a camel on the beach. Whose camel is it?

Aslam : I think it's that little boy's camel. Obviously (‘it is clear that’) it is someone's (camel). Sometimes there are tourists here. They like to sit on a camel.

Helen : And what lovely weather! Neither hot nor cold.

Aslam : Yes. In (the month of) November the weather is usually good. Come on, Helen Sahiba. Have a ride (sit) on a camel.

Exercise 6.1

1 ہوتی ہے 2 ہے 3 ہیں' ہوتے ہیں 4 ہوتے ہیں 5 ہے' ہوتے ہیں

Dialogue 2

John : Hamid, since we are in Clifton today, so show us the school. You study (read) here, don't you.

Hamid : Yes, but today is Saturday. Our school is closed.

John : It doesn't matter. At least show us where you study.

Hamid : All right, but Clifton is quite a big area. My school is a bit far from here.

Aslam : It's all right. Fortunately, we have our car (with us) today. In the car it's only (a road of) five minutes. Come on, sit in the car. But wait a minute. I haven't got the key. Who's got (the key)? Someone's got it. Bilqis. Do you have the key?

Bilqis : Yes. Don't worry. I have it.

Aslam : Why do you have the key?

Bilqis : It's with me because ('for this reason that') you always forget everything. Do you have (any) money with you today?

Aslam : Yes, I'll have a look now ... no, I haven't got any money.

Bilqis : There you are (see)! You forget the key, you forget the money! So it's good that I have money. Come on. I've got the key, so today I'll drive!

Exercise 6.2

1 True 2 True 3 False 4 False 5 False

Dialogue 3

John : Good heavens! (Bravo!) What a splendid school, Hamid. What sort of children study here?

Aslam : Mostly the children of middle-class families study here. Unfortunately, the children of poor people do not study here. There are poor people in every country in the world. But what can you do? Someone is rich, someone is poor.

John : I think the education (of) here is good.

Aslam : Yes. Usually in the big schools of Karachi the education is very good. Hamid, tell John Sahib what you study, and which subjects you like.

Hamid : We study all kinds of subjects. From among languages, English,

Urdu and Arabic. In addition to this, history, geography, science, etc.

John : And do you like English?

Hamid : Yes. English is quite easy, but Arabic is very difficult.

Exercise 6.3

رحیم : السلام علیکم، خان صاحب۔ کیا آپ بھی یہاں اسٹیشن پر ہیں؟ ریل گاڑی کتنے بجے پہنچتی ہے؟

خان : میرے خیال سے تین بجے آتی ہے۔ کیا آپ آج کام پر نہیں ہیں؟

رحیم : جی نہیں، آج چھٹی ہے۔ عام طور پر چار نومبر کو چھٹی ہوتی ہے نا؟

خان : اچھا، کیوں؟

رحیم : وزیر کی سالگرہ ہے۔اس لئے چھٹی ہے۔

خان : واہ ! واہ ! وزیر بہت بڑے آدمی ہیں۔ ان کی سالگرہ پر چھٹی ہوتی ہے؟

رحیم : ضرور۔ دیکھیے، ریل گاڑی وہاں ہے۔ اس میں ہمارے وزیر صاحب ہیں۔

R : Hello, Khan Sahib. You're also here at the station? What time does the train arrive?

K : I think it comes at 3 o'clock. Aren't you at work today?

R : No. There's a holiday today. There's usually a holiday on the 4th of November, isn't there?

K : Really. Why?

R : It's the minister's birthday. That's why there's a holiday.

K : Bravo! The minister is very great man. Is there a holiday on his birthday?

R : Of course! Look. The train's there. Our minister's in it.

Answers: 1 b 2 b 3 a 4 a 5 a 6 b

Exercise 6.4

1 کی طرح 2 سے 3 پاس 4 کو 5 پر

Exercise 6.5

پانچ نومبر کو، بارہ بجے، دو جنوری کو، نو اور سولہ = پچیس، اکتیس اکتوبر، میری سالگرہ ستائیس اپریل کو ہے۔ مہینے میں کبھی تیس دن ہوتے ہیں اور کبھی اکتیس دن، پچیس روپے، ایک روپے میں سو پیسے ہیں۔

Exercise 6.6

1 نقشے پر آٹھ (۸) شہر ہیں۔

2 لاہور پنجاب میں ہے۔

3 اسلام آباد لاہور سے کوئی دو سو میل دور ہے۔

4 حیدر آباد ملتان سے کوئی پانچ سو میل دور ہے۔

5 کراچی بحیرۂ عرب پر ہے۔

Unit 7

Dialogue 1

Rahim : Hello, John Sahib. How are you? What are you doing these days?

John : Hello (it is your prayer), Rahim Sahib. These days I'm quite busy. We are preparing to go to Lahore.

Rahim : Really. When are you going?

John : Perhaps next week. On the 10th. We are still not certain.

Rahim : How are you going? By train or by air?

John : We intend to go (there is an intention of going) by train. What do you think?

Rahim : This is good, because on the 10th my sister and her husband are going to Lahore by train. Go with them.

John : This is very good, but we don't have tickets or reservations. Where does one get tickets? Can you get them from the station (where are tickets got?, are they got from?)?

Rahim : No. Don't go to the station. There's always bother there. I'll do it like this. A good friend of mine works in a travel agency here. I'll telephone him today. Don't worry. So, this means – two tickets Karachi – Lahore, in first class, for the 10th. All right?

John : Rahim Sahib, thank you very much.

Rahim : No problem! Telephone me this (today) evening. Do you have my number?

John : No, I don't.

Rahim : All right, so write (it): 10593 Now I am going somewhere (to one place). (Can I take my) leave?

John : Thank you very much, Rahim Sahib. Goodbye.

Exercise 7.1

1 لڑکا آئس کریم کھا رہا ہے۔
2 لڑکی کتاب پڑھ رہی ہے۔
3 آدمی ٹیلیفون کر رہا ہے۔
4 یہ دو آدمی ریل گاڑی میں بیٹھ رہے ہیں۔
5 عورت کھانا پکا رہی ہے۔

Dialogue 2

John : Hello! This is John speaking (I am John speaking). Is Rahim Sahib at home?

Begam Rahim : Yes. One minute. I'll just call him. He's coming.

Rahim : Hello, John Sahib. Listen. There is (one) good news. I have your tickets with me. My friend is a very cunning fellow! You can always get tickets from him easily. I don't know how. I never ask. Well, this means that you are going next week, on the 10th, at eight in the morning.

John : Thank you, Rahim Sahib. This is your and your friend's kindness.

Rahim : Then tell me John. What are you doing this evening? Are you going out somewhere?

John : No. At this moment we are in the hotel. Usually we have the evening meal here.

Rahim : Right. Don't eat there. Come here for dinner. This evening my sister and her husband are also coming. Meet them. What's the time now? It's seven o'clock, isn't it? So you come at eight.

John : Thank you, Rahim Sahib. We'll arrive at eight sharp.

Dialogue 3

Rahim : Come in, John Sahib. Come in, Helen Sahiba. Please sit down. Meet my wife. Her name is Fatima. And this is my sister, Kausar, and my brother-in-law, Qasim Sahib. He is a native of Lahore. They are going with you next Thursday. Qasim Sahib knows everything about Lahore. Qasim Sahib, you know that John and Helen are our English friends. Both are doctors in England. And both speak very good Urdu.

Qasim : Tell me, John Sahib. Where do you intend to stay in Lahore?

John : So far I don't know. I suppose in some hotel.

Qasim : In Lahore there are many good new hotels but my favourite hotel is an old English hotel. It is near Mall Road. Right in the centre. I'll give you the telephone number. Ring there tomorrow and give my name.

Exercise 7.2

1 میں مصروف ہوں اور اسلام آباد جانے کی تیاری کر رہا ہوں / کر رہی ہوں۔

2 جی نہیں میرا ریل گاڑی سے جانے کا ارادہ ہے۔

3 جی ہاں۔ مجھے معلوم ہے۔ مجھے ٹکٹ کہاں سے ملتے ہیں۔

4 بہت شکریہ ' رحیم صاحب۔ میں ٹھیک آٹھ بجے ٹیلیفون کرتا / کرتی ہوں۔

Exercise 7.3

فاطمہ آداب عرض ہے ' کوثر۔ آج آپ کیا کر رہی ہیں۔

کوثر کچھ نہیں۔ آج میں گھر پر ہوں۔ اس وقت میں کھانے کی تیاری کر رہی ہوں۔

فاطمہ اچھا۔ آپ کیا پکا رہی ہیں؟

کوثر میں زیادہ نہیں پکا رہی ہوں۔ روٹی ' مرغی ' چاول۔

فاطمہ کیا آج شام کو آپ کو فرصت ہے؟

کوثر جی نہیں ہم لوگ باہر جا رہے ہیں۔ کھانے پر۔

فاطمہ تو کل صبح آپ کیا کر رہی ہیں۔ کیا فارغ ہیں۔

کوثر جی ہاں۔ میں فارغ ہوں۔

فاطمہ اچھا تو مجھے ٹھیک نو بجے فون کیجیے۔ خدا حافظ۔

Fatima : Hello, Kausar. What are you doing today?

Kausar : Nothing. I'm at home today. At the moment I'm preparing lunch.

Fatima : I see. What are you cooking?

Kausar : I'm not cooking much. Bread, chicken, rice.

Fatima : Do you have some time this evening?

Kausar : No. We're going out to dinner.

Fatima : Then what are you doing tomorrow morning? Are you free?

Kausar : Yes. I'm free.

Fatima : Good. Then phone me at nine sharp. Goodbye.

Answers: 1 b 2 b 3 a 4 a 5 b

Exercise 7.4

1 ہیلو۔ یہ نمبر چھے صفر چار نو پانچ (۶۰۴۹۵) ہے؟
2 قاسم صاحب تشریف رکھتے ہیں؟
3 میرا نام بل براؤن / میری جونز ہے۔ میں اگلی جمعرات کو لاہور جا رہا / رہی ہوں‘ میں امریکن ہوں۔
4 کیا آپ کو معلوم ہے کہ پہلے درجے کا ریزرویشن کہاں سے ملتا ہے۔
5 بہت شکریہ۔ آپ کی مہربانی ہے۔ میرا نمبر لیجیے۔ اور آج شام کو مجھے ٹیلیفون کیجیے۔

Unit 8

Dialogue 1

John : Hello, sir.

Manager : Hello, Mr Smith. How are you? Are you having a good time in Karachi? (a good time is passing?)

John : Yes, we are having very good days here (good days are passing). We like your hotel very much. Tomorrow morning we are going to Lahore, and we shall stay there for about ten days.

Manager : I see. How will you go? By train or by air?

John : We shall go by train. The train will depart from the station at eight a.m. (in the morning). Therefore, we have to get up early. Can one get a taxi from here easily?

Manager : Yes. There will be no problem. I'll call a taxi for you at seven. Before going, have breakfast. Will you have breakfast in the room?

John : This will be very good. And give me the bill by this (today) evening. I have to go out now for two (or) three hours. I'll come back at about six.

Manager : All right. Mr Smith. You go. By six o'clock all will be ready. Will you have dinner here this evening?

John : No, we are going to friends. We shall have dinner wth them.

Manager : Very well, sir. I shall be (remain) here in the evening. If you need anything else, then tell me.

John : Thank you. We'll meet again in the evening.

Dialogue 2

John : Hello, sir. Thank you for the breakfast. I have to pay (give you money) for it.

Manager : No, Mr Smith. It's no trouble. It's on (from the side of) the hotel. And here is (some) fruit for the journey. Take (it). This is also from us.

John : Oh, you are taking too much trouble! Thank you very, very much. We shall always remember your hotel (will remain a memory to us).

Manager : Where is your luggage? Is it in the room?

John : Yes. There are three suitcases. But they are quite heavy.

Manager : All right. You sit here. I'll call the porter. He'll bring the luggage and put it in the taxi. You have plenty of time. Before going will you have (drink) tea or coffee?

John : No, thank you. I think that we'll be off now, because we have to meet friends at the station. They are going to Lahore with us.

Manager : After Lahore, what do you intend? Will you go home from there?

John : No, we shall go from there to Delhi and stay for two weeks in India.

Manager : I see. You will like Delhi a lot. Delhi is the homeland of my family. That is I am a native of Delhi. It's a very splendid city.

John : I am sure that Delhi is very splendid. But first of all we shall see Lahore. Right. That's our taxi driver, isn't it? So, we'll be off. Once more, thank you very, very much. We shall meet again.

Manager : Come again some time. Goodbye.

Exercise 8.1

1 پڑھنی ہیں 2 دینے ہیں 3 کرنی ہے 4 کرنا ہے 5 جانا ہے
6 بلانا ہے

Dialogue 3

Taxi driver : Where do you have to go, sahib? Do you have to go to the station?

John : Yes. We are going to Lahore. From which platform does the train depart? You probably know (you will know).

Taxi driver : Yes, sahib. There's no problem. I'll call the porter for you. The station is not very far from here. It's only twenty minutes (a road of 20 minutes). You are English, aren't you? How do you know Urdu (how does Urdu come to you)?

John : Well, I'm learning Urdu. A lot of Urdu speakers live in England.

Taxi driver : Yes, I know. My elder brother lives in Manchester. I shall also go there.

John : I see. When do you intend to go?

Taxi driver : There are always intentions, sahib, but one needs money, doesn't one? I'm a taxi driver. I don't earn much. But one day I shall certainly go there. Look. The station is here.

John : Oho! What a big crowd! How shall we get (arrive) to the platform?

Taxi driver : It's no problem, sahib. I'll call the porter. He will put (seat) you in the train. Give him ten rupees. No more.

John : And how much money do I have to give you?

Taxi driver : Well. Give [me] twenty-five rupees. See that man? He's your porter.

John : Thank you very much. Goodbye.

Exercise 8.2

1 جی ہاں، میں لاہور جا رہا (رہی) ہوں۔
2 میرے پاس صرف دو سوٹ کیس ہیں۔
3 جی ہاں۔ ریل گاڑی کتنے بجے روانہ ہوگی؟
4 بہت شکریہ۔ مجھے آپ کو کتنے پیسے دینے ہیں؟

Exercise 8.3

1 کھانی 2 اٹھنا 3 پڑھنی 4 کرنا 5 جانا

Exercise 8.4

1 Ten 2 1630 rupees 3 Five times 4 309 rupees 5 22 rupees 6 3921 rupees

Unit 9

Dialogue 1

Qasim : John Sahib, hello! Where were you? You weren't on the platform. I was very worried.

John : Hello, Qasim Sahib. Excuse (me). But there was such a big crowd. It's difficult, isn't it? In such a crowd, you can't see anyone (anyone does not come into view).

Qasim : Well, never mind. The important thing is that you are here. The compartment is quite comfortable, isn't it? And there will only be the four of us (we shall only be four people). There won't be anyone else. Are you enjoying Pakistan (is Pakistan coming pleasing)?

John : We're enjoying it very much. In Karachi our hotel was very good. The food was good, the people were good, and the hotel manager was an especially kind person. We have many new friends.

Qasim : In Lahore you will find (will be acquired) many more friends. The people of Panjab are very hospitable. Good heavens! Where's my wife? Five minutes ago she was on the platform with (her) (lady) friends. Now I can't see her anywhere (she does not come into view). You sit here. I'll look for her. The train will depart in (after) five minutes.

John : Qasim Sahib, don't be anxious. Look, she is coming.

Qasim : Kausar! Where were you? Were you with (your) friends? Come on. Get (sit) in the compartment. The train is going now.

Exercise 9.1

1 تھے 2 تھے 3 تھیں 4 تھیں 5 تھا

Dialogue 2

John : (Why), Qasim Sahib. Are you a native of Lahore?

Qasim : No. I am originally from Multan. Multan is also in Panjab and not very far from Lahore. First, I was in the army. Namely, I was a soldier for (from) ten years. After that I was in Hyderabad Sindh and Karachi. Nowadays I do business in Lahore. Today our train will pass through Hyderabad and Multan. Tomorrow morning at about eight o'clock we shall arrive in Lahore.

John : Lahore is smaller than Karachi, isn't it?

Qasim : Yes. Lahore is the biggest city in (of) Panjab, but it is much smaller than Karachi. I think the population of Lahore is about three (to) four million ('thirty, forty lakhs'). Karachi's population is very big. First, Karachi was the capital of Pakistan. As you know our capital is now Islamabad.

John : Is Islamabad far from Lahore?

Qasim : No, it is not all that far. In the train it is about five hours' journey. Islamabad is quite a new city, and much smaller than Lahore. Karachi is the biggest city in (of) Pakistan. But in my opinion Lahore is the most interesting and pleasant. What's the time now? It's ten o'clock. In (after) a short while we shall arrive at Hyderabad. There we shall have (drink) tea.

Exercise 9.2

1 گاڑی کراچی، حیدر آباد، سکر، رحیم یار خان، بہاول پور اور ملتان سے گزرتی ہے۔

2 پہلا اسٹیشن حیدر آباد ہے۔

3 چھے سو پچیس (۶۲۵) میل دور ہے۔

4 جی ہاں، زیادہ سردی ہوتی ہے۔

5 پاکستان کا دارالحکومت اسلام آباد ہے۔ لاہور سے ایک سو چالیس (۱۴۰) میل دور ہے۔

Dialogue 3

Qasim : Well, at last we are in Lahore. You must be (will be) very tired. But your hotel is not all that far from here. We'll take (sit in) a taxi and we'll take you as far as the hotel.

John : Thank you, Qasim Sahib, but please don't trouble yourself. You must be tired too. You go straight home. We'll easily get to (arrive at) the hotel.

Qasim : It's no trouble. Your hotel is on our way. You will see that your hotel is a very interesting building. It means that the building is interesting. First, it was the house of some English general. And English troops were there. Now it's a hotel. The rooms are very big and comfortable. It's an old hotel but I think old hotels are more interesting than those new hotels. Come on, let's get in the taxi. We'll go straight to your hotel. Have something to eat there and have a good rest. And tomorrow morning I'll come to you. I'll show you Lahore.

John : Thank you very much, Qasim Sahib. But will you have time tomorrow?

Qasim : Yes. I shall be free (there will be leisure) all day long. It's Saturday tomorrow, isn't it? I don't work on Saturday. Usually in Pakistan there's a holiday on Saturday. Look, your hotel is here on the left. On the right is Mall Road. This is the biggest and most splendid road in (of) Lahore. Go now. Have a rest and we shall meet tomorrow, *inshallah*.

John : Thank you, Qasim Sahib. Goodbye.

Exercise 9.3

1 5; 2 1; 3 6; 4 7; 5 2; 6 4; 7 3

Exercise 9.4

1 آرہا/رہی ہوں 2 تھے 3 پکائیں گی 4 اٹھتے ہیں 5 نہاتیں/نہاتی ہیں
6 پڑھنا 7 لاؤ 8 دیکھوں گا/گی 9 بولتے ہیں

Exercise 9.5

1 بڑا' پرانا 2 چھوٹا 3 مزےدار 4 مشکل 5 امیر

Unit 10

Dialogue 1

Qasim : Hello, John Sahib, Can I come in?

John : Hello. Yes, Qasim Sahib. Please come in. Will you have tea? Shall I order tea? What a splendid hotel this is! Not one room but three rooms. Here is the sitting room; there is the bedroom (sleeping room); and at the back is a very big bathroom.

Qasim : And how was your day yesterday. I think that after the journey you were very tired.

John : Yes. Well, all day long we were in the hotel. In front there is a very beautiful garden. There is every kind of comfort (rest). And what fine weather it is! It is colder (there is more cold) in Lahore in comparison with Karachi, isn't it?

Qasim : Yes, in Panjab in (the month of) November it is colder. But all day long it is sunny (there is sunshine). So, you tell (me). What shall we do today? Shall we go out?

John : If you are free (if there is leisure to you) (then) we shall look around Lahore (do a tour of Lahore). Can you show us the most important streets and buildings?

Qasim : Yes, with great pleasure. If you tell me what you especially want to see (then) I shall show you.

John : I think we might start (let us start) with the Badshahi Mosque. They say that the Badshahi Mosque is the biggest mosque in (of) the world, don't they?

Qasim : I'm not certain, but it must be (will be) one of the biggest (from among the biggest) mosques. At least it is bigger than Delhi's Jami' Mosque. All right. Let's have tea quickly and get going.

Dialogue 2

John : So this is the Badshahi Mosque. It's really a vast mosque. Qasim sahib, tell (me). Whose mosque is it?

Qasim : It's Aurangzeb's mosque. You will recall that Aurangzeb was the son of Shahjahan, and the most famous building of Shahjahan is the Taj Mahal. The Taj Mahal is in Agra. They were both Mughal kings and in the time of the Mughals three cities, namely Lahore, Delhi and Agra, were the most important capitals.

John : Can we go inside?

Qasim : Of course. There is no problem. If your wife puts a shawl or scarf on her head, it will be good.

John : This means that ladies can enter the mosque.

Qasim : Why not? From the point of view of Islam all human beings are equal. Look, the door is there. Come on, let's go.

Helen : What a splendid mosque it is! There are eight high minarets and three white domes. The colour of the walls is red. And how clean and tidy it is! But there are very few people here.

Qasim : Yes, but at the time of prayers there's a great crowd. A hundred thousand people can pray (read prayer) here.

Helen : Can I take a photograph?

Qasim : Of course, but don't take it from here. The sun is in front of you. If you go to that side, a good picture will come out.

Dialogue 3

Helen : The Badshahi Mosque was really very beautiful, and how interesting are the streets of this area! It seems that we are seeing the stories of the Arabian Nights (*Alf Laila*). If I close (my) eyes (then) I can see old Baghdad (Baghdad comes into view).

Qasim : Do you like Lahore better than Karachi?

Helen : I won't say that. I can say this much that it is quite different.

Qasim : Very well then, let's go on (forward) and before lunch I'll show you the old city. There is a very famous bazaar. It's name is Anarkali. Anarkali, in the time of the Mughals, was an unfortunate girl. She was a famous singer and dancer. But her life was sad. Her tomb is in the Old Fort. If you want to go to Anarkali on foot (then) we shall cross the old city. You will be able to see everything.

Helen : Yes. Let's go on foot. The weather is lovely and I am neither hungry nor thirsty (to me there is neither hunger nor thirst). I am only in love with this beautiful city (to me there is love from).

Qasim : All right, let's go on foot. But in (after) an hour you will be certainly be hungry (hunger will be). In Anarkali I know a (one) very good restaurant. Excuse me. I am also interested in old buildings, but in this world food (bread) is also an important thing!

Exercise 10.1

1 میں اگلی جمعرات کو ریل گاڑی سے اسلام آباد جانا چاہتا/ چاہتی ہوں۔

2 ریل گاڑی لاہور سے کتنے بجے روانہ ہوتی ہے اور اسلام آباد کتنے بجے پہنچتی ہے؟

3 کیا ہوٹل آسانی سے ملے گا؟ ایک رات کے لئے کتنے پیسے دینے ہیں؟

4 اسلام آباد میں سب سے دلچسپ چیزیں کیا ہیں؟

5 مجھے اتوار کو لاہور واپس آنا ہے کیونکہ اگلے ہفتے میں ہوائی جہاز سے دہلی جا رہا/ رہی ہوں

Exercise 10.2

1 سکتے ہیں 2 آتی ہے 3 کھائیں 4 ہوتی ہے 5 رہتے ہیں

6 منگواؤں؟ 7 رہتے ہیں۔

Exercise 10.3

1 False 2 False 3 True 4 False 5 True 6 False 7 True

Unit 11

Dialogue 1

Qasim : Well, John. Are you here alone? Isn't Helen here, then?

John : Yes. I was thinking that I would write one (or) two letters. This morning my wife is wandering around Anarkali. She is buying some clothes with the wife of the hotel manager. This room is so comfortable that I was thinking I would take full advantage of my wife's absence. I am very frightened of bazaars.

Qasim : Yes, Helen was telling me that you don't like wandering around ('in') shops.

John : This is true. Shall I order tea?

Qasim : That's a very good idea. Let's drink tea and have a chat. John, I was thinking that since you are in Lahore, then I would show you my village. My village is towards Shaikhupura. I used to live there in my childhood. I always remember (my) childhood.

John : So, you originally come from a village?

Qasim : Yes. Most Pakistanis live in villages. How good my childhood was! We used to play in the fields, eat the very best of food. At that time everything used to be good. It's possible we may go the day after tomorrow. Our village is not all that far.

John : Very well. We'll certainly make arrangements to go. Tell me, Qasim, what were you doing yesterday evening? Your telephone was ringing. It seemed that you were not at home.

Qasim : Yes, we were at a party. My wife was singing there.

John : Really. Does your wife sing?

Qasim : Yes. Come to the house some time and listen.

Dialogue 2

Qasim : Hello, John. I haven't called at an awkward moment?

John : No, Qasim. We are ready. Today the weather is very good. It was raining last night, wasn't it?

Qasim : Yes. It doesn't usually rain in November. Well, It's getting nice and sunny ('a good sunshine is coming out'). Come on, let's go. Get into the car.

John : Shaikhupura's not so far from here, is it?

Qasim : No, it's about 34 miles away. Towards the north. If you go east from here, then you come to the Indian border ('the border will come'). If you go further on from Shaikhupura, then you'll arrive at Islamabad. Further on from there is Peshawar and the North West Frontier. But that's quite far. Islamabad is about 160 miles from Lahore.

John : Is Shaikhupura an old town?

Qasim : In the 17th century Jahangir used to live there and used to hunt in the nearby jungle. His fort is still there.

John : And is your village large?

Qasim : It's quite a big village. My relations still practise agriculture there. As you know, the meaning of 'Panjab' is 'the Land of the Five Rivers'. The land is very fetile. My family has been ('is') resident there since the 18th century. Before Partition, Muslims, Hindus and Sikhs all lived together there. But now there are only Muslims. As I was telling you the day before yesterday, the world changes very fast. *Inshallah*, in the next century we shall be able to live more happily. Look, our village is coming into view. Come on, I'll introduce you to my relations and we'll have a good dinner.

Exercise 11.1

1 افغانستان ہے۔

2 چار صوبے ہیں۔ سندھ، بلوچستان، پنجاب، سرحدِ شمال مغرب، حیدر آباد، کوئٹہ، اسلام آباد، پشاور۔

3 حیدر آباد سندھ، ملتان۔

4 شمالی ہندوستان میں۔

5 جنوبی ہندوستان میں۔

6 کلکتہ

7 سندھ میں

8 لاہور میں۔ جی ہاں۔ دہلی کی جامع مسجد سے بڑی ہے۔

9 بحیرۂ عرب

10 بنگلہ دیش میں۔

Exercise 11.2

1 پہنچیں 2 کریں 3 کروں 4 کریں 5 جائیں 6 پڑھو

7 منگواؤں

Unit 12

Dialogue 1

John : Hello, Bilqis, Tell me. How are you?

Bilqis : Really, it's John. How are you? Did you get to Lahore safely?

John : Yes, thank you. All's well here. Lahore is really a splendid place. Is Aslam there?

Bilqis : Yes. I'll call him now. There you are. He's coming.

Aslam : John! I'm very pleased. What are you doing these days?

John : We're very busy. The day before yesterday we went to Shaikhupura to see Qasim's village. That was really very interesting. Yesterday we went to visit Jahangir's tomb.

Aslam : And how's the weather?

John : It's colder here than Karachi. They say that in winter it's (usually) quite cold in Panjab. The day before yesterday, it rained for a little while. After that the sun came out, and it was sunny ('sunshine remained') all day long.

Aslam : And what's your intention?

John : In three days' time ('after three days'), that is on Tuesday, we're going to Delhi. We'll go by air, because we don't have all that much time.

Aslam : Right. I've never been ('gone') to Delhi. You know that Delhi is

Bilqis' home town. Can you do a job for me? An old friend of ours lives near Chandni Chowk. Go and meet him and give ('say') him our greetings. His name is Sharif Ahmad and he lives in *Kucha-e Rahman.* The house number is 1045. Any rickshaw driver will show you the way ('road').

John : Yes, Aslam. I shall certainly do that (work).

Aslam : And what's your programme today?

John : We're going to lunch at the place of some friends. Yesterday we met them ('a meeting came about with them') in a tea shop. After that, they'll take us to the banks of the Ravi.

Aslam : OK, John. Have a good time ('stroll around well') and write to us from Delhi. Bon voyage!

Exercise 12.1

1 اسلم صاحب پانچ بجے آئے۔

2 وہ بادشاہی مسجد کی سیر کرنے گئے۔

3 راوی کے کنارے لے گئے۔

4 شیخو پورے کے آس پاس کے جنگل میں۔

5 آگرے جانے کا انتظام کریں گے۔

6 چار بجے آئے گی۔

7 گاؤں میں گزرا۔

Dialogue 2

Qasim : Hello. At last you are (present) here. I passed by at about five, but you were not in the room.

John : I'm sorry, Qasim. We went out. I have just (now) come. Five minutes ago, Helen was chatting to the manager's wife. It seems that they have gone somewhere. They'll come in a little while.

Qasim : Where did you go today?

John : Yesterday evening we were sitting in a tea shop, and we met a person there. He's a lawyer in the court here. He at once began to ask how we know Urdu. After that we went to his house and met his family (members). His wife was preparing the food, so (then) we joined in the dinner. We arrived at the hotel at about 12 pm. As you were saying, Panjabi people are very hospitable.

This afternoon we met again and went to walk by the banks of the Ravi. I'm sorry that I couldn't phone you.

Qasim : Oho! New friends, new habits! You couldn't phone me ('us')! I began to think that you had gone to India without my permission.

John : Please forgive (me), Qasim. This is our mistake.

Qasim : No, John. It was only a joke. I'm very happy ('it is a matter of much happiness') that you like our Panjabi brothers. So, are all your preparations for going to India complete?

John : We're almost ready. We shall have plenty of time. The plane goes at about eleven.

Qasim : OK I'll come here at eight tomorrow morning, and take you (up) to the airport. Goodbye!

Exercise 12.2

میرا نام اقبال احمد ہے۔ میں کراچی کا رہنے والا ہوں۔ پچھلے ہفتے میں پہلی بار لاہور گیا تھا۔ موسم بہت خوشگوار تھا۔ نہ گرمی نہ سردی تھی اور دن بھر دھوپ رہی۔ جمعرات کو میں دوستوں کے ہاں کھانا کھانے گیا تھا۔ وہاں ایک مشہور وکیل سے ملا۔ وہ کہنے لگے! 'اقبال صاحب' آپ کام کرنے لاہور کیوں نہیں آتے؟' لیکن میں لاہور میں رہ نہیں سکتا۔ میرے سب رشتے دار کراچی میں ہیں اور میری بیگم کو پنجاب کا موسم پسند نہیں ہے۔

My name is Iqbal Ahmad. I originally come from Karachi. Last week I went ('had gone') for the first time to Lahore. The weather was very pleasant. (It was) neither hot nor cold and it was sunny ('sunshine remained') all day long. On Thursday evening, I went to have dinner at my friends'place. There I met a famous lawyer. He said ('began to say'): 'Iqbal Sahib, why don't you come to work in Lahore?' But I cannot live in Lahore. All my relations are in Karachi. And my wife does not like the climate/weather of Panjab.

1 وہ کراچی کے رہنے والے ہیں۔

2 وہ لاہور گئے تھے۔

3 لاہور میں نہ سردی تھی نہ گرمی تھی۔

4 وہ دوستوں کے ہاں گئے تھے۔

5 وہاں ایک مشہور وکیل سے ملاقات ہوئی۔

6 آپ کام کرنے لاہور کیوں نہیں آتے؟

Exercise 12.3

1 جی ہاں' یہ کون صاحب بول رہے ہیں۔
2 معاف کیجیے۔ میں بازار میں خریداری کر رہا تھا / رہی تھی۔
3 میں کوئی چھے بجے آیا / آئی۔
4 مجھے کتنے بجے آنا ہے / میں کتنے بجے آؤں؟
5 مجھے بہت خوشی ہو گی۔ میں ضرور آؤں گا / آؤں گی۔

Exercise 12.4

1 پڑھتے ہیں 2 کر رہے ہیں 3 نہاتا تھا 4 پڑھ رہے تھے 5 کہیں گی
6 نکلیں 7 ملے ہیں 8 چکی تھی

Unit 13

Dialogue 1

John : Excuse me, is this queue for Delhi?

Officer : Yes. Please wait in the queue. Your flight is at 11.25. Is this your luggage?

John : Yes. Two suitcases and one bag.

Officer : Did you pack the luggage yourself? Are you taking things for anyone else?

John : No. We packed it ourselves. All the things are just our things.

Officer : Very well. Come! Show your tickets and passports. After that you will be able to go straight into the lounge. Tell me. Where (from) did you learn Urdu?

John : First of all I learnt Urdu in London with friends. These days we are travelling in the subcontinent. In Karachi and Lahore we had a lot of practice in speaking Urdu ('much practice came about').

Officer : Very well, Mr Smith. I'm very pleased to have met you ('having met you much pleasure has come about'). Very few foreigners speak such good Urdu. Go on. You have quite a lot of time.

John : What's the time now? My watch (has) stopped.

Officer : Now it's twenty to eleven. No. Sorry. Quarter to eleven.

John : And what time do we arrive at Delhi?

Officer : It's not a very long flight. You'll arrive about quarter past, half past twelve. Did you enjoy Lahore?

John : (We) enjoyed it very much. I think we saw absolutely everything. We shall always remember Pakistan. So, there's the announcement for ('of') our flight. Goodbye. *Inshallah*, we'll meet again.

Exercise 13.1

1 کیں 2 کی 3 دیکھا 4 کھایا 5 کیا 6 پڑھی 7 باندھا

Dialogue 2

Hostess: *Assalamu 'alaikum.* Please ('having done kindness') show (me) your boarding pass. Your seats are there on the right.

John : Thank you. I understand ('understood'). 18 and 19, near the window. But look. There are two men sitting in our seats. What's happened? 'I'll go ('having gone') and have a word. Excuse me. It seems that you are sitting in our seats. 18 and 19.

Man : Really? I'm sorry. What you say is quite right. One minute and we'll shift from here. Are you going to Delhi?

John : I think we are all going to Delhi. Otherwise, we're sitting in the wrong plane.

Man : That's true. Today my brain is not working well. I didn't sleep (last) night. Yesterday evening I went to meet friends, and we were chatting till four in the morning. Having gone home, I quickly packed my luggage and came straight to the airport. It doesn't matter. Having arrived in Delhi, I'll have a good rest. But at home there's my wife, children and relations. They never let me have a rest ('give me to rest'). Rest is 'forbidden' at home! I'm very hungry. Last night I didn't eat anything. This morning I didn't even drink tea. You know, life is sometimes very difficult. Every morning, having got up early, I go to work. In the evening, having arrived home, I want to eat. Do I get food ('is food acquired')? I get nothing. My wife sits all day long with her friends. She comes ('having come') home and says: 'I'm tired. You make the dinner yourself. I also get tired. I'm thirsty now as well. Don't they give tea on this flight? I'm a poor man! Sometimes I think I'll go ('having gone') to Britain and work.

Once I tried to go, but they didn't give me a visa. Brother, what can I say to you? Look. That girl is bringing tea. Thanks be to Allah! But she's going back. Won't we get tea? Alas! Alas!

Exercise 13.2

1 میں اب گھر جا کر کھانا کھاؤں گا۔ (جا کے)
2 کراچی جا کر فہمیدہ سب رشتے داروں سے ملی۔ (جا کے)
3 کتاب پڑھ کر حامد نے آرام کیا۔ (پڑھ کے)
4 سامان باندھ کر / باندھ کے ہم ہوائی اڈے گئے۔
5 ٹیکسی میں بیٹھ کر / بیٹھ کے وہ ڈرائیور سے باتیں کرنے لگے۔

Exercise 13.3

1 4; 2 6; 3 1; 4 7; 5 2; 6 3; 7 5

Exercise 13.4

کل صبح سویرے اُٹھ کے ہم صبح ساڑھے آٹھ بجے ہوائی اڈے پہنچے۔ ہوائی جہاز دس بجنے میں بیس منٹ پر جانے والا تھا۔ میں نے اپنی بیگم سے کہا: 'چلیں' ہمارے پاس کافی وقت ہے۔ سب سے پہلے ایک کپ چائے پینے جائیں۔ سیدھے ریستراں میں جا کر ہم نے چائے منگوائی' چونکہ ہم نے ناشتہ نہیں کیا' میں نے اپنی بیگم سے کہا: 'مجھے بھوک لگی ہے۔ میں کھانا بھی منگواوں؟ کتنے بجے ہیں' انہوں نے پوچھا۔ 'پونے نو بجے ہیں' میں نے کہا: 'ہم یہاں آدھے گھنٹے کے لئے بیٹھ سکتے ہیں۔ اس کے بعد ہم سامان لے کر لاؤنج کی طرف جا سکتے ہیں۔' قطار زیادہ لمبی نہیں تھی۔ پاسپورٹ دکھا کر ہم لاؤنج میں گئے۔ ساڑھے نو بجے تھے۔ ہماری پرواز پچاس منٹ کے بعد روانہ ہو گی' میں نے کہا: آج شام کو ہم دہلی میں ہوں گے۔ سفر مبارک ہو!

Unit 14

Dialogue 1

John : At last we have arrived at Delhi. Let's look for a taxi and go straight to the hotel. I've got the address of the hotel. It's on Raj Path. Let's have a little food there. After that we'll visit the Red Fort and the Jami' Mosque.

Helen : John. Why are you talking to me in Urdu? Have you forgotten English?

John : No. I was thinking that since we have come to the homeland of

Urdu, we ought to talk only in Urdu. Urdu was born in the lanes and alleys of Delhi, wasn't it?

Helen : You've really gone mad. Well, it doesn't matter. Let's talk only in Urdu. I have no objection. My Urdu is better than your Urdu.

John : That taxi's standing there. Eh Sardarji! Is the taxi empty?

Sardar : Yes, sir. Get in. Where do you want to go?

John : We have to go to the Raj Path. Do you know where the Imperial Hotel is?

Sardar : Yes, sir. Get in. Where are you coming from?

John : We're coming from Lahore.

Sardar : I see. Lahore is my native place. After Partition in (19)47, my family moved ('was transferred') here. My childhood was spent there.

John : A lot of Sikhs live in Delhi, don't they?

Sardar : Yes. All sorts of people live in Delhi. There are Hindus as well, and the Muslims live mainly in the old city, that is by Chandni Chowk. You speak good Urdu. You're not Pakistanis?

John : No, we're from England. There we have many Indian and Pakistani friends. Therefore, I learnt Urdu.

Sardar : Excellent! Here's your hotel ('hotel has come').

John : How much money shall ('may') I give you?

Sardar : Well, give me 60 rupees.

John : OK. Here you are. Thank you. *Inshallah*, we'll meet again.

Dialogue 2

John : At last we've got to the hotel. I'm very tired. We've done a great deal today. In the morning we came from Lahore to Delhi. In the afternoon we visited the Red Fort and the Jami' Mosque. It's now half past seven. Come on let's have a bite to eat ('food and things').

Helen : I'm sorry, John. I'm a little unwell. I'll lie down for a little while.

John : I thought ('was thinking') that you were very quiet. You look a bit tired. What's the matter with you?

Helen : I don't really know ('I don't understand anything'). I've got a headache. I've got a bit of a temperature ('fever') and I've started to get diarrhoea ('diarrhoea began to be').

John : I think I'll try to call a doctor. You lie down. I'll go to the reception and ask someone.

(John returns in a short while)

John : There you are. It's OK ('it's become'). The doctor will come at once. They phoned from here. Listen. There's someone at the door. I think it must ('will') be the doctor.

Doctor : Hello! I've heard that you speak Urdu. My name is Dr Sharma. Tell me. What's the matter?

Helen : Hello, Doctor, I'm ('have become') a bit unwell. I've got stomach trouble. I have diarrhoea, and a terrible headache. It seems I also have a fever.

Doctor : I see ('understood'). You lie down on the bed and I'll have a look. Indeed, your temperature is 104. Just show your tongue. You seem a bit tired. It's possible that it is because of the change in the climate. I'll give you some antibiotics. And take care with what you eat and drink ('in eating and drinking').

Helen : Thank you, Doctor. How much do we have to give you?

Doctor : That's quite all right. You are our guests. Please rest for a day, and when your health improves ('will become better'), have a good visit. I'm off now. Goodbye.

Exercise 14.1

1 اس کے سر میں درد ہے۔

2 اس کو زکام ہے۔

3 اس کا بازو ٹوٹا ہے۔

4 اس کو بخار ہے۔

5 اس کے پیٹ میں گڑبڑ ہے۔

6 اس کی ٹانگ ٹوٹی ہے۔

Exercise 14.2

ڈاکٹر : آیئے، خان صاحب۔ فرمایئے۔ میں آپ کی کیا خدمت کر سکتا ہوں؟

خان : دو دن سے میری طبیعت ٹھیک نہیں ہے۔ خاص طور پر سر میں درد ہے اور پیٹ میں ذرا گڑبڑ ہے۔

ڈاکٹر : اچھا۔ زبان دکھائیے۔ بتائیے۔ پیچش ہے؟ بخار ہے؟

خان : اب تک پیچش نہیں ہوئی۔ لیکن معلوم ہوتا ہے کہ تھوڑا سا بخار ہے۔

ڈاکٹر : اچھا، دیکھ لیں گے۔ ہاں، آپ کا درجۂ حرارت ایک سو ہے۔ میرے خیال سے یہ پانی کی وجہ سے ہے۔ جب پانی پیتے ہیں تو احتیاط برتنا چاہیے۔ خیر میں آپ کو کچھ اینٹی بایوٹک دوں گا، اگر آپ کی طبیعت ٹھیک نہ ہو تو دو دن کے بعد میرے پاس پھر آئیے۔

1 Headache and stomach trouble 2 Does he also have diarrhoea and fever 3 100 4 Drinking water 5 Antibiotics 6 Come back in two days' time

Exercise 14.3

1 میں سن انیس سو ساٹھ میں (۱۹۶۰ء) میں پیدا ہوا تھا/ہوئی تھی۔

2 سوا دس بجے ہیں ۱۰.۳۰

3 ہوائی جہاز کوئی ساڑھے سات بجے روانہ ہوتا ہے ۷.۳۰

4 ہمیں وہاں پونے پانچ بجے تک پہنچنا چاہیے۔ ۴.۴۵

5 کتنے بجے ہیں؟ پانچ بجنے میں سولہ منٹ باقی ہیں۔ ۴.۴۴

6 اب گیارہ بج کر اٹھارہ منٹ ہو رہے ہیں۔ ۱۱.۱۸

Exercise 14.4

1 آگیا 2 پہنچ گیا تھا 3 نکل گئے 4 سو گئیں 5 ریل گاڑی پہنچ گئی ہے۔

Exercise 14.5

1 دے دوں 2 کھالیا 3 بھیج دوں گا 4 پڑھ لی 5 سیکھ لی تھی

Unit 15

Dialogue 1

John : Hello! Are you Sharif Ahmad Sahib?

Sharif : Yes. And your name ('honourable title')?

John : My name is John Smith. You don't know me. I hope I haven't called at an inconvenient moment. The matter is this (that) two (or) three weeks ago I was in Karachi, and there I met Muhammad Aslam Khan. He gave me your address and told me ('said to me') that, while (being) in Delhi, I should meet you. I should have telephoned you, but I didn't have your number.

Sharif : I see. You know Aslam Sahib? I am very well acquainted with his wife's family. Come in please, and tell me everything in detail. And where do you come from? How long have you been in Delhi ('you Delhi having come how many days have come about')?

John : You can perhaps guess that I am English. In England I have many Indian and Pakistani friends. (While) staying with them, I have managed to learn a little ('little much') Urdu.

Sharif : Your Urdu is very good, as Allah wished! And when did you meet Aslam Sahib?

John : As soon as I arrived (in) Karachi I met him. As I was walking in the city, I stopped him, and asked him ('enquired from him') where Victoria Road was ('is'). He immediately invited me to his home ('gave an invitation to come'). He is a very kind (*šarīf* 'honourable') person.

Sharif : I am also Sharif ('Honourable'); that is, my name is *Sharif.* Come on, I'll get you (some) tea. I have a small request. You must know ('you will know') that between India and Pakistan relations are generally not good. I shall give you my new book. If, as soon as you arrive in England, you can send (it) by air mail to Aslam, I shall be most indebted to you ('I shall be your limitless debtor'). I don't know how much it will cost ('how much cost will be'), but I shall give you two hundred rupees.

John : No, Sharif Sahib. Give me the book, and as soon as I land in London, I'll post it.

Exercise 15.1

1 جلی ہوئی روٹی 2 پہنچتے ہی 3 رہتے ہوئے 4 چلتے چلتے 5 ہوتے ہوئے

Dialogue 2

John : Sharif Sahib, tell me something about yourself and about your life. Do you originate from Delhi?

Sharif : No. I was born in Muradabad. That place is usually called the birth place of Urdu. When I first (of all) came to Delhi, (then) I was admitted into a college, and there I acquired my initial education. After doing BA, I was admitted into the Urdu Department of Delhi University, and while studying there I got my MA. In 1970 I got employment in the Department of Urdu, and from then on I have been teaching ('am teaching') Urdu literature. That is I have been teaching there for almost thirty years ('while teaching 30 years have come about').

John : Obviously there must ('will') be many students of Urdu.

Sharif : Yes. There are not only Indian, but foreign students also. There are Japanese, Americans, Russians etc. When you have ('will have') time, (then) come to the department. Will you have time tomorrow evening?

John : Yes. Can I bring my wife as well?

Sharif : Certainly. (From) among the foreign students, there is an American who speaks as well in Urdu as you speak. There is a Japanese student whom you will be very pleased to meet. Come whenever you please ('at which time you wish, come'). Tomorrow at five o'clock there will be a discussion about emigrants. That is there will be a conversation about the problems of Indian and Pakistani emigrants who are settled in Europe and America ('which emigrants about their problems'). Can you give a little speech?

John : Ahmad Sahib! I have never made a speech in Urdu, but I'll try.

Exercise 15.2

1 اُردو میں اسے اونٹ کہتے ہیں۔
2 اردو میں اسے ریل گاڑی کہتے ہیں۔
3 اردو میں اسے گاڑی کہتے ہیں۔
4 اردو میں اسے گھر کہتے ہیں۔
5 اردو میں اسے کتاب کہتے ہیں۔

Exercise 15.3

1 True 2 False 3 True 4 False 5 False

Exercise 15.4

جان : معاف کیجئے۔ میرے پاس دو چھٹیاں ہیں۔ میں یہاں سے ٹکٹ لے سکتا ہوں؟

کلرک : جی ہاں۔ کون سے ملکوں کے لئے ہیں۔
جان : ایک انگلستان کے لئے اور ایک امریکہ کے لئے۔
کلرک : انگلستان کے لئے پینتیس (۳۵) روپے اور امریکہ کے لئے چالیس (۴۰) روپے۔
جان : اور ایک چھوٹا سا پارسل ہے۔ یہ مراد آباد کے لئے ہے۔ اس کو بھی یہاں سے بھیج سکتا ہوں؟
کلرک : جی ہاں۔ لیکن آپ نے اس کو کپڑے میں باندھا ہے؟
جان : جی ہاں۔ یہ دیکھیے۔
کلرک : آپ نے فارم بھر لیا پارسل کے لئے؟
جان : جی نہیں۔ آپ مجھے فارم دے سکتے ہیں؟ اور مجھے ایک تار بھیجنا ہے۔
کلرک : تار وہاں سے بھیج سکتے ہیں۔ لیجیے۔ یہ فارم آپ کے پارسل کے لئے ہے۔

Answers: 1 Two 2 England and America 3 40 rupees 4 Wrapped it in cloth 5 Muradabad 6 No 7 To send a telegram

Exercise 15.5

1 کس 2 جو 3 کسی 4 جس 5 جن 6 کس 7 کسی 8 جن

Exercise 15.6

1 میں نے لندن میں دوستوں کے ساتھ رہتے ہوئے اردو سیکھ لی۔
2 جی ہاں انگلستان میں بہت ہندوستانی اور پاکستانی تارکینِ وطن رہتے ہیں۔
3 ان میں سے بہت لوگ دفتروں اور کارخانوں میں کام کرتے ہیں۔
4 آپ مجھے ان کا پتہ دیجئے اور میں خوشی سے ان کو دے دوں گا/دوں گی۔

Appendix 1
Numerals

Numbers to read: 0–10

صفر	۰	*sifr*	0	چھے	۶	*che*	6
ایک	۱	*ek*	1	سات	۷	*sāt*	7
دو	۲	*do*	2	آٹھ	۸	*āṭh*	8
تین	۳	*tīn*	3	نو	۹	*nau*	9
چار	۴	*cār*	4	دس	۱۰	*das*	10
پانچ	۵	*pāṅc*	5				

Numbers to read: 11–20

گیارہ	۱۱	*giyāra*	11	سولہ	۱۶	*sola*	16
بارہ	۱۲	*bāra*	12	سترہ	۱۷	*satra*	17
تیرہ	۱۳	*tera*	13	اٹھارہ	۱۸	*aṭhāra*	18
چودہ	۱۴	*cauda*	14	انیس	۱۹	*unnīs*	19
پندرہ	۱۵	*pandra*	15	بیس	۲۰	*bīs*	20

Numbers to read: 21–30

اکیس	۲۱	*ikkīs*	21	چھبیس	۲۶	*chabbīs*	26
بائیس	۲۲	*bāīs*	22	ستائیس	۲۷	*satāīs*	27
تیئیس	۲۳	*teīs*	23	اٹھائیس	۲۸	*aṭhāīs*	28
چوبیس	۲۴	*caubīs*	24	انتیس	۲۹	*untīs*	29
پچیس	۲۵	*paccīs*	25	تیس	۳۰	*tīs*	30

Numbers to read: 31–40

اکتیس	۳۱	*iktīs*	31	چھتیس	۳۶	*chattīs*	36
بتیس	۳۲	*battīs*	32	سینتیس	۳۷	*saiṅtīs*	37
تینتیس	۳۳	*taiṅtīs*	33	اڑتیس	۳۸	*aṛtīs*	38
چونتیس	۳۴	*cauṅtīs*	34	انتالیس	۳۹	*untālīs*	39
پینتیس	۳۵	*paiṅtīs*	35	چالیس	۴۰	*cālīs*	40

Numbers to read: 41–50

اکتالیس	۴۱	*iktālīs*	41	چھیالیس	۴۶	*cheālīs*	46
بیالیس	۴۲	*beālīs*	42	سینتالیس	۴۷	*saiṅtālīs*	47
تینتالیس	۴۳	*taiṅtālīs*	43	اڑتالیس	۴۸	*aṛtālīs*	48
چوالیس	۴۴	*cavālīs*	44	انچاس	۴۹	*uncās*	49
پینتالیس	۴۵	*paiṅtālīs*	45	پچاس	۵۰	*pacās*	50

Numbers to read: 51–60

اکیاون	۵۱	*ikyāvan*	51	چھپن	۵۶	*chappan*	56
باون	۵۲	*bāvan*	52	ستاون	۵۷	*satāvan*	57
ترپن	۵۳	*tirpan*	53	اٹھاون	۵۸	*aṭhāvan*	58
چوّن	۵۴	*cauvan*	54	انسٹھ	۵۹	*unsaṭh*	59
پچپن	۵۵	*pacpan*	55	ساٹھ	۶۰	*sāṭh*	60

Numbers to read: 61–70

اکسٹھ	۶۱	*iksaṭh*	61	چھیاسٹھ	۶۶	*cheāsaṭh*	66
باسٹھ	۶۲	*bāsaṭh*	62	سڑسٹھ	۶۷	*saṛsaṭh*	67
ترسٹھ	۶۳	*tirsaṭh*	63	اڑسٹھ	۶۸	*aṛsaṭh*	68
چونسٹھ	۶۴	*cauṅsaṭh*	64	انہتر	۶۹	*unhattar*	69
پینسٹھ	۶۵	*paiṅsaṭh*	65	ستر	۷۰	*sattar*	70

Numbers to read: 71–80

اکہتر	۷۱	ikhattar	71	چھہتر	۷۶	chihattar	76
بہتر	۷۲	bahattar	72	ستہتر	۷۷	sathattar	77
ترہتر	۷۳	tirhattar	73	اٹھہتر	۷۸	aṭhattar	78
چوہتر	۷۴	cauhattar	74	اناسی	۷۹	unāsī	79
پچھتر	۷۵	pachattar	75	اسی	۸۰	assī	80

Numbers to read: 81–90

اکیاسی	۸۱	ikyāsī	81	چھیاسی	۸۶	cheāsī	86
بیاسی	۸۲	beāsī	82	ستاسی	۸۷	satāsī	87
تراسی	۸۳	tirāsī	83	اٹھاسی	۸۸	aṭhāsī	88
چوراسی	۸۴	caurāsī	84	اننوّے	۸۹	unanavve	89
پچاسی	۸۵	pacāsī	85	نوّے	۹۰	navve	90

Numbers to read: 91–100

اکیانوے	۹۱	ikyāṅve	91	چھیانوے	۹۶	cheāṅve	96
بیانوے	۹۲	beāṅve	92	ستانوے	۹۷	satāṅve	97
ترانوے	۹۳	tirāṅve	93	اٹھانوے	۹۸	aṭhāṅve	98
چورانوے	۹۴	caurāṅve	94	ننانوے	۹۹	nināṅve	99
پچانوے	۹۵	pacāṅve	95	سو	۱۰۰	(ek) sau	100

Appendix 2
Relations

دادا	*dādā*	paternal grandfather
نانا	*nānā*	maternal grandfather
والد	*vālid*	father
باپ	*bāp*	father
والدہ	*vālida*	mother
ماں	*māṅ*	mother
چچا	*cacā*	paternal uncle
ماموں	*māmūṅ*	maternal uncle
پھوپی	*phūpī*	paternal aunt
خالہ	*xālā*	maternal aunt
بھائی	*bhāī*	brother
بہن	*bahin*	sister
بھتیجا	*bhatījā*	nephew (brother's son)
بھتیجی	*bhatījī*	niece (sister's daughter)
بھانجا	*bhāṅjā*	nephew (sister's son)
بھانجی	*bhāṅjī*	niece (sister's daughter)

Cousins are usually referred to simply as بھائی 'brother' بہن 'sister'. If it is necessary to specify to which side of the family they belong, the adjectives چچازاد *cacāzād* 'born of the paternal uncle' and ماموں زاد *māmūṅzād* 'born of the maternal uncle' may be added:

چچا زاد بھائی	cousin (paternal uncle's son)
ماموں زاد بہن	cousin (maternal uncle's daughter)

GRAMMATICAL INDEX

Numbers after the entries refer to the units in which the topics are first introduced and further discussed.